Office 365 with SharePoint Online Cookbook Solutions

Maximize your productivity with Office 365 and SharePoint Online

Alex Pollard

www.bpbonline.com

First published: 2023

Published by BPB Online
WeWork
119 Marylebone Road
London NW1 5PU

UK | UAE | INDIA | SINGAPORE

ISBN 978-93-55518-392

www.bpbonline.com

Dedicated to

My beloved wife **Nikole** *and My Daughter* **Uliana**

&

My Mom

Tatyana Pashkevych

About the Author

Alex has a Master's degree in Computer Sciences, and more than 12 years of experience in web development and programming for Microsoft platform and applications. He has worked as an IT Consultant and Software Engineer in the area of Collaboration Environments, SharePoint development, and Migrations to the Cloud.

Alex started his journey by setting up and configuring SharePoint for large financial organizations and banks, back when it was SharePoint 2007 as Windows SharePoint Services (wss) 3.0. Since then, he has worked with various SharePoint platforms for on-premise environments 2007, 2010, 2013, 2016, and 2019, as well as Office 365 and SharePoint online. From his vast experience, Alex attained a deep knowledge of SharePoint and related products from administration, Development, Configuration, and Support angles. Once Alex gained enough experience, he opened his own IT Consulting company. Nowadays, he works with large enterprise companies from Fortune 500 and national government agencies. Alex holds multiple Microsoft certifications, is a public speaker, and continues growing the business and providing services to the company's clients.

About the Reviewers

❖ **Oleksandr Vedmid's** career in IT spans over 20 years in various roles, from Developer to Software Architect. Development is his true passion, and he has been involved in various projects throughout his entire career, in different technical and business areas, with a major focus on the implementation of reporting and collaboration portals, based on the Microsoft stack of technologies: O365, SharePoint, Microsoft Flow, and PowerApps.

❖ **Leslie Rivera** is an ambitious expert at anything Microsoft. With over twenty years of experience, she has dedicated her life to helping others by identifying opportunities to improve productivity and streamline processes through M365 products. Her talent for bridging past and future technologies helps her deliver quantifiable solutions to stakeholders. Her goal is to develop and affect change with technology. When not at work, Leslie enjoys time with family, watching HGTV, and aspires to retire in peace on the beach one day.

❖ **Andre Galitsky** is a collaboration architect and consultant, specializing in Microsoft SharePoint and related technologies. He has more than twenty years of IT industry experience, and since 2006, he has focused almost exclusively on Microsoft SharePoint solutions. He has been involved in a number of large-scale SharePoint implementations for both private and government clients, affecting thousands of users and many terabytes of content.

Acknowledgement

I would like to express my gratitude to the many people who have supported me throughout the process of writing this book on Office 365 and SharePoint overview. First and foremost, I want to thank my wife and daughter for their unwavering encouragement and support throughout this journey. Without them, I could not have accomplished this feat.

I also want to extend my sincere thanks to the Chiron LLC development team and all colleagues that provided me with the tools and resources necessary to learn and develop my skills in Office 365. Your support has been invaluable.

Lastly, I want to acknowledge the contributions of Yaroslav Masyuk, Oleksandr Vedmid and Denys Saveliev, whose technical expertise and keen eye helped to ensure the accuracy and quality of this book. Thank you to all who have supported and encouraged me along the way.

My gratitude also goes to the team at BPB Publications for being supportive enough to provide me with enough time to finish the book and for collaborative work on its editing and enhancements.

Preface

In this book, you will get an in-depth understanding of the Microsoft Office 365 (O365) platform from various angles such as Implementations, Set Up, Administrations, Out of the Box (OOB) development, custom solutions development, and business process automation. We will start with a high-level platform overview and what it is used for and then slowly continue diving deeper into the topic and have some practice samples. We will also look at a wide variety of technologies and techniques associated with O365 and induced applications scuh as SharePoint, OneDrive, Exchange, Teams, and so on. The book will be useful to people who are learning about Microsoft Office 365 as well as professionals who would like to switch their focus from other similar platforms or want to enhance O365 knowledge.

You will learn how to use technologies and frameworks such as PowerApps, Power Automate, SharePoint Designer, InfoPath, Office 365 Admin center, SQL and Security and Compliance center, as well as React, SPFX, PnP and PowerShell.

Chapter 1: Outline of Microsoft 365 – discusses what Microsoft Office 365 is; what it is used for and what is its main purpose. We will also cover how companies all over the world use Office 365 for their needs and what the main difference between on-premise and online versions of Microsoft apps is.

Chapter 2: Prologue to SharePoint Online – reviews the evolution path of SharePoint. We will cover where the idea of creating SharePoint came from and how it evolved from wss 3.0 to SharePoint online, which is used globally nowadays. We will review the high-level administration, configuration, and security capabilities of SharePoint online and how they can be used in real-world projects.

Chapter 3: Working with Present-day Destinations in SharePoint Online – will dive deeper into the topic of SharePoint. Here, we will discover what components SharePoint consists of and what the main pieces in the puzzle are; how to set up the right permissions so that users would have access to the information they need; how to protect and secure your organization's data, and more.

Chapter 4: Working with Records in SharePoint Online – overviews SharePoint and its capabilities even further. How often have you seen situations where documents are supposed to be retained for 5 or 10, or even more years? This is where the Records management feature in SharePoint comes in. Here, we will review in more detail what records management is; how to configure it for your specific case; and how to protect and preserve your data for the years ahead.

Chapter 5: Working with Archive Libraries in SharePoint Online – discusses some built-in and custom features available in SharePoint, that helps to free up space and keep data organized, by periodically archiving some information. The chapter reviews them and lets the reader find how to properly organize, manage and archive data to make sure your collaboration environment always stays up to date and easy to navigate and find the right piece of information.

Chapter 6: OneDrive for Business – discusses what OneDrive is, and why we should use it when we have SharePoint available already. The same as SharePoint, OneDrive is available as a part of the Office 365 suite, and it also has its own desktop client for a more convenient user experience. In this chapter, you will learn the main difference in purpose between SharePoint and OneDrive, what to use when, and what features are available similar and different between them.

Chapter 7: Search in Microsoft 365 – discusses Search, which is one of the core functions of any platform. Here you will learn how to get the best out of the SharePoint online search. You will become familiar with search templates, crawling, metadata, search results templates, indexing, and other core capabilities of SPO search. After a proper configuration, users will be able to find documents effectively, fast, and in a reliable way.

Chapter 8: Microsoft Groups – explores how essential it is to set up correct permission levels and organize users accordingly, in order to build a proper governance model in the Office 365 environment. The most common way to manage groups is via Active Directory (AD) groups. But let us see what Office 365 groups can offer instead, and how they can supplement AD functionality. In this chapter, you will learn how to set up Office 365 groups, where to manage them, and how to properly organize users.

Chapter 9: Microsoft Teams – discusses how, with more and more people switching to remote work every day, the need of tools that would support instant chatting and meeting capabilities has dramatically increased. When it comes to a collaboration, Microsoft Teams covers all aspects such as chatting, meeting, calendars, as well as approvals and file management. In this chapter, we will overview what are the main capabilities of Microsoft Teams. You will create your own Teams channel, configure permissions, and add supporting tabs and materials to your channel.

Chapter 10: Power Platform and Citizen Development – discusses Power Platform, which is the new low-code solution from Microsoft to allow users to develop applications and workflows and automate business processes. The beauty of any low-code solution is that no coding skills are needed from the user working on the functionality. Hence, development can be done by regular employees with no or minimal training provided. Power Platform is a combination of applications that includes PowerApps (with Canvas, Model Driven, Power Portals, Dataverse) and Power Automate (with Flows and solutions). This chapter will cover how regular users can use all of the apps and what are the best ways for organizations to utilize various development approaches.

Chapter 11: Stream – explores the whole idea behind Stream, that is, to provide an application integrated with Microsoft 365 suite that can store videos, where users can create their channels and publish various media files assigning metadata to them. This chapter will cover all these and review how Stream can be integrated with other Microsoft 365 apps such as SharePoint or Teams.

Chapter 12: PowerApps – dives deeper into the PowerApps topic. As you already know, there are multiple different versions of PowerApps: Canvas and Model Driven. Information can be stored in SharePoint, Dataverse, SQL or even at Excel. We will review how to build simple Canvas and Model Driven app. You will learn how to connect your app to the proper data source, how to operate and manipulate the data from there and add various validations to the form.

Chapter 13: Power Automate – dives deeper into Power Automate, and discusses how to build various versions of Flows: running on start, on modify, or scheduled. You will learn a few basic actions commonly used to automate processes in Power Automate, as well as review connections to API and how to make queries directly from the Flow.

Chapter 14: Power BI – discusses PowerBI as a powerful tool for creating dashboards, analytics reports, and data visualization. It will also explore PowerBI licensing, PowerBI Desktop, how to create reports and publish them, and how to integrate and prepare reports back to SharePoint and make them visible to other users. Moreover, the chapter will overview different data sources and connectors available in the tool and how filters, sorting, and different views can be implemented based on your needs.

Chapter 15: Office 365 Admin Center – goes through the administration and management of the applications using the Microsoft 365 Admin center. It includes various admin centers and their capabilities to configure policies, set up users and manage billing.

Chapter 16: Security and Compliance Policies – explores the topic of security in the Microsoft 365 ecosystem, that covers all applications included in the suite. It discusses how to protect your environment from unwanted data leakage or information sharing with external sources, how to set up an environment in a way that would be compliant with policies such as HIPA, and all possible applications starting from SharePoint and finishing with Exchange. You will also learn about eDiscovery, Labels and other tools available as a part of the Security and Compliance Center.

Chapter 17: Term Store and Content Sorts in SharePoint Online – discusses Term Store, that helps to expand metadata capabilities and navigation options. On Term Store, terms aka managed metadata, can be created in a proper structure and later be assigned to specific documents or items in SharePoint, or can even be used to build the navigation. In this chapter, you will learn how to access Term store, create Term groups and Terms, and later use them for your content or navigation management needs.

Chapter 18: Custom Solutions Development SPFX – explores how SharePoint offers advanced customization when it comes to updating features based on the company's needs, compared to what SPO can offer out of the box. That is why SPFX solutions might be needed. Using React, Angular or any other JavaScript framework of your choice, you can develop custom web-parts, custom look and feel, dashboards, reports, and much more. In this chapter, we will review the history of customization support for various SharePoint platforms and what approaches are available nowadays.

Chapter 19: PnP, PowerShell and Scripting – reviews the main scripting languages supported by Microsoft 365, like PowerShell, PnP, CSOM, and even CAML. Using scripts, Admins can generate reports faster, retrieve and operate with data in the platform, set up policies and much more, all from cmd interface.

Code Bundle and Coloured Images

Please follow the link to download the
Code Bundle and the *Coloured Images* of the book:

https://rebrand.ly/v0s4n26

The code bundle for the book is also hosted on GitHub at **https://github.com/bpbpublications/Office-365-with-SharePoint-Online-Cookbook-Solutions**. In case there's an update to the code, it will be updated on the existing GitHub repository.

We have code bundles from our rich catalogue of books and videos available at **https://github.com/bpbpublications**. Check them out!

Errata

We take immense pride in our work at BPB Publications and follow best practices to ensure the accuracy of our content to provide with an indulging reading experience to our subscribers. Our readers are our mirrors, and we use their inputs to reflect and improve upon human errors, if any, that may have occurred during the publishing processes involved. To let us maintain the quality and help us reach out to any readers who might be having difficulties due to any unforeseen errors, please write to us at :

errata@bpbonline.com

Your support, suggestions and feedbacks are highly appreciated by the BPB Publications' Family.

Did you know that BPB offers eBook versions of every book published, with PDF and ePub files available? You can upgrade to the eBook version at www.bpbonline.com and as a print book customer, you are entitled to a discount on the eBook copy. Get in touch with us at :

business@bpbonline.com for more details.

At **www.bpbonline.com**, you can also read a collection of free technical articles, sign up for a range of free newsletters, and receive exclusive discounts and offers on BPB books and eBooks.

Piracy

If you come across any illegal copies of our works in any form on the internet, we would be grateful if you would provide us with the location address or website name. Please contact us at **business@bpbonline.com** with a link to the material.

If you are interested in becoming an author

If there is a topic that you have expertise in, and you are interested in either writing or contributing to a book, please visit **www.bpbonline.com**. We have worked with thousands of developers and tech professionals, just like you, to help them share their insights with the global tech community. You can make a general application, apply for a specific hot topic that we are recruiting an author for, or submit your own idea.

Reviews

Please leave a review. Once you have read and used this book, why not leave a review on the site that you purchased it from? Potential readers can then see and use your unbiased opinion to make purchase decisions. We at BPB can understand what you think about our products, and our authors can see your feedback on their book. Thank you!

For more information about BPB, please visit **www.bpbonline.com**.

Join our book's Discord space

Join the book's Discord Workspace for Latest updates, Offers, Tech happenings around the world, New Release and Sessions with the Authors:

https://discord.bpbonline.com

Table of Contents

CHAPTER 1
Outline of Microsoft 365

"Teamwork is the ability to work together toward a common vision. The ability to direct individual accomplishments toward organizational objectives. It is the fuel that allows common people to attain uncommon results."

- Andrew Carnegie

Introduction

More than a decade ago, at the time when the author started working with SharePoint, Windows SharePoint Services (WSS 3.0) to be precise, it was the race for leadership in the corporate market between Microsoft, Google, Box, and a few other platforms. It became obvious that big enterprise companies and government agencies are overloaded with paperwork. With evolving technologies in the web space, there is a massive market for setting up and organizing proper collaboration workspace. After all these years, we can see that Microsoft got a strong position in the Collaboration workspace (as it usually had with Windows, MS Office, and all other tools for corporate space).

In this chapter, we will start our journey from the Microsoft 365 overview, understand why it is so popular that every enterprise company uses its capabilities, and discover more of the history and pros and cons between the on-premises platform and cloud-based version.

Structure

In this chapter, we will cover the following topics:

- The need for Microsoft 365
- Main capabilities of Microsoft 365
- On-premise versus online
- Licensing in Microsoft 365
- Setting up your own tenant

Objectives

This chapter will discover what Microsoft Office 365 is, what it is used for, and its primary purpose. We will also cover how companies worldwide are using Office 365 for their needs and the main difference between on-premise and online versions of Microsoft apps.

The need for Microsoft 365

Let us assume you are a large organization's Chief Technology Officer or Vice President of technology. What would your day-to-day tasks and problems you have to deal with be? Suppose we are talking about a "large organization". In that case, you probably have around ten thousand employees in your company, and you are responsible for ensuring they have the best tools and technologies available to complete their work daily. When employees complete their daily activities, they usually:

- Communicate with each other
- Work together on some documents
- Filling up forms
- Doing reviews
- Preparing reports
- Receiving and giving calls
- Attending meetings
- Sending emails
- Work on tasks and report their progress to managers, and so on.

Therefore, as a top-level executive and a good leader, you would be looking for ways to increase your employee's productivity, as you know it will directly impact your company sales and product quality. The equation is pretty simple; this higher productivity means more profit for the company and faster business development. So, it is a win-win game, employees do less work (or more work for the same amount of time), and the company receives more profit and develops faster.

This is precisely where Microsoft 365 comes into play. Let us check what activities employees commonly do and how Microsoft 365 can help boost their productivity.

Communicate with each other, receive and give calls, attend meetings: Microsoft Teams can help satisfy all the needs. Teams are included in all basic licenses, which we will review in more detail in the coming chapter. It is an excellent tool for setting up the entire collaboration environment. In fact, it is such a great tool and combines so many features that many companies switch all of their communication and document management needs to Teams. We will review its main capabilities in the next chapter.

Work together on documents: SharePoint and OneDrive are also included in all basic licenses and provide outstanding capabilities to create, store, share, and work together on documents. SharePoint would be a better fit for documents and materials shared across multiple people or departments. Meanwhile, OneDrive is a perfect workplace for personal and work-related documents.

Fill up forms, and do reviews: Power Platform is available to satisfy this need. Office 365 forms might be handy for creating forms or simple surveys. But if you are looking for more advanced capabilities, PowerApps would be a great fit with multiple data-source connectors available that will allow you to retrieve and store information in different places such as Excel, SharePoint lists, databases, 3rd party platforms like Salesforce, and so on. Moreover, Power Automate running in the background will help automate sending notifications and emails to persons needed, requesting approvals or reviews, handling status updates, and much more. Power Apps and Power Automate are big topics that we will cover separately in this book.

Send emails: Well, we have all used Outlook. But guess what? It is a part of Microsoft 365 as well. Outlook is the application and interface that allows users to work with their emails. Microsoft Exchange is the engine that handles all mail deliveries, rules, and filters. It is available in all Microsoft 365 licenses and provides a custom domain email address, Outlook client, and other features.

The list can go on and on. Thus, in our next chapter, we will cover the main capabilities of Microsoft 365 and do a high-level overview of all included applications and features.

For now, though, let us return to our Chief Technology Officer role and see why we would like to use Microsoft 365 that much. You see, M365 is a suite of applications included and available to you, based on your license and the money you spend per user per month. Your end goal is to increase productivity and your employee's performance. So, why would you use multiple tools, support them, and have different teams to complete upgrades and solve issues, when you can have all the tools you need in one place?

That is precisely what Microsoft 365 is about! Plus, it is cloud-based, so you do not need to host your infrastructure and maintain servers. It is all done by Microsoft! Users need to use the browser or available desktop apps, and voila! All tools are at your fingertips!

Meanwhile, if you are cautious about security and compliances and want to maintain your infrastructure, an on-premises version of all apps is always available as an alternative. You can even have a cloud version and an on-premises and set up a Hybrid environment. However, we will talk later about it.

Main capabilities of Microsoft 365

As discussed, Microsoft 365 (or Office 365) is a suite of apps available to you based on the purchased license. The minimal basic license includes apps, such as:

- Outlook
- Exchange
- OneDrive
- OneNote
- Teams
- SharePoint
- MS Office (Word, Excel, PowerPoint, and so on)
- PowerApps
- Power Automate

More advanced and add-on licenses may include apps, such as:

- Publisher
- Access DB
- Project

- Yammer
- Stream
- Forms
- Visio
- Planner
- Power BI, and so on.

The whole idea behind Microsoft 365 platform is to bring all applications together and provide users with a unified interface where they can easily switch between apps, and applications can exchange information with each other. This approach offers users a great user experience and endless capabilities for developers (REST API, GRAPH API).

Figure 1.1 features the Microsoft 365 welcome screen:

Figure 1.1: *A Microsoft 365 welcome screen and Home page*

Figure 1.2 features the available apps within Microsoft 365:

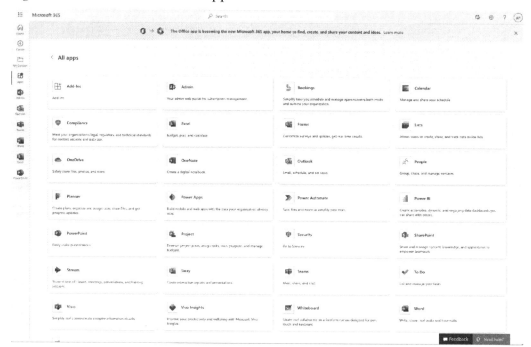

Figure 1.2: *A Microsoft 365 app listed on the left side*

As you can see in the preceding *Figure 1.2*, all the apps are available to you from the home page.

Just navigate to **https://portal.office.com** and sign in with your corporate account (if you do not have one, we will review how to set up a sandbox environment at the end of this chapter).

Let us now review each application on a high level to understand its advantages and why they are included in Microsoft 365.

Outlook

Microsoft Outlook is a personal information manager that allows you to send and receive emails. It includes a calendar to set and schedule meetings, create tasks, and store names and other people's contact information. The cool thing about it is that it can be managed by the admin team and define which features, add-ons, and options are available to you, have integration with contacts from **Active Directory** (**AD**), and give you the ability to see other people schedules and availability from your calendar. On top of that, built-in security, configurable **Data Loss Prevention** (**DLP**) policies, and security rules will make it a very safe place for you to work.

Exchange

Exchange is the mail, calendar server, and dedicated network resource management program. It runs in the background and is responsible for all mail delivery processes and rules. Using Exchange admin, the team can enforce rules and policies, which will be applied to the email inside Outlook and Calendars.

OneDrive

OneDrive is a file hosting and documents storage service. It allows users to share and synchronize their files from various devices such as PC, mobile, and file systems into the cloud and back. OneDrive has a OneDrive sync client that can be installed on any OS (Windows, Mac OS, IOS, Android) and synchronizes files back and forth between cloud storage and other connected devices.

OneNote

OneNote is a note-taking application. It allows individual users or entire teams to take and organize notes, store valuable text information, and share it between different members. All information is synchronized to the cloud and available on various PC, mobile, and online platforms through the browser. Users can create separate sections and pages within the app to store and organize information efficiently.

Teams

Microsoft Teams is a collaboration and messaging app for organizations and individual use. It provides an interface and workspace for real-time communication, meetings, calls, chats, and file sharing. It is a unified platform to get all your work done. Thanks to Teams integrations with MS Office and SharePoint, you can create Word, Excel, and other files from Teams. Edit, share, and work simultaneously on files right from it at the same time as having chats and calls and scheduling meetings through the calendar at the same place.

SharePoint

SharePoint is a web-based collaboration platform for document management and business process automation. There are various versions available historically:

- SharePoint 2003
- SharePoint 2007
- SharePoint 2010
- SharePoint 2013

- SharePoint 2016
- SharePoint 2019
- SharePoint Online

When we are working with Microsoft 365, we are constantly dealing with the latest and greatest version available, which is SharePoint Online. All other versions are server-based. We will cover more on SharePoint and its capabilities in the upcoming chapters.

MS Office

Microsoft Office is a suite of applications designed to help complete common tasks on a computer. Office includes the following:

- Word
- Excel
- PowerPoint
- Access
- Outlook
- Publisher
- Visio

It can be installed as the whole suite of apps together, or each app can be installed separately. They are available for various platforms such as PC, Mac, Mobile, and Online. For the Online version, you need to use your browser, and no installation is required.

PowerApps

PowerApps is a low-code data platform with various apps, services, and connectors that provides a rapid development environment to build custom applications for various business needs. As a low-code solution, PowerApps is designed for *citizen developers or power users* that do not necessarily have coding skills or previous application development background. PowerApps are mainly forms and UI interfaces for data input and storage (in Dataverse).

Figure 1.3 features the PowerApps Canvas application designer:

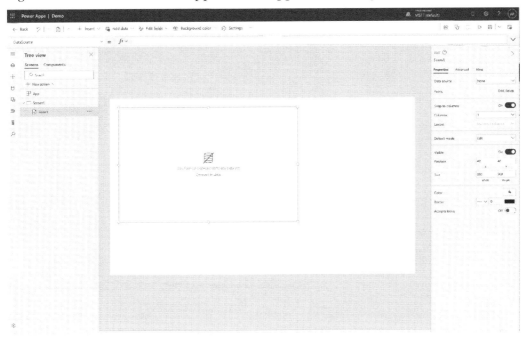

Figure 1.3: *PowerApps Canvas application designer*

Power Automate

Power Automate, similar to PowerApps, is a low-code platform for Automation and workflow development logic. It allows to extend capabilities of automation and gives the ability for *citizen developers or power users* to quickly build workflows for process automation, approvals, and email notifications. *Figure 1.4* features the Power Automate Flow designer:

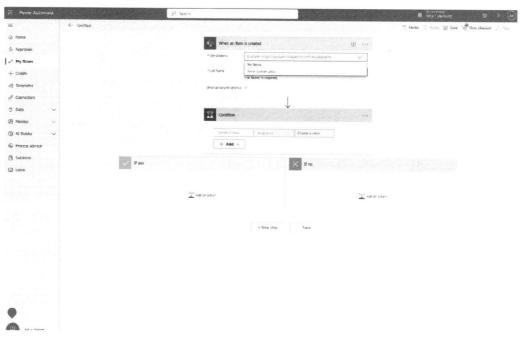

Figure 1.4: *Power Automate Flow designer*

On-premise versus online

This topic is about Microsoft 365 itself (as it is a purely online-based suite of applications), although it is more about the applications included in the M365. Let us take SharePoint and Microsoft Office as our example applications to explain the difference between on-premise and online-based versions.

On-premise application is something that is physically hosted on your servers and infrastructure. Thus, it is also referenced as server-based. Online, on the other head, is something hosted in the cloud and located on the servers of 3rd party providers such as Microsoft (Azure or M365), Amazon (AWS), and others. Thus, the main difference is that it is either hosted on your equipment or someone else's.

Let us take a closer look at a SharePoint example and see the basic components needed. To set up your own infrastructure and deploy SharePoint, we need the following:

- Application server with matching requirements on hardware. If you plan to have a massive infrastructure, you would need a few of them.

- Windows Server Operational system.

- Database as MS SQL.

- Load Balancer, preferably.

- Separate Search server.

- Active Directory with a configured user and their profiles.

- To make SharePoint available outside of your Intranet network, you would need to do additional configurations.

- You would need to have a team of Administrators to patch Windows, Databases, and SharePoint itself and to maintain your environment up-to-date and protected.

For SharePoint Online (part of Microsoft 365), you would need the following:

- Purchase licenses for M365.

- Choose your domain name.

- You might need to have the admin make sure to set up security policies and requirements.

Thus, you can see how much less hustle and effort is required to maintain an Online environment. Microsoft is taking care of the initial setup, configuration, and provision. You get a ready-to-use suite of apps (remember, it is not just SharePoint included) in a matter of minutes. More than that, you will not need to take care of patching and your infrastructure maintenance.

However, there are also some disadvantages coming with the Online version. You do not have direct access to the database or logs, which might be very handy from time to time. If something goes wrong in your environment, you would need to work with the Microsoft support team and rely on them rather than fixing issues yourself.

The main advantage of the on-premise version of the applications is security and compliance. If you want to have full control of your data and take full responsibility for its safety, you do not trust any other 3rd party providers enough to store sensitive information. The on-premise version is the right choice. Moreover, you have full control of system logs, audits, and databases.

If you want to have the best of both worlds, a Hybrid environment is a right option for you. It definitely increases the cost as you need to pay for the Online version, and you also get your own on-premise infrastructure. However, you get full control and a safe place to store sensitive data and an online version for overall convenient user. The search can be configured to look through the documents or users on both environments.

Microsoft Office applications such as Word, Excel, PowerPoint, and so on, can also be on-premise and installed directly to your PC or mobile device. They can also be Online-based versions. The online version is convenient as it allows users to create, edit, and work on their documents directly through the browser, and no installation of MS Word or MS Excel is needed on your machine. As a downside, some functionality such as macros in Excel or particular formulas, might be limited in the Online-based version. As a rule of thumb, Office Online is good for documents preview and basic edits. Meanwhile, if you need to work on heavy documents, it is better to open them in the desktop-based version of the app. Online version of apps also has the autosave enabled all the time and synchronize all the changes automatically back to the source where the file is stored.

Licensing in Microsoft 365

All Microsoft licenses can be defined, based on the size of your business. There are four main categories:

- Home and family
- Business
- Enterprise
- Government

In most of these options, they include the same basic set of apps such as Office applications, OneDrive, Teams, and so on. The higher the tier you go, the more applications will be available in the subscription, and the more will the price increase.

All the available packages can be found at the **https://www.microsoft.com/en-us/microsoft-365**. If you go to the Products section on the menu, you will see all available packages and types of licenses.

Home and Family is the most basic plan that costs either $100/year and includes 6-person licenses. Or costs $70/year just for one person. Applications included are as follows:

- Word
- Excel
- PowerPoint
- OneDrive

- Outlook
- OneNote

Figure 1.5 features the home and family licenses:

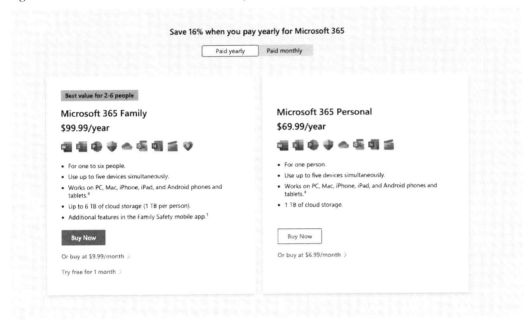

Figure 1.5: *Home and Family licenses*

Business licenses are the next tier of plans. It is more expanded as now in addition to the Office apps, you also get SharePoint, Exchange, and in some plans, Access and Publisher. Now, instead of buying a license for the whole year, you will pay per license per month for each user. The good news is that you can combine multiple plans and for some users, assign one license, and for others, different.

The business tier includes the following plans:

- Basic: $6/user/month
- Apps for business: $8.25/user/month
- Standard: $12.50/user/month
- Premium: $22/user/month

Figure 1.6 features the Business licenses:

Figure 1.6: *Business licenses*

Enterprise and Government licenses are somewhat similar.

They can all be broken down into plans like:

- E3 (G3 – government)
- E5 (G5 – government)

The main difference between them will be a set of security policies and functionality available within the apps. The Government tier is stricter on the data protection rules and where and how infrastructure should be hosted. Thus, the Government tier tends to get updates later than the Enterprise environment and sometimes has limited applications or functionality available, although with higher security. Moreover, it is worth mentioning that G-type licenses and Government environment are available only to government agencies on a local, state, and federal level. You will not find information about government licenses on the website itself. The government acquisition team usually works directly with Microsoft to set those up.

The set of applications is extended in E/G licenses, as is the cost. You still would pay for the user per month license.

The following *Figure 1.7* features the enterprise licenses:

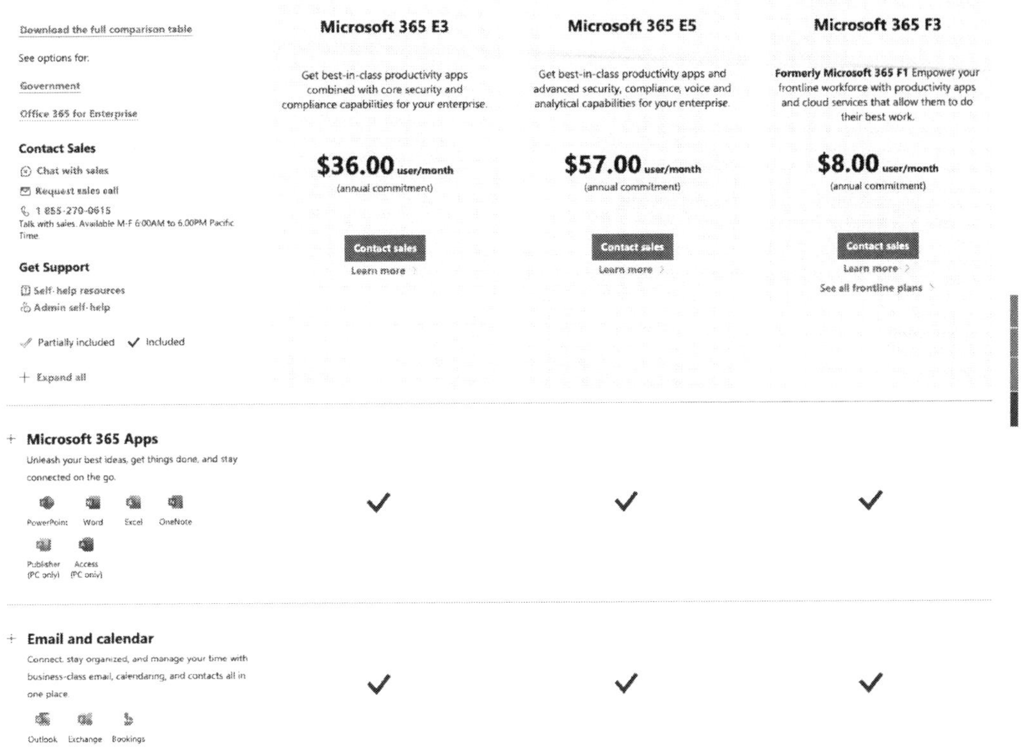

Figure 1.7: Enterprise licenses

It is worth mentioning that it does not matter what type of license tier or plan you have. You can also purchase additional apps and include them in your tenant for a different cost.

Setting up your own tenant

Through this book, we will conduct reviews of various applications and features and will do practical exercises. Thus, it is required for the reader to have a workplace where you can take a look at the apps and become familiar with the functionality. Luckily for us, Microsoft provides an option for a Microsoft 365 Sandbox Development environment, where all solutions we are looking for are available.

As the first step in your browser, go to the **https://developer.microsoft.com/en-us/ microsoft-365/dev-program**

You would need to create a new Microsoft email and account to set everything up. Follow the given steps:

1. Once you landed on the Developer Program site at the top right corner, click on the **Sign In** option, as shown in *Figure 1.8:*

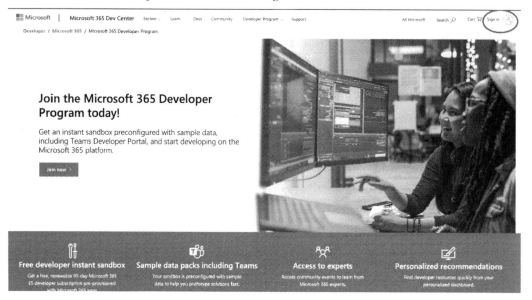

Figure 1.8: Sign In at the Microsoft Developer program site

2. You will see the option '**No account? Create One!**'. Click on it, as shown in *Figure 1.9:*

Figure 1.9: Creating a Microsoft account

3. Next, you will see a similar window asking for your email address. Select the option **Get a new email address**.

4. Choose the desired account name and domain, as shown in *Figure 1.10*:

Figure 1.10: Creating a new email

5. In the subsequent few screens, follow the prompts to set up the password and fill out any information required.

6. After the email is created, you will be automatically redirected back to the Developer Program page. As the last step, click on the top right corner of your profile icon and select the option **Add Name**. Add your name and give it about 30 minutes to synchronize. Take a break here.

7. Afterward, go back to the Developer Program page and click the **Join Now** button in the middle of the screen.

8. You will be asked to provide your region information. Then select the type of use as **Personal Use** and select all of the checkboxes and apps on the next

screen. After that, you will see the plans option. Select **Instant Sandbox** and click **Next**. Create admin usernames. Refer to *Figure 1.11:*

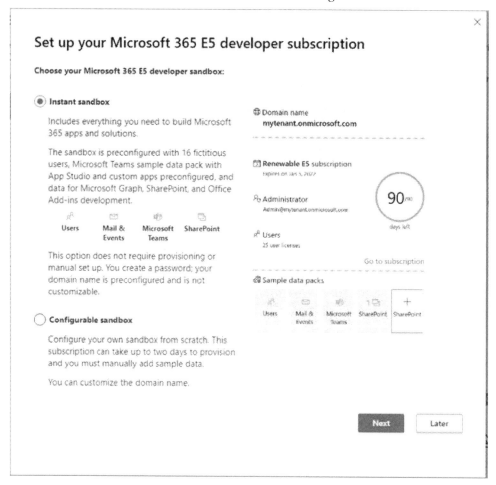

Figure 1.11: Selecting Sandbox plan

Note: Sandbox environment will be available for only 90 days free of charge. Then, you can either set up the new one or get your own license and subscription.

9. Confirm your phone number with the code from a text message.

10. Click **Go to Subscription**.

11. You will see M365 home page. Down the road, you can go here directly by typing **https://portal.office.com** in your browser. Use your newly created account to sign in.

From the home page, click on the top left corner of the screen where you have squares, and you will see applications available. Click on *Admin* to go to the admin center, as shown in *Figure 1.12:*

Figure 1.12: *Access admin center from the home page*

In the admin center, you will see different Admin centers available for you, such as:

- Security
- Compliance
- Exchange
- Azure
- SharePoint
- Teams

We will review capabilities and features of each center later in this book.

Figure 1.13 features the Microsoft 365 Admin Center:

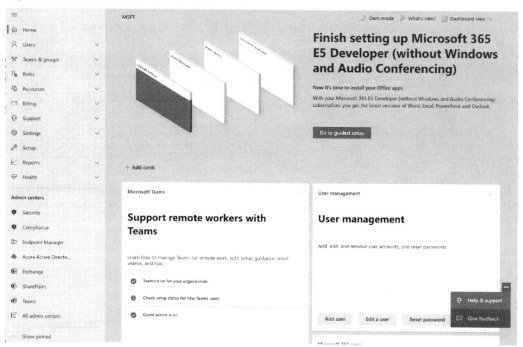

Figure 1.13: *Microsoft 365 Admin Center*

Let us click on the **Billing** dropdown and select **Licenses**. On that screen, you will see how many licenses and which type you have available. It should show you E5 license.

Now click the **Users** dropdown in the left menu and select **Active Users**. You will be able to see all demo accounts automatically provisioned for you there. You can use it to play around in the environment. If you click on any of the funds, it will show you that profile information, assigned licenses and roles.

Click again at the top left corner on squares and select the **All apps** option. It will show you all applications available to you in Microsoft 365 with your E5 license. Try find SharePoint, OneDrive, and Teams. Click on each one of them and take an initial look at the interface and become familiar with it.

Conclusion

In the first chapter, we discovered what Microsoft 365 is, what it is used for, and its main advantages. You became familiar with the on-premise and online versions of applications and learned the difference and pros and cons between them. Now you should be aware of the different licensing packages available and have your very own Microsoft 365 sandbox environment. In conclusion, Microsoft 365 is an online suite of applications available to you based on your license type. Primary applications are SharePoint, Teams, OneDrive, and Office.

Points to remember

- Microsoft 365, also known as Office 365, is an online platform with various apps. What applications are available depends on your subscription.

- All of the applications inside the M365 suite are available to you via browser. Some applications, such as Office apps, can be installed on your machine as a desktop version.

- Different license types are available based on your needs: Home, Business, Enterprise, and Government.

- The main advantage of M365 compared to on-promise infrastructure is that it is easier to maintain, as Microsoft executes most maintenance tasks. As a disadvantage, you have less control over the database and back end of the system.

- SharePoint, OneDrive, Teams, and Power Platform are the leading solutions widely used inside M365.

Join our book's Discord space

Join the book's Discord Workspace for Latest updates, Offers, Tech happenings around the world, New Release and Sessions with the Authors:

https://discord.bpbonline.com

CHAPTER 2

Prologue to SharePoint Online

"Paper is no longer a big part of my day. I get 90% of my news online, and when I go to a meeting and want to jot things down, I bring my Tablet PC. It's fully synchronized with my office machine, so I have all the files I need. It also has a note-taking piece of software called OneNote, so all my notes are in digital form."

- Bill Gates

Introduction

In the first chapter of the book, we briefly covered what Microsoft 365 is and what applications are a part of it. You noticed that SharePoint is one of the biggest applications from that list. Let us dive deeper into the SharePoint topics and discover what capabilities it holds, what features are available inside, and what are the best practices based on Microsoft recommendations.

Structure

In this chapter, we will cover the following topics:

- SharePoint history

- Collaboration environments with cutting-edge technologies built on SharePoint

- Why use SharePoint online nowadays?

- Practical examples on SharePoint Online

Objectives

In this chapter, we will review the evolution path of SharePoint. We will cover where the idea of creating SharePoint came from and how it evolved from **Windows SharePoint Services 3.0 (WSS 3.0)** to SharePoint online, which is used globally nowadays. We will review the high-level administration, configuration, and security capabilities of SharePoint online and how they can be used in real-world projects.

SharePoint history

The idea of SharePoint came from the Office Server. The initial application was built based on Exchange with Digital Dashboard and some graphical interface. Its target was to provide a simple, yet effective collaboration solution that could be used by regular company employees, up to executive management. The solution package was coming in the form of some Office Server extensions and provided additional collaboration features and functionality compared to the regular Office. It all happened in the beginning of 2000 – 2002.

In the digital era, when all documentation is stored on personal computers and exchanged more constantly via emails, there was a new niche opening to provide one centralized place, where all documents could be stored, and automation could be built on top of that.

As it always happens, the system did not stay in one place and constantly evolved. Users around the globe found SharePoint more and more useful and attractive. It took approximately five years for Microsoft to push solutions to the companies and get leading positions out there in the enterprise market.

Microsoft Office SharePoint Server (MOSS) 2007 and SharePoint server 2010, are really when mass adoption started to happen. Both versions were installed and hosted on a server running Windows Server OS, SQL Database, and **Internet Information Services (IIS)** on the back. User synchronization and user profiles were stored in the company's **Active Directory (AD)**.

Figure 2.1 features the interface of SharePoint Server 2007:

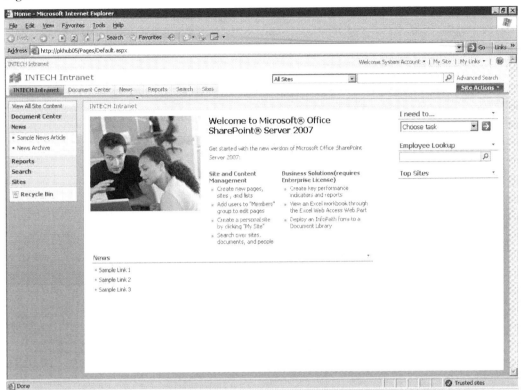

Figure 2.1: *A SharePoint 2007 home screen*

As more and more companies were adopting SharePoint, Microsoft came up with 'different package' options. So, based on the features you need, company size, and budget, multiple versions are able for purchase and installation in SharePoint 2010 (on-premises):

- SharePoint Foundation 2010 (free of charge)

- SharePoint Server 2010 (was an extended version of Foundation for commercial use)

- SharePoint Enterprise 2010 (the most reach on features and the most expensive version)

Changes in end-user functionality added in the 2010 version of SharePoint (on-premises) included:

- New UI with Fluent Ribbon, using wiki pages rather than 'web-part pages' and offering multi-browser support.

- New social profiles and early social networking features.

- Updated Central Administration, where admins could manage the majority of configuration instead of using IIS directly.

- Sandboxed Solutions and client-side object-model APIs for JavaScript, Silverlight, and .NET applications.

- Business Connectivity Services, Claims-based Authentication, and Windows PowerShell support for easier scripting and command executions for bulk operations.

- SharePoint Designer (a desktop application to manage sites, lists, forms and workflows) was introduced in the 2010 version.

Figure 2.2 features the interface of SharePoint Enterprise 2010:

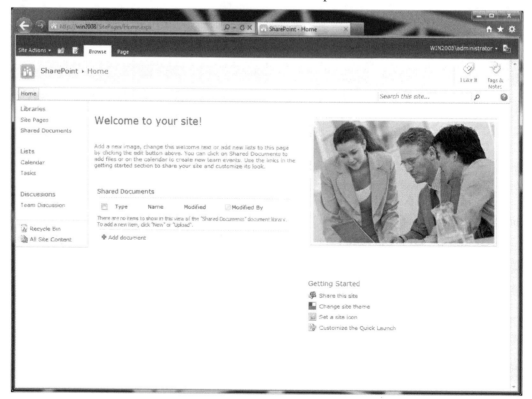

Figure 2.2: A SharePoint 2010 home screen

You can see from the preceding figure how the interface evolved and became much cleaner in the 2010 version. Moreover, all the additional features available made it a really great and agile platform for development and customization, and provided the ability to tailor it towards the client's specific needs.

The next released versions of SharePoint were more mature and advanced:

- SharePoint 2013

- SharePoint 2016

- SharePoint 2019

- SharePoint Online became available somewhere around 2012 as part of Office 365 (known as Microsoft 365 nowadays). Microsoft released the first technical preview to a select group of partners in early 2012 and the public beta in July of 2012. The final version came out in October 2012. Office 365 SharePoint Online was out at the end of February 2013.

New features for updated versions are also included, and they are as follows:

- Cross-browser drag & drop support for file uploads/changes

- Follow/Share buttons

- OneDrive for Business (initially SkyDrive Pro) replaces MySites and Workspaces

- Audit center (service called eDiscovery)

- Rebuilt and improved search capabilities

- Updated **User Interface** (**UI**)

- Updated SharePoint Designer version 2013

- New REST API introduced

- Hybrid Improvements

- Modern sites and page layouts

- Communication sites and site templates

Collaboration environments with cutting-edge technologies built on SharePoint

There are quite a few companies using and adopting SharePoint to their needs in the world. As a matter of fact, all Fortune 500 companies from the United States and government agencies are using it: E&Y, Deloitte, Qualcomm, TCS, IRS, NIH, and many more, to name a few.

With SharePoint Online, Azure, API services developers and administrators can integrate multiple platforms together and build one eco-system that will work perfectly for the company. For instance, the company might be product-oriented and needs to have the ability to track incoming invoices and their statuses. All the invoices in this case can be stored in some bookkeeping software, such as Quickbooks from Intuit and then, using Webhooks, can be synchronized with Power Automate to the Dataverse in Microsoft 365. Information from Dataverse can be synchronized to the SharePoint list on the accounting site. So, this would allow accountants to quickly get access to the data they need, to proceed with their work execution, and would eliminate the need to switch back and forth between multiple systems.

On top of that, reports can be built to display valuable information, and infographics and data could be exported into PDF or Excel format. It is all up to your imagination and requirements. The possibilities are endless. The core functionality for authentication, storage, and navigation are already there, and so you can keep building on top of that. Utilizing Out of Box features and tools, a lot of things can be done and achieved. For everything else, custom options are always available. We have a separate dedicated chapter on customizations, covering some available basic and advanced options.

With proper administration and configuration from the admin side, companies nowadays might not even need any customization to be applied directly to SharePoint. There are a lot of data connectors available out of the box. Moreover, if those provided for free are not enough, a premium package is always an option for an additional payment. At an extra cost, a premium package would cover custom connectors with all API and data integrations you might need to develop and deploy.

Why use SharePoint online nowadays?

There are a few significant reasons why SharePoint is an excellent platform to use today. Let us review the main ones, which are noted as follows.

Document storage and collaboration

First of all, SharePoint is an excellent tool for document storage. Built-in functionality for version tracking, metadata, and a vast amount of storage that can be extended if needed, makes it an all-in-one tool for all your document management needs. Content owners and site admins can configure how many versions of each document should be stored. Each version can be reviewed and restored on a need basis. Moreover, the content approval and review options are available before the document gets published and becomes visible to everyone.

Agile permissions configuration would allow content owners to define permissions on different levels such as site, library, folder, or document itself, if needed. Hence, users who have access will be able to see the content, and who do not have the access, will be given an Access Denied message. Content can also be shared with external users and links to the documents can be configured to give ready-only, edit, or temporary access, that will expire soon. You can also invite external users and manage who should have access to your tenant from the admin panel.

Refer to *Figure 2.3:*

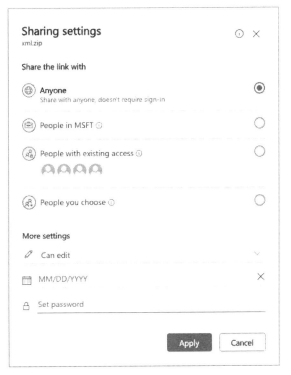

Figure 2.3: Sharing settings configuration for external users

Co-authoring

There are various situations when you need to work together with someone on a document, especially in the corporate world. It can be a new proposal, quarterly report, or anything else.

Previously, you would make your portion of updates in the file, then send it to someone else, and they will do their updates. This back and forth will continue until work on the document is done. Or everyone works with their document copy, and then all changes should be merged. Either way, the process was a headache, and the more people you have working on the same document, the more headache you get.

When all documentation is available online, there are more possibilities to work on the document together. The co-authoring feature in SharePoint, OneDrive, Teams, and pretty much all office documents, allows you to work together with your colleagues on the same document simultaneously. All users will be able to see who else logged in to the document and see what changes they are making in real time.

Refer to *Figure 2.4:*

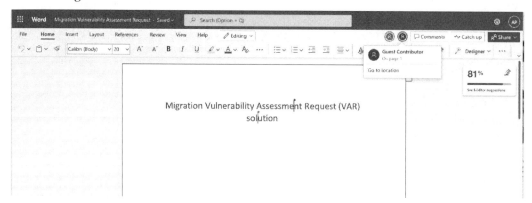

Figure 2.4: *Co-authoring view of the MS Word document*

You can see multiple cursors shown in the text, and you can see in the top right corner who else is working on the document with you. If the link was shared with external users, they would be displayed as 'Guest Contributor'; otherwise, you will see the name of the person from your organization.

Automation

After you finish working on the document, it might need to go through the review and approval process. There are multiple ways in which automation can be implemented. There is an option available for document review configured directly from the library level. Power Automate Flow is available if the process requires going through multiple approves, and different statuses should be captured. Either way, automation can save you a lot of time and paper by not printing those documents and getting signatures or sending a bunch of emails to whoever should review the document. Different approval processes can be configured, based on the document types and their location. We will cover more of it in *Chapter 13, Power Automate.*

Refer to *Figure 2.5:*

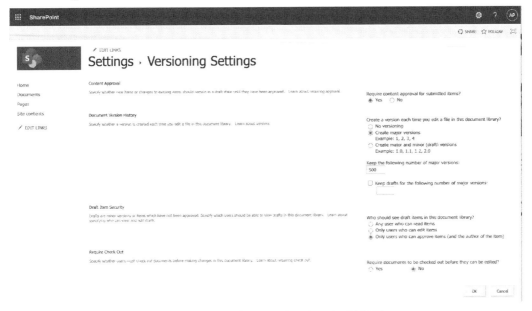

Figure 2.5: *Version and Approval settings in SPO Library*

Document retention

If your organization or government has any compliance rules stating that some documents should be retained for a specific time, then SharePoint can help with this too. As the majority of the document will be stored inside SharePoint, it offers a document retention option too. Out-of-the-box configuration allows admins to set up rules that will make a copy of the document or copy it to a dedicated site. Moreover, it will declare it as a record, preventing unauthorized document deletion or modification. Different rules can be configured based on the type of document. Documents can be retained for different periods of time. After time passes by, the document can be either automatically deleted or archived in another place. This feature is called 'Records Management' and is available for configuration from the Document Library setting in SharePoint itself.

Data loss prevention

Admins can set up a set of rules that will constantly be running and tracking all documents, emails, and chats on teams and other places to make sure information stays protected. This is especially handy and important for **Personal Protected Information** (PPI) and **Personal Identification Information** (PII). Those documents, emails or content that was identified by the system to store any of the sensitive information, will be sent to the admin team for review and can even be locked from further modifications, sharing, or deletion until a decision is made.

There is much more to cover for the features available in SharePoint Online, which will help make your workplace more protected, secure, and efficient. We will cover them in the following chapters. But even with those five covered before, you can see how SharePoint is a potent tool for collaboration and document management.

Practical examples on SharePoint Online

Let us go back to the Sand Box environment you configured before. Login to **https://portal.office.com** with the email and password you set up, and let us go to SharePoint from the home page. To do so, click on the squares in the top left corner and select SharePoint from the list of available applications.

Figure 2.6 features SharePoint application access from the M365 home page:

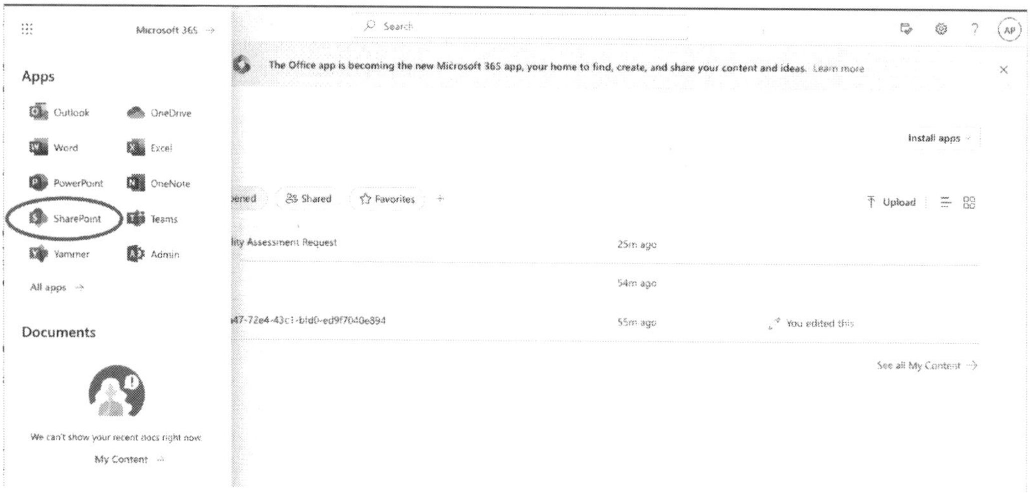

Figure 2.6: *How to access SharePoint from the M365 home page*

SharePoint will open in the new browser tab. As we are working with the newly set up environment, no sites will be available to you. So, let us create one!

At the top right corner, you will see two options available:

- Create a site (will create new site collection)
- Create news post (will create a news article)

Click on the **Create a site** option.

It will show you the pop-up on the right side of the screen, letting you choose from two templates: **Team site** or **Communication site**. You can read in the description right there what they both are intended to be used for. The bottom line is:

- A *Team site* is for the team, and a new team and O365 group (we will review groups in more depth later in the book) will be created in the Teams application. The site will be connected to that team. Its primary purpose would be to work with people from your team on some documents or items.

- A *Communication site* is similar, but it will be better suited for the Department site or some site, where various teams inside the organization should communicate. It has a different set of permissions, navigation, and additional features available. It also will NOT be connected to the Teams application.

Figure 2.7 features available SharePoint site templates when you create a new site. Please refer to the following figure:

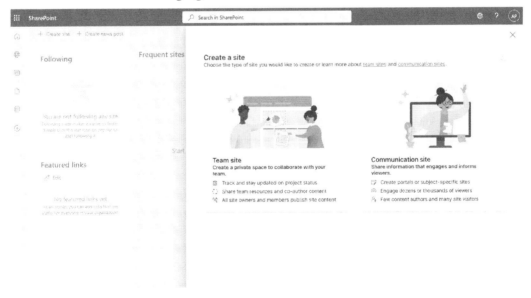

Figure 2.7: *SharePoint site templates choices*

Please note that once the site is created and it is tied to the template you selected, there is no direct way to change it later on. So, make the right choice from the beginning.

Otherwise, you would need to re-create a site and re-migrate all the content, which might be extra hustle if the site was used for an extended period of time and there is much content there. Alternatively, use a PowerShell script which will add additional complexity.

Let us select the **Communication site** option.

Name your site as you wish; all names are available at this moment. But down the road, if a site with the same name already exists, SharePoint will give you an error message and prompt you to create a site with a different name or change the site URL manually. This happens because when you create a new site, its URL will be defined based on its name, and each site URL should be unique. It is good to note that if you delete a site, the URL will not become available until deletion renders throughout the environment, which can take up to 24 hours. Please refer to the following figure:

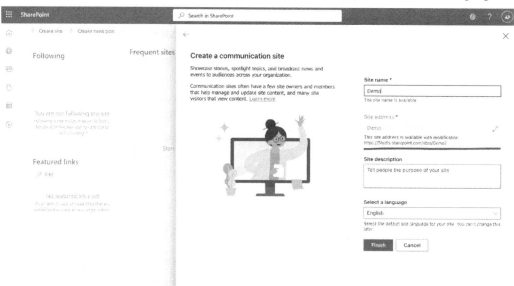

Figure 2.8: *Error message showed up if the site with the same URL already exists*

After you provide the site name, you can select the language it will be created based on. The default language will be selected based on your user profile's local configuration.

Once the site is created, you will see its Home page. Please note how URL is structured.

You have your domain name in the first part *someName***.sharepoint.com**. Then it follows with the **/sites/***siteName* indicating that this is the new Site Collection inside SharePoint online. This means that it has its own set of permissions and rules applied.

In the top right corner of the site, you will see a gear icon. Click on it and select **Site Contents**.

Figure 2.9 features the **Site Contents** link from the **Settings** menu:

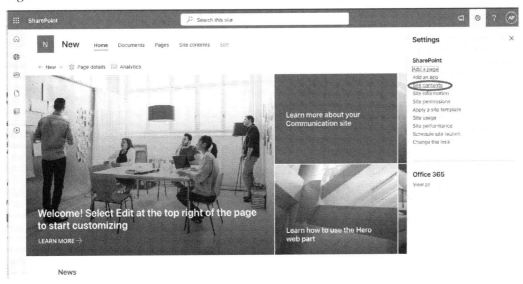

Figure 2.9: *Site Contents link from the setting menu*

It will open your Site Content page, where you can see all applications added to your site.

The view is broken down to show Content (by default when you land on the page), and you can see all of the subsites from this page too.

Figure 2.10 features the **Site contents** page and shows how you can switch between Contents and Subsite:

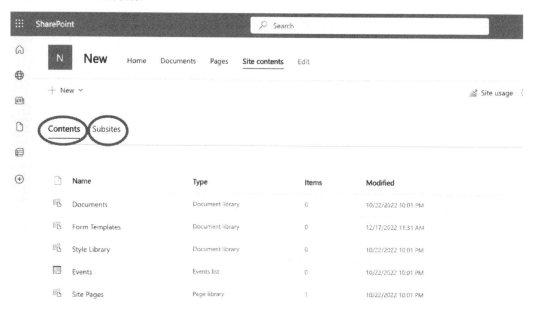

Figure 2.10: Contents and Subsite views

As you can see from the page itself, it will show you the entity name, its type, how many items are stored inside, and what is the last modified date.

There are a few main types of entities used in the SharePoint:

- Document library (store documents and media files)
- Lists (designed as a table to store information)
- Page library (stores pages available on your site)
- Application (custom apps installed on the site)

Let us create a new Document library on our site. Click on the **New** link at the top right corner and select **Document Library**, as shown in *Figure 2.11*:

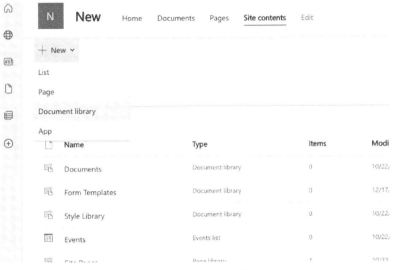

Figure 2.11: *the new Document Library creation*

Provide your Library name (as you wish) and click **Create**.

The new library will be created, and you will see that you can create or upload new documents there.

If you click at the top right corner on a gear icon and select **Site Contents**, you will see that your newly created library will be displayed on the list there.

Another way to quickly access Site contents is from the top menu. You should see the link available there by default. So, to do fewer clicks, you can use the link from the menu, as it will bring you to the exact same place.

Figure 2.12 features **Site Contents** links from the menu:

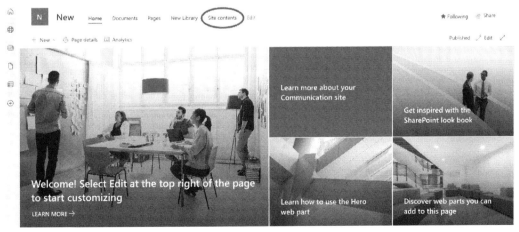

Figure 2.12: *Site Contents links from the menu.*

You see in Site Contents that there is also a Subsites view available. However, by default, it does not allow you to create a subsite underneath your site. This is a default configuration in the M365, and so there is nothing wrong with your environment. We will discover how to enable subsite creation in the coming chapter when we cover Admin Center for SharePoint.

We took some simple steps here to create the new site and document library, but it should give you an understanding of the structure and how SharePoint online works. In the next chapter, we will dive deeper into the different elements and features available in SharePoint and cover the difference between them.

Conclusion

Good job on setting up your first site and document library in the new tenant! Now, you should be familiar with the SharePoint history, what different versions there are, and how SharePoint evolution happened. You also know that you can implement pretty much anything on your SharePoint environment and integrate it with various third party systems and apps, based on your needs. We covered five main advantages of SharePoint online and how it helps organizations and users to be more efficient and build a more secure environment.

Points to remember

- SharePoint started as an Office extension.
- There are server versions of SharePoint (on-premise): SharePoint 2007, SharePoint 2010, SharePoint 2013, SharePoint 2016, and SharePoint 2019. SharePoint Online is also available as part of Microsoft 365.
- SharePoint online is always patched and up to date as Microsoft takes care of SharePoint Online maintenance.
- There are Out of box and custom components available inside SharePoint that will help you build any functionality you need and do integrations with third party systems.
- SharePoint is a powerful tool that provides users with document storage, collaboration and automation capabilities.

Join our book's Discord space

Join the book's Discord Workspace for Latest updates, Offers, Tech happenings around the world, New Release and Sessions with the Authors:

https://discord.bpbonline.com

## CHAPTER 3

Working with Present-day Destinations in SharePoint Online

> "Developer testing is an important step towards accountability. It gives developers a way to demonstrate the quality of the software they produce."
>
> *- Kent Beck*

Introduction

You might be asking: "what are the present-day destinations?". In our case, it is some components and main blocks SharePoint online in constructed from. Let us review those blocks and gain a deeper understanding of the overall SharePoint online structure and its features and components.

Structure

In this chapter, we will cover the following topics:

- SharePoint structure: Site collections, Sites, Lists, Libraries
- Governance and permissions
- Navigation
- Managed metadata
- Practical tasks

Objectives

After overviewing what SharePoint is, let us dive deeper into the topic in this chapter. Here, we will discover what components SharePoint consists of and the main pieces in the puzzle, and how to set up the correct permissions so that users can access the information they need. Lastly, we will also learn how to protect and secure your organization's data, and more.

SharePoint structure - Site collections, Sites, Lists, Libraries

You know that there are multiple components in SharePoint, such as applications, lists, sites, groups, and so on. But do you have a clear picture of how the whole architecture is built and what is the hierarchy between those components?

Let us look at the following diagram to explain better and visualize it.

Figure 3.1 features the hierarchy structure of SharePoint online components:

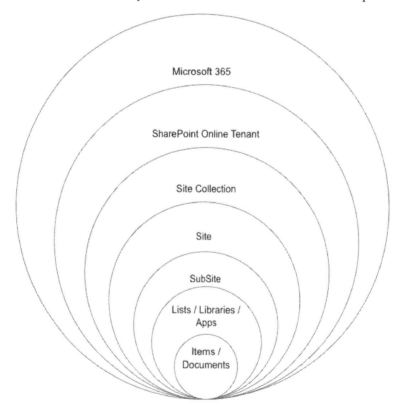

Figure 3.1: *SharePoint online visual Structure representation*

We can see how nested the structure is and how one component is included inside other components. For example, you can have one SharePoint online tenant, and there might be multiple site collections in it, which may have numerous sites under them with various lists, and so on.

Figure 3.2 features a simple Site collection diagram:

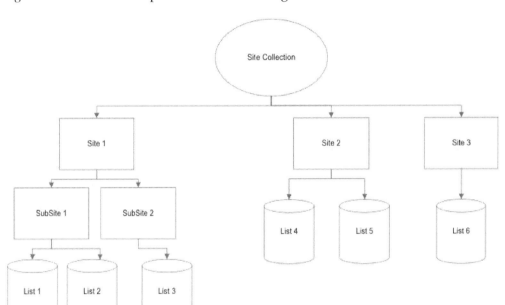

Figure 3.2: SharePoint online site collection diagram

Such a structure can be expanded and scaled on any level. Like a Database with tables, there will always be some root components at the end. In our case, those components are list items or files inside document libraries. Anyway, let us not go too deep into the weeds, as technical diagrams can quickly become complicated, and we do not want to spend much time analyzing them. Let us define the main components of SharePoint online and discover what they are about.

SharePoint Online Tenant

SharePoint Online (SPO) Tenant is a workplace where all your sites and configurations are stored. There is only one tenant per Microsoft 365 environment. When you set up the new environment, you are prompted to select the name of your tenant, and it will be reflected in the URL. For instance, if we name our environment *AlexTest*, then URL of the SharePoint will look like:

https://alextest.sharepoint.com

The part highlighted in bold will be changed, based on the company name or environment name you selected when initially setting up your subscription with Microsoft. It also could not be changed or renamed down the road. If we decide to change our name and have it as AlexDemo, then our URL accordingly would be:

https://alexdemo.sharepoint.com

> **Note: To update the tenant name, we would need to create a new tenant and set up a separate subscription with Microsoft (remember, you cannot rename your environment or change the URL after it is made). Thus, it is crucial to set up everything right from the first time. Otherwise, you might migrate and move all your content around to the new tenant.**

Site collection

A site collection is a group of logically related sites. The HR department might have different divisions inside it, such as Hiring, Benefits, Jobs, Policies, and so on. Similarly, it might be the Accounting department or IT department also. In this case, it makes sense to have a separate site collection for HR and any other department for better structure alignment and logical implementation. Whenever you create a new site collection, you will see sites in the URL before your site collection name. That a clear indication of a site collection. The URL, in this case, will look like:

https://alextest.sharepoint.com/sites/HR

Refer to *Figure 3.3:*

Figure 3.3: Tenants and site collection in a URL

So, looking at it, you will know that you are at the *AlexTest* tenant on the HR site collection.

Site and subsite

Now, as we are on the HR site collection, we need to drill it farther down. What options are there? If our HR department is small, then we may stay on a site collection level and create some lists and pages right there. But if we have multiple divisions inside the HR department, then it would be a mess managing over one thousand pages all in one place. That is why it would make sense to separate them logically and have separate sites for Hiring, Benefits, and other divisions. Sites can contain subsites, and there is no limitation on how deep you can go. So, there might be a structure such as a site collection | site | subsite | subsite | subsite, and so on. It is up to you as an admin, to decide what structure you would like to implement and which one will work the best in your situation.

Again, looking at the URL, you can quickly understand on what level you are and what component you are working with. If we are on the Hiring site of HR site collection, it would look like this:

https://alextest.sharepoint.com/sites/HR/Hiring

If the Hiring site has a subsite Contractors, then the URL will be as follows:

https://alextest.sharepoint.com/sites/HR/Hiring/Contractors

Pretty much any new forward slash and site name would indicate the structure of your site collection.

List

The list is pretty much a database table. You can also think about it as an Excel data set, where you can create columns and then populate rows. Information stored in the list (each row) is called a list item. Items can consist of different columns and store information inside them. You can create columns of different types, specify the structure, and store data in it. Lists can be of various types such as Task list, data log list, calendar or in the majority of cases, it is just custom lists with users' own defined columns and views.

Column types in SharePoint are adjusted to be more user-friendly and intuitive compared to the database types. There are 15 types of columns in the SharePoint list, and they are:

- Single Line of Text
- Multiple Lines of Text
- Number
- Location
- Date and Time
- Yes/No
- Person or Group
- Hyperlink

- Choice

- Image

- Currency

- Lookup (information already on this site)

- Calculated (calculation based on other columns)

- Task Outcome

- Managed Metadata

They should be pretty intuitive and it is up to you as a content owner to decide what is the right column type for you to store the data in. There are also Look Ups that allow you to pull information from other lists and link items between lists in this way. Please refer to the following figure:

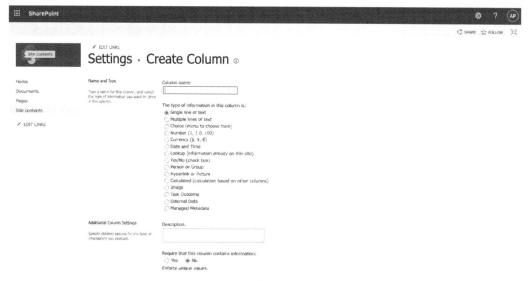

Figure 3.4: New columns creation view and options for the column type

Then from the columns, you can create views and pick what columns to display in the view. By default, the newly created column will be added to the default view unless a checkbox is unchecked. Maybe you do not need to see all of the columns and data related to the item. Then, you can choose to hide other unnecessary columns to not present the information on the page until you click on the list item. There, you will be able to see all the data inside the columns.

Be aware that there are some limitations with lists. Although SharePoint can store up to 30 million items when a list view displays more than 5,000 items, you will get the "The attempted operation is prohibited because it exceeds the list view threshold enforced by the administrator" error. Therefore, you would need to think about creating various views with filters to limit the number of items you show per view.

When a list, library, or folder contains more than 100,000 items, you cannot break permissions inheritance on the list, library, or folder. You also cannot re-inherit permissions on it.

It is always best practice to limit Lists and Libraries to 5,000 items.

Library

Library, based on its structure and logic, is very similar to the list. You can also create columns there and populate them with metadata and create views to display columns you need, or apply filters to the data you want to see. The main difference is what we store in the library. It is designed to store documents, media files, or any other documentation. If list items are text-based data, the library is media-based data. So, if you need to store documents related to their information such as, Title, Author, approval status, owning department, and so on, then you will select Library to store it. You can use all metadata associated with documents to create views and filter what documents you will show in each view.

Moreover, in SharePoint, whenever you create a new site, there is by default created a Site *Pages* library. It stores site Pages, and it is only one per site. Thus, you always know where to find your Pages if you want to update content on them. That library is called 'Pages' or 'Site Pages' (in older versions of SharePoint).

Pages are like website pages, where you can navigate between them, see different text and content on them, and interact with applications. Pages can present multiple lists or libraries on them and text with images. You build pages using web parts. There are also various types of web parts available, depending on what content you would like to present on the page. It can be Text, Links, Lists and Libraries, Videos, buttons, and so on. The default pages available out of the box are Page, Article Page, Welcome Page and Error Page. Please refer to the following figure:

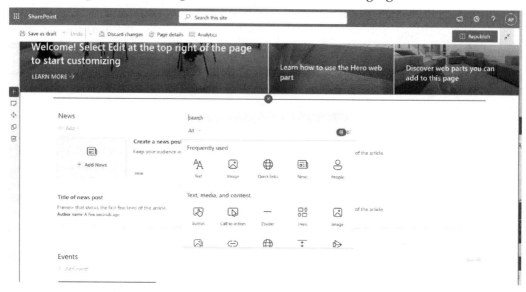

Figure 3.5: View of some of the available modern interface web parts

SharePoint user interface

There are two types of User Interfaces in SharePoint online:

- Modern (default one)
- Classic

Classic interface is still supported as it is coming from a previous version of SharePoint and it is mainly related to pages available for you, and web parts you can use to build those pages. Modern UI is more simplified, clean, and robust, while Classic UI gives you more options for customizations and implementations.

The majority of all new sites in SharePoint Online are built on the Modern UI as we never know for how long Microsoft supports the Classic one. Moreover, if you want to use some new technologies such as embedding PowerApps on pages, such options are rolled out only to a Modern UI. Thus, for all the sites and pages, you will create in the future, it is recommended to use Modern User Interface. Furthermore, it is worth mentioning that there is no simple way to convert a Classic UI page into a Modern UI, and in such cases, the classic page should be rebuilt manually from scratch into the Modern one. The other option would be to use PowerShell scripting to do so, but it is not always giving you too accurate results.

Overall Modern and Classic UI applied to:

- Site Content look

- Pages and available web-parts

- Lists and Libraries views

Even if your site is created on the Modern UI for Lists and Libraries, you can always switch back to the Classic UI by clicking on the link in the bottom left corner of the List or Library. Please note that this option is not available for Pages.

There 9 key differences between Classic vs Modern interface are as follows:

- **Home pages:** The Modern Team site homepage features news, quick links, and site activity capabilities. It also automatically displays recent activity on the site, such as files uploaded, changes made, lists and libraries created, and so on, and has a better responsive mobile user interface experience. The Classic Experience web parts are segmental components, and so you have greater control over the placement of elements and script execution. However, because it is developed on the ASP.NET platform, the user has a slower rendering experience, and there are challenges with custom JavaScript code.

- **Team Sites:** When you create a classic team site, web parts for announcements, a calendar or links are automatically added to the home page. Modern sites are connected to Microsoft 365 groups. Not only do the homepage features include news, quick links, site activity, and a document library, it also automatically displays recent activity on the site, such as files uploaded, changes made, lists and libraries created, and more, offering faster site provisioning and color customization.

- **M365 Tool Integration:** The integration support with Microsoft 365 app has been the biggest difference between classic and modern sites. This has revolutionized SharePoint as the all-around home base platform, allowing users to collaborate and create lists for calendars, announcements, tasks, and more, while SharePoint takes care of the content management processes.

- **SharePoint Document Lists & Libraries:** As an integral part of SharePoint, the modern version offers an improved user interface. Unlike the classic version, the newest version allows you to download multiple files at once as a Zip file. With features like customized list and column view, sorting and grouping columns, quick change of file info, pinning documents at the top, it provides better usability.

- **Power Automate:** Classic SharePoint workflows had limitations requiring extensive developer resources to process automation. You can easily access

Power Automate right from the toolbar in lists and libraries, making it that much easier for end users to create their own robust workflows.

- **SharePoint News:** In Classic SharePoint, to create a news feed you would have to customize a master page, add CSS code, and develop web parts to create a compelling News page. The Modern experience has an intuitive user interface and a cleaner look for a more dynamic experience. Users can effortlessly add graphics to their announcements or news posts.

- **In-Line Editing:** The classic experience, even the smallest task such as renaming a document or item, redirects you to another page. The Modern SharePoint allows users to view updates and make edits in real-time without redirection.

- **Mobility:** SharePoint has come a long way. Nowadays, users need to access site data and documents from their mobile phones, tablets or laptops. Classic SharePoint pages and interfaces were not mobile-friendly and offer poor user experience. Modern SharePoint offer's responsive design out of the box.

- **Sites and Search:** Classic SharePoint offers both communication and publishing sites. Whereas Modern does not offer publishing sites that required more development. The communications sites of the modern share point are easy to edit and update without any programming experience. The search function is also better as it shows suggestions based on your history as you type and offers personalized search results. Search is so robust it searches the text inside the documents.

Governance and permissions

In SharePoint, there is a very flexible Governance structure with multiple levels of permissions. Firstly, Microsoft 365 environment is connected to the company's **Active Directory** (**AD**), and that is how users within the organization get access to all applications and are able to authenticate with Microsoft. However, AD is not the only option to store user profiles. Users can also be created directly inside Microsoft 365, and then the profile will be stored in the Azure AD that is used by Microsoft 365 as a backend.

So, as a first step, users in order to be able to access your environment, should have profiles created either in the organization's on-premises Active Directory or inside Azure Active Directory (or inside Microsoft 365, which is the same). Creating users in the Azure AD, you are able to provide access to external to your organization users and specify 'friendly domains' that should have access to your environment, once they log in with their credentials.

The *second* level of permissions is **Admin roles** assigned to a user. There are a variety of Admin roles inside Microsoft 365. They can all be found and configured within the **Users**pages, and roles can be assigned to a user directly.

Figure 3.6 features major available Administrator roles inside Microsoft 365:

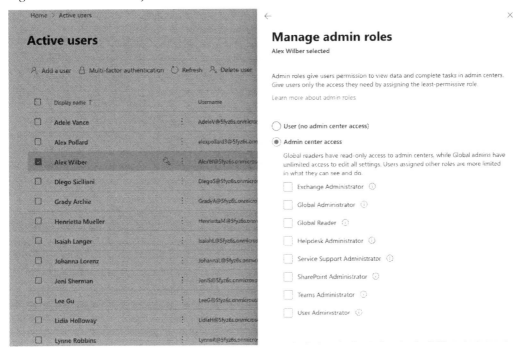

Figure 3.6: *Features major available Administrator roles inside Microsoft 365*

The major administrator roles are as follows:

- **Global administrator:** This role will give you access to all admin centers inside Microsoft 365, billing, users, and all features available. It is recommended you have between 2-4 Global admins, as giving too many users this access is a high-security risk. The person who signed up for Microsoft online services are automatically Global Admins.

- **SharePoint administrator:** This role will give you access to SharePoint and OneDrive Admin Centers. You will be able to see all site collections created within the tenant and will be able to assign yourself as the admin there. Moreover, all other functionality for administration related to policies and configuration for SharePoint and OneDrive will be available to you.

- **Exchange administrator:** This role will give you access to the Exchange Admin center, and you will be able to configure various rules and policies related to the Exchange and mailboxes.

- **Security and compliance roles:** There are several different roles under this category that will give you access to a Security and Compliance center, where you will be able to configure policies for data loss protection, and compliance rules that will apply to the content inside all of the Microsoft 365 applications.

As you can see in the preceding *Figure 3.6*, there is a checkbox next to each Administrator role. This means that multiple Administrator roles can be assigned at the same time and can be combined for different users, based on the need and access needed.

The *third* level of roles is a **Site Collection Admin** role. This role is assigned directly from the site and gives a user access to all of the features and content on the site. Even if there are unique permissions assigned to some of the content, users with the Site Collection Admin role will still be able to see that content. This is a unique ability available only to this role.

The next and *fourth* level of permissions is **access given to a specific site**. Usually, when you create a new site, there are three groups created by default:

- Owner group (Full Access)
- Members group (Contribute Access)
- Visitor group (Read Access)

You get different access levels, Full, Contribute and Read, within site. There are also Design and Edit permissions available, but they are usually used less often than the previous three. The New Custom level of permissions can be created for the site-by-Site Collection Admins can be accordingly assigned to the group. The site collection administrator(s) has full control on all the sites and subsites of the site collection. Moreover, the primary site collection administrator receives administrative email alerts.

Figure 3.7 features default permissions available on any SharePoint online site:

Figure 3.7: *Default permissions available on any SharePoint online site*

Table 3.1 features out-of-the-box permission levels:

Full Control	Has full control.
Design	Can view, add, update, delete, approve, and customize.
Edit	Can add, edit and delete lists; can view, add, update and delete list items and documents.
Contribute	Can view, add, update, and delete list items and documents.
Read	Can view pages and list items and download documents.
Approve	Can edit and approve pages, list items, and documents.
View Only	Can view pages, list items, and documents. Document types with server-side file handlers can be viewed in the browser but not downloaded.

***Table 3.1**: Out-of-the-box permission levels*

If the new custom level of permissions is created, the admin can choose what kind of actions users with that permission will be able to do.

Figure 3.8 features various actions available when configuring custom permissions level:

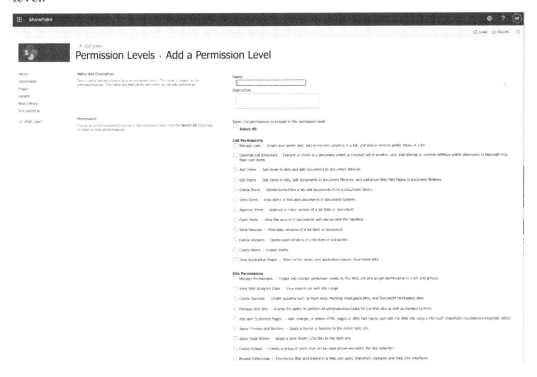

***Figure 3.8**: Various actions available when configuring custom permissions level*

Let us come back to the 'onion' diagram to see the relations and hierarchy between permissions, groups, and users.

Figure 3.9 features relations between permissions, groups, and users:

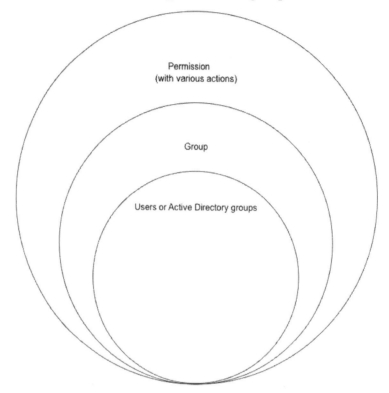

Figure 3.9: *Relations between permissions, groups, and users*

The diagram can be explained in the following steps:

1. Actions grouped together define a permission.

2. Permission can be assigned to a SharePoint Group.

3. Users or Active Directory groups can be added inside the SharePoint Group and will inherit the permission level of that group.

It is worth mentioning that users can be assigned directly with a level of permission without being added to a SharePoint Group. It has its downside. Assigning permissions directly to users is not only time-consuming, but it can also have a negative effect on permission management with conflicting permission levels. You will quickly end up in a messy situation where it will be hard to find users in the list of site permissions and/or difficult to troubleshoot when users have accessibility errors. So, follow best practices and use SharePoint Groups to grant permissions to users.

You might be wondering what the difference between SharePoint Group and Active Directory group is. They both contain users and both can be granted permissions inside SharePoint. The main thing is that you are able to see users inside the SharePoint group right within SharePoint. So, you can add, edit and delete them from that group right there. With the Active Directory group, you can only see the name of the group but no insights into users who belonged to that group. To find out users inside the AD group, you would need to go to Active Directory from the server, and usually, it is only IT Admins who have access to it.

So, the rule of thumb is: if you want to have more flexibility and manage all users and their permissions by yourself, go with SharePoint groups.

If you want less of a headache and more of a process to obtain permission to access the site and that request should go through the IT Admin team, use Active Directory groups and the users there will be managed by your IT department. But be aware that the biggest issue with utilizing AD groups in SharePoint is that you cannot view the AD group membership. This makes it very difficult to determine exactly who has access to what. Also external users are not allowed in AD groups. Finally there is no access request system with AD groups.

Similarly, to SharePoint groups, there are Microsoft 365 groups. Those are used for 'Teams' sites, and there are only Owners and Member access available for them on the site.

The next *fifth* level of permissions is **access to List, Library, or Page**. They all by default, inherit permissions from the site level, but the inheritance can be broken, and unique permissions can be assigned to them. This is usually done if there is some information inside the list or library that should be accessible or visible only for specific people, and everyone else within the site should not have access to it.

Similarly, to the previous one, there is a *sixth* level of permission but on the level down. Libraries contain folders and documents within them, and Lists contain list items. Those can have a unique level of permissions too. There is sometimes a need to have unique permissions on a specific document or folder that everyone else would not be able to see it as it might store sensitive documents.

Please note, both the *fifth* and *sixth* level of permissions might create a mess in your site governance structure very quickly. If you imagine that you already have permissions on the site and then unique permissions on the library, and going deeper there are some documents with unique permissions on them, it will be very hard for you as a content owner to identify such documents if you have hundreds of thousands of them. There are some tools such as Sharegate and PowerShell scripts that can help with such reports, as well as identifying documents/folders/items with unique permissions. However, all of it is going to induce nothing but a headache! Thus, it is always a best practice to limit unique permissions level only down to the list or library and not go deeper. All other items should inherit permissions from the top level.

Moreover, there is a *seventh* level of permission that can be identified. It is a link that is shared to give access to a specific document, folder, or item. These links are usually shared with users who do not have access to the site, list, or library, or with external users to give them the ability to see the content of the file or folder.

Visually, all seven levels of permissions can be described as a hierarchy, where the top level has all the access, and the bottom one has very limited access. Remember that the Site Collection admin gives users access to all of the items within the site, even with broken inheritance. Meanwhile, if you have even 'Full Access' permission on the site, you might not see some items that have unique permissions. With the Admin role (*level 2*) you also might not have access to some sites if you are not granted permission to them directly. But you always have access to the SharePoint admin center, where you can look-up the site and assign yourself as a site collection admin to that site.

Figure 3.10 features seven levels of the permissions hierarchy:

Figure 3.10: *Seven levels of the permissions hierarchy*

Navigation

Navigation on SharePoint consists of a few various elements, such as:

- There is a *Top-level navigation* available across the pages, and can be inherited from one site to its subsites.

- Then, there is *Left navigation* available across the site. The main difference between left navigation from top-level navigation is that it is not inherited between site and subsite, and is unique to each site level. It is displayed on the left of the page rather than at the top.

- There are also buttons, links and hero web parts available on the page itself, that also provides users with the ability to navigate between sites and pages inside SharePoint Online.

So, all together combined, these three elements provide users with navigation capabilities. *Figure 3.11* shows top-level navigation:

Figure 3.11: Top-level navigation

Figure 3.12 shows both top-level and left navigation:

Figure 3.12: Top-level and left navigation

Figure 3.13 shows the hero web part, button and links used for navigation on the page:

Figure 3.13: *The hero web part, button and links used for navigation on the page*

It is pretty easy to set up and configure navigation on a page using buttons or links. You just add the needed web part on the page – provide a link, set a name, and add an image if needed.

For the top-level and left navigations, you have two sub-levels available. This allows you to group some links together in categories. To modify the navigation, you would need to click on **Edit** that is next to the top level or left navigation accordingly (only users with appropriate permissions will see the Edit button to modify the top or left navigation accordingly).

Figure 3.14 shows the edit view of the left navigation:

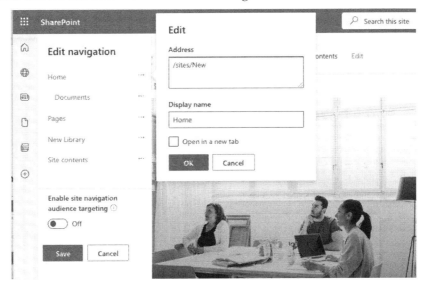

Figure 3.14: *Edit view of the Left navigation*

One more important feature that is available for all links, including buttons and links on a page, is *Audience targeting*. If you want some of the links or a group of links, or buttons to be visible only to specific people, you can enable a switch **Enable audience targeting**, and it will allow you to define what SharePoint or Microsoft groups should have access to that link. Everyone inside that group will have access to the link. Please note that there is a limitation that only 10 groups can be added per link to be able to see it.

Managed metadata

Metadata is information that describes something or characterizes something. For instance, you might have a document. Document title or author would be metadata in this case. That is why inside document libraries, you can create columns and store information there about documents, which is also called metadata.

Managed metadata is the functionality inside SharePoint online, to create metadata that can be used and reused across different sites, libraries, and in navigation. Managed metadata consists of a few elements:

- Term store
- Term group
- Term set
- Term

Terms are your metadata. Multiple terms can be added to the Term set. Term sets can then be grouped into Term groups. All Term groups are included in the Term store.

You can access your term store from any SharePoint site where you have site collection admin permissions or directly from the SharePoint admin center. To access the Term store at the site collection level, simply go to the **Site Settings** and under the **Site Administration** category, select the **Term Store Management** link. You can manage the Term Store at the tenant level to provide a Global Navigation for all site collections. *Figure 3.15* shows the term store view:

Figure 3.15: *Term store view*

Once there, you will see two categories in the menu: Global term groups and Site level term groups. Global groups will be available across all the sites in your tenant, and Site groups will only be available on a specific site.

After terms, term sets, and term groups are configured, they can be used on the site. As we mentioned before, there are multiple ways to use them. Firstly, you can go to any document library or list, and create a 'managed metadata' type column. You will be prompted which term set or term group to pull and display in that column. It will look like a choice field where the user can select either one or multiple terms from the term set you selected.

Once configured, users will be able to select those terms, which will be visible in the library or list view as tags attached to the document. They can later be used to filter views and quickly find documents based on them, as well as also be used in search.

For example, you can create a term group called HR term group and make it available only on the HR site collection. Then you may create a term set inside related to Benefits. Inside it, you can create terms such as Dental, 401k plan, health insurance, and so on. In this way, you will get a structure like this:

- HR term group
  - ○ Benefits (term set)

- Dental (term)
- 401k (term)
- Health Insurance (term)

In addition to Benefits term set, you can add Jobs and Hiring, Onboarding and create other related items.

Then you go to the HR site collection, and inside the documents, go to library, to add a column of 'managed metadata' type and select your HR term group. Now, all the documents uploaded to that document library can be tagged if they are related to Dental benefits or Onboarding or anything else.

Based on those tags, you would be able to quickly find documents needed, based on the related term, or build a view that will display all documents related to the Health insurance plan, while another documents will be hidden.

Similarly, based on the Term groups and term sets, you can build top-level navigation. Users can click on the corresponding term and will be redirected to the page that contains information related to that term or to the library showing all documents related to that term.

Practical tasks

In this chapter, we covered a lot of theory material about SharePoint's basic components and features. To strengthen your knowledge, let us do some practical tasks.

In the browser on your PC, log in to your tenant at **https://portal.office.com** or the new URL is **https://www.microsoft365.com** using the username and password you configured before. Once logged in inside the list of all applications, select SharePoint and navigate to the site you created in *Chapter 2, Prologue to SharePoint Online*.

Let us **set up a subsite** for that site. Follow the given steps:

1. In the top right corner, click on the gear icon and select Site Contents.

2. It will bring you to the contents page. From there, at the top left corner click on '**New**' and select the '**Subsite**' option.

    a. There is a chance that 'Site' option is not available for you, as you have a new environment. Microsoft disables it by default, since according to best practices, they recommend to limit creating of subsite and only use site collections for new site creation. Then, if you need to connect multiple sites together, you can create a Hub site that will share navigation and information between all of those sites.

If you do not have Subsite option available, follow steps 3-5, otherwise you can skip to step 6.

3. To enable site creation, click on the top right corner and select the squares icon. From there, select Admin application. Once in the Admin center in the left navigation, click on 'Show all' and select SharePoint Admin center.

4. In the SharePoint Admin center, select **Settings** in the left navigation. Once the page loads at the bottom of it, you will see an option to switch to a classic settings page. Click on it.

5. A new page with all available settings will open to you. In the middle of the page, find the **Subsite Creation** section. Select **Enable sub site creation for all sites** and click on OK. You have a link there to learn more about hub sites as well. It is recommended to visit it and read about hub sites.

Figure 3.16 shows the substitute enabling settings:

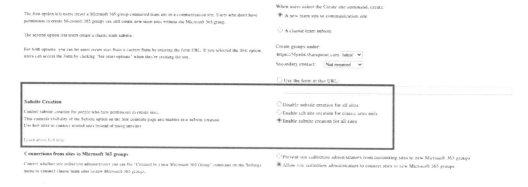

Figure 3.16: Subsite enabling setting

6. Once the configuration is updated, go back to your site, where you will create a new subsite. Refresh the page and click on '**New'** at the top left corner. Now you should see the Subsite option – click on it. Fill out all parameters there, such as site name and URL, and click on OK. You will see the new subsite created under your site.

On your newly created site, let us **modify the Documents document library** a little. Follow the given steps:

1. In the top right corner, click on the gear icon and go to **Site Contents**.

2. Find **Documents** there and click on the library name. You will be redirected to the Documents document library.

3. Upload some test documents in it. You can just drag and drop the file or in the top left corner, select the **Upload** button and select the document from

the PC. You can also create a new one right there in the library if you do not have any documents to upload.

4. Now, when the document is in the library, let us create a couple of new columns to assign some metadata to the document. Next to the **Modified By**, click on **Add Columns**. Select column type **Choice** and click **Next**. Name your column Category (or any other name you would like to use).

Figure 3.17 shows the new column creation in a document library:

Figure 3.17: New column creation in a document library

5. You are provided with three choices as options, inside your choice column, under Site Settings (**Site information | View all site settings**). You can click on each choice name and rename them to whatever you want; you can also delete and add choices right from here too. For now, let us leave them as they are: Choice 1, Choice 2, and Choice 3.

6. Click **Save**. You will see your column was added to the view and you can now see it.

7. Let us create another one with the 'person' type. Name it as Owner and click **Save**.

8. Next, select your document, and click a bit to the left from the document name (do not click on the name as the document will open). Click on the 'i' icon in the right corner after the document is selected. There you will see all the properties/metadata associated with the document. Your two newly create columns will be there too.

Figure 3.18 shows the properties panel in the document library:

Figure 3.18: *Properties panel in the document library*

9. Assign Choice 1 category to the document and set yourself as the owner. Inside the owner column, just start typing your name and SharePoint will show you the associated user profile. Changes will be automatically saved.

10. Now upload or create a few more documents and add them to the library. Assign some categories and owners to them too. As the next step, we will create a new view to show only documents where Category equals 'Choice 1', and set yourself as the owner of the document.

11. A little to the left from the 'i' icon we used before, you will see a dropdown called **All Documents**. Click on it. Select **Create new view** and you will be asked for the view name. Name it as Category – Choice 1. Remove the checkbox at the bottom from **make this default view** option. The view will be created. Now click on the same dropdown one more time (it will say Category – Choice 1 now) and select **Edit current view** option.

12. You will see the page where you can configure your view and change its parameters. At the top, you can select what columns should be displayed in your view and you can set the order in which they will be displayed. Select checkboxes next to the ID and Version column so that they will be added to the view. Then scroll down.

13. You have options to configure sorting, filtering, and grouping. We will add a Filter. In a Filter section from the first dropdown, select **Category**, and in the

second drop-down, choose **is equal to** and set value Choice 1. For a second filter, select from a drop-down "Owner" 'is equal to' and type [ME]. Switch the radio button between filter to 'And'.

Figure 3.19 features filter configuration for the view.

Figure 3.19: *Filter configuration for the view*

Thus, you configured a filter that will show you all documents with Category = Choice 1 and where you were set as an owner. [ME] is the dynamic expression in SharePoint used for filters. It will automatically define who is the currently logged-in user, and will set his name into the filter. So, different users will see results where they were set as owners. If you need to display only documents related to a specific person, then you would need to type that person's name in the filter instead. Scroll all the way down on the page and click on the **OK** button.

Now your new view has a filter in it and will only show you documents matching to the filter.

Let us take a look at permissions. Follow the given steps:

1. Click on the gear icon in the top right corner and select **Site settings**. It also can be shown as Site Information, depending on which page you are. If you see Site Information, click on it and select **view all site settings** at the bottom of the window.

2. The Site settings page will open. At the top left column, you will see second link **Site Permissions**. Select it. You will see that there are three groups created on your site as we discussed before: for Owners, Members, and Visitors.

3. At the top ribbon, you will see **Manage parent** and **Stop inheriting permissions** options. This means your subsite currently has the same permissions as the main site.

4. Click on **Stop Inheriting permissions**, which will show you the pop-up. Click on OK. SharePoint will prompt you to create three new groups for your site. Click on OK again.

5. Go back to the **site settings** | **site permissions** page. Now at the top ribbon, you will see that your site has unique permissions, and whatever changes to permissions will be done on the top-level site, will not impact your subsite as it is now managed as a separate entity.

6. At any moment, you can click **Delete Unique permissions** from the top ribbon, and then your subsite permissions configuration will be lost and it will start inherit permissions form the top site again.

Conclusion

In this chapter, you learned about major SharePoint online components such as site collections, sites, lists, libraries, navigation, views and permissions. Altogether, it might be a bit challenging to remember, so you are encouraged to always have your SharePoint sandbox environment open and take the steps described in the book. This will make the learning process much easier and faster. Remember about the nested structure of tenants | site collections | subsites | lists and libraries. We also discussed how permissions work and are inherited from one level to another.

Points to remember

- There are different levels of permissions in SharePoint online: Tenant level admin roles, Site Collection admin, Site permissions, List and Library unique permission, Items and Documents level permissions.

- There are two types of User Interfaces in SharePoint online: Modern, which is the default one, and Classic.

- Web parts are blocks for building pages.

- There is a Top level and Left page navigation.

- There are 7 levels of permissions: Active Directory, Admin roles, Site collection Admin, Site Access with groups, List and Library level permissions, Items and Documents level permissions, and shared links.

- Managed Metadata is designed to be used across the site or globally across all sites.

- You can build tags in lists and libraries or create navigation with managed metadata.

- Managed metadata includes: Term Store, Term Sets, Term groups, Terms.

## CHAPTER 4

Working with Records in SharePoint Online

> "Documents create a paper reality we call proof."
>
> *- Mason Cooley*

Introduction

Records management is coming from compliance. Whenever you work with any paperwork that can be used later for the audit, that documentation or any related records should be retained. If we still worked with physical papers, we would organize them together and store them in the dedicated archives facility. As everything is digital in SharePoint online, the method stays the same, but only for digital paperwork.

Structure

In this chapter, we will cover the following topics:

- Records Management
- Content types for records
- Site columns

- Information management policies
- Labels
- Data Archival

Objectives

In this chapter, we will overview SharePoint and its capabilities even further. How often have you seen situations where documents are supposed to be retained for 5 or 10, or even more years? This is where you will be introduced to the Records management feature in SharePoint.

In this chapter, we will review in more detail what records management is, how to configure it for your specific case, and how to protect and preserve your data for the upcoming years.

Records management

Any file can be a record. The extension does not matter. As long as you need to maintain the file for a specific period, based on compliance, it can be declared as a record. When we are talking about records management in SPO, there are two ways to store records:

- In Place Records
- Records in a specific location

In-place records mean that files will be declared as records, based on the defined set of rules, and stored in the original location where they were created for a specific portion of time. The benefit of this approach is that you keep the original site and placement of the file unchanged. Still, as a downside, your libraries may become messy with all that outdated content staying there.

Another option is to have a dedicated place, such as a Records Center site, where all declared records from different locations will be saved. In this case, you have a separate area (such as a physical facility), where all your records are stored. When you create this rule, you can define if the document should be moved over or if a copy of the document should be created and stored.

The place where you store records can be a dedicated Records Center site, a dedicated record storing library or list, or even an associated content type.

Based on Microsoft's best practices, whenever you implement records management, creating a records management plan and rules for your organization is recommended.

There are multiple tools available in the marketplace that can help automate records management and declaration. Such tools can be easily integrated into your Microsoft 365 environment and work together with SharePoint, OneDrive, Teams, and Exchange. Overall, all rules can be configured directly from the website or list/ library.

Modern approach for records management includes Security and Compliance center. Retention labels can be configured from the admin center and automatically applied to the content. Admins can specify application labels that will be applied. For example, you can create a label that will be applied only at SharePoint. Another label can be applied to SharePoint, OneDrive, and Teams. So, configurations are very flexible. We will cover more of the functionality related to labels and how to configure them in the Security and Compliance center chapter.

After any document or item is declared as a record, some common rules usually occur. Records cannot be deleted or changed by a regular user. It can appear only after the admin approves the action. Multiple-level approval processes can also be configured before any change can happen to the record.

Content types for records

Content types define different types of documents. For instance, the file might have a commonly used word template. To make it easier for users and not create a template every time in SharePoint online when needed, you can create a content type based on that template. So, next time the user goes to the library and creates a word document, he can make it based on the content type, and all fields and information will already be in that document. Thus, you can have different content types for word documents, excel, or any other kind of document or item.

When we declare such documents as records and move them to the Records Center site, they can be placed into different document libraries and lists, based on the Content-type they are built on. This provides an extra level for proper storage and records organization. Thus, you can later find the information and documents you are looking for much faster.

When you create a new site collection, it includes some predefined default content types. The main default content types are as follows:

- *Document* and *Folder* for document libraries
- *Item* for lists
- *Event* for calendar

You can create custom content types, based on the different templates you use or based on any other needs. The thing is that each custom content type will have a parent. At the end of this parent hierarchy, default content types will always be at the end. If you would create a content type based on the Invoice and name it as 'Invoice,' you will be prompted to select a parent content type. In this case, *Document* default content type makes the most sense to be assigned as a parent, as an invoice is also a document.

Content types are usually created and managed either by admins on specific sites or by site owners on the sites they own. Content types can be made via **Site Settings | Site Content Types**.

Figure 4.1 features the creation of the new content type:

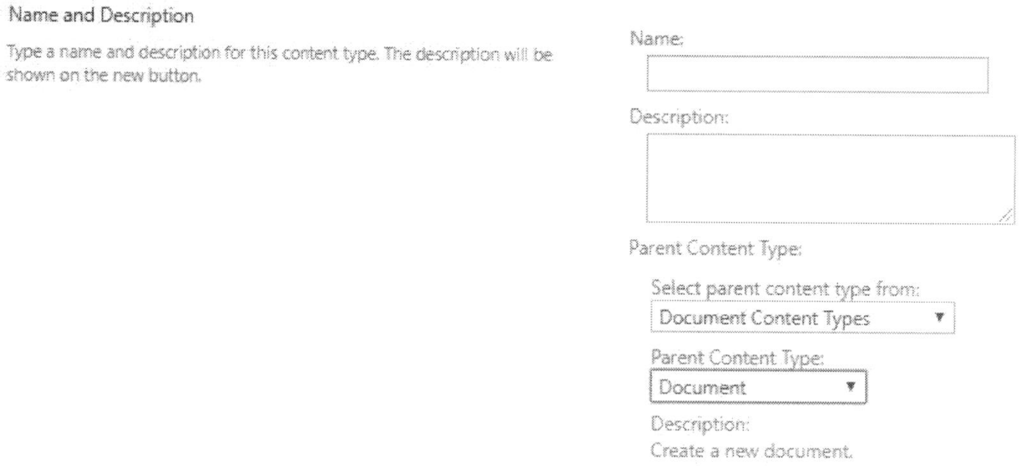

Figure 4.1: *The creation of the new content type*

As you can see, content types can be organized into Content-Type sets that logically align them. Then, the parent content type should be selected for every new custom content type created. Once you make a new content type, it can be edited, and new columns can be added, including those from the Managed Metadata. Supporting custom content types is a feature that is configured directly from each list or library. By going to List or Library Settings and then to Advanced settings, their admin can select if the custom content types should be supported. They can then add content types from the list available on that site.

Site columns

Columns are used to help group, categorize or track records and other items. Columns contain the information and are assigned a specific data type, similar to when we added them to the lists and libraries. Information in columns, as we stated before, called metadata, describes associated items. Based on the stored information, you can build list views, apply filters and search based on it. When you created a column last time, you did it directly from the library by clicking on 'Add column' and selecting the data type for that column. You also have the option to add columns from the list of Site Columns.

Site columns are added from the site collection level. The process is pretty similar. It is only site columns that are not associated with any list or library when you create them. They can then be added and reused across various lists and libraries. Moreover, search rules can be built, based on site columns, to determine what information should be searchable.

To create a site column, you would need to go to **Site Settings | Site Columns**.

Figure 4.2 features **Site columns** link from **Site Settings**:

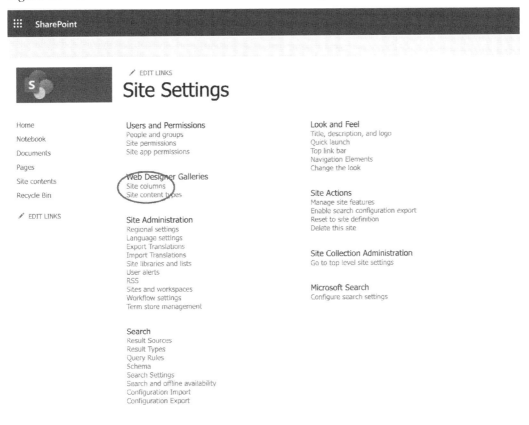

Figure 4.2: *Site columns link from site settings*

Site columns are grouped into categories and can be added to different content types. For example, you can add a site column to a content type for a record. To do that, follow the given steps:

1. From the home page of the Records Center site, click **Settings**, and then click **Site Settings**.

2. In a SharePoint group-connected site, click **Settings | Site Contents**, and then click **Site Settings**.

3. In the Web Designer Galleries section, click **Site content types**.

4. On the Site Content Types page, click the site content type that you want to configure.

5. After you have either selected a site content type from the parent site, or created a new site content type, click **Add from existing site columns**, on the selected site content type page, in the Columns section.

6. On the **Add Columns to Content Type** page, in the **Select Columns** section, select the group that you want to filter on from the Select columns from list.

7. Select the column that you want to add from the Available columns list, and then click **Add**.

8. In the **Update Lists** and **Site Content Types** section, specify whether the child site content types that inherit from this site content type will be updated with your changes.

9. After you finish adding the columns you want, click on **OK**.

To summarize, site columns are reusable columns that can be used across various lists and libraries on the site. This will save you time down the road to not do the same configuration over and over again in different lists or libraries. Moreover, site columns can be added into the content types.

Information management policies

One way to manage information in SharePoint Online is through the use of policies. Information management policies are rules used to manage how content is created, used, and deleted in SharePoint Online. These policies can be used to help ensure that the content is organized, up-to-date, and compliant with company standards and regulations.

Several types of policies can be implemented in SharePoint Online, including the following:

- **Retention policies**: These policies help organizations manage the lifecycle of their content, by specifying how long content should be retained and what should happen to it when it reaches the end of its retention period. Retention policies can be used to retain content for a specified number of days, months, or years, or until a specific date or event occurs. When a retention policy is triggered, the content can be deleted, moved to an archive, or marked as a record (to indicate that it should not be deleted or modified).

- **Classification policies**: These policies help organizations classify and label their content, making it easier to manage and find. Classification policies can be used to apply labels to content based on its type, sensitivity, or other characteristics. Labels can be used to trigger retention policies or to apply restrictions on how the content can be accessed or shared.

- **Auditing policies**: These policies enable organizations to track and audit changes to content, helping to ensure compliance and protect against unauthorized access or modifications. Auditing policies can be used to track actions such as view, edit, or delete, and can be configured to capture specific types of content or activities.

- **Deletion policies**: These policies specify when and how content should be deleted from SharePoint Online. Deletion policies can be used either to delete content that is no longer needed or to free up storage space. Deletion policies can be triggered based on a specific date or event, or can be set to delete content that has not been accessed or modified in a certain period of time.

By implementing these policies in SharePoint Online, organizations can more effectively manage and protect their content and ensure compliance with internal and external regulations. To implement them in SharePoint Online, you must use the Compliance Center in the Microsoft 365 admin center. From there, you can create and manage policies and view reports on policy activity.

Follow the given steps for a general overview of the process, using Security and Compliance center:

1. Sign in to the Microsoft 365 admin center.

2. Go to the Compliance Center by clicking on the **Compliance** icon in the left-hand navigation menu.

3. In the Compliance Center, click on the **Information governance** tab.

4. Click on the **Policies** tab, and then click on the **Create policy** button.

5. On the **Create policy** page, select the type of policy you want to create (retention, classification, auditing, or deletion).

6. Follow the prompts to configure the policy settings, such as the name of the policy, the content it applies to, and the action to be taken when the policy is triggered.

7. When you have finished configuring the policy, click on the **Save** button to create the policy.

It is important to note that it is required, as appropriate permissions are always required to create and manage policies in the Compliance Center. Otherwise, users may need to contact their Microsoft 365 administrator for assistance.

Information management policies can be created for multiple different content types within a site collection or for a specific list or library. If you configure information policies on a site and not through a security and compliance center, then you first would need to go to the **Site Settings** | **Site Features** and activate Site Policy feature there.

There are several reasons why organizations use information management policies in SharePoint Online, and they are as follows:

- **To ensure compliance with internal and external regulations:** Many organizations are required to retain certain types of content for a specified period of time, or to follow specific guidelines for handling sensitive information. Information management policies can help organizations meet these requirements by automating content retention, classification, and auditing.

- **To reduce risk and protect against data loss:** By specifying how content should be handled and deleted, organizations can reduce the risk of data loss due to accidental deletion or expiration of retention periods.

- **To improve content management and organization:** Classification policies can help organizations label and categorize their content, making it easier to find and access. Auditing policies can help organizations track changes to content, helping to ensure that it is accurate and up-to-date.

- **To free up storage space:** Deletion policies can be used to delete content that is no longer needed, or that has reached the end of its retention period, helping to free up storage space.

Overall, information management policies can help organizations more effectively manage, protect, and organize their content in SharePoint Online.

Labels

In Microsoft 365, *Labels* are a way to classify and tag content, making it easier to manage and find. Labels can be applied to documents, sites, lists, and other types of content in SharePoint Online. Several types of labels can be used in SharePoint Online, including the following:

- **Sensitivity labels:** These labels are used to classify content based on its sensitivity or confidentiality. Sensitivity labels can be used to help protect sensitive information, such as financial or personal data, from unauthorized access or sharing.

- **Metadata labels:** These labels are used to classify content based on its attributes or characteristics, such as type, department, or location. Metadata labels can be used to help organize and categorize content, making it easier to find and access.

- **Retention labels:** These labels are used to classify content based on its retention period or how long it should be retained before being deleted or archived. Retention labels can be used to help organizations meet compliance requirements by specifying how long certain types of content should be retained.

To create and manage labels in SharePoint Online, you must use the Compliance Center in the Microsoft 365 admin center, as with information policies. From there, you can create and manage labels, as well as apply labels to content. Labels can be applied manually, or they can be applied automatically using classification policies.

Labels can be a useful tool for managing and organizing content in SharePoint Online. Here are a few reasons why organizations might use labels:

- **To classify and categorize content:** Labels can be used to classify and categorize content based on its sensitivity, type, or other characteristics. This can make it easier to find and access content, and can help improve the overall organization of content in SharePoint Online.

- **To protect sensitive information:** Sensitivity labels can be used to classify and protect sensitive information, such as financial or personal data, from unauthorized access or sharing. This can help organizations meet compliance requirements and reduce the risk of data breaches.

- **To automate retention and deletion:** Retention labels can be used to classify content, based on its retention period and can be configured to trigger retention or deletion policies when the retention period expires. This can help organizations manage the lifecycle of their content and free up storage space.

Labels are however, not specific to SharePoint Online. They can be applied to a document and content in OneDrive, Yammer, and other applications. Historically, labels are used in many different contexts and systems, including file systems, email systems, and social media platforms. In these systems, labels are used to categorize and organize content and can often be used to trigger actions or apply restrictions on content.

Overall, labels can be a helpful tool for managing and organizing content in Microsoft 365 and SharePoint Online, and can help organizations improve compliance, protect sensitive information, and automate content management processes.

Data Archival

Data archival is the process of preserving and storing data for long-term retention, typically for legal, compliance, or historical purposes. In SharePoint Online, there are a few different options for archiving data.

Retention policies in SharePoint Online can be used to specify how long content should be retained and what should happen to it when it reaches the end of its retention period. Retention policies can be configured to move content to an archive, delete it, or mark it as a record (to indicate that it should not be deleted or modified). Refer to the following:

- **In-place archiving**: In-place archiving is a feature of SharePoint Online that allows organizations to store content in a separate location within the same SharePoint Online site. This can be useful for preserving content that is no longer actively used, but still needs to be retained for legal or compliance purposes.

- **Content export**: SharePoint Online allows organizations to export content from a site or library as a package, which can then be stored on a local drive or network share. This can be useful for creating a backup of content or for transferring content to a different system or location. You can also use tools such as Sharegate or DocAve to manually move content between sites and place it on a dedicated site.

The archival process can also be automated using workflows. Logic can be defined inside Power Automate – that documents after a specific period of time or after the retention period, will be moved to a separate site or 3rd party system. In this case, Flow can be configured to run every day and check all of the documents, records or items on a specific site or library. If it then finds some present even beyond the retention period, they will be moved. Different scenarios can be implemented based on your needs.

Follow the given steps for a general overview of how you might use Power Automate to archive content in SharePoint Online:

1. Create a new Power Automate workflow.

2. Add a trigger to the workflow to specify when it should be activated. For example, you might use a trigger such as "When an item is created or modified" to start the workflow when a new item is added to a SharePoint list, or when an existing item is modified.

3. Add an action to the workflow to specify what should happen when the trigger is activated. For example, you might use an action such as "Move to folder" to move the item to an archive folder when the trigger is activated.

4. Configure any additional actions or conditions as needed. For example, you might use a condition to check the value of a metadata field before deciding whether to move the item to the archive folder.

5. Save and activate the workflow.

The best approach to archiving data in SharePoint Online will depend on the specific needs and requirements of your organization. Here are a few factors to consider when deciding how to archive data in SharePoint Online:

1. **The type of data being archived:** Different types of data may have different retention and compliance requirements and may need to be archived differently. For example, sensitive or confidential data may need to be stored in a more secure location, while less sensitive data may be suitable for storage in a less secure location.

2. **The volume of data being archived:** If you have a large volume of data that needs to be archived, you may need to use a more automated approach to ensure that the process is efficient and scalable.

3. **The frequency of data archived:** If you need to archive data regularly, you may want to consider using a workflow tool such as Power Automate to automate the process.

4. **The location and accessibility of the data:** You may want to consider where the data will be stored and how it will be accessed when deciding on an archiving approach. For example, suppose you need to store the data in a secure location and ensure it is only accessible to authorized users. In that case, you may need to use a more sophisticated archiving solution.

Again, the best approach to archiving data in SharePoint Online will depend on your specific needs and requirements. It may be helpful to consult with a content owner or department director, to determine the best approach for your organization.

Practical tasks

Let us login again to your tenant and do some configuration related to the records management. As the first step, we will create a records management site. To do so in SharePoint Online, you will need to have the appropriate permissions (which you are as a Global admin) and follow these steps:

1. Sign in to Microsoft 365 using your account.

2. Create a new site collection. However, this time, we will do it in a different way – via the Admin center, as we need to use additional templates. From the top left corner, click on squares and select the Admin application.

3. In the left navigation, select **Show All** and then **SharePoint**.

4. It will open the SharePoint admin center for you. In the left navigation under sites section, select **Active Sites**.

5. In the top ribbon, select **Create**.

6. You will see two default templates which are **Team site** and the **Communication site**. We need more templates and so, at the bottom of the pop up, select **Other Options**.

Figure 4.3 features additional templates selection during site creation.

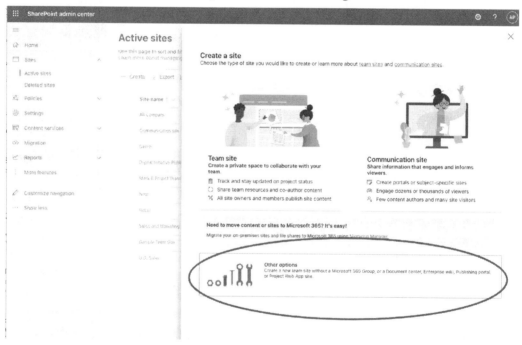

Figure 4.3: *Additional templates selection during site creation*

7. In the left corner, you will see a dropdown, where it says **Choose a template**. Select **Content center** from the list of available templates. On the right side, name the site as you would like. In our case, we will name this as 'Records Center'. Put yourself as a primary administrator and click on **Create**.

Now your site should be created, and if you refresh your Active Sites page in the admin center, you will see it in the list of available sites. Click on its URL and you will be redirected to the site. Go to the Site Contents of that site and you will see that the structure of the site is slightly different comparing to the Communication or Teams site. You do not have a default 'Documents' document library but get a few others instead.

We can use 'Files' library to store our records there or you can create new library as we did before.

As you have a place where the content can be stored, we can configure some rules and policies now. There are a couple of ways as to how that can be done:

- Using Compliance center.

- On the site itself (classic UI method).

As we are trying to use new approaches based on the best practices, we will use Compliance center in the following example. The reader is nonetheless encouraged to research how records management rules can be configured on a site itself, on their own. There are a lot of articles from Microsoft and different blogs available on this topic.

Now follow the given steps for retention policy creation from the Compliance center:

1. At the top left corner, click on squares and select **Admin** app.

2. From the **Admin** center, click on **Show All** in the left navigation and select **Compliance**.

3. The Compliance center will open. There are a lot of features and functionality available that we will cover more in depth later. For now, select **Policies** from the left navigation. Click on **Retention** category.

Figure 4.4 features retention policy creation from the Compliance center:

Figure 4.4: *Retention policy creation from the Compliance center*

4. The new page will load. In the top ribbon, select **Create retention** policy.

5. The first screen will ask for the name of the policy and its description. Name your policy as 'Records policy' or in some similar way.

6. The next screen will prompt to select the type of policy, that is, *Adaptive* or *Static*. We will select *Static* type for this example. Click **Next**.

    a. You will see a list of location available to apply this policy. As we have covered previously, there are a lot of applications where policy can be implemented. We will select only SharePoint for this exercise. Make sure that all other applications Status is Off.

    b. In the 'Included' column, you will see the value 'All Sites' which means this policy will be applied to all site. We do not want our policy to be applied for all sites. Click on Edit link there and paste your newly created site URL there.

Figure 4.5 features the configuring site where policy should be applied:

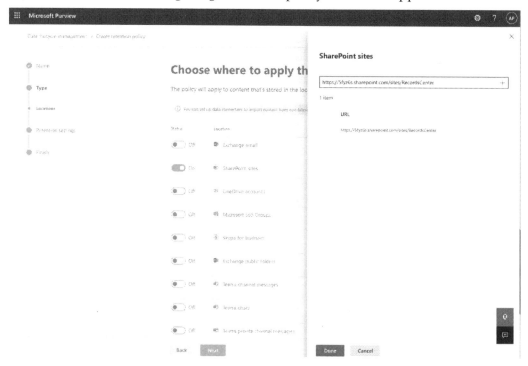

Figure 4.5: *Configuring site where policy should be applied to*

7. You can select multiple sites if needed. Click **Done** and then Next.

8. On the following screen, you will see a few configuration options: for how long document should be retained, from when it was created or last modified,

and what should happen after the retention period is over. You will have multiple choices to select from in form of radio buttons. Check them all out and select the option you like.

9. Then you will see a summary screen, where you can click **Finish** to create your policy. Once created, it will be available in the list of all policies in the Compliance center.

For more flexibility and more agile functionality, Labels can be applied on top of Policies. You can determine if a document should be moved to another location or anywhere else. We will cover it in *Chapter 16, Security and Compliance Policies*.

Conclusion

In this chapter, you learned about how to work with Records in SharePoint online. We covered what Records are and why we need to use them. We discussed that records can be placed in a dedicated Records Center site and created our own Record Center during practical tasks. Moreover, you learned about various content types and that they can be applied for records management, and policies can be created based on the content type. Site columns can be helpful in saving time and creating common columns that can later be used in various lists and libraries and added to content types. Information management policies can be used to retain documents and content based on compliance rules, and Labels can be used to provide a more flexible functionality on retention. At the end of the process, your data can be archived using the same retention rules or using automated tools like Power Automate.

Points to remember

- Any file can be a record.

- Records can be stored in-place or moved to a specific location or site.

- Content types are a reusable collection of metadata (information about the content), workflow, and behavior settings for a specific type of content. Content types allow organizations to manage and organize their content in a consistent and structured way.

- Site columns are reusable piece of metadata (information about the content) that can be used to describe and classify content. Site columns can be used to add consistent, structured information to content types, lists, and libraries in SharePoint Online.

- Information policies can be different types and are generally used to ensure compliance with internal and external regulations.

- Labels are metadata tags that can be applied to content and based on them, rules can be created to reattain or move the data.

- Data can be archived using retaining policies and moved to a dedicated location or can be deleted. Another way to automate the process is to use Power Automate Flow and define the logic there.

Join our book's Discord space

Join the book's Discord Workspace for Latest updates, Offers, Tech happenings around the world, New Release and Sessions with the Authors:

https://discord.bpbonline.com

## CHAPTER 5

Working with Archive Libraries in SharePoint Online

> **"An archive is the repository of a society's past, the place where its records are kept and preserved."**
>
> *- Timothy Ferris*

Introduction

Some information should be periodically archived to free up space and keep data organized. This can be done using some built-in and custom features available in SharePoint. Let us review them and find out how to properly collect, manage and archive data to ensure your collaboration environment always stays up to date, is easy to navigate and find the correct information.

Structure

In this chapter, we will cover the following topics:

- Lists and Libraries archival process
- Archiving using Flow
- Archiving using records management
- Manual Data Archival

Objectives

In this chapter, we will review and dive deeper into the archival process to see how whole lists and libraries could be archived using Out of the Box and 3rd party tools. We will build our own Power Automate Flow to move data on a condition, from one place to another and will also use records management to move files between sites. SharePoint also has a built-in feature to move a file or copy it to another location, and so, we will look at how that too works. At the end of this chapter, you will know various ways to archive data and approaches available for data archival.

Lists and Libraries archival process

In SharePoint Online, lists and libraries can be configured to use retention policies to automate the archival process. As we covered in a previous chapter, a retention policy is a set of rules that specifies how long the content should be retained and what should happen to it when it reaches the end of its retention period. You even configured one policy yourself in the Complaint center.

To configure a list or library to use a retention policy in SharePoint Online, you will need to follow the given steps:

1. Sign in to SharePoint Online as a site owner or administrator.

2. Go to the list or library that you want to configure.

3. Click on the **Settings** gear icon, and then click on **List settings** (for a list) or **Library settings** (for a library).

4. Under **Permissions and Management**, click **Information management policy settings**.

5. On the **Information management policy settings** page, select the retention policy you want to apply to the list or library.

6. Click on the **OK** button to apply the policy.

Once the retention policy has been applied to the list or library, it will be used to all items in the list or library. When an item reaches the end of its retention period, it will be deleted or moved to an archive, depending on the settings specified in the retention policy. This is the classic UI approach that was there for a while.

To manually archive a list in SharePoint Online, you will need to follow these steps:

1. Sign in to SharePoint Online as a site owner or administrator.

2. Go to the list that you want to archive.

3. Click on the **Settings** gear icon, and click on **List settings**.

4. Under **Permissions and Management**, click on **Save list as template**.

5. On the **Save as Template** page, enter the template's name and description.

6. Under **Include Content**, select the **Include Content** option.

7. Click on the **OK** button to create the template.

The list will be saved as a template, and the template will be added to the "Solution Gallery" for the site. You can then download the template to your local drive or move it to a different site or location.

Templates are a great tool as they allow quickly creating a template of a list or library structure, with an option to include all the content.

To access list templates on a SharePoint Online site, you will need to have the appropriate permissions and follow these steps:

1. Sign in to SharePoint Online as a site owner or administrator.

2. Go to the site where the list templates are stored.

3. Click on the **Settings** gear icon, and then click on **Site contents**.

4. In the **Site Contents** page, click on the **Solution Gallery** link in the **Web Designer Galleries** section.

In the **Solution Gallery**, you will see a list of all the available list templates for the site. You can click on the name of a template to view its details, or click on the **Create** button to create a new list based on the template. You can also download list template and later upload it to template gallery on another site or even another tenant.

It is possible that the **Save list as template** option is not available in the list settings for certain SharePoint Online sites because it has been disabled by the site administrator. This option can be disabled at the site level or at the organization-wide level (across all sites).

If you do not see the **Save list as template** option in the list settings, it is likely that it has been disabled for the site. In this case, you will need to contact the site administrator or your Microsoft 365 administrator to request that the option be enabled.

It is also possible that the option is not available because the list contains certain types of content or features that cannot be included in a list template. For example, lists that contain lookup columns that reference other lists cannot be saved as templates.

Overall, the availability of the **Save list as template** option in the list settings will depend on the specific settings and permissions for the site, as well as the types of content and features in the list. Some of the modern site templates like Team site, will not have Save list (or library) as a template option in them. The only way to create a template in this way would be to use the pnp script, which you can get using the following steps:

1. Install the SharePoint PnP PowerShell module on your local machine.

2. Connect to your SharePoint Online tenant using the Connect-PnPOnline cmdlet.

3. Navigate to the site where the list that you want to save as a template is located.

4. Use the Save-PnPListTemplate cmdlet to create a list template based on the list.

Here is an example of the syntax you would use to save a list as a template using the Save-PnPListTemplate cmdlet:

```
Save-PnPListTemplate -Identity "MyList" -FileName "MyListTemplate.stp"
-IncludeContent
```

This example creates a list template based on the list named "**MyList**", and saves it as a file named "**MyListTemplate.stp**" in the current directory. The "**-Include-Content**" parameter specifies that the existing items in the list should be included in the template.

List templates can be created and used in SharePoint Online in the following ways:

- **Predefined list templates:** SharePoint Online includes a number of predefined list templates that you can use to create lists for common business scenarios, such as tasks, events, contacts, and issues. These templates include predefined columns and settings that are tailored to the specific business needs of each scenario.

- **Custom list templates:** You can create custom list templates by saving an existing list as a template. To create a custom list template, you will need to have the appropriate permissions and follow these steps:

  1. Go to the list that you want to save as a template.

  2. Click on the **Settings** gear icon, and then click on **List settings**.

  3. Under **Permissions and Management**, click on **Save list as template**.

  4. On the **Save as Template** page, enter a name and a description for the template.

  5. Under **Include Content**, select the **Include Content** option if you want to include the existing items in the list in the template.

  6. Click on the **OK** button to create the template.

Custom list templates can be used to create new lists with the same structure and behavior as the original list.

The last option to archive the list or library would be to just go to the list/library settings and rename it to List Name – Archive or in some similar way. You can also change permissions on the list level to break the inheritance and set them all to read-only. In this way, only site collection admins will be able to make changes to the list and content, and everyone else will have permission to read the content.

Archiving using flow

There are several ways to archive documents using Power Automate Flow. Flow can run only on a specific library based on the schedule that you set. So it can run every day or once a week or each hour. The limitation is that you cannot run the flow on the entire site, site collection or tenant. For that purpose, you might want to consider Azure Jobs that are executed on a scheduled basis and have more functionality available. But let us discover how Flow can help us with the archival process; there are a few approaches available:

- **Move documents to an archive library:** You can use a Power Automate flow to move documents from a specific library to an archive library. This flow can be triggered by a certain event, such as when a document has not been modified in a certain number of days, or when a document reaches a certain age by running a scheduled flow. Once the document is moved to the archive library, you can use another flow to clean up and delete the unnecessary documents.

- **Copy documents to external storage:** Another approach is to copy the documents to an external storage such as Azure Blob Storage, then delete the original copy. This can be done using a flow that triggers when a new document is added to a library; the flow then copies the document to Azure Blob storage and deletes the original document. Or it also can be a scheduled flow that will check all documents on the library based on a specific condition like created date + 4 years from that date.

- **Create a Backup:** You can create a Backup of the documents to an external storage service, and Azure Blob storage is a popular option. This approach allows you to easily restore data, in case of disaster recovery. Additionally, you can use Azure Policy to keep your backup data for a specific period of time before deletion.

- **Email Archival:** If you are dealing with emails, you can create a flow that archives emails from a specific mailbox to a specific folder in SharePoint or OneDrive, or a specific container in Azure Blob storage.

It is important to note that depending on the size of your organization, the number of documents you are archiving, the requirement for the archiving process and how long you need to retain the data, you may need to consider different approach. Moreover, it is recommended that you should regularly review and update your archiving policies and configurations to ensure that they meet the needs of your organization and comply with any regulatory requirements.

Here is an example of a Power Automate flow that can be used to archive documents from a SharePoint library to an archive library:

1. Create a new Power Automate flow using the **Scheduled** trigger. This trigger will start the flow every day by default at midnight.

2. Add a **SharePoint - Get file properties** action; this action will retrieve the properties of the documents inside the library you are going to crawl.

3. Add a condition to check if Today's data is greater than **Modified** date of the document for 360 days.

4. If the condition is true, add a **SharePoint - Move file** action. This action will move the document from the original library to the archive library, the URL of which, you can specify in the action itself.

5. If the condition is false, then just skip the file.

6. Finally, add a **Send an email** action to notify the relevant parties that the document has been archived and moved.

You can test and fine-tune this flow as per your need. This is just a basic example, to give you a high-level overview of the process. For example, you can add additional conditions to check for different properties of the document, such as its content type or the user who created it. We will create similar Flow in the Practical tasks section of this chapter.

Archiving using records management

We have already covered a big portion of records management, policies, labels, and archival included in the previous chapter. But let us recap to make sure nothing is forgotten.

Records management is a process of organizing, storing, preserving, and disposing of records and documents in a systematic way.

A few steps on how to archive documents using records management in SharePoint are described as follows:

- **Create a records center site.** The first step is to create a records center site in SharePoint. A records center site is a special type of site designed specifically for records management. It has built-in features for managing records and allows you to create custom retention policies.

- **Create a retention policy.** Once the records center site is created, you can create a retention policy for the documents (or it can be done directly from the Compliance center). A retention policy defines how long a document should be kept before it is eligible for the deletion or archiving. The retention policy can be created for all documents or for specific document types.

- **Move documents to the records center.** You can use Power Automate flow or Labels rules to move documents from other SharePoint sites to the records center. You can also set up content organizer rules to automatically route documents to the records center based on their content type or other properties.

- **Review and dispose.** After the documents are moved to the records center, you can review them and dispose of those that are no longer needed. The review process can be automated using workflows, and custom SharePoint columns, or you can use out-of-the-box records management features in SharePoint.

- **Archiving.** Once the documents are no longer needed and the retention period is over, the documents will be automatically moved to the archive. The archive can be external storage or a special archive library within the records center site. You can also use Azure Content Management policies to handle your archival process.

It is important to note that records management is a complex process and it is important to define and follow a consistent and systematic approach. Moreover, it is recommended to prepare documentation on the defined process, in order to make sure anyone can follow it and be familir with it.

Manual data archival

SharePoint (and similarly OneDrive and Teams) have a few built-in features that would allow you to move data manually from one location to another. There are a few different ways to move data manually in SharePoint, depending on the specific requirements of your solution. Here are a few common approaches:

- **Drag and drop.** You can use the drag-and-drop feature to move files and folders from one location to another within the same SharePoint site or between different SharePoint sites. Simply select the file or folder you want to move, hold down the left mouse button and drag the file or folder to the desired location.

- **Move or Copy.** You can use the move or copy feature to move or copy files and folders from one location to another. This can be done by selecting the file or folder you want to move or copy, and then going to the **File** menu and choosing **Move** or **Copy** option from the top ribbon in the document library. This approach will work within one site collection or hub site.
  - o **Important to check Check Out/Check In configuration**. If you are working with documents that are checked out, you can check them in and move them to a different location. Go to the document you want to move, click on the ellipses (...) and choose **Check In** option and then move it to the desired location.

- **SharePoint Designer.** SharePoint Designer is a powerful tool that allows you to perform more advanced operations, such as moving data between lists or libraries. You can use the **Copy List Item** or **Move List Item** actions in SharePoint Designer to move data between different lists or libraries. SharePoint Designer slowly becomes decommissioned and less and less used for development but still stays a great tool with features that might be handy in day-to-day operations.
  - o It is important to note that when you move data, it is a good practice to double-check the permissions on the destination location, to ensure that the users who need to have access to the data will have it after the move.
  - o Additionally, if you are moving large amount of data, it is recommended to plan the operation in a non-peak hour, and also inform the stakeholders about the move, to avoid any confusion and to ensure that the data will be accessed after the move.

- **3rd party tools.** One of the good examples and most commonly used 3rd party tools for migration is Sharegate. ShareGate is a software company that provides tools for content migration and management in Microsoft SharePoint and Microsoft Teams. Their products include ShareGate Desktop, a tool for migrating content between SharePoint environments, and ShareGate Apricot, a tool for managing and governing SharePoint and Teams content. ShareGate's

- Products are designed to help organizations simplify and automate the process of migrating content to SharePoint and managing it once it is there. They also have options for deploying and managing Office365 and Microsoft Teams. They are considered one of the leading player in the market of such tools.

Here are some general steps for using ShareGate Desktop to move files:

1. Install ShareGate Desktop on your computer and launch the application.

2. Connect to the source and destination SharePoint environments. You can do this by entering the URLs for the sites and providing your credentials.

3. Select the files or folders that you want to move by using the user interface. You can also use the filtering options to select specific files based on different criterias.

4. Choose the destination location in the destination SharePoint environment.

5. Choose the migration options you want to use, such as preserving permissions or maintaining version history.

6. Start the migration process by clicking the **Migrate** button. ShareGate will copy the selected files from the source environment to the destination environment.

7. Monitor the migration process to see the status of the files as they are being moved. ShareGate provides detailed log and report of the migration.

8. Once the migration is completed, you can verify that the files have been moved correctly and that the metadata and permissions have been preserved as desired.

Sharegate is a great tool for small and bulk migrations, archiving files and running reports on permissions and content. This all comes with additional cost of course. The price for sharegate tool can be checked on their official website but usually, it stays around $5,000 per license per year.

Figure 5.1 features the interface of a Sharegate tool:

Figure 5.1: *The interface of a Sharegate tool*

Practical tasks

Let us jump right into it and create a template of the library and restore from it. Follow the given steps:

1. The first thing, as always, is to login into your Microsoft 365 account at portal.office.com.

2. Next, go to SharePoint admin application from there.

3. Select **Sites | Active** Sites on the left navigation.

4. Click on **Create** at the top ribbon and select **Other Options** from the pop-up at the bottom.

5. In the left corner of the Select template, dropdown, select **More templates** at the bottom. The new tab will open.

6. Fill out site name and URL in the required fields and set yourself as the admin. The example of the site name can be **Classic**. Select **Team site (classic)** template. Remember the URL of the site you creating.

Figure 5.2 features the screen of Classic Team Site creation:

Create Site Collection

Title	
Web Site Address	https://5fyz6s.sharepoint.com /sites/
Template Selection	2013 experience version will be used Select a language: English Select a template: Collaboration | Enterprise | Publishing | Custom Team site (classic experience) Developer Site Project Site Community Site A site with a classic experience on the home page and no connection to a Microsoft 365 Group.
Time Zone	(UTC-08:00) Pacific Time (US and Canada)
Administrator	
Server Resource Quota	0 resources of 0 resources available

OK

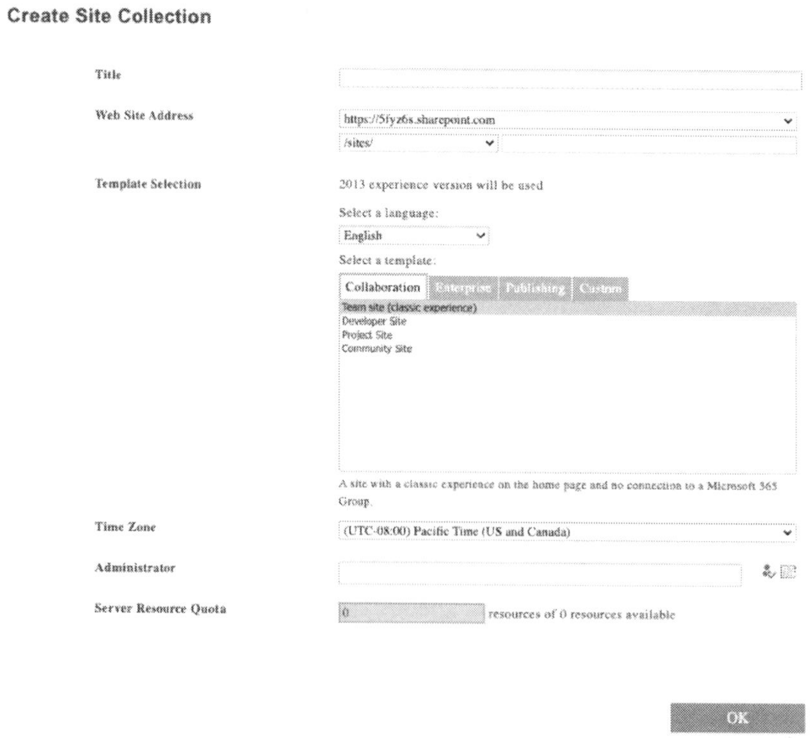

Figure 5.2: The screen of Classic Team Site creation

7. Next wait for a couple of minutes for the site to provision and navigate to the URL you just created.

   This will be the Team site on a classic experience. This will allow us to create a template of the list/library and re-create it on the same site. All modern sites have templates functionality limited as PnP script should be used instead. We will cover PnP approach later in this book. You can see right away that Classic UI page looks different from the one you created before in the Modern UI. Some web-parts a different too.

8. To proceed with a template creation in the left navigation, click on **Documents**.

9. You will be redirected to the document library.

10. Upload a few test documents in it or create them right from the library.

11. After documents are uploaded, click on the gear icon in the top right corner and select the **Library Settings** option.

12. On a library settings page in the right column **Permission and Management**, select the option **Save document library as template**.

13. Fill out all of the fields and select checkbox **Include Content** at the bottom.

14. Click **OK**.

Figure 5.3 features the screen saving library as a Template:

Figure 5.3: *Screen saving library as a Template*

List template will be created and you will see a confirmation screen. On a same screen in the text, you will see **List template gallery** link. Click on it and it will redirect you to the templates gallery page. You will see your newly created template there. As you selected the option to **Include content** when created the template – all previously uploaded documents will be stored in that template too.

15. As the next step, click in the top right corner on the gear icon and select **Site Contents**.

16. At the bottom left corner select **Return to classic SharePoint** link. It will change the interface from modern to classic.

17. Click on **Add and app** button.

18. Use search below Site Contents words and type your template name there.

Figure 5.4 features creating a library from the previously saved template:

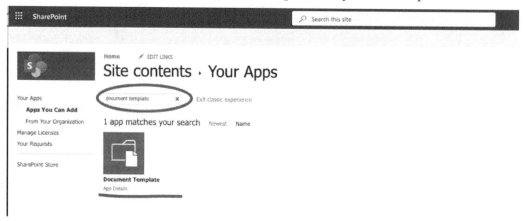

Figure 5.4: *creating a library from the previously saved template*

19. Click on the template name and set your new list name in the pop-up.

20. Click **Create**.

You will be redirected back to the Site Contents page where you can see your newly created library from the template. If you click on it, you will see that all of your documents are saved there.

In this way, lists or libraries templates can be created and restored later on the same site or site collection. If you need to move the template to another site collection or tenant, then you can do that too. Each site collection has its own List Templates Gallery. So, in order for the list to be recreated, template should be uploaded there. You can go to Site Settings and look for the 'List Templates'. There will be all your templates (same page you accessed before). If you click on the template name it will be downloaded to your local machine.

In the same way, you could go to a different site collection – site settings – list templates and upload it there using drag and drop or the 'upload' feature from the top ribbon. Then create a list from the site content – add an app, in the same way as we did above.

The next practice task would be to move documents from one place to another.

You can stay at the same site. Click on the Documents link in the left navigation and create a couple more documents in it. Follow the given steps:

1. Select the first newly created document (do not click on the document name but rather click slightly left from the document icon to highlight it.

2. You will see '**Move to**' and '**Copy to**' become available in the top ribbon. If you do not see those options there, you may zom out of your browser or increase size of the browser window. Otherwise, you can click on three dots in the top rubbon and options will be available there.

Figure 5.5 features document highlight and options Move to and Copy to available in the top ribbon:

Figure 5.5: *Document highlight and options Move to and Copy to available in the top ribbon*

3. For selected dcocument, click on **Move to** option.

4. Pop up will be prompted and you can select from the left side what site document should go to, and on the right, what library it should be moved to. You can use breadcrumbs to move between folders, libraries and site contents view

Figure 5.6 features '**Move to**' pop-up with configurations:

Figure 5.6: *'Move to' pop up with configurations*

5. After you finished your final destination, click on **Move here** button at the bottom.

The document will be removed from your library and placed into the other one you selected. You can do this operation with multiple documents or folders. But do not select too much content at once, as this feature does not work too well with bulk data.

Now highlight another document you created and select **Copy to** option from the ribbon.

Select destination library and click on the **Copy here** button at the bottom. In this case, document will stay in your library and copy will be created in the other one.

Lastly, let us review a migration tool like Sharegate. It used on a lot of migration related projects and pretty well known between developers and admins. Go to **sharegate.com** and at the top right corner, click on **Start a free trial** button. Fill out your information and email (you can use the same account you using form Microsoft 365 or your personal one). Go through account creation process answering question and at the end download 'Sharegate Desktop' tool.

You would need to install it on your machine and login with the newly created account. You might need to confirm your email before your free 14 day trial will be started.

After it is downloaded, and the trial activated in the left menu, go to **Migration** menu and select **Content migration** option. Structure migration option is a good fit when you move entire site or libraries between different locations, but if you want to move only specific document, '**Content migration**' option will work the best. Provide the URL of the site you are moving the file from and credentials you are using to login. Then do the same for the destination site where you want to move files to (just follow the prompts).

Connections will be established and you will see 2 columns where on the left will be your source site and on the right, the destination one. You can select any documents and move them from site to another and see how it works.

Sharegate is a very powerful tool and can move content in bulk. So, do not be afraid to move hundreds gigabytes of data if needed. Well, in your case it is just going to be a few files most likely, but it is always good to know what it is capable of. You are encouraged to check out '**Structure migration**' option and '**Move file from local storage**'.

Conclusion

In this chapter, you got more insights on content management, migration and archival. We discovered multiple approaches that include old-fashion templates, modern UI move and copy files feature, and 3rd party tool discovered on example of Sharegate. When you will work with the content, it will be up to you to decide what approach suits you better based on situation and tasks you have. As a rule of thumb, it is usually for small size content movement that built-in capabilities are used. If you are looking to move content larger than 100 GB in size, you might want to consider using some tool.

Points to remember

- Lists and Libraries can be archived using information policies, templates or PnP script.

- Automation can be achieved using Power Automate Flow.

- You can also archive lists and libraries by renaming them and setting read-only permissions on them

- There are two buil-in features available in Modern UI: 'Move to' and 'Copy to'.

- 3rd party tools such as Sharegate, are designed for a large size migrations and reports.

- There are a couple of other approaches available. Check out on the internet how to move files using '**Open file in explorer**' feature. There is also a free migration tool available from Microsoft called **SharePoint Migration Tool** (**SPMT**).

Join our book's Discord space

Join the book's Discord Workspace for Latest updates, Offers, Tech happenings around the world, New Release and Sessions with the Authors:

https://discord.bpbonline.com

Chapter 6
OneDrive for Business

"The most important thing is to keep the stuff that you care about most—the stuff you truly care about—close to you, either on your computer or on a backup disk."

-Steve Jobs

Introduction

What is OneDrive, and why use it when you have SharePoint available already? Well, that is just what we are going to discover. The same as SharePoint, OneDrive is available as a part of the Office 365 suite as well as it has its own desktop client for a more convenient user experience. In this chapter, you will learn the main difference in purpose between SharePoint and OneDrive, what to use when, and what features are available similar and different between them.

Structure

In this chapter, we will cover the following topics:

- OneDrive vs SharePoint
- OneDrive Sync Client

- Files on demand
- OneDrive retention policies after document deletion
- Admin access to OneDrive

Objectives

In this chapter, we will review the OneDrive application, compare it to SharePoint and cover what differences between them. At the end of this chapter, you will learn about the OneDrive sync client, how to install and use it, how to synchronize files from the cloud to the local machine and vice versa. You will configure Files on Demand to learn how this feature works and will see how retention policies can be applied to OneDrive. In the end, we will cover OneDrive Admin Center and what configurations are available there.

OneDrive vs SharePoint

OneDrive and SharePoint are both Microsoft 365 products, but they serve different purposes.

OneDrive is a cloud-based storage and file-sharing service that allows users to store, access, and share files from anywhere. It is primarily designed for personal use, though it can also be used in a business use. It is up to you as a user to decide what type of content you want to store there. As OneDrive is integrated with Microsoft Office 365, it allows users to collaborate on documents with others in real time.

SharePoint, on the other hand, is a more comprehensive content management and collaboration platform. It is designed for businesses and organizations to store, organize, and share information, such as documents, lists, and web pages as we reviewed in the previous chapter. SharePoint also includes features such as document management, workflow, and business intelligence. SharePoint can be used to create intranet sites, extranet sites, and it also allows for creating custom solutions for specific business needs.

Figure 6.1 features a schema on what product to use when:

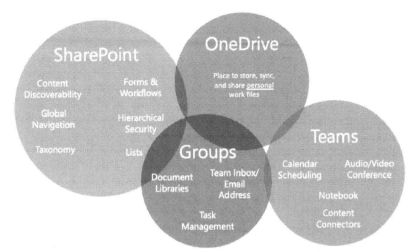

Figure 6.1: *Schema on what product to use when*

Here are a few key differences between OneDrive for Business and SharePoint Online:

- OneDrive is focused on personal storage and file sharing, while SharePoint is focused on enterprise content management, business process automation, and collaboration.

- OneDrive for Business is primarily used by individual users to store their personal or work-related files. On the other hand, SharePoint Online is used by teams and organizations to collaborate on the document everyone works on.

- OneDrive for Business is integrated with Microsoft Office 365 and allows for real-time collaboration on documents, while SharePoint Online offers more advanced collaboration features, such as shared calendars and lists, and support for custom workflows and forms.

- OneDrive for Business allows for personal storage and sharing of files, while SharePoint Online allows for creating and customizing sites, managing documents and workflows, and also provides more advanced collaboration features.

- SharePoint storage quota is usually defined by the admin, while every user in OneDrive for business gets 1TB of storage by default.

- OneDrive for Business allows for syncing files and folders to a user's device and has access to the files when not connected to the internet. SharePoint Online also allows for this, but it is more focused on the central storage and access of files in the cloud, it also allows for creating custom solutions to access the files offline.

- OneDrive itself can be imagined as one document library that allows you to create views, folder structure, permissions and so on. However, the primary intent of use is just for you. While in SharePoint, you can create multiple libraries, lists, and pages.

- Power Automate as a workflow platform can work with both SharePoint and OneDrive and free connectors are available out of the box for both platforms.

To avoid confusion, you should also know that there is OneDrive *Personal* and *OneDrive for business* versions. The Personal one usually comes with the Windows installed machines and is dedicated for a personal documents usage. The Business version comes as a part of the Microsoft 365 platform, includes more storage, that is, 1TB, and is dedicated to be used for your documents related to a business.

Here are a few key differences between the Personal version and For Business one:

- OneDrive is primarily designed for personal use, while OneDrive for Business is designed for use in a business context.

- OneDrive is free to use with some limitations on storage, while OneDrive for Business is a paid service that is included as part of Microsoft 365.

- OneDrive has a simpler user interface and is more focused on file storage and sharing, while OneDrive for Business has a more complex interface and includes additional features such as document management, workflow, and business intelligence.

- OneDrive is accessible to anyone with a Microsoft account, while OneDrive for Business requires a work or school account with license.

OneDrive application is available on PC, Mac and mobile devices running IOS and Android.

OneDrive Sync Client

The OneDrive sync client is a software application that allows users to synchronize their OneDrive files between their computer and the cloud. The OneDrive sync client allows users to work with their OneDrive files as if they were stored locally on their computer while also keeping them backed up and in sync with the cloud. It is compatible with Windows and Mac computers.

The OneDrive sync client works by creating a special folder on the user's computer, usually called "OneDrive" or "OneDrive - [Organization Name]", which is connected to the user's OneDrive account in the cloud. Any files or folders that are added to this folder are automatically synced to the cloud and made available on other devices where the user has installed the sync client. This allows users to access their OneDrive files from any device and work on them even when they are offline.

The OneDrive sync client also allows users to share files and folders with others, collaborate on documents in real-time, and restore previous versions of files. It also allows to set up selective sync (fils on-demand feature), which means that users can choose which folders and files to sync to the device and which to keep only on the cloud.

Figure 6.2 features OneDrive sync client view on the local machine:

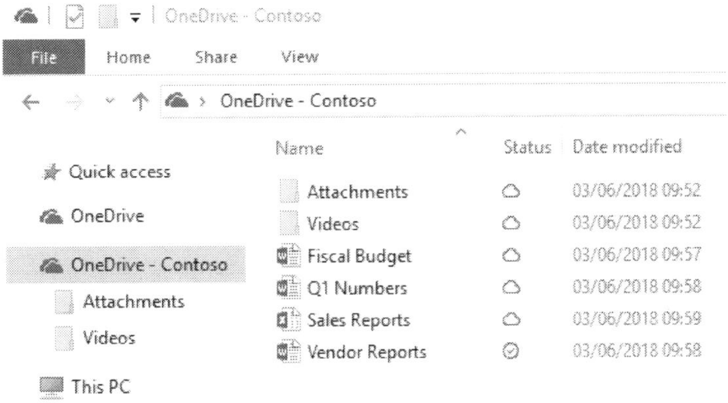

Figure 6.2: *OneDrive sync client view on the local machine*

The client software runs on the user's computer, and it creates a special folder that is connected to the user's OneDrive account in the cloud. This folder, as mentioned previously, is called the "OneDrive folder" or "OneDrive - [Organization Name]". Any files or folders that are added to this folder are automatically synced to the cloud and made available on other devices where the user has installed the sync client. This allows users to access their OneDrive files from any device and work on them even when they are offline.

The OneDrive sync client has several features that are designed to make it easy for users to access and work with their OneDrive files. Some of these features include:

- **Real-time syncing:** The sync client automatically syncs files and folders between the user's computer and the cloud as soon as they are added, modified, or deleted. This allows users to access their most up-to-date files from any device.

- **File and folder sharing:** The sync client allows users to share files and folders with others, and collaborate on documents in real-time. Users can also set permissions for others to view, edit or just read-only access.

- **Version history:** The sync client keeps a record of previous versions of files, so users can easily restore an older version of a file if they need to.

- **Selective sync:** The sync client allows users to choose which folders and files to sync to the device and which to keep only on the cloud. This feature is especially useful for users who have limited storage space on their device.

- **Conflicts resolution:** In case of conflicts between the same files being edited by different users, the OneDrive sync client will automatically detect and resolve the conflicts.

- **Security:** The sync client encrypts files before uploading to the cloud, and also allows for setting up two-factor authentication for added security.

Overall, the OneDrive sync client is a powerful tool that allows users to access and work with their OneDrive files from their computer, while also keeping them backed up and in sync with the cloud. It also offers additional features such as file and folder sharing, version history and selective sync, making it a convenient and efficient way to work with cloud-based files.

Files on demand

Files On-Demand is a feature of the OneDrive sync client that allows users to access all of their OneDrive files from their computer without having to download them all to the local storage. With Files On-Demand, files are still stored in the cloud, but they can be accessed as if they were stored locally on the computer. This feature is especially useful for users who have limited storage space on their devices or who need to access a large number of files that they do not frequently use.

When Files On-Demand is enabled, the OneDrive folder on the user's computer will display all of the files and folders that are stored in the user's OneDrive account, but they will not take up space on the computer. Instead of downloading the entire file, only a placeholder file will be downloaded, which will take up minimal space. When the user opens a file, the actual content of the file will be downloaded on demand.

Users can also choose to make certain files or folders always available offline, which means that the full file will be downloaded to the local storage and will be available even when the device is not connected to the internet. This allows users to access their files quickly even if they do not have internet connection.

Files On-Demand feature is available for Windows and Mac users and it allows for better management of the storage space on their device while providing easy access to their OneDrive files.

The OneDrive sync client uses a set of icons to indicate the status of files and folders in the OneDrive folder on the user's computer. Here is a brief description of the most common icons that you might see:

- **A green checkmark:** This icon indicates that the file or folder is up to date and has been synced successfully between the computer and the cloud.

- **A blue cloud:** This icon indicates that the file or folder is available online-only. This means that the file or folder is stored in the cloud but not downloaded to the local storage. This is the state of the files when Files on Demand feature is enabled.

- **A blue cloud with a white checkmark:** This icon indicates that the file or folder is available online-only, but it is also set to be always available offline. This means that the file or folder is stored in the cloud and will be downloaded to the local storage.

- **A white checkmark on a blue background:** This icon indicates that the file or folder is currently being synced between the computer and the cloud.

- **A white X on a red background:** This icon indicates that there is a problem with the file or folder, and it is not currently syncing. The user should check the file or folder for issues and resolve them.

- **A yellow triangle with an exclamation mark:** This icon indicates that there is a conflict with the file or folder. This can happen when the same file is being edited by different users at the same time. The user should resolve the conflict by choosing which version of the file to keep.

- **A white arrow pointing up and down:** This icon indicates that the file or folder is set to be shared with other people.

These are the most common icons that you might see when using the OneDrive sync client, but please keep in mind that the appearance of the icons might vary depending on the device and operating system you are using.

Figure 6.3 features OneDrive sync client folder with icons and file property pop up open:

Figure 6.3: *OneDrive sync client folder with icons and file property pop-up open*

OneDrive retention policies after document deletion

OneDrive for Business allows administrators to set retention policies for deleted files and folders. These policies can be used to automatically delete files and folders that have been deleted by users after a certain period of time. This can help organizations comply with regulatory requirements and to free up storage space.

When a file or folder is deleted in OneDrive for Business, it is moved to the user's recycle bin. By default, files and folders that are deleted by users will be retained in the recycle bin for 93 days. After this period, they will be permanently deleted and will not be able to be restored. Administrators can set a retention policy to automatically delete files and folders from the recycle bin after a shorter period of time, depending on the organization's needs.

Retention policies can be set at the tenant level, meaning they will apply to all users in the organization, or they can be set at the site collection level, which means that they will apply to a specific group of users.

Two types of retention policies can be set in OneDrive for Business:

- **Default retention policy:** This policy applies to all files and folders that are deleted by users, unless a custom retention policy is applied to them.

- **Custom retention policy:** This policy is applied to specific files or folders, and it overrides the default retention policy. This can be useful if there are certain files or folders that need to be retained for a longer period of time, or if they need to be permanently deleted.

In the Compliance Center, administrators can set and manage policies related to data retention, eDiscovery, and data governance. OneDrive for Business is integrated with the Compliance Center, which means that administrators can use the Compliance Center to set and manage retention policies for files and folders that are stored in OneDrive for Business. This can include setting policies for automatically deleting files and folders after a certain period of time, and also for preserving files and folders for a specific period of time.

Additionally, the Compliance Center also provides eDiscovery feature which allows administrators to search for and export specific files and folders from OneDrive for Business, as well as other Office 365 services, for compliance or legal purposes.

The Compliance Center also provides data governance features such as data loss prevention, data classification, and Azure Information Protection, which can be used to protect sensitive data that is stored in OneDrive for Business. For example, administrators can set policies to prevent sensitive data from being shared outside of the organization, or to encrypt files that contain sensitive information.

So there are multiple rules will be applied to the data stored in the OneDrive. Policies specified in the OneDrive admin center and policies set from the Security and Compliance center.

Admin access to OneDrive

The OneDrive Admin center in Office 365 is a web-based tool, similar to other Admin Centers. It allows administrators to manage and configure OneDrive for Business for your organization. The OneDrive Admin center provides a centralized location for managing settings, policies, and user access to OneDrive for Business.

With the OneDrive Admin center, administrators can perform a variety of tasks, such as:

- Setting storage limits for individual users.

- Managing external sharing settings, such as setting up guest access or creating sharing links.

- Managing the retention policies for deleted files and folders.

- Managing the OneDrive sync client settings.

- Viewing usage reports and activity logs for OneDrive for Business.

- Setting policies for data loss prevention, data classification, and Azure Information Protection.

- Managing access to the OneDrive Admin center for other administrators.

The OneDrive Admin center is accessible to Office 365 global administrators and SharePoint administrators, who have the necessary permissions to manage OneDrive for Business in their organization.

Additionally, the OneDrive admin center also allows to create and manage user profiles, so that the administrators can view user's activity, usage and storage information, they can also assign licenses, reset passwords and manage access to OneDrive. It also allows managing group policies, such as setting up sharing and collaboration settings, retention policies, and access to the service.

In summary, the OneDrive Admin center in Office 365 provides a centralized location for administrators to manage and configure OneDrive for Business for their organization. It allows them to set policies, manage user access, and view usage and activity reports, while also allowing the management of user profiles and group policies, which helps them to make sure that the service is being used in a compliant and secure manner.

Sometimes OneDrive Admin center is not visible in the Office 365 admin center, but you can always access it via the SharePoint admin center. OneDrive Admin center is built on top of SharePoint, so you can access it via the SharePoint admin center by going to the Settings menu there.

Practical tasks

Let us go and provision your OneDrive (launch it for the first time).

As usual, first, go to **portal.office.com** and sign in with your Microsoft account.

After logging in from the list of available applications, select **OneDrive**.

When you launch it for the first time, it may take a few seconds to open as the profile is configured.

Figure 6.4 features a web view of the OneDrive for Business:

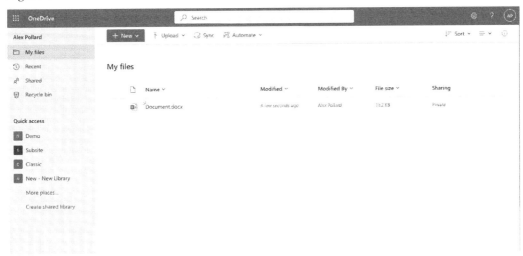

Figure 6.4: *Web view of the OneDrive for Business*

Next, create a document or upload a few documents there. The process is the same as with a SharePoint library. Use drag and drop, upload, or a new button.

After documents are added, you can configure sync. Technically, you would be able to set up sync even without documents, but it is just that we could see the effect right away.

Click on the **Sync** button at the top ribbon. It should give you a prompt to open OneDrive. Click on **Yes** or the **Open OneDrive** button. Next, you will see a OneDrive set up window on your desktop. Configure the path where you would like to store files and follow other prompts. It may also ask you to enter your account pior to selecting the path where all the files will be stored.

Figure 6.5 features a OneDrive sync client configuration screen:

Figure 6.5: *OneDrive sync client configuration screen*

You should be able to see files you uploaded before they are already added to the newly created folder for OneDrive.

Try to delete, change and upload some files directly in the folder and check how they will appear in the browser version. Same goes the other way. If you change or add any documents in the browser, they will appear in your OneDrive folder on the desktop. While you are doing this exercise, pay attention to the icons next to the files. Depending on a state, if the file is downloaded or staying on the cloud, you will see different icons.

Next, create a few folders in OneDrive.

On your desktop, in a status bar, find OneDrive icon and right click on it and select **Settings**.

Figure 6.6 features a OneDrive sync client configuration panel from a status bar:

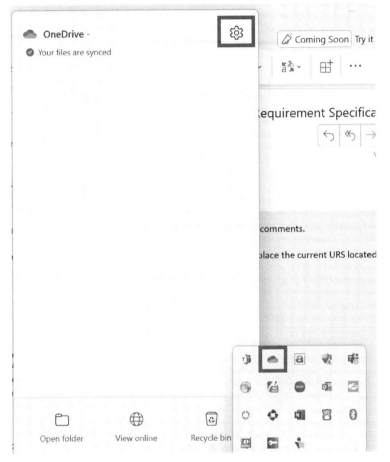

Figure 6.6: *A OneDrive sync client configuration panel from a status bar*

In the settings window in the left navigation, click **Account**. There, you will see an option **Choose folders**. That is the 'files on demand' feature. You will be able to select what folder should be visible on your local machine. In this way, you optimize space taken by your files. Moreover, you always can access all of them via browser and web version.

After you delete your files, they will be placed in the recycle bin. The default configuration is that they will stay there for 93 days, but you can always change it via the Admin center. Recycle bin will be available only via browser. So, after you delete files from the desktop, they will go to the recycle bin in Microsoft 365. To view them or restore, you can go to OneDrive from the browser and in the left navigation, click on the 'Recycle Bin' link.

Conclusion

In this chapter, you learned about OneDrive product and the major difference between OneDrive and SharePoint. We discovered OneDrive sync client and configured one on our own. The Files on Demand feature helps users select what fields and folders should be synced and visible to the local machine. Moreover, all files can always be accessed via the web version of OneDrive. Multiple retention policies can be applied to the OneDrive. Some rules and policies are configured directly from the OneDrive and SharePoint admin centers, some are inherited from the Security and Compliance center.

In summary, OneDrive is a personal storage and file sharing service that is primarily designed for personal use, while OneDrive for Business is a cloud-based storage and file sharing service that is designed for use in a business context and includes additional features such as document management, workflow, and business intelligence.

Points to remember

- OneDrive is for the personal files that you work on and SharePoint is for files you collaborate with others on.

- There is OneDrive for business that comes as a part of Microsoft 365 and there is a OneDrive personal version, that comes with Windows OS.

- By default, there is 1TB of storage per user in OneDrive for business.

- Sync client synchronize files between web, mobile and desktop versions for the same account.

- Files on Demand feature helps users to select files and folders that should be visible on the desktop version.

- Policies can be applied from OneDrive admin center or Security and Compliance center.

Join our book's Discord space

Join the book's Discord Workspace for Latest updates, Offers, Tech happenings around the world, New Release and Sessions with the Authors:

https://discord.bpbonline.com

CHAPTER 7

Search in Microsoft 365

"Search is not only about finding the information you're looking for, it's also about discovering new things you never knew existed. It's a journey of exploration and discovery."

- Sundar Pichai

Introduction

Search is one of the core functions of any platform. In this chapter, you will learn how to get the best out of the SharePoint online search. You will become familiar with search templates, crawling, metadata, search results templates, indexing, and other core capabilities of SPO search. After a proper configuration, users will be able to find documents effectively, fast, and in a reliable way.

Structure

In this chapter, we will cover the following topics:

- SharePoint online search
    - Search results templates
    - Search web-parts

    o PnP search

    o Search configurations

Objectives

In this chapter, we will review SharePoint online search functionality and its configurations. The results you get from the search can be adjusted and tailored to your needs. You will also find out how search results templates can be customized, and thus the format of displayed content from the search results will have another look and fill. There are multiple search-related web-parts that can be connected to each other and we will learn how to do that. PnP search is the new functionality available in SharePoint online and we will see how to use PnP-related web-parts as well as what configurations they have.

SharePoint online search

SharePoint Online search uses a powerful search engine that can index and search through a wide variety of content, including documents, lists, libraries, and web pages. The search engine uses various algorithms and techniques to return the most relevant results, based on an user's query. It also uses machine learning to understand the intent behind the query and return results that match the user's intent.

SharePoint Online search also includes several advanced features that make it even more powerful and easy to use. Some of these features include:

- **Query suggestions:** SharePoint Online search provides query suggestions as users type, which can help them find what they are looking for, more quickly.

- **Refiners:** SharePoint Online search allows users to filter search results by various criteria, such as date, author, or document type.

- **Best bets:** SharePoint Online search can be configured to promote certain results for specific queries, also known as Best Bets, which can help users find the most relevant results more quickly.

- **Search results customization:** SharePoint Online search allows customizing the search results page by adding or removing web parts, and also allows to create custom display templates to show the results in a specific format.

- **Search analytics:** SharePoint Online search provides analytics that allow administrators to see how users are interacting with the search feature, including what queries are being used, what results are being clicked on, and more.

- **Search connectors:** SharePoint Online search allows to connect and search external sources such as external websites, SharePoint on-premises, and other external systems.

Here are a few ways to use SharePoint Online's search capabilities:

- **Simple keyword search**: Users can enter a keyword or phrase into the search bar and press enter. SharePoint Online will return all results that match the keyword or phrase in the search results.

- **Advanced search:** Users can use advanced search operators to refine their search results. For example, they can use the "site:" operator to search within a specific site or the "filetype:" operator to search for specific file types.

- **Search by content type**: Users can filter their search results by content type, such as document, image, or video. This can help them find the specific type of content they are looking for.

- **Refiners:** Users can use refiners to filter search results by various criteria, such as date, author, or document type. This can help them narrow down their search results to find the most relevant information.

- **Preview:** Users can preview the contents of a document before opening it by hovering over the result.

- **Search for People:** Users can search for people in the organization by using the "people:" operator.

- **Search for sites:** Users can search for sites within the SharePoint environment by using the "site:" operator.

- **Search for answers:** SharePoint Online search uses natural language processing, so that users can type in questions and get answers from the search results.

These are just a few examples of the ways you can use SharePoint Online's search capabilities, to find the information you need quickly and easily. As a user, you can experiment with different search queries and operators, to find the most relevant results for your specific needs. Additionally, SharePoint Online's search capabilities can be customized to meet the specific needs of different organizations and users.

Search results templates

SharePoint Online's search results page can be customized by using search result templates. These templates allow administrators to change the way search results are displayed to users and to add additional information to the search results page.

There are two types of search result templates:

- **Display templates:** These templates control the way the search results are displayed on the page. They can be used to change the layout of the search results, add additional information to the results, and even display results in different formats, such as a gallery or a list view.

- **Item templates:** These templates control the way individual search results are displayed. They can be used to add additional information to the search results, such as the author of the document or the last modified date.

Search result templates can be created and managed by administrators using the SharePoint Designer tool or using client-side rendering techniques. These templates are written in HTML, JavaScript, and CSS, and so, some level of coding knowledge is required to create and manage them. Once created, the templates can be associated with a specific search result type and applied to the search results page.

For example, if you want to show the search results in a gallery view, you can create a new display template that shows the results in a grid format and then associate that template with the search results page. Alternatively, if you want to show additional information such as the author of the document, you can create an item template that shows this information and associate it with the search results page.

Search result templates are a powerful way to customize the search results page and provide users with additional information that can help them find the information they need, quickly and easily. It is an important tool to improve the search experience for the users.

SharePoint Online's modern **User Interface (UI)** provides a streamlined, responsive design that makes it easy to customize the search results page. The modern UI allows administrators to make changes to the search results page, using the SharePoint Online user interface without the need for coding or SharePoint Designer.

Here are a few examples of how you can customize the search results page in the modern UI:

- **Web parts:** SharePoint Online's modern UI allows administrators to add, remove, and configure web parts on the search results page. This can include adding a search box, adding a search results web part, or adding a web part that shows search refinements.

- **Layouts:** SharePoint Online's modern UI allows administrators to change the layout of the search results page, such as switching between a list view and a gallery view.

- **Custom display templates:** SharePoint Online's modern UI allows administrators to create custom display templates for the search results page. These templates can include additional information, such as the author of the document or the last modified date, and can be used to change the way the search results are displayed.

- **Search filters:** SharePoint Online's modern UI allows administrators to create custom search filters that can be used to refine the search results. These filters can include things such as date range, content type, and author.

- **Customizable result types:** SharePoint Online's modern UI allows administrators to create custom result types that can be used to display search results in different formats. This can include things such as showing search results as cards or as a list view.

- **Search analytics:** SharePoint Online's modern UI allows administrators to view analytics for the search results, such as the number of searches performed, the most popular search terms, and the click-through rate for the search results.

SharePoint Online's modern UI provides a streamlined and user-friendly way to customize the search results page, which allows administrators to create a more efficient and effective search experience for the users.

The modern **User Interface (UI)** in SharePoint Online uses web technologies such as HTML, JavaScript, and CSS for customization.

The **Hypertext Markup Language (HTML)** is used to structure the elements on the page and to create the layout of the search results page.

JavaScript is used to add interactivity and dynamic behavior to the search results page. For example, JavaScript can be used to create custom search filters, to create custom display templates, or to add custom functionality to the search results page.

Cascading Style Sheets (CSS) is used to control the styling and layout of the search results page. It can be used to change the colors, fonts, and spacing of the elements on the page, and it can also be used to create responsive design.

The above mentioned technologies are widely used in web development and are supported by most modern web browsers. To customize the modern UI templates in SharePoint Online, it is necessary to have a basic understanding of these technologies, and in some cases, some experience in web development is necessary to create custom templates and custom functionality.

It is also worth mentioning that **SharePoint Framework (SPFx)** is a page and web part model that provides full support for client-side SharePoint development, allowing developers to use modern web technologies and tools in creating their solutions. With SPFx, developers can use common libraries such as React, Angular, and Knockout.js to build web parts and other customizations.

Search web-parts

There are many different web parts related to the search. To optimize the learning process, we will cover them from Classic UI and Modern UI sides as they are different in both cases.

In the classic UI of SharePoint Online, there are several web parts that can be used to customize the search results page. These web parts can be added to the search results page or any other page that you want to have search capabilities. They allow administrators to add additional functionality and information to the search results page. Here are a few examples of search web parts that are available in the classic UI:

- **Search box:** This web part allows users to enter a search query and perform a search. It can be configured to show or hide the search box, search suggestions, and search refinement options.

- **Search results:** This web part shows the search results based on the search query entered by the user. It can be configured to show the results in different formats, such as a list view or a table view.

- **Search refinement:** This web part allows users to filter the search results by different criteria, such as date, author, or content type.

- **Search paging:** This web part allows users to navigate through the search results by page.

- **Search statistics:** This web part shows statistics about the search results, such as the number of results returned and the time it took to perform the search.

- **Best bets:** This web part shows a list of promoted results for specific queries, known as Best Bets, which can help users find the most relevant results more quickly.

- **Search navigation:** This web part allows users to navigate through the search results using a hierarchical navigation structure.

- **Search visualization:** This web part allows users to visualize the search results in a graphical format, such as a chart or a map.

These web parts can be added, removed, and configured to work together to meet the specific needs of different organizations and users.

In the modern UI of SharePoint Online, there are also several web parts that can be used to customize the search results page. Here are a few examples of search web parts that are available in the modern UI:

- **Search box:** This web part allows users to enter a search query and perform a search. It can be configured to show or hide the search box, search suggestions, and search refinement options.

- **Search results:** This web part shows the search results, based on the search query entered by the user. It can be configured to show the results in different formats, such as a list view or a gallery view.

- **Search filters:** This web part allows users to filter the search results by different criteria, such as date, author, or content type.

- **Search paging:** This web part allows users to navigate through the search results by page.

- **Search refiners:** This web part allows users to refine the search results by different criteria, such as date, author, or content type.

- **Search verticals:** This web part allows users to search within a specific area of interest, known as search verticals, which can help users find the most relevant results more quickly.

- **Search analytics:** This web part allows administrators to view analytics for the search results, such as the number of searches performed, the most popular search terms, and the click-through rate for the search results.

- **Search people:** This web part allows users to search for people in the organization.

- **Search sites:** This web part allows users to search for sites within the SharePoint environment.

There is one more web part that uses search capabilities to crawl the content and return results, but is more content rather than search oriented. Highlighted Content is a web part in SharePoint Online that allows users to display specific items or pages on the SharePoint site, based on certain criteria. This web part can be used to promote content, such as news articles, blog posts, or important documents, that are most relevant to the users.

The highlighted content web part can be configured to show items or pages from different sources, such as lists, libraries, or pages. You can also specify which items or pages to display, based on certain criteria, such as the content type, the author, or the date modified. Additionally, you can customize the layout and design of the highlighted content web part to match the branding of your SharePoint site.

This web part can be used in the classic UI and modern UI, and it gives the ability to promote content that you want to be highlighted, and it can be used to show the content in different ways, such as a carousel, a list, or a grid. It is a great way to make sure that users see the most important content on your SharePoint site.

The highlighted content web part can be added to any page on the SharePoint site, including the homepage, and it can be configured to show different types of content, such as news articles, blog posts, or important documents. It is a powerful way to promote relevant content to users and improve the user experience on the SharePoint site.

PnP search

Patterns and Practices (PNP) Search is a community-driven initiative that provides guidance and resources for working with SharePoint search. The PNP Search initiative is focused on providing solutions and best practices for common search scenarios, such as creating custom search results pages, customizing search web parts, and integrating search with other services and applications.

PNP Search is an open-source project, which means that developers can contribute to the project and share their solutions and best practices with the community. The project provides a wide range of resources, such as code samples, tutorials, and documentation, that can help developers and administrators to work with SharePoint search more effectively.

PNP Search is built on top of SharePoint search, and it is a collection of libraries, samples, and documentation that helps developers to work with the search functionality in SharePoint. It offers a lot of functionality such as:

- Providing a simplified way to work with search results and result sources.

- Providing a simplified way to work with search queries and query rules.

- Providing a simplified way to work with search-managed properties and refinements.

- Providing a simplified way to work with search analytics and search reporting.

PNP Search is a great resource for developers and administrators who want to work with SharePoint search more effectively and efficiently. It can help them create custom search solutions that meet the specific needs of their organization and users, and it can also help them learn about the best practices for working with SharePoint search.

The basic search functionality provided by SharePoint allows users to search for content within a SharePoint site or tenant, but it may be limited in terms of customization and integration with other services and applications. PNP Search provides additional functionality that can be used to extend and enhance the basic search functionality provided by SharePoint.

Here are a few examples of how PNP Search is different from the basic search functionality in SharePoint:

- **Simplified API:** PNP Search provides a simplified API that can be used to work with search results, result sources, queries, and query rules. This API can help developers work with search more efficiently and effectively.

- **Additional functionality:** PNP Search provides additional functionality that can be used to extend the basic search functionality provided by SharePoint. For example, it provides a way to work with search managed properties and refinements, search analytics and reporting, and creating custom search solutions.

- **Community-driven:** PNP Search is a community-driven project, which means that developers can contribute to the project and share their solutions and best practices with the community. This can help developers learn from the experiences of others and to find solutions to common search scenarios.

- **Resources:** PNP Search provides a wide range of resources, such as code samples, tutorials, and documentation, that can help developers and administrators to work with SharePoint search more effectively.

In summary, PNP Search is an open-source project that provides additional functionality and resources for working with SharePoint search. It is built on top of the basic search functionality provided by SharePoint and provides a simplified API, additional functionality, community-driven solutions and resources to help developers and administrators to work with SharePoint search more effectively and efficiently.

Search configurations

There are several search configurations that you can do in SharePoint Online. Let us cover them.

- **Result sources**: Result sources allow you to specify the scope of your search, such as specific lists, libraries, or sites. You can also create custom result sources that can be used to search external content, such as a database or a web service.

- **Query rules**: Query rules allow you to create custom actions that are triggered when a specific search query is entered. For example, you can create a query rule that promotes certain content for a specific search query or that redirects the user to a specific page.

- **Managed properties:** Managed properties allow you to control how content is indexed and how it is displayed in the search results. For example, you can create custom managed properties that can be used to display additional information in the search results, such as the author or the last modified date.

- **Refiners:** Refiners allow you to create custom filters that can be used to refine the search results. For example, you can create a refiner that allows users to filter the search results by date or by author.

- **Search analytics**: Search analytics allow you to view statistics about the search results, such as the number of searches performed, the most popular search terms, and the click-through rate for the search results.

- **Search visualization:** Search visualization allows you to visualize the search results in a graphical format, such as a chart or a map. This can be a powerful way to understand the data and the results.

- **Result types:** Result types allow you to create custom display templates for different types of content, such as documents, images, or videos. This allows you to control how the search results are displayed and to provide additional information to the users.

In SharePoint Online, the search crawl is the process by which the search engine indexes the content of the SharePoint site or tenant. The search engine uses a web crawler to scan the content of the SharePoint site and to extract information about the content, such as the title, the author, the last modified date, and the keywords. This information is then used to create an index of the content, which is used to provide search results to users.

The search crawl can be configured in various ways to control how content is indexed and how it is searched. Here are a few examples of how you can configure the search crawl:

- **Crawl schedules:** You can configure the crawl schedule to specify how often the search engine should crawl the content of the SharePoint site. For example, you can configure the search engine to crawl the content every day or every week.

- **Crawl rules:** You can configure crawl rules to specify which content should be crawled and which content should be excluded from the search index. For example, you can configure the search engine to crawl only certain lists, libraries, or sites, or you can configure the search engine to exclude certain content, such as test content or sensitive information.

- **Start and end addresses:** You can configure the start and end addresses to specify the range of URLs that the search engine should crawl. For example, you can configure the search engine to start crawling at the homepage of the SharePoint site and to end crawling at a specific page.

- **Authentication:** You can configure the authentication settings to specify how the search engine should authenticate with the SharePoint site. For example, you can configure the search engine to use Windows authentication or forms-based authentication.

- **Content sources:** You can configure content sources to specify the type of content that the search engine should crawl. For example, you can configure the search engine to crawl only SharePoint content, or you can configure the search engine to crawl external content, such as a database or a web service.

- **Crawl log:** You can check the crawl log to see the status of the search crawl; this can give you information about the number of items that were crawled, the number of items that were indexed, and any errors that occurred during the crawl.

Remember when we covered site columns? Site columns are reusable columns that can be used across multiple lists and libraries within a site or across multiple sites in a site collection. Site columns can be used to store metadata about content, such as the author, the last modified date, or the keywords. This metadata can then be used to provide additional information in the search results and to improve the search experience for users.

When it comes to search, site columns can be used in several ways and they are explained as follows:

- Site columns can be used as managed properties. Managed properties allow you to control how content is indexed and how it is displayed in the search results. You can create custom managed properties based on site columns, and thus, you can use them to display additional information in the search results, such as the author or the last modified date.

- Site columns can be used as refiners. Refiners allow you to create custom filters that can be used to refine the search results. You can create refiners based on site columns, so users can filter the search results by different criteria, such as date, author, or content type.

- Site columns can be used as query rules. Query rules allow you to create custom actions that are triggered when a specific search query is entered. You can create query rules based on site columns, and so, you can promote certain content for a specific search query or redirect the user to a specific page based on the site columns.

- Site columns can be used as part of the result types. Result types allow you to create custom display templates for different types of content, such as documents, images, or videos. You can use site columns as part of the conditions to apply a specific result type to the search results which allows you to control how the search results are displayed and to provide additional information to the users.

In summary, Site columns can be an important part of the search configuration and help in providing more relevant search results to users. As site columns are reusable, it is easy to maintain and can be used across multiple lists and libraries, which can help to ensure that the metadata is consistent and accurate. It can be used to improve the search experience for users by providing additional information in the search results and by making it easier to refine and navigate the search results.

In SharePoint, list indexing refers to the process of adding a list's content to the search index, so that it can be searched and returned as part of the search results. When a list is indexed, the search engine extracts information about the list items, such as the title, the author, the last modified date, and the keywords. This information is then used to create an entry in the search index for each list item, so that it can be searched and returned as part of the search results.

There are several ways to configure list indexing in SharePoint. By configuring the list indexing correctly, you can ensure that the content of the lists is properly indexed and that it can be searched and returned as part of the search results. This can help to improve the search experience for users by making it easier for them to find the content they need. Additionally, by configuring the display and refinement options, you can make the search results more relevant and user-friendly.

Sometimes, you might need to create custom refiners to have more agility in searching results. To create custom refiners in SharePoint, you can use the following steps.

1. **Create a managed property:** A refiner is based on a managed property, and so you first need to create a managed property that will be used as the refiner. You can do this by going to the SharePoint Site Setting and navigating to the **Search** section, and then click on **Managed Properties**. Then, you can create a new managed property and specify the settings such as the name, type, and mapping.

2. **Configure the refiner:** Next, you need to configure the refiner itself. You can do this by going to the SharePoint Site Settings and navigate to the **Search** section. Then click on **Refiners**. Here, you can create a new refiner and specify the settings such as the name, the managed property to use as the refiner, and the display name.

3. **Apply the refiner to the search results:** Once you have created and configured the refiner, you need to apply it to the search results. You can do this by going to the SharePoint Site Setting, navigate to the **Search** section, and then click on **Result Types**. Here, you can create a new result type and specify the settings such as the name, the condition, and the refiners to use.

4. **Test the refiner:** Finally, you should test the refiner by performing a search and checking if the refiner is working correctly and if the search results are being refined as expected.

It is also possible to use tools such as PnP PowerShell or the SharePoint Framework to create refiners programmatically. This can be useful when you need to create multiple refiners or if you have a complex refiner configuration. We will cover the use of PowerShell and PnP script later on in the book.

Keep in mind that after you create a refiner, it may take a while for it to start working, since it is needed to wait for the next crawl to happen. In SharePoint online, you do not have a control when the crawl starts and you cannot start it manually. Usually however, it happens overnight.

Additionally, you can use the Search Query Tool to test the refiner and check the results. This way, you can troubleshoot any issues that might arise during the configuration process.

Practical tasks

As usual, let us begin by logging in to the Microsoft 365 portal with your account.

Go to SharePoint and navigate to the previously created site (it can be the first site you created; it will be in the Modern UI).

Once on the SharePoint site at the top, find a search bar and try to search for any documents you previously uploaded to the site. Note that the search bar is always available from any page in SharePoint, but the context of the search can be changed depending on where you are currently. For instance, if you are at some page, search will be looking for search results across the site. However, if you are using search from the list or library, it will return you results from that list or library accordingly, and then give you the option to search on the entire site.

Figure 7.1 features a Search bar at the top of the page with search suggestions:

Figure 7.1: *The search bar at the top of the page with search suggestions*

Next, let us take a look at a search configuration and properties.

In the top right corner of the site, click on the **Settings** gear and select **Site Settings** (or **Site Information | View All site** settings).

Then in the **Site Collection Administration** column, you will find various links that allow configuring search schema, parameters, and settings.

Click on **Search Settings** first. From the Search settings, you can configure Search Center URL or set a custom search results page. Search Center is a separate site that you can create and there is a dedicated template for that in the Classic UI. The Search Center is designed to improve the search experience for the users by providing a centralized location for searching and browsing content. It also allows to configure and customize the search results and the search experience.

So, let us create a custom search result page and do some customization on how the results look like.

1. First, at the top right corner, go to **Site Contents** and from there, go to **Site Pages**.

2. Click on the **New – Site Page** and name it 'Search' or as you like.

3. On the page, hover your mouse on the web part area and click on the plus icon.

4. Look for the search box and search results web part and add them to the page.

Figure 7.2 features a new Search page with an available web parts view:

Figure 7.2: *New Search page with an available web parts view*

5. Add both web parts to your newly created page. Add also Search filters web part.

6. For the Search results web part, select edit, and a window will open on the ride side of the screen.

There were be 3 screens on that window, where you can make configurations. Firstly, search query keywords. By providing these keywords, you can determine what results should be displayed by default, when a user lands on your page. In the majority of cases, we do not configure this as it is blank by default and then we are showing results that match the criteria from the search box. However, there are some cases where this functionality might be very neat.

Search query keywords are used to construct the search query that is sent to the search engine. They can include keywords, phrases, property filters, and other search syntax. The search engine will then use these keywords to find and return the matching results.

You can use the Search Results web part to create a search experience that is tailored to the needs of your users by using different query keywords. For example, you can use query keywords to filter results by content type, by author, or by date. You can also use query keywords to boost or demote certain results based on specific criteria.

You can also use query variables to add dynamic functionality to your search results. For example, you can use the **SearchBoxQuery** variable to include the text entered in the search box to your query, or the **Site** variable to limit the search results to the current site.

You can also use query rules to improve the search results and these rules can be set to promote or demote certain results, based on specific keywords or phrases.

Here are a few examples of search query keywords that you can use in the Search Results web part in SharePoint:

- **Keywords:** You can use keywords to search for specific words or phrases in the content. For example, "SharePoint training" will return results that contain both "SharePoint" and "training" in the content.

- **Property filters:** You can use property filters to filter results by specific properties, such as the content type, the author, or the last modified date. For example, "`contenttype:document`" will return only results that are of the content type "document".

- **Boosting and demoting:** You can use the boosting and demoting feature to give more relevance to certain results. For example, you can boost the results that contain the word "urgent" by using the syntax "urgent^2"

- **Logical operators:** You can use logical operators to combine different keywords and filters. For example, you can use "AND", "OR", "NOT" to refine the search results. For example, "SharePoint AND training NOT urgent" will return results that contain both "SharePoint" and "training" but not "urgent".

- **Query variables:** You can use query variables to add dynamic functionality to your search results. For example, you can use the {SearchBoxQuery} variable to include the text entered in the search box to your query, or the {Site} variable to limit the search results to the current site.

- **FAST query language (FQL):** You can use FQL to create more complex queries by using the FAST Query Language. This allows you to use advanced syntax and operators, such as wildcards, proximity, and synonyms.

Now, as you know how queries work, click **Next** at the bottom of that window and it will take you to a second screen. There you can configure the query template, set sorting order and define properties that will be used for sorting. As the last option, you will see connect to a search refiners web part. Remember you added filters web part to the page. So, this is how results will be connected to those filters and will show proper results based on those filters.

Figure 7.3 features the second screen of search results with the highlighted option to connect to filters web part:

Figure 7.3: The second screen of search results with the highlighted option to connect to filters web part

A query template that you can see at the top of this screen is a predefined search query that can be used to retrieve specific results from the search index. Query templates are defined using search query keywords, which are used to specify the search criteria for the results.

In SharePoint, you can use query templates to create custom search experiences for your users. For example, you can create a query template that retrieves all documents that were last modified in the last 30 days, and use this template to display a list of recent documents on a page.

Here is an example of a query template syntax that you can use in SharePoint:

Code snippet:

```
{searchTerms} contenttype:document modified:>={Today-30}
```

This query template uses the following elements:

- **{searchTerms}**: This variable is replaced by the search terms entered by the user in the search box.

- **contenttype:document**: This is a property filter that will return only results of content type "document".

- **modified:>={Today-30}**: This is a property filter that will return only results that have been modified in the last 30 days.

- This query template will return all documents modified in the last 30 days, and will include the search terms entered by the user in the search box.

Now, if you click **Next**, you will see the third and last screen for search results configuration. There, you can set a title for the web part and select the layout in which results will be displayed. You can also edit a template. This requires some coding skills. Overall, markup is pretty straight forward as it is HTML, combined with search tags. The tags and columns that you search upon, can be configured on the same screen at **Edit Columns** section.

Figure 7.4 features the view of the Edit results template:

Figure 7.4: *view of the Edit results template*

A results template is a file that defines the layout and presentation of the search results. It is based on HTML, CSS and JavaScript and allows you to control how the search results are displayed to the users.

You can edit a results template in SharePoint in several ways:

- **Using the built-in templates:** SharePoint provides a set of built-in templates that you can use to display the search results. You can edit these templates to suit your needs.

- **Creating custom templates:** You can create your own custom template from scratch using HTML, CSS and JavaScript.

- **Editing the existing templates:** You can edit the existing templates to suit your needs.

When you edit a results template, you can control the layout of the search results, the way the results are displayed, and the information that is displayed for each result. For example, you can choose to display the title, the author, and the last modified date for each result.

It is important to note that editing the results templates require some knowledge of web development, and it is recommended to work with an experienced developer or to use the built-in templates whenever possible.

Here is an example code snippet of a simple results template that you can use in SharePoint:

```
<div class="search-result">
  <h2><a href="{Url}">{Title}</a></h2>
  <div class="meta">
    <span class="author">{Author}</span>
    <span class="date">{LastModifiedTime}</span>
  </div>
  <p>{HitHighlightedSummary}</p>
</div>
```

This template uses a few basic HTML elements to define the layout of the search results, and it uses a combination of placeholders and variables to display the information of each result.

The placeholders in curly braces, such as **{Url}**, **{Title}**, **{Author}**, **{LastModifiedTime}**, and so on, are replaced by the values of the corresponding properties of the search results.

This template displays the title of the result as a link to the item, the author and the last modified date, and a summary of the item.

Keep in mind that this is just a simple example, and you can create more complex templates to suit your needs. You can add more properties and format the layout in a way that better suits your needs.

Once you have created or edited a results template, you need to apply it to the search results web part to display the results. You can do this by editing the search results web part and specifying the template to use.

You can click on **Finish** to finish setting up your search results. This should give you a working search page and you can go back to settings and set up this page as a default for all results.

Conclusion

In this chapter, you learned about SharePoint Online Search capabilities. You discovered and learned about search results templates, various types of search web parts and open source practices from PnP search. There are multiple configurations that can be done directly from the SharePoint site that includes list and library settings where you can set if results from there should appear in search, and configurations in Site settings that allow you to define search schema and other parameters. Search Center can be configured as a separate site where results from various sites will be shown.

Points to remember

- Search is a powerful tool with agile configuration.

- A separate dedicated site can be created, such as a Search Center to show results from all sites in your tenant.

- You can use site columns to determine search results.

- You can create a custom page using search web parts and set that page as a default in setting for all search results to be displayed.

- You can use Filters web part to give users and ability to narrow down search results.

- Search results template can be adjusted and layout configured based on the html structure.

Join our book's Discord space

Join the book's Discord Workspace for Latest updates, Offers, Tech happenings around the world, New Release and Sessions with the Authors:

https://discord.bpbonline.com

## CHAPTER 8

Microsoft Groups

> **"Groups are the way we can multiply our effectiveness, our creativity, and our ability to get things done."**
>
> *- Jon Katzenbach*

Introduction

To build a proper governance model in Office 365 environment, it is essential to set up correct permission levels and organize users accordingly. The most common way to manage groups is via **Active Directory** (**AD**) groups. However, let us see what Office 365 groups can offer instead and how they can supplement AD functionality. In this chapter, you will learn how to set up Office 365 groups, where to manage them, and how to properly organize users.

Structure

In this chapter, we will cover the following topics:

- Office 365 Groups
- Office 365 Groups vs. Active Directory vs. SharePoint groups
- Different types of Office 365 groups

- Administration of Office 365 groups

- Dynamic rules in Office 365

Objectives

In this chapter, you will learn about Microsoft 365 groups. There are multiple types of groups and we will review them. We will cover the differences between M365 groups, active directory and SharePoint groups. As always, we will cover the admin part to understand how groups are managed and can be organized in a proper way. There are different rules that can be implemented to make groups dynamic and add people automatically into them, based on the conditions.

Office 365 groups

Office 365 Groups is a feature in Office 365 that allows users to create and manage groups of people, such as teams or project groups, and the resources associated with them, such as shared mailboxes, calendars, and document libraries. Office 365 Groups is a cross-application feature that enables collaboration across multiple Office 365 services, such as Outlook, SharePoint, OneNote, Planner, Power BI, PowerApps, and so on.

One of the key features of Office 365 Groups is the ability for users to easily create and manage groups within the Office 365 platform, without the need for IT involvement. Office 365 Groups can be created and managed through the Outlook web app, the Outlook desktop client, or the Office 365 admin center.

Once a group is created, its members have access to a shared mailbox, calendar, OneNote notebook, and a SharePoint site, where they can collaborate on documents, tasks, and other resources. Additionally, Office 365 groups can be integrated with other apps and services, such as PowerApps, Power BI, and Stream, to extend the capabilities of the group.

Office 365 Groups also provides features such as guest access, which allows external users to be added to a group, and dynamic membership, which allows group membership to be managed through **Azure Active Directory** (**AAD**) security groups or Microsoft Teams.

There are a few ways to create a new Office 365 Group in Office 365, and they are as follows:

- Using the Outlook Web App:

- o Log in to **Outlook Web App (OWA)** and click on the "+" icon next to the navigation bar.

- o Select "**Group**" from the drop-down menu.

- o Fill in the required information for the group, such as the name, the description, and the members.

- o Click on "**Create**" to create the group.

- Using the Outlook Desktop Client:

  - o Open Outlook and click on the "**Home**" tab.

  - o Click on "**New Group**" in the "New Items" section.

  - o Fill in the required information for the group, such as the name, the description, and the members.

  - o Click on "**Create**" to create the group.

- Using the Office 365 admin center:

  - o Log in to the Office 365 admin center and navigate to the "**Groups**" section.

  - o Click on "**Create a group**"

  - o Fill in the required information for the group, such as the name, the description, and the members.

  - o Click on "**Save**" to create the group.

After you create a new group, the members will receive an email inviting them to join the group and access the shared resources. Once the members join the group, they will have access to the shared mailbox, calendar, OneNote notebook, and SharePoint site associated with the group.

It is important to note that the process may slightly change depending on the version of the license you have for the Office 365. Additionally, depending on the organization's settings, proper permissions might be needed for users to create a new group.

Figure 8.1 features the teams and groups page in the Microsoft 365 Admin Center:

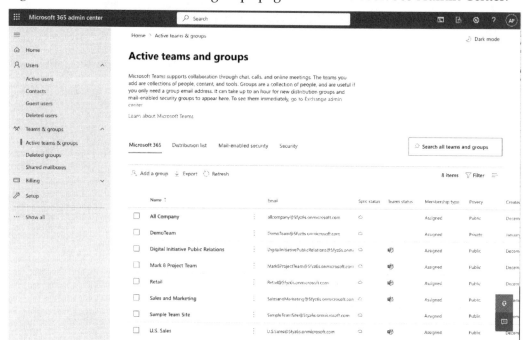

Figure 8.1: *Teams and groups page in the Microsoft 365 Admin Center*

Once you are a member of an Office 365 group, you can access and work with the group's resources in Outlook in the following ways:

- **Shared mailbox**: Each Office 365 group has a shared mailbox associated with it. You can access the shared mailbox by opening Outlook and clicking on the "**Mail**" tab. The shared mailbox will be listed under your personal mailbox. You can use the shared mailbox to send and receive emails, schedule meetings, and manage tasks as a group.

- **Shared calendar:** Each Office 365 group also has a shared calendar associated with it. You can access the shared calendar by opening Outlook and clicking on the "**Calendar**" tab. The shared calendar will be listed under your personal calendar. You can use the shared calendar to schedule meetings, events, and appointments as a group.

- **Shared OneNote notebook:** Each Office 365 group also has a OneNote notebook associated with it. You can access the notebook by opening Outlook. Click on the "**Groups**" tab, and select the group, and then click on "**Notebook**" tab. You can use the notebook to take notes, brainstorm ideas, and collaborate with the group members.

- **SharePoint site:** Each Office 365 group also has a SharePoint site associated with it. You can access the SharePoint site by opening Outlook. Click on the "**Groups**" tab, and select the group, and then click on "**Files**" tab. You can use the SharePoint site to store, organize, and share files and documents with the group members.

By working with O365 groups in Outlook, you can easily access and collaborate on group resources, communicate with group members and schedule meeting and events. Additionally, you can access the group resources through the Outlook web app, and so you can work with them from anywhere.

In summary, Office 365 Groups is a feature in Office 365 that allows users to create and manage groups of people and the resources associated with them. It further enables collaboration across multiple Office 365 services. The ease of use and the integration with other apps and services, make it a powerful tool to improve collaboration and communication in an organization.

Office 365 Groups vs. Active Directory vs. SharePoint groups

Office 365 Groups, Active Directory groups, and SharePoint groups are all different types of groups that can be used in different scenarios, for different purposes and with different features.

Active Directory (**AD**) groups are a feature of the Active Directory domain service that is used to manage user and computer accounts in a Windows domain. AD groups are used to manage permissions and access to resources within the domain, such as shared folders, printers, and applications. AD groups are typically used to manage user access to resources on-premises, and they do not have direct relation with Office 365 services.

SharePoint groups are a feature of SharePoint that are used to manage permissions, and access to resources within a SharePoint site collection. SharePoint groups are used to manage user access to resources such as lists, libraries, and web pages. SharePoint groups can be created and managed directly in SharePoint and can be used to manage access to resources within SharePoint only.

Office 365 Groups, on the other hand, are a feature of Office 365 that allows users to create and manage groups of people and the resources associated with them across multiple Office 365 services such as Outlook, SharePoint, OneNote, Planner, Power BI, PowerApps, and more. Office 365 Groups are used to manage user access to resources such as shared mailboxes, calendars, and document libraries, and enable collaboration across multiple Office 365 services. Office 365 Groups are typically used to manage user access to resources in the cloud, and they can be integrated with other apps and services.

It is possible to add an Office 365 group as a member of a SharePoint group.

When you create an Office 365 group, a SharePoint site is automatically created for the group. The members of the Office 365 group are automatically added as members of the associated SharePoint group with the default permission level.

You can also add an existing Office 365 group as a member of an existing SharePoint group. This can be done by going to the SharePoint site. Navigate to the "**Settings**" gear icon, "**Site Settings**", "**People and groups**" and then "**Add group**. Select the Office 365 group you want to add.

It is important to note that adding an Office 365 group as a member of a SharePoint group does not grant the members of the Office 365 group any additional permissions. The members of the Office 365 group will have the same permissions as the Office 365 group has been granted on the SharePoint site.

It is also worth noting that by adding an Office 365 group as a member of a SharePoint group, you are allowing the members of the Office 365 group to access and collaborate on resources within the SharePoint site. However, it does not affect the functionality of the Office 365 group itself, and the members of the Office 365 group will still be able to access the resources associated with the Office 365 group such as the shared mailbox, calendar, and OneNote notebook.

It is also possible to add an AD group as a member of a SharePoint group, but it requires a little bit more configuration than adding an Office 365 group.

To add an AD group to a SharePoint group, you will need to create a SharePoint group and then add the AD group as a member of that group. Follow the given steps:

1. **Create a SharePoint group:** Go to the SharePoint site, navigate to the "**Settings**" gear icon, "**Site Settings**", "**People and groups**" and then "**New**" to create a new group.

2. **Add the AD group as a member:** Once the SharePoint group is created, go to the "**People and groups**" page, then select the SharePoint group you just created. Next, go to the "**Settings**" menu and select "**Add Users**".

3. Use the browser to navigate to the location of the AD group, select the group and confirm the selection.

It is not possible to manage the members of an AD group directly from a SharePoint group. SharePoint groups and AD groups are managed separately and have different management interfaces.

When you add an AD group to a SharePoint group, you are giving the members of the AD group the same permissions as the SharePoint group has been granted on the SharePoint site. However, you cannot manage the members of the AD group directly from SharePoint. The members of the AD group will still be managed using the Active Directory Users and Computers management console or other AD management tools.

To manage the members of the AD group, you will need to use the appropriate tools and procedures for managing AD groups, such as the Active Directory Users and Computers management console or other AD management tools.

It is worth noting that SharePoint groups and AD groups serve different purposes and have different capabilities. While AD groups are used to manage access to resources within a Windows domain and for authentication, SharePoint groups are used to manage access to resources within a SharePoint site collection.

Additionally, you can use Office 365 groups to manage access to resources across multiple Office 365 services and enable collaboration among users. Furthermore, you can add AD groups as members to an Office 365 group, and this way, you can have an easy management of group members and their access to different resources.

Figure 8.2 features groups relations in Microsoft 365 and SharePoint:

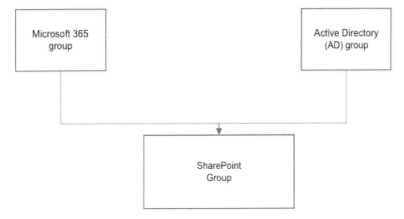

Figure 8.2: *Groups relations in Microsoft 365 and SharePoint*

Different types of Office 365 groups

There are several types of Office 365 groups that you can create in Office 365, each with its own unique features and capabilities, and they are as follows:

- **Outlook group:** An Outlook group is a group that is primarily used for email communication. When you create an Outlook group, a shared mailbox and calendar are created for the group, and members can use the shared mailbox to send and receive emails, schedule meetings, and manage tasks as a group.

- **Team:** A team is a group that is primarily used for collaboration. When you create a team, a SharePoint site, OneNote notebook, and a shared calendar are created for the group, and members can use the SharePoint site to store, organize, and share files and documents; the OneNote notebook to take notes, brainstorm ideas; and the shared calendar to schedule meetings, events, and appointments as a group.

- **Yammer group:** A Yammer group is a group that is primarily used for social communication and collaboration. When you create a Yammer group, a Yammer network is created for the group, and members can use the network to have conversations, share files and links, and collaborate on projects and ideas.

- **Plan:** A Plan is a group that is primarily used for project management. When you create a Plan, a SharePoint site, OneNote notebook, and a Planner plan are created for the group, and members can use the SharePoint site to store, organize, and share files and documents; the OneNote notebook to take notes, brainstorm ideas, and the Planner plan to manage tasks and projects as a group.

- **Power BI group:** A Power BI group is a group that is primarily used for data visualization and analytics. When you create a Power BI group, a SharePoint site, and a Power BI workspace are created for the group, and members can use the SharePoint site to store, organize, and share files and documents, and the Power BI workspace to create, share, and collaborate on data visualizations and reports.

All these types of groups have the ability to collaborate, communicate and share resources, in common. The main difference among them is the primary focus and the set of tools that come with each one of them. Additionally, you can customize the groups and add or remove tools according to your needs.

An Office 365 group can only be one type at a time. Each type of Office 365 group comes with its own unique set of features and capabilities.

For example, an Outlook group has a shared mailbox and calendar, while a Team group has a SharePoint site, OneNote notebook, and a shared calendar. A Yammer group has a Yammer network, and a Plan group has a SharePoint site, OneNote notebook, and a Planner plan.

It is not possible to have an Office 365 group that combines the features of multiple group types, such as having a shared mailbox and a SharePoint site in the same group. However, you can customize the groups, add or remove features and tools according to your needs, but the group will still be of the same type.

Additionally, you can create multiple groups of different types and connect them together. For example, you can create a Team group and add an Outlook group as a member, and this way, the members of the Outlook group will be able to access the shared resources of the Team group.

It is worth noting that Office 365 groups are dynamic and flexible, and you can customize them to suit your organization's needs and workflows.

Administration of Office 365 groups

There are several ways to administrate Office 365 groups in Office 365, including the following:

- **Office 365 admin center**. You can use the Office 365 admin center to manage and administrate Office 365 groups. You can use the Office 365 admin center to create, edit, and delete groups, add and remove members, and assign group owners. You can also use the Office 365 admin center to set policies for groups, such as expiration policies, and to view usage statistics for groups.

- **Azure AD portal.** You can use the Azure AD portal to manage and administrate Office 365 groups. You can use the Azure AD portal to create, edit, and delete groups, add and remove members, and assign group owners. You can also use the Azure AD portal to set policies for groups, such as expiration policies, and to view usage statistics for groups.

- **PowerShell.** You can use PowerShell to manage and administrate Office 365 groups. You can use PowerShell to create, edit, and delete groups, add and remove members, and assign group owners. You can also use PowerShell to set policies for groups, such as expiration policies, and to view usage statistics for groups.

- **Microsoft Graph API.** You can use Microsoft Graph API to manage and administrate Office 365 groups programmatically. You can use Microsoft Graph API to create, edit, and delete groups, add and remove members, and assign group owners. You can also use Microsoft Graph API to set policies for groups, such as expiration policies, and to view usage statistics for groups.

- **Third-party tools.** There are also third-party tools available that can help you manage and administrate Office 365 groups, such as ShareGate or AvePoint. These tools can help you automate and streamline group management tasks, such as creating and deleting groups, adding and removing members, and managing group policies.

There are several best practices for managing and administrating Office 365 groups, and they are as follows:

- Create and communicate clear guidelines for creating and using Office 365 groups within your organization. This can include guidelines for naming groups, what types of groups to create, and how to use the different tools and features of groups.

- Assign one or more group owners for each group. Group owners are responsible for managing the group and ensuring that it is being used in accordance with your organization's guidelines.

- Regularly review the membership of each group and remove members who are no longer active or needed. This can help keep groups organized and ensure that only the necessary people have access to group resources.

- Monitor the usage of Office 365 groups to ensure that they are being used effectively and in accordance with your organization's guidelines.

- Set policies for Office 365 groups, such as expiration policies, to ensure that groups are being used in accordance with your organization's guidelines.

- Use automation tools and scripts to manage Office 365 groups. This can help you automate and streamline group management tasks, such as creating and deleting groups, adding and removing members, and managing group policies.

- Provide training and resources to help users understand how to effectively use and manage Office 365 groups.

- Have a backup plan in place to preserve the data and settings of the groups, especially if the group is important or contains sensitive information. In this way, you can restore the group in case of an accidental deletion or data loss.

It is important to note that Office 365 groups are dynamic and flexible, and these best practices are not set in stone. They can be adapted and changed, depending on the organization's needs and workflows.

Dynamic rules in Office 365 groups

There are several reasons why you might want to automatically populate Office 365 groups, and some of them are explained as follows:

- **Streamline management:** Automatically populating Office 365 groups can help streamline the management of groups and reduce the workload of group owners and administrators. By automating the process of adding and removing members, you can save time and reduce the possibility of human error.

- **Scalability:** Automatically populating Office 365 groups can help you scale your group infrastructure to meet the needs of a growing organization. As your organization grows, you can use dynamic groups to automatically add new members to groups based on specific attributes, such as location, department, or job title, without having to manually add them one by one.

- **Improve collaboration:** Automatically populating Office 365 groups can help improve collaboration within your organization, by ensuring that the right people are added to the right groups. By using dynamic groups, you can ensure that members of a specific department or project team are automatically added to the appropriate groups, which can help improve communication and collaboration within the team.

- **Security:** Automatically populating Office 365 groups can help improve security by ensuring that only authorized users have access to sensitive information. For example, you can use dynamic groups to automatically add members to a group, based on their security clearance, which can help ensure that only authorized users have access to sensitive information.

- **Compliance:** Automatically populating Office 365 groups can help you comply with regulatory requirements, by ensuring that only authorized users have access to sensitive information. For example, you can use dynamic groups to automatically add members to a group, based on their role or responsibilities, and ensure that only users with the appropriate clearance or certification can access sensitive data.

It is worth noting that while automatically populating Office 365 groups can bring a lot of benefits, you should be aware of the limitations and potential issues that can arise, such as missing attributes to be used for population, conflicts between different population mechanisms, performance issues on large scale, and so on.

Office 365 groups can be dynamically populated using various methods, and they are as follows:

1. **Azure Active Directory (AAD) Dynamic Groups:** You can use Azure Active Directory Dynamic Groups to automatically add and remove members from an Office 365 group, based on specific attributes, such as location, department, or job title. AAD Dynamic Groups use a query to match users to the group based on their attributes, and the group membership is updated automatically when the user's attributes change.

2. **PowerShell:** You can use PowerShell scripts to automatically add and remove members from an Office 365 group. You can use PowerShell to query Azure Active Directory for user information, such as location, department, or job title, and then use that information to add or remove users from the group.

3. **Microsoft Graph API:** You can use the Microsoft Graph API to programmatically manage group membership. You can use the API to query Azure Active Directory for user information, such as location, department, or job title, and then use that information to add or remove users from the group.

4. **Third-party tools:** There are also third-party tools available that can help you manage and administrate Office 365 groups, such as ShareGate or AvePoint. These tools can help you automate and streamline group management tasks, such as creating and deleting groups, adding and removing members, and managing group policies, including dynamic population of the group.

You should test the scripts and methods used for dynamic population before applying them to production environment, to ensure that they are working as expected and not causing any unwanted behavior.

Practical tasks

Now it is time to switch to some practice. Open Microsoft 365 portal and log in with your credentials. Select the Admin app once there, and follow the given steps:

1. In the Office 365 admin center, navigate to the "**Groups**" section. This section can be found in the navigation menu on the left-hand side of the screen.

2. In the "Groups" section, you will see a list of all the Office 365 groups that have been created in your organization. You can use the search bar at the top of the page to search for specific groups by name.

3. To access the settings for a specific group, click on the name of the group in the list. This will open the group settings page, where you can manage various aspects of the group, such as members, settings, and policies.

In the group settings page, you will be able to see the different options available to you as an administrator, such as:

- Adding or removing members.

- Changing the group's type.

- Changing the group's settings.

- Managing group policies.

- Viewing usage statistics.

You can also use the Azure AD portal to access Office 365 groups. In that case, the process would be similar, and you would navigate to the "Groups" section and search for the group you want to administrate.

Now, let us create a new group from the admin center.

1. Click on the "+" button or the "**Create**" button to create a new group.

2. Fill in the required fields for the group, such as the group name, group type, and group owner and members.

3. Select the group's settings and policies, such as expiration policies, email delivery options, and membership approval settings.

4. Click "**Create**" or "**Save**" to create the new group.

It is worth noting that, when you create a new group, you will be prompted to select the type of group you want to create.

Figure 8.3 features the screen of anew Office 365 group creation:

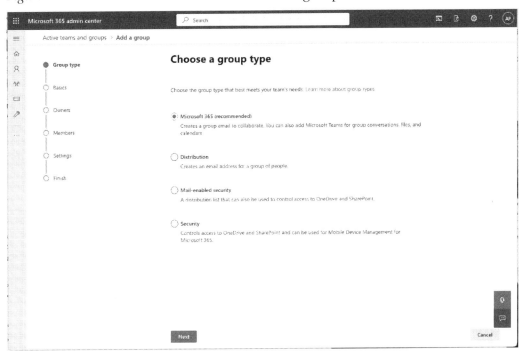

Figure 8.3: *Screen of a new Office 365 group creation*

The different types of groups that you can opt to create are as follows:

-   **Outlook:** A group that includes a shared inbox, calendar, and a team site.

-   **Team:** A group that includes a team site, a SharePoint document library, a OneNote notebook and a planner plan.

-   **Yammer:** A group that includes a Yammer network and a team site.

- **Plan:** A group that includes a Planner plan, a SharePoint document library and a OneNote notebook.

You can select the group type you like. Each group type has its own set of features and capabilities. Additionally, we can customize the group settings and policies to suit your organization's needs and workflows.

At the end, you will be prompted to select if the group is Public or Private.

The main difference between public and private Office 365 groups is the level of access and visibility of the group's resources and members. Refer to the following points:

- **Public groups:** Public Office 365 groups are visible to all users in the organization and anyone can see the group's resources, such as the group's conversations, files, calendar, and members list. Users can also request to join a public group without the need for approval. Public groups are useful when you want to share information and collaborate with a large number of users within your organization.

- **Private groups:** Private Office 365 groups are only visible to the members of the group and the group's resources are not visible to non-members. Private groups are useful when you want to share information and collaborate with a specific set of users, such as a project team, and you want to restrict access to the group's resources. Users can request to join a private group, but the request must be approved by a group owner or administrator.

So now you have the new group created and you can manage it form the Groups section in the Admin center. If you click on your newly created group name and there you will be able to see owners and members. At any time, if new members need to be populated, you can do it from there.

Let us set the rule to populate our group dynamically, based on the rules we set up. Follow the given steps:

1. Go to the Azure portal. In your browser, navigate to **portal.azzure.com** and use your account to log in if prompted.

2. Once in Azure, use the search bar at the top and look for the **'groups'** there.

Figure 8.4 features search for the 'groups' in the Azure portal:

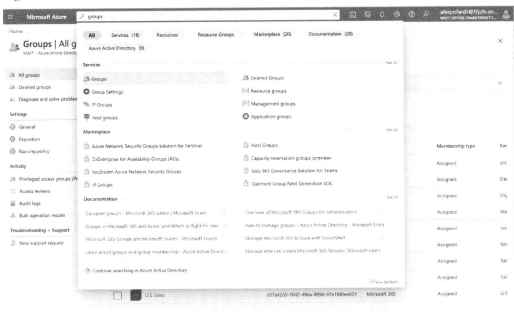

Figure 8.4: *Search for the 'groups' in the Azure portal*

3. Select **groups** from the search menu and you will be directed to the page where you will see all of your groups, plus the newly created one too. Click on your created group name.

4. In the left navigation, click on the '**Properties'** link.

5. We would need to change Membership type from Assigned to Dynamic User.

Figure 8.5 features the switching of a group type to Dynamic:

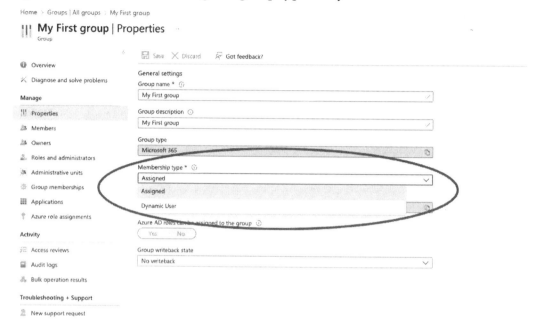

Figure 8.5: *Switching of a group type to Dynamic*

6. Once switched, you will see a link a little below that field name '**Add Dynamic query**'. Click on it.

7. You can build a query as City equals Los Angeles or anything you would like.

8. Finalize your changes and click **Save** in Azure.

9. You can go back to your Microsoft 365 portal now and create a couple of users from the Admin center and set them a city such as Los Angeles (or you can modify existing users).

10. If you go back to the group members, you will see that users will be added there dynamically, based on the configured rule from Azure.

You should also test the dynamic membership rule before applying it to a production environment, to make sure that it is working as expected and not causing any unwanted behavior.

Additionally, you can use PowerShell scripts or Microsoft Graph API to create dynamic groups and manage their membership, which is useful for automating the process and for large scale scenarios.

Conclusion

In this chapter, you learned about Microsoft 365 groups and the major differences between groups, AD groups and SharePoint permission groups. We also covered various type of Microsoft 365 groups and what they are used for. Now you should know where to go in the Admin center to create a new group and how set up a dynamic rule for the group from the Azure portal. In summary, Office 365 Groups is a feature in Office 365 that allows users to create and manage groups of people and the resources associated with them, and it enables collaboration across multiple Office 365 services. The ease of use and the integration with other apps and services makes it a powerful tool to improve the collaboration and communication in an organization.

Points to remember

- Microsoft 365 groups are groups designed for collaboration.
- There are various types of M365 group: M365, Distribution, Mail-enabled, and Security.
- M365 groups can be Public or Private.
- AD groups and M365 groups can be added inside SharePoint permission groups.
- You can manage M365 groups in Admin center, Azure, Outlook or using a PowerShell script.
- You can populate users manually into M365 group or set a dynamic rule.

Join our book's Discord space

Join the book's Discord Workspace for Latest updates, Offers, Tech happenings around the world, New Release and Sessions with the Authors:

https://discord.bpbonline.com

CHAPTER 9
Microsoft Teams

"Teamwork is the ability to work together toward a common vision. The ability to direct individual accomplishments toward organizational objectives. It is the fuel that allows common people to attain uncommon results."

- Andrew Carnegie

Introduction

With more and more people switching to remote work every day, the need of tools that would support instant chatting and meeting capabilities has dramatically increased. When it comes to collaboration, Microsoft Teams covers it all, from chatting, meetings and calendars to approval and file management.

All of these and much more can be done in Microsoft Teams. In this chapter, we will get an overview of the main capabilities of Microsoft Teams. You will also create your own Teams channel, configure permissions, and add supporting tabs and materials to your channel.

Structure

In this chapter, we will cover the following topics:

- Microsoft Teams Online and Desktop clients

- Teams overview: teams, channels, chats, files

- Teams management in the Admin center

- Teams add-ons

- Approval processes integration with Teams

Objectives

In this chapter, you will learn about Microsoft Teams. We will review Web, Desktop, and mobile versions of the app. The reader will then become familiar with Teams structure, and learn about channels, and will apply knowledge from the previous chapter about Groups. We will review the Admin center and what policies and configurations can be applied inside Teams. Then, we will see how Teams functionality can be expanded with 3rd party add-ons and automation processes.

Microsoft Teams Online and Desktop clients

Microsoft Teams is a collaboration and communication platform that is part of the Microsoft Office 365 suite of services. It is designed to help teams work together more effectively by providing a centralized hub for communication, collaboration, and organization.

Some of the key features of Microsoft Teams include the following:

- **Chat:** Teams allow users to communicate with each other through instant messaging, both one-on-one and in group chats.

- **Video and audio conferencing:** Teams include built-in support for video and audio conferencing, allowing users to hold meetings and presentations with other users, both within and outside of their organization.

- **File sharing and collaboration:** Teams includes a built-in document library, allowing users to store, share, and collaborate on files.

- **Integrations:** Teams can be integrated with other Microsoft Office 365 services, such as SharePoint, OneNote, and OneDrive, as well as with a wide range of third-party services, such as Trello, Asana, and many more.

- **Customization**: Teams can be customized to fit the needs of different teams and organizations, with the ability to add apps, connectors, and bot.

- **Security and compliance**: Teams is built on Microsoft's enterprise-grade security and compliance platform, providing robust security and compliance features, such as data encryption, multi-factor authentication, and eDiscovery.

Teams is a powerful communication and collaboration platform that can help teams work together more efficiently and effectively, by providing a centralized hub for communication, collaboration, and organization. It can be integrated with other services, and it has a good level of security and compliance features.

Microsoft Teams has three main client options: web, desktop, and mobile. Each of these clients provides access to the same set of features and functionality, but with some variations to cater to different usage scenarios and devices.

- **Web client:** The web client is the version of Teams that can be accessed through a web browser, such as Chrome, Firefox, or Edge. It does not require any installation, and it can be accessed from any device with an internet connection. The web client provides access to all of the core features of Teams, such as chat, video and audio conferencing, file sharing, and integrations.

- **Desktop client:** The desktop client is a version of Teams that can be installed on a Windows or Mac computer. It provides the same core features as the web client but with additional capabilities such as background blur, custom background and more. It also provides notifications, and can run in the background even when the application is closed.

- **Mobile client:** The mobile client is a version of Teams that can be installed on a mobile device, such as a smartphone or tablet. It provides access to core features such as chat, video and audio conferencing, file sharing, and integrations, but with a user interface optimized for the smaller screens of mobile devices. The mobile client also offers the ability to join meetings and make calls on-the-go, as well as the ability to access files offline.

The web, desktop and mobile clients are designed to work together seamlessly, providing users with a consistent experience across devices, and allowing them to switch between devices without interruption. Additionally, all clients are updated regularly to include new features and improvements.

It is possible to log in to multiple accounts on Microsoft Teams, but it will depend on the client you are using and the type of account. The different types of client are :

- **Web client:** In the web client, it is possible to log in to multiple accounts using different web browsers or private/incognito windows. Each browser window or tab can be logged in to a different account. However, it is worth noting that you will have to sign out of one account before signing in to another one, as the web client does not support logging in to multiple accounts at the same time.

- **Desktop client:** The desktop client for Windows and Mac does NOT support logging in to multiple Business accounts simultaneously. However, you can add multiple personal accounts by clicking on your profile picture in the top-right corner of the client and then selecting "**Add account**". Once you have added multiple accounts, you can switch between them by clicking on your profile picture and selecting the account you want to use. Unfortunately, this feature as of Q1 of 2023 is not available for business accounts. So, the web version will be more helpful if you need to maintain multiple accounts at the same time.

- **Mobile client:** The mobile client supports logging in to multiple accounts, but it will depend on the type of account you are using. If you are using a personal Microsoft account, you can add multiple accounts by going to the settings menu of the mobile app, and selecting the "Switch accounts" option. It will work with Business accounts too. If you are using an Azure AD account, you can use the same process, but it will depend on the device and operating system capabilities.

It is important to note that when you log in to multiple accounts on Teams, you will be able to see and access all the teams, channels, and conversations associated with each account. However, you will not be able to access the same team, channel or conversation simultaneously.

Additionally, it is worth mentioning that you should use a different browser or a different device for a different account, as it will help you avoid confusion and keep your work separate.

Figure 9.1 features a desktop version of the Teams client:

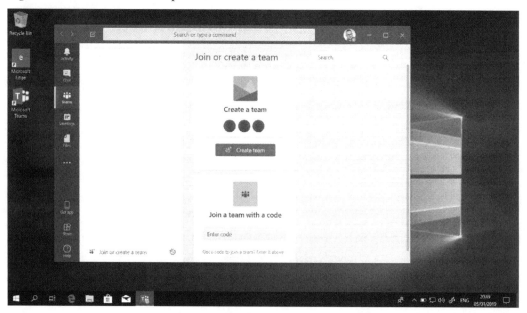

Figure 9.1: *Desktop version of the Teams client*

Teams overview: teams, channels, chats, files

Microsoft Teams is a collaboration and communication platform that is designed to help teams work together more effectively. It includes several key features that allow teams to communicate, collaborate, and organize their work, and they are as follows:

- **Teams:** A Team is a collection of people, conversations, files, and tools that are brought together to work on a specific project or goal. Teams are organized around channels, which are the primary way for team members to communicate and collaborate.

- **Channels:** Channels are dedicated sections within a team for specific topics, projects, or groups of people. Each channel has its own set of conversations, files, and tools, and team members can join and leave channels as needed. Channels are meant to help organize the conversations and files within a team, and can be used to create focused spaces for different topics, projects, or departments.

- **Chats:** Chats are the primary way for team members to communicate with each other in Teams. They can be one-on-one conversations, or they can be group chats with multiple people. Chats allow team members to send messages, share files, and make audio and video calls with each other.

- **Files:** Files in Teams are stored in a shared library that is accessible to all team members. Teams integrate with other Microsoft Office 365 services such as OneDrive and SharePoint, so that team members can work on files together in real-time, and easily share files with other teams and services.

Teams provides a central hub for communication and collaboration, with teams, channels, chats, and files as the main components that allow team members to work together. Teams are organized around channels, which help to keep conversations and files organized and focused. Chats provide the primary way for team members to communicate and collaborate, and files are shared through a shared library that is accessible to all team members.

It is worth noting that, teams, channels, chats, and files are not the only features in Teams; it also includes other features such as meetings, apps, and integrations that make it a powerful tool to help teams work together effectively.

Meetings, calendar, and scheduling are also important features in Microsoft Teams. They allow team members to schedule and conduct virtual meetings, as well as manage their availability and schedule. Here is a brief description of each of these features:

- **Meetings:** Teams includes built-in support for virtual meetings, including audio and video conferencing, screen sharing, and recording. Meetings can be scheduled in advance or started on-demand, and can include team members both inside and outside of an organization. Additionally, Meetings can be scheduled via Outlook or Teams, and the attendees receive calendar invites with all the necessary details.

- **Calendar:** Teams include a calendar feature that allows team members to view their upcoming meetings and events, as well as schedule new ones. The calendar can be accessed directly within Teams, and it can also be integrated with other calendar services such as Outlook, Google Calendar, and iCal.

- **Scheduling assistant:** Scheduling Assistant is a feature that helps to schedule meetings by showing users all the attendees' availability and suggesting the best time for the meeting. It also allows to see the people's location, and the time zone they are in.

- **Tasks:** Teams also includes a built-in task management feature that allows teams to create and assign tasks, set deadlines, and track progress.

- **Notes:** Teams have a feature that allows team members to take and share notes during meetings, and keep track of important information discussed.

Meetings, calendar, scheduling, tasks, and notes are also important features of Teams. They allow team members to schedule and conduct virtual meetings, manage their availability, schedule and take notes during meetings, as well as keep track of important information discussed. These features are integrated with other Office 365 services such as Outlook, and they help teams to stay organized, productive, and on schedule.

Figure 9.2 features a new meeting scheduling screen:

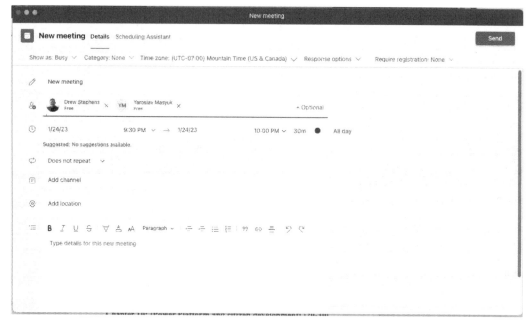

Figure 9.2: New meeting scheduling screen

It is also possible to have a phone number on Microsoft Teams. Teams integrates with Phone System, a component of Microsoft 365 or Office 365 that enables you to make and receive calls using Teams, and also allows to manage phone numbers, call routing, voicemail and call groups.

With Phone System, you can get a phone number for your organization and assign it to users, or you can also port your existing phone numbers to Teams. Once you have a phone number, users can make and receive calls using the Teams client on their computer or mobile device, and manage their voicemail and call routing settings.

Additionally, Teams also integrate with Direct Routing, which allows you to connect your own **Public Switched Telephone Network (PSTN)** carrier to Teams, and use your own phone numbers. With Direct Routing, you can use Teams to make and receive calls to phone numbers outside your organization, as well as manage and route calls to different users and groups.

The availability of phone numbers and calling plans may vary depending on the country or region, and the specific Office 365 or Microsoft 365 plan you have. Some plans include calling plans that provide phone numbers and calling minutes, while others may require you to purchase a separate plan or add-on.

When a meeting is scheduled in Teams, the organizer has the option to provide a dial-in number and conference ID for the meeting. Attendees can then call into the meeting using this dial-in number and conference ID, allowing them to join the audio portion of the meeting without needing to use a computer or internet connection.

Teams also supports phone audio conferencing, which allows you to add a dial-in number to your meetings. This dial-in number can be used by attendees to join your meetings by phone, even if they do not have internet access.

If your organization has a Phone System in place, you can also join a meeting by calling the Phone System and entering the conference ID. If you are calling from an external number, you will need to enter the conference ID, and then press the pound key.

It is worth noting that the availability of dial-in numbers and phone audio conferencing may vary, depending on the country or region, and the specific Office 365 or Microsoft 365 plan you have. Some plans include a dial-in number and calling minutes, while others may require you to purchase a separate plan or add-on. Additionally, some meetings may not have the dial-in number available and the attendees will only be able to join through the computer or mobile device.

However, there are a few notes worth mentioning. By default, the phone number to join your Teams meetings by phone will not be available as it is coming as add-on and requires an additional license. There are a few reasons why you may not see a phone number added to your Teams meeting invites, and they are as follows:

- **Phone system or calling plan is not enabled:** In order to have the ability to schedule meetings with dial-in numbers, you need to have a Phone System or Calling Plan enabled in your Office 365 or Microsoft 365 subscription. If you do not have one of these plans, you will not be able to schedule meetings with dial-in numbers, and attendees will not see a phone number in the meeting invites.

- **Phone system or calling plan is not assigned to the user:** Even if your organization has a Phone System or Calling Plan enabled, it may not be assigned to the user who is scheduling the meeting. In this case, the user will not be able to schedule meetings with dial-in numbers, and attendees will not see a phone number in the meeting invites.

- **Dial-in numbers are not available in your country or region:** The availability of dial-in numbers and phone audio conferencing may vary depending on the country or region, and so, if your organization is located in a country or region where dial-in numbers are not available, you will not be able to schedule meetings with dial-in numbers.

- **The meeting organizer did not enable the dial-in numbers:** Even if your organization has a Phone System or Calling Plan enabled, and it is assigned to the user, the meeting organizer can choose not to enable the dial-in number while scheduling the meeting.

If you are certain that you have a Phone System or Calling Plan enabled and assigned to the user, dial-in numbers are available in your country or region, and the meeting organizer did enable the dial-in numbers, there might be an issue with the service or an error that occurred during the scheduling process. In this case, you can try to schedule the meeting again or contact the support team for further assistance.

You can schedule Teams meetings in two ways: either from the Teams client itself or from the Outlook.

You can schedule a Microsoft Teams meeting from Outlook by following the given steps:

1. Open Outlook and click on the "**Calendar**" tab.

2. Click on the "**New Teams Meeting**" button located in the "**Home**" tab. Alternatively, you can also click on "**New Meeting**" button and then select "**Teams Meeting**" from the options.

3. In the "**Meeting**" tab, add the required information such as subject, location, start and end time, and invitees.

4. You can also set the meeting options like "**Recording**", "**Presenters**" and "**Attendees**".

5. Once you have set all the options and added the invitees, click on "**Send**" to schedule the meeting.

6. The attendees will receive an email with a link to the meeting. They can join the meeting by clicking on the link, or they can join by phone if the organizer enabled the dial-in number.

Figure 9.3 features a new Teams meeting scheduling from the Outlook Calendar view:

Figure 9.3: *New Teams meeting scheduling from the Outlook Calendar view*

Teams management in the admin center

The Microsoft Teams section of the Microsoft 365 admin center allows you to manage your organization's Teams settings and configurations. As a global admin or teams service admin, you can access the Teams admin center by going to the Microsoft 365 admin center, clicking on **Show all**, and then selecting Teams.

In the Teams admin center, you can perform tasks such as the following:

- **Manage user licenses:** Assign or remove licenses for Teams, and view the usage of your licenses.

- **Manage policies:** Create, edit, and delete policies that control features such as who can create teams, and what features are available to users.

- **Manage devices:** View and manage the devices that are used to access Teams, such as IP phones and conference room devices.

- **Manage calling and meeting policies:** Control settings such as who can make PSTN calls, and who can schedule meetings with dial-in numbers.

- **Manage meeting settings:** Configure settings such as whether anonymous users can join meetings, and whether attendees can join before the host.

- **Manage messaging policies:** Configure settings such as whether users can send messages to external contacts, and whether users can delete messages.

- **Manage compliance:** View and manage compliance settings for Teams, such as retention policies, eDiscovery, and archiving.

- **Manage Teams usage reports:** View usage reports for Teams, such as the number of active users, and the number of calls and meetings.

- **Manage guest access:** Control settings such as whether external users can join teams and channels, and whether team owners can add external users.

- **Manage live events:** Create and manage live events such as virtual conferences, webinars and town halls.

The Teams admin center is a powerful tool that allows you to manage and configure many aspects of Teams, from user licenses to compliance settings, and it is the one-stop-shop for global admin or teams service admin to manage their organization's Teams experience.

Teams add-ons

Microsoft Teams allows users to install and use various add-ons to enhance the functionality of the platform. These add-ons can be installed from the Teams store, and they can be used to integrate with other apps and services, such as Trello, Asana, and Salesforce, among others. Some of the add-ons available include the following:

- **Trello for teams:** This add-on allows users to create and manage Trello boards directly from Teams, thus making it easier to collaborate on projects.

- **Asana for teams:** This add-on allows users to create and manage Asana tasks and projects directly from Teams, making it easier to track and manage work.

- **Salesforce for teams:** This add-on allows users to access Salesforce data and functionality directly from Teams, making it easier to track and manage customer interactions.

- **Polls for teams:** This add-on allows users to create and conduct polls directly within Teams, making it easy to gather feedback and make decisions.

- **Translator for teams:** This add-on allows users to translate text and speech in real-time, making it easier to communicate with people who speak different languages.

These are just a few examples, but there are many other add-ons available, each with its own unique set of features and capabilities. There are several categories of add-ons, including:

- **Productivity:** Apps that help with tasks such as scheduling, note-taking, and project management.

- **Communication:** Apps that enhance the way team members communicate, such as through video conferencing or instant messaging.

- **Integrations:** Apps that integrate with other tools and services, such as Salesforce, Trello, and Asana.

- **Business:** Apps that help with tasks such as expense tracking, invoicing, and HR management.

These add-ons can be added by going to the Teams app store and browsing through the various offerings, or by searching for a specific app. The app can then be added to a team or channel, and team members can use its functionality within the context of their conversations. Some apps may require additional configuration or setup before they can be used.

Additionally, Microsoft Teams allows third-party developers to create custom apps using the Microsoft Teams platform. This way, organizations can tailor apps to their specific needs and workflows, and can also share and distribute these custom apps with other organizations.

To submit your own add-on for Teams, you will need to first create it using the Microsoft Teams platform, which includes the Microsoft Teams JavaScript client SDK and other tools and resources. Once your add-on is developed and tested, you can submit it for review by Microsoft. The process for submitting an add-on can vary, depending on the region and platform, but typically involves creating a listing in the Microsoft Teams App store and providing details about your add-on such as its capabilities, screenshots, and a privacy statement. The Microsoft Teams developer documentation provides more information on the process of creating and submitting add-ons for Teams, including the necessary steps and requirements.

Figure 9.4 features Microsoft Teams Apps add-ons store:

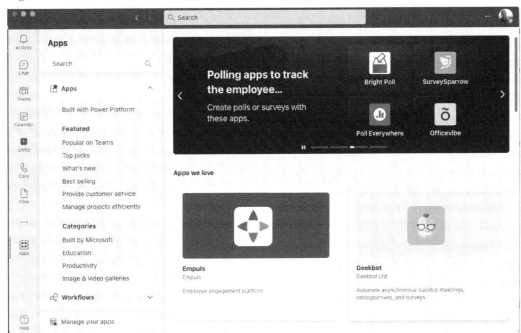

Figure 9.4: *Microsoft Teams Apps add-ons store*

Please note that allowing the use of add-ons in a specific organization, ultimately depends on the policies and restrictions set by the organization's IT administrators. You as an admin have an ability to control what add-ons are available to be installed by users within the organization. If you are developing an add-on for Teams, you will need to work with your organization's IT administrator to ensure that it meets their requirements and is approved for use within the organization.

Approval processes integration with Teams

In Microsoft Teams, you can use the built-in approval workflows to request and track approvals for various types of content, such as documents and messages. Approval workflows can be set up and managed by users with appropriate permissions, such as team owners or members with admin roles.

When a user requests approval for a piece of content, the designated approvers will receive a notification and can review the content and approve or reject it. The user who requested the approval will also be notified of the outcome.

Approval workflows can also be customized with the use of Microsoft Power Automate, a service that allows you to automate workflows and business processes using a wide range of connectors, including connectors for Teams. With Power Automate, you can create custom approval flows that include additional steps, such as sending notifications to other users or adding the approved content to specific channels.

It is important to note that the approval process and use of add-ons would depend on the policies and regulations of the organization, as well as the configuration of a specific Teams environment.

Potential approval scenarios using Teams include the following:

- Approval of documents or content shared within a team or channel. This could include approvals for documents, images, or other types of content shared within a team or channel.

- Approval of meeting requests or calendar events. This could include approvals for scheduling meetings, webinars, or other events.

- Approval of expenses or purchase requests. This could include approvals for expense reports, purchase orders, or other types of financial requests.

- Approval of vacation or time off requests. This could include approvals for vacation time, sick leave, or other types of time off requests.

To set up an approval process in Teams, you can use the built-in approval app or create a custom approval flow using Power Automate. The specific steps to set up an approval process will depend on the type of approval scenario you are trying to implement, but generally, the process will involve the following steps:

1. **Identify the type of approval needed:** This could be for a document, expense report, time off request, and so on.

2. **Create an approval form:** This could be a simple form with the necessary fields for the approval request, such as a title, description, and attachments.

3. **Create an approval flow:** This can be done using Power Automate, where you can specify the steps in the approval process, such as who needs to approve the request, any conditions that need to be met, and what actions need to be taken when the request is approved or denied.

4. **Test the approval flow:** Before rolling out the approval process to your organization, it is a good idea to test it with a small group of users, to ensure that it is working as expected.

5. **Roll out the approval process:** Once the approval process is tested and working correctly, you can roll it out to your organization. Make sure to provide clear instructions on how the process works and who to contact if there are any issues.

6. **Monitor and maintain the approval process:** Regularly monitor the approval process to ensure that it is working correctly and make any necessary adjustments.

In order to access all requests awaiting your approval in Teams, you will need to use the Approvals feature. This feature allows you to view, manage, and take action on approval requests that have been sent to you. To access the Approvals feature, you will need to open the Teams app and navigate to the Approvals tab in the navigation menu. This will display a list of all pending approval requests. You can then select a request to view its details, and take action by approving or rejecting the request. Additionally, you can also set up notifications to be alerted when new approval requests are sent to you.

Figure 9.5 features the Approvals feature in the Microsoft Teams app:

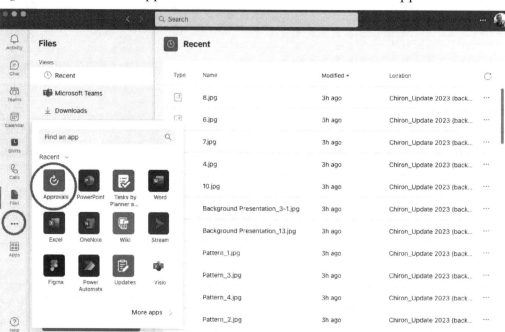

Figure 9.5: Approvals feature in the Microsoft Teams app

Practical tasks

Let us now review some features of Microsoft teams in Microsoft 365. Follow these steps:

1. Login to **portal.office.com** with your account.

2. Once on the home page, from the list of available applications, select **Teams**.

Figure 9.6 features web version of teams from the Microsoft 365 home page:

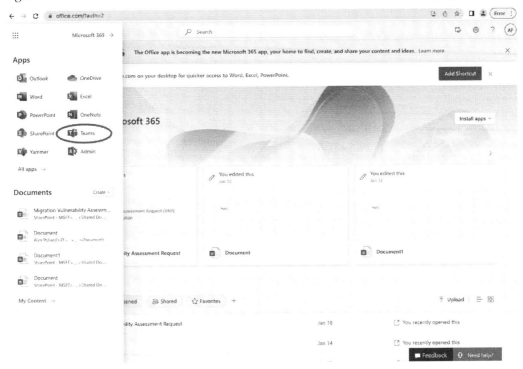

Figure 9.6: *Web version of teams from the Microsoft 365 home page*

Once you access Teams, you will be prompted to install the Desktop client or use the web app instead. Feel free to choose whatever option you like more.

Please note that the Teams web app is generally feature-rich and provides most of the functionality that is available in the desktop app. However, there may be some limitations when compared to the desktop app, such as the following:

- Some advanced calling and meeting features may not be available in the web app.

- The web app may have slightly lower performance compared to the desktop app.

- Some third-party apps and add-ons may not be available in the web app.

- Some advanced administrative controls may not be available in the web app.

However, Microsoft is continuously working to improve the web app and bring it closer to the functionality of the desktop app. It is worth noting that the majority of the features are available in both versions, and the web app is well suited for most scenarios. It is also supported in most major web browsers.

No matter whatever version you selected on the left navigation in Teams, click on '**Teams**'. It will bring you the view of some pre-created teams and channels inside them. These are available as a part of the Development plan that we are using to have the environment. Let us create a new team and some channels inside by ourselves, by following the given steps:

1. At the bottom, click on the "+" button to create a new team.

2. Select "**Create a new team**" from the options that appear.

3. Choose the type of team you want to create (for example, "**Class team**," "**Organization team**" "**Professional learning community**" and so on).

4. Give your team a name, and add a description if desired.

5. Choose whether the team will be private or public.

6. Select the members you want to add to the team.

7. Click "**Create**" to create the new team.

8. Once the team is created, you can add channels within the team by clicking on the three-dot menu and selecting "**Add channel**".

9. Give the channel a name and set the privacy level, and then click on "**Create**" to create the channel.

10. Once you have the channel, you can add members to the channel, and start posting messages and files.

Figure 9.7 features new team creation on Teams web:

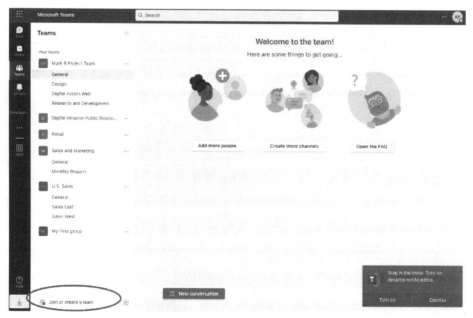

Figure 9.7: *New team creation on Teams web*

While you were creating a team and channel, you were prompted to add members to the team or channel.

To configure permissions for an existing channel or team in Microsoft Teams, follow the given steps:

1. Click on the three dots icon next to the team or channel name, and then select "**Manage team**" or "**Manage channel**".

2. In the "**Manage team**" or "**Manage channel**" window, you will see the "**Settings**" tab. Click on it.

3. Under the "**Settings**" tab, you will see the "**Permissions**" section. Here, you can choose to customize permissions for team members or guests, or you can use the default settings.

4. To customize permissions, click on the "**Customize permissions**" button. From there, you can select the specific permissions you want to grant or revoke for team members or guests.

5. Once you have made your changes, click on "**Save**" to apply them.

In Microsoft Teams, there are several different levels of permissions that can be assigned to users within a team or channel. These levels include Member, Guest, and Owner.

*   A **Member** is a user who is a full member of the team and has access to all of the team's content and features. Members can create and edit channels, add and remove other members, and perform other team management tasks.

*   A **Guest** is a user who has been added to a team as a guest. Guests have access to the team's channels and content, but they do not have the same level of permissions as members. They cannot create or edit channels, add or remove other users, or perform other team management tasks.

*   An **Owner** is a user who has been designated as the owner of a team. Owners have full control over the team and all its content and settings. They can add and remove members and guests, create and edit channels, and perform other team management tasks. They also have access to team settings and can configure settings such as team name, description, and permissions.

Once the channel is created, you can post messages there and exchange messages with potential team members. Post a message on a channel. Once posted, you have an option to edit or delete your message. Click on the three dots next to the message, and select the **Edit** option (select **Delete** if you want to delete it). You will then be able to make changes to your message. Please note that it will mark the message as **Edited** in the corner.

Figure 9.8 features message edit functionality:

Figure 9.8: *Message edit functionality*

Next, let us add a new tab to our channel. Click on one of those icons above your message that says '**Add tab**'. Search for **Document library** there.

Figure 9.9 features adding new Document library into the channel:

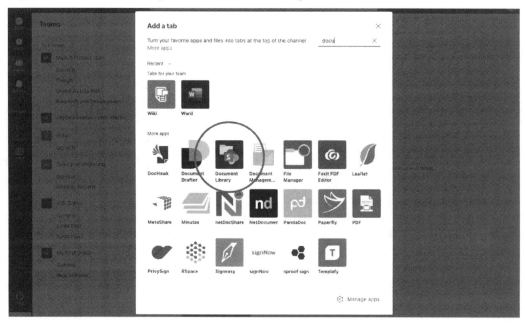

Figure 9.9: *Adding new Document library into the channel*

One document library is added to the channel. You can store and exchange files on your teams channel with our channel members. Depending on the Public or Private channel, all team members will automatically have access to your channel or should be invited one by one accordingly.

Look and play around in Teams to observe the functionality, alerts and different apps available in there. The major features will be Chat, Calendar (integrated with your Exchange and Outlooks), Teams and Activity.

To manage various policies and configurations, you need to go to the Teams Admin centre. Follow the given steps:

1. Click on the squares in the top left corner and click on the "**Show all**" button.

2. Select Admin.

3. From the list in the left navigation, click on **Teams Admin center.**

4. The Teams admin center will open and you can use it to manage and configure various settings for your organization's teams and channels.

Alternatively, you can also access the Teams admin center by going to the URL "**https://admin.teams.microsoft.com**" and sign in with your credentials.

Figure 9.10 features the Teams admin center view:

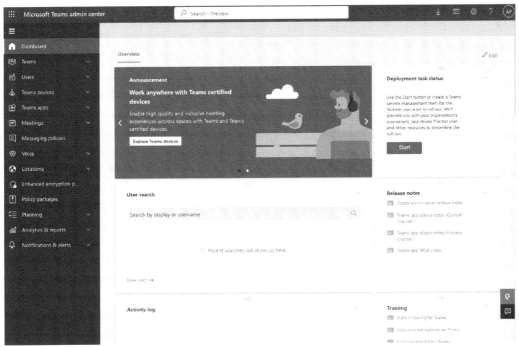

Figure 9.10: *Teams admin center view*

The Teams admin center allows you to configure various settings for your organization's Teams deployment. Some of the things you can do in the Teams admin center include:

- **Manage teams and channels:** You can create, edit, and delete teams and channels, as well as set permissions for them.

- **Manage users and groups:** You can add, remove, and manage users and groups within your organization, as well as assign licenses and roles.

- **Manage devices:** You can manage devices that are used to access Teams, such as setting up device policies and managing device compliance.

- **Manage app settings:** You can configure settings for apps that are integrated with Teams, such as SharePoint and OneNote.

- **Manage call and meeting settings:** You can configure settings for audio and video calls, as well as meetings, such as setting up call routing and managing call quality.

- **Manage messaging settings:** You can configure settings for instant messaging and chat, such as setting up policies for instant messaging and managing message retention.

- **Manage compliance and security:** You can set up policies and compliance requirements for data governance and security, such as managing eDiscovery and setting up data loss prevention policies.

- **Monitor and troubleshoot:** You can monitor the health and usage of Teams in your organization, as well as troubleshoot issues that may arise.

- **Global settings:** You can manage settings that apply to all of your organization's Teams users, such as settings for Office 365 groups, guest access, and more.

These are just some examples of the things you can do in the Teams admin center, but depending on your organization's needs, there may be other options available to you as well.

Explore on your own to see what configurations and features available for you.

One of the other features we discussed in this chapter was adding the phone to your Teams. Microsoft provides some trial plans for 30 days that we could use to test them out. To set it up, follow the given steps:

1. Log in to the Microsoft 365 admin center (root admin center).

2. Go to the Billing section of the admin center.

3. Under the **Products & services** section, find the Microsoft Teams listing and select it.

4. Select the **Add-ons** tab and look for the **Phone System** add-on.

5. Select the number of phone licenses you want to purchase and follow the prompts to complete the purchase.

Conclusion

In this chapter, you learned about Microsoft Teams and the different client versions available for PC, mobile and web. We covered some major differences between them as well as common features and functionality. You learned about teams, channels, chats, calls and add-ons available for Teams. We also covered the Teams admin center and reviewed some of its functionality. In conclusion, Microsoft Teams is a collaboration and communication platform that allows teams to work together in a seamless and efficient way. It offers features such as chat, voice and video calls, file sharing, and integration with other Microsoft apps. Teams also allows for customization through the use of add-ons, which can enhance the functionality of the platform. Teams can be accessed through a web client, desktop app, and mobile app, and it allows for guest access and permissions management. Teams can also be managed through the Teams Admin Center, which allows administrators to configure settings, assign licenses, and access telemetry data. With its wide range of features and customization options, Microsoft Teams is a powerful tool for teams to collaborate and work together effectively.

Points to remember

- Microsoft Teams comes for Desktop, mobile and web.

- Chats, Calendar, Teams, and Files are some of the major Teams features.

- You can add a phone number to your account in Teams and use it for calls by acquiring a license form the M365 Admin center.

- There is a separate Admin center for Microsoft Teams that allows you to configure policies and manage configurations. Moreover, you can view reports and metrics there.

- There are Public and Private channels that can be created in Teams.

- When you create a new Team, a new 'Teams' template site is created in SharePoint, where all the documents and notes associated with that team will be stored.

Join our book's Discord space

Join the book's Discord Workspace for Latest updates, Offers, Tech happenings around the world, New Release and Sessions with the Authors:

https://discord.bpbonline.com

## CHAPTER 10

Power Platform and Citizen Development

> **"Low-code is the democratization of technology. It allows anyone, not just developers, to create, deploy and run applications."**
>
> *- Marc Benioff*

Introduction

Power Platform is the new low-code solution from Microsoft to allow users develop applications and workflows and automate business processes. The beauty of any low-code solution is that no coding skills are needed from the user working on the functionality. Hence, development can be done by regular employees with no or minimal training provided. Power Platform is a combination of applications that includes the following:

- PowerApps
  - Canvas
  - Model Driven
  - Power Portals
  - Dataverse

- Power Automate
  - Flows
  - Solutions

In this chapter, we will cover how regular users can use all of the apps and what are the best ways for organizations to utilize various development approaches.

Structure

In this chapter, we will cover the following topics:

- Power Platform
- Citizen development
- PowerApps overview
- Power Automate overview

Objectives

In this chapter, we will review a low-code platform from Microsoft. Power Platform includes multiple applications inside it, such as PowerApp, Power Automate, and Power BI. We will review them all and learn the differences between different types of applications and workflows. Citizen development is the development done by power Users (non-developers). Thus, we will review what kind of applications can be developed by something without coding logic and what are enhanced options available for devs.

Power Platform

Microsoft Power Platform is a low-code, no-code platform that allows users to create custom business applications, automate workflows, and integrate with other Microsoft products, such as Dynamics 365 and Office 365. The Power Platform includes three main components:

- Power Automate
- Power Apps
- Power BI

The Power Platform is designed to be accessible to non-technical users. It can help organizations build custom solutions quickly and easily, without the need for significant development resources.

You can access Power Platform by browsing to **https://make.powerapps.com**, **https://flow.microsoft.com**, and **https://powerbi.com**. You can also use Power Apps, Power Automate and Power BI from within Microsoft Teams and Dynamics 365.

Microsoft 365 plans are included into the license with Office 365 E3 and E5, Dynamics 365, and Dynamics 365 for Customer Engagement.

The Power Platform is a collection of tools and services that, on the back-end, are built on top of Microsoft Azure and Dynamics 365.

Power Automate is a workflow automation tool that allows users to create automated processes using a drag-and-drop interface. This can include tasks such as sending emails, updating data, or creating tasks in other systems. Users can also create custom connectors to integrate with other systems and services.

Power Apps is a low-code development platform that allows users to create custom business applications for web and mobile devices. This can include forms, data entry screens, and other custom interfaces. Power Apps also includes pre-built connectors to common services, such as Office 365 and Dynamics 365, as well as the ability to create custom connectors to other systems.

Power BI is a business intelligence tool that allows users to create interactive visualizations, reports, and dashboards from various data sources. This can include data from Excel, SharePoint, Azure, and other systems. Power BI also includes pre-built connectors to common data sources such as Dynamics 365 and Salesforce.

There are different license options available for the Power Platform, each of which grants access to different features and capabilities, and they are explained as follows:

- **Power Automate Plan 1 and Plan 2:** These licenses are designed for users who need to create and run automated workflows. Plan 1 includes basic automation capabilities, while Plan 2 includes more advanced features, such as data loss prevention and the ability to run workflows on-premises.

- **Power Apps Plan 1 and Plan 2:** These licenses are designed for users who need to create and run custom business applications. Plan 1 includes basic app-creation capabilities, while Plan 2 includes more advanced features such as custom connectors and the ability to create and run model-driven apps.

- **Power BI Pro and Premium:** These licenses are designed for users who need to create and share interactive visualizations, reports, and dashboards. Power BI Pro is a per-user license that allows users to create and share reports, while Power BI Premium includes additional features such as the ability to share reports with external users and additional scalability options.

- **Power Apps and Power Automate per app and per flow:** This allows to pay for specific functionality and use case.

Some Power Platform features and capabilities may also require additional Dynamics 365 or Office 365 licenses. It is also important to mention that the Power Platform is continuously updated with new features, capabilities, and integrations. Thus, it is worth keeping track of new releases and updates to the platform, by visiting the Power Platform website and reviewing official documentation from Microsoft.

In the Power Platform, an environment is a container for all the data, connectors, and customizations that make up your organization's apps, flows, and portals. Environments allow you to separate and manage different aspects of your organization's operations, such as development, testing, and production.

When you create an environment, you also create a set of default connectors that allow you to connect to data sources and services. Additionally, you can create custom connectors, which allow you to connect to other data sources and services.

You can create multiple environments in Power Platform, each with their own set of connectors and customizations. This allows you to maintain separate development, testing, and production environments. This can help you ensure that changes made in one environment do not affect the others, as well as to ensure data security and compliance.

In terms of managing environments, as an administrator, you can add users, assign roles, and control access to environments in Power Platform. This can be done through the Power Platform admin center. Additionally, you can also use Power Automate and Power Apps Studio to create and manage flows, apps, and portals in the environment.

Various environments allow you to separate your development, testing, and production resources, and to manage access and permissions for different teams and users.

Examples of environments include:

- **Development environment:** This is where developers create and test their apps, flows, and connectors. It is typically used for internal testing and experimentation.

- **Test environment:** This is where you test your apps, flows, and connectors before deploying them to production. It allows you to validate that your solutions work as expected and to find and fix any issues.

- **Production environment:** This is where you deploy your final apps, flows, and connectors for use by end-users. It is typically used for customer-facing solutions.

There can be a few potential use cases for environments such as the ones mentioned as follows:

- An organization that wants to develop a custom app for their sales team to use, would create a development environment to build and test the app, and a production environment to make the app available to the sales team.

- A company that wants to automate its business processes using Power Automate, would create a development environment to create and test their flows and a production environment to make the flows available to their users.

- A team that wants to build a custom connector to connect to an external system. They would create a development environment to build and test the connector and a production environment to make the connector available for use in other solutions.

Environments are key part of the Power Platform; it enables you to create a segregation of resources and access controls for different teams and users. It also enables you to work on different versions and stages of your apps, flows, and connectors. Moreover, it allows you to manage costs and usage of resources separately.

Figure 10.1 features environment selection in the Power Automate portal:

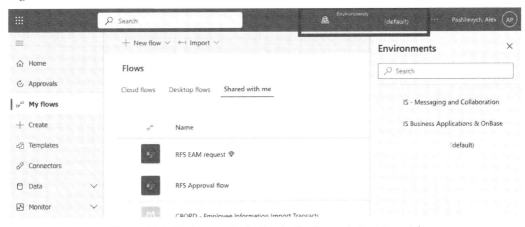

Figure 10.1: *Environment selection in the Power Automate portal*

To manage your environments, you will first need to navigate to the Power Platform admin center. Once there, you can create new environments, assign users to them, and configure settings such as app and flow limits.

You can also use the Power Platform admin center to manage the data within your environments. This includes the ability to create and manage connection references, which are used to connect to external data sources, as well as managing data policies and data loss prevention settings.

Another important aspect of environment management is security. In the Power Platform admin center, you can set up and manage user roles, which determine what actions a user is allowed to take within an environment. Additionally, you can set up and manage security policies, such as multifactor authentication and conditional access, to ensure that only authorized users can access your environments.

You can also use the Power Platform admin center to monitor and troubleshoot your environments. This includes monitoring usage and performance, and accessing diagnostic logs to help identify and resolve issues.

It is also worth noting that each environment in the Power Platform is associated with a tenant, which is the top-level container for all the resources used by an organization. Tenants can be used to manage and organize environments, and to control access to the resources within them.

In the Power Platform admin center, you can manage various settings for your organization's Power Platform environment. Some examples of the types of settings you can manage include the following:

- **Environments**, as we already discussed. You can create and manage different environments, such as production, development, and test environments, and assign users and teams to each environment.

- **Connections**: You can create and manage connections to external data sources, such as Dynamics 365 and SharePoint, that can be used in Power Automate flows and Power Apps.

- **Data Loss Prevention (DLP)**: You can set up policies to prevent sensitive data from being shared or stored in certain ways, such as by setting up rules to block certain types of data from being included in email attachments.

- **Governance**: You can set up policies to govern how users can create and use Power Automate flows and Power Apps, such as by setting limits on the number of flows or apps that a single user can create.

- **Security**: You can manage security settings for the Power Platform, such as by setting up multi-factor authentication for users, and managing access to the Power Platform for external users.

- **Monitoring**: You can monitor the usage and performance of the Power Platform, such as by viewing usage reports and monitoring the health of the platform.

- **Access**: You can manage access to the Power Platform by giving access to users and teams, and manage user roles and permissions.

- **Licensing**: You can manage licenses for Power Apps, Power Automate and Power Virtual Agents.

- **Integration**: You can manage the integration between Power Platform and other Microsoft services, such as Dynamics 365 and SharePoint.

- **Customization**: You can customize the Power Platform to suit your organization's needs, such as by customizing the look and feel of the platform, and customizing the functionality of the platform.

Figure 10.2 features Automate Platform Admin center:

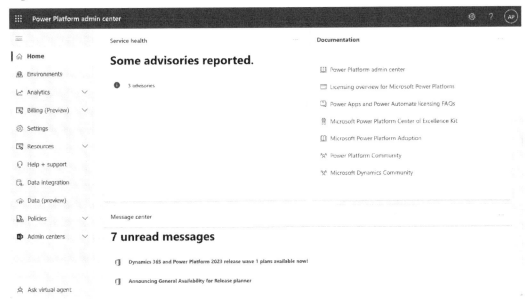

Figure 10.2: *Power Automate Admin center*

In the Power Platform admin center, you can monitor the health of your environments by viewing the environment status, which provides an overview of the current state of your environments, including any issues or errors. Additionally, you can view environment usage metrics, such as the number of active users and the number of API calls, to help you understand how your environments are being used and identify any potential performance issues.

To access environment health information in the Power Platform admin center, you need to have the Power Platform admin or environment admin role. Once you have access, you can navigate to the **Environments** page to view the environment status and usage metrics. You can also set up alerts to notify you of any issues or errors with your environments, so that you can quickly respond to them.

You can also use the Power Automate or Power Apps monitor to see the usage and performance of your flows and apps across your environments. This way you can make sure that your apps and flows are running smoothly, check the errors, and monitor the performance.

Additionally, you can also use third-party monitoring and logging tools to monitor your environments and gather additional information about their health and performance.

There are many third-party tools available for monitoring the health and performance of Power Platform environments. Here are a few examples:

- **PowerApps checker:** This tool allows you to validate your PowerApps and Flows for best practices and common issues. It can also identify performance bottlenecks and provide recommendations for improvement.

- **Power Platform governance:** This tool provides a set of governance and management capabilities for Power Platform, including environment management, data governance, and compliance.

- **Power Platform Audit Log Analyzer:** This tool allows you to analyze and search the audit logs for your Power Platform environments, providing visibility into user activity and changes made to your environment.

- **Power Platform Health Monitor:** This tool provides real-time monitoring of your Power Platform environments, including performance metrics, error tracking, and alerting.

- **Power Platform Management Suite:** This tool offers a set of management and governance capabilities for Power Platform, including environment management, security, and compliance.

These are just a few examples. There are many other third-party tools available to help you monitor and manage your Power Platform environments. The best tool for you will depend on your specific needs and requirements.

Overall, managing environments in the Power Platform is an important aspect of any organization's deployment. By creating and managing environments, you can separate different stages of development, manage data, set up security, and troubleshoot issues.

Citizen development

You might be wondering what citizen development means. Citizen development refers to the practice of empowering non-technical users, such as business users or "citizens," to create and modify their own software applications using low-code or no-code development platforms. This approach aims to enable users to quickly and easily create the applications they need, in order to support their business processes, without relying on IT or professional developers. By empowering citizens to take an active role in software development, organizations can improve the speed and efficiency of application delivery, as well as increase user engagement and adoption.

In the context of the Power Platform, citizen development refers to the ability for business users to create their own custom solutions and automate their own workflows using the Power Platform's low-code and no-code tools, such as PowerApps, Power Automate, and Power Virtual Agents. These tools allow users to create custom apps, automate business processes, and build chatbots, all without writing any code. By empowering business users to create their own solutions, the Power Platform enables organizations to become more agile, responsive, and efficient.

In particular, citizen development refers to the idea of empowering non-technical users, such as business analysts or department heads, to create their own business applications and automate their own processes, without the need for IT involvement. This is achieved through the use of low-code or no-code platforms. In our case, it is the Power Platform, which provides a drag-and-drop interface and pre-built templates for creating apps and automating workflows.

One of the main benefits of citizen development is that it allows organizations to quickly and efficiently address business needs that would otherwise require IT resources and time.

With citizen development, business users can create their own applications and automate their own processes, which can lead to increased productivity, cost savings, and faster time-to-market.

For example, a sales department might use Power Platform to create a custom CRM application, that tracks leads and sales data, allowing them to better manage their pipeline and close deals faster. Another example would be a HR department, that could use Power Platform to create an onboarding application that streamlines the process of onboarding new employees. This can help reduce the workload on HR and IT staff, while also improving the new-hire experience.

Another example could be a field service team that could use Power Platform to create a mobile app, that allows technicians to access customer information, view service history, and update job status while they are on the field. This can help improve service quality and efficiency, while also reducing the need for technicians to return to the office to update job status.

Citizen development can also allow organizations to experiment with new ideas and technologies at a low cost. With Power Platform, business users can quickly create prototypes of new apps and workflows, and then we test them with real users to see if they are viable. This allows organizations to validate ideas and identify opportunities for innovation, without incurring the costs of a full-scale development project.

However, there are also some potential downsides to citizen development. One concern is that business users may not have the same level of technical expertise or understanding of security and compliance requirements, as their IT staff. This could lead to applications and workflows that are not secure, compliant, or scalable.

Another concern is that citizen development can lead to an increase in the number of custom applications and workflows within an organization, which can make it difficult for IT to manage and support them. This can lead to silos of information and integration issues, which can negatively impact data quality and overall business performance.

Therefore, it is important for organizations to have proper governance and oversight in place, to ensure that citizen-developed applications and workflows meet security, compliance, and scalability requirements. This can include providing training and resources to business users on best practices for development, as well as having IT review and approve citizen-developed applications and workflows before they are deployed.

Office Hours is a dedicated meeting that allows IT professionals to set specific times during which, they are available to answer questions and provide support to users. These meetings usually scheduled once or twice per week for about an hour and repeat every week. This practice can be particularly useful in organizations where there are many citizen developers who may not have the same level of technical expertise as IT professionals.

One way to use Office Hours in the context of the Power Platform, is to set aside specific times during which, citizen developers can ask questions and receive guidance on how to use the platform. This can help to ensure that citizen developers are able to get the help they need when they need it, and can help to reduce the number of support tickets that IT needs to handle.

Another way to use Office Hours is to set up virtual or in-person sessions where IT professionals provide training and demos on specific features or use cases of the Power Platform. This can help to educate citizen developers on how to use the platform more effectively and increase their productivity.

Additionally, Office Hours can be used as a way for IT to gather feedback from the citizen developers on how to improve the platform, or to gather ideas for new features or functionality. This can help IT to better understand the needs of the citizen developers and make the platform more user-friendly.

The pros of having citizen developers in the organization, is that they can help to drive innovation, by creating new apps and automating business processes quickly, which can help the organization to be more efficient and productive. Additionally, citizen developers can help to reduce the workload of IT by taking on tasks such as app development and data integration.

On the other hand, one of the cons of having citizen developers in the organization is that they may not have the same level of technical expertise as IT professionals, which can lead to issues with data security, compliance, and overall app quality. This is why having Office Hours can help to address these concerns by providing a way for IT professionals to provide guidance and support to citizen developers.

So, to summarize, Office Hours is an effective way to provide support and guidance to citizen developers in the context of the Power Platform. By setting aside specific times during which IT professionals are available to answer questions and provide training, organizations can help to ensure that citizen developers are able to use the platform effectively and efficiently, while also reducing the workload of IT.

In conclusion, citizen development can be a powerful tool for organizations that want to quickly and efficiently address business needs while also encouraging innovation and experimentation. By leveraging low-code or no-code platforms such as Power Platform, organizations can empower business users to create their own applications and automate their own processes. However, it is important for organizations to have proper governance and oversight in place, to ensure that citizen-developed applications and workflows meet security, compliance, and scalability requirements.

PowerApps overview

Microsoft PowerApps is a service that allows users to create custom business applications without writing code. These applications, known as PowerApps, can be used to automate business processes, connect to data sources, and create custom forms and workflows.

PowerApps can be used to create three types of apps:

- **Canvas app:** This type of app allows you to create an app from scratch by dragging and dropping controls onto a canvas. It gives you full control over the layout and design of the app, and you can add custom logic and formulas to the app's controls.

- **Model-driven app:** This type of app is based on a data model that you create in **Common Data Service (CDS)**. A Model-driven app is a more powerful and flexible than canvas app; it can be used to build business application with advanced features such as business process flows, and business rules.

- **Portal (Pages):** This type of app allows users to create public-facing websites for external users (such as customers or partners) to access data, forms, and workflows.

To develop PowerApps, you can use the PowerApps Studio, which is a visual development environment that allows you to create, test, and publish your apps. It runs on both Windows and Mac.

You can start by creating a new app and choosing the type of app you want to create. Once you have created your app, you can add controls, such as buttons and text boxes, to the canvas and customize their properties. You can also add custom logic and formulas to your app's controls, such as calculating a total or performing data validation.

To connect your app to data, you can use the connectors available in PowerApps, which allow you to connect to a wide range of data sources, including Excel, SharePoint, Dynamics 365, and many more. You can also use custom connectors to connect to other data sources.

You can also use PowerApps Studio to test your app and make sure it behaves as expected. Once you have finished developing your app, you can publish it and make it available to other users.

PowerApps is a powerful tool that allows you to create custom business applications quickly and easily, without needing to write any code. It can be used to automate business processes, improve data collection and management, and increase productivity. With the help of PowerApps, you can create a variety of apps to suit different business needs, such as customer management, inventory management, task management and more.

In addition to using the PowerApps Studio, you can also develop PowerApps from a browser by using the PowerApps web editor. That is a more common approach. The web editor is a simplified version of the PowerApps Studio, and it allows you to create and edit apps from a web browser. It is a good option for users who do not have PowerApps Studio installed on their machine or for those who prefer to work in a browser.

Figure 10.3 features PowerApps portal:

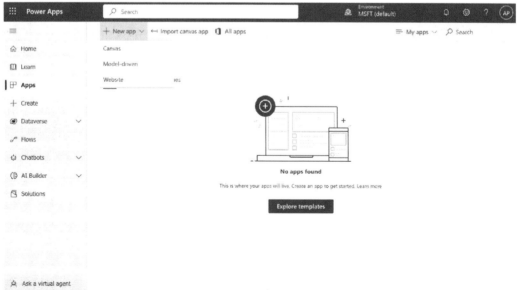

Figure 10.3: *PowerApps portal*

When deciding whether to use a canvas app or a model-driven app, it is important to consider the specific requirements of your app and the level of complexity it will require.

Canvas apps are best used for simple apps that do not require a lot of data or advanced functionality. They are also a good option for creating prototypes or proof-of-concepts quickly. Canvas app gives you full control over the layout and design of the app and you can add custom logic and formulas to the app's controls, which is great for creating custom business solutions.

Model-driven apps, on the other hand, are best used for more complex apps that require a lot of data and advanced functionality. They are built on top of the **Common Data Service** (**CDS**), which provides a centralized data model that allows you to manage and relate data in a consistent way. Model-driven apps allow you to create advanced features such as business process flows, and business rules, which can be very useful for building business applications.

It is worth noting that you can also combine the two types of apps, and use a canvas app to create a user interface that communicates with a model-driven app to handle data and business logic.

Canvas apps do provide a high degree of flexibility in terms of the user interface, allowing you to virtually create any layout or design you want. You can use the drag-and-drop interface in PowerApps Studio to add and customize controls, and then use formulas and custom logic to add functionality to your app. This makes canvas apps well-suited for creating custom business solutions or for prototyping and proof-of-concepts.

Model-driven apps, on the other hand, provide a more structured and data-centric approach to app development. They are built on top of the **Common Data Service** (**CDS**), which provides a centralized data model that allows you to manage and relate data in a consistent way. Model-driven apps also provide a set of pre-built components, such as forms, views and charts that you can use to quickly build an app.

While the interface of a model-driven app is more limited compared to a canvas app, it can handle more complex data and business logic, and also provides a set of advanced features such as business process flows and business rules, which can be very useful for building business applications.

The structure of a canvas app in PowerApps is based on screens, controls, and formulas, as explained as follows:

- A screen is a container for controls and represents a specific view or page in the app. Screens can be added to an app by using the Screens pane in PowerApps Studio.

- Controls are the individual UI elements, such as text boxes, labels, buttons, and galleries, that you add to a screen. You can add controls to a screen by using the Insert tab in PowerApps Studio.

- Formulas are used to add custom logic and calculations to the app. They can be used to define the behavior of controls, set properties, and perform calculations. Formulas can be added to controls by using the formula bar in PowerApps Studio.

To create a simple canvas app in PowerApps, you can follow these general steps:

1. Open PowerApps app from the M365 portal.

2. Add a new screen to the app by using the Screens pane.

3. Add controls to the screen by using the Insert tab.

4. Set properties for the controls, such as their position and size, by using the Properties pane.

5. Use formulas to define the behavior of the controls and add custom logic to the app.

6. Test the app by clicking the "Preview" button in PowerApps Studio.

7. Finally, you can publish the app and share it with others.

Here is an example of a simple app that allows users to enter their name and email address and submit the form:

1. Create a new screen and add a label, a text input, and a button control to the screen.

2. Set the text property of the label to "Enter your name and email".

3. Set the placeholder property of the text input to "Name" and set the text property of the button to "Submit".

4. Add another text input control and set the placeholder property to "Email".

5. In the formula bar, set the **OnSelect** property of the button to a formula that uses the Collect function to add the name and email to a collection.

6. Test the app by clicking the "Preview" button in PowerApps Studio.

Please note that this is a very simple example. However, canvas apps can be much more complex and sophisticated, depending on the requirements of the app.

Figure 10.4 features PowerApps Canvas app builder view:

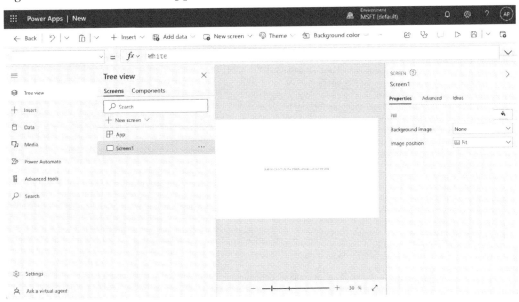

Figure 10.4: *PowerApps Canvas app builder view*

Layouts

Canvas app layouts in PowerApps refer to the way that controls are arranged on a screen. There are several different layout options available in PowerApps, each with its own advantages and use cases.

Here are a few of the most commonly used layout options in PowerApps:

- **Stack layout:** This layout arranges controls vertically or horizontally, one on top of the other. It is useful for creating simple forms or for laying out controls in a single column or row.

- **Table layout:** This layout arranges controls in a table format, with rows and columns. It is useful for creating data-driven apps or for displaying data in a tabular format.

- **Grid layout:** This layout arranges controls in a grid format, with rows and columns. It is useful for creating responsive designs that adjust to different screen sizes and orientations.

- **Flow layout:** This layout allows controls to flow automatically based on the available space, and it is useful for creating responsive designs that adjust to different screen sizes and orientations.

- **Absolute layout:** This layout allows controls to be positioned at specific coordinates on a screen, and it is useful for creating custom designs and for fine-tuning the position of controls.

In addition to these layout options, you can also use grouping controls, such as the Gallery and Form controls, to create more complex layouts. These controls allow you to repeat a layout for each item in a data source, and can be used to create data-driven apps that display information from a database or other data source.

When you are designing a canvas app, you can choose the layout that best suits the requirements of your app, and use the layout options in combination to create the desired user interface.

When designing a canvas app for mobile and tablet devices, there are a few things to keep in mind to ensure that your app looks and works well on these smaller screens.

One of the most important things to consider is screen size. Mobile and tablet screens are generally smaller than desktop screens, so you will need to make sure that your app's layout and controls are optimized for these smaller sizes. This may involve using different layout options or adjusting the size and position of controls to ensure that they are visible and easy to use on a smaller screen.

Another important consideration is touch input. Mobile and tablet devices use touch input instead of mouse and keyboard, and so, you will need to make sure that your app's controls are large enough to be easily tapped and that the app's navigation is intuitive and easy to use with touch.

Responsive design is a key aspect to consider when designing a canvas app for mobile and tablet devices; this allows the app to adapt to different screen sizes, orientations and resolutions. This can be achieved by using the flexible layout options in PowerApps, such as the Grid layout or the Flow layout, that can be set to automatically adjust the position and size of controls based on the available space.

In addition to the above, you can also use the Device check and Device functions to add functionality that is specific to mobile and tablet devices. For example, you can use the Device function to detect whether the app is running on a mobile or tablet device and then use this information to change the app's behavior or layout accordingly.

Formulas

In PowerApps, formulas are used to create calculations and logic in your canvas app. Formulas are written in a language called the PowerApps Formula Language, which is similar to Excel formulas.

You can use formulas in a variety of places in a canvas app, including controls, formulas, and variables. For example, you can use a formula to set the value of a control, to define a variable, or to perform a calculation. There is a dedicated area at the top of the builder where you right those formulas in. We will do a few examples later on, during the practice in this chapter. For now, here are a few examples of formulas you can use in a PowerApps canvas app:

- **Setting the value of a control:** You can use a formula to set the value of a control, such as a text box or label. For example, the following formula sets the value of a text box called "TextBox1" to the current date and time:

```
Text(Now(), "mm/dd/yyyy hh:mm:ss")
```

- **Conditional logic:** You can use formulas to perform conditional logic, such as showing or hiding a control, based on a certain condition. For example, the following formula shows a label called "Label1" if a checkbox called "Checkbox1" is checked:

```
If(Checkbox1.Value = true, true, false)
```

- **Perform calculation:** You can use formulas to perform calculations, such as adding, subtracting, multiplying and dividing. For example, the following formula calculates the total cost based on quantity and price:

```
Quantity.Value * Price.Value
```

- **Concatenation:** You can use formulas to concatenate two or more values or text together. For example, the following formula concatenates first name and last name together:

```
FirstName.Value & " " & LastName.Value
```

- **Validation:** You can use formulas to validate input fields, such as making sure a field is not empty, or that the input is in the correct format.

It is important to note that formulas in PowerApps are case-sensitive and must start with an equal sign (=). Moreover, you need to pay attention to the data types that you are working with, for example if you are trying to add a number with a text you should convert one of them to match the other.

It is a good practice to test your formulas with different inputs and expected results. PowerApps provides a formula bar where you can test and verify your formulas before you use them in your app.

Date and Time format

In PowerApps, date and time values are stored in **Coordinated Universal Time (UTC)** format. This means that when you capture a date or time value in an app, it is automatically converted to UTC before it is stored.

For example, if you use the **Now()** function to capture the current date and time, it will return the current date and time in UTC format.

When you display a date or time value in an app, it is automatically converted to the user's local time zone. This ensures that the date and time values are displayed correctly regardless of the user's location.

You can use the **DateTimeValue** function to convert a date and time value from one time zone to another. For example, if you want to convert a date and time value from UTC to **Eastern Standard Time** (**EST**), you can use the following formula:

```
DateTimeValue(DateTimeValue("date/time value in UTC").UTCToLocal("EST"))
```

It is also worth noting that you can use the **TimeZone** function to get the current timezone or list of all the supported timezones in the PowerApp.

As a best practice, it is recommended to use UTC date and time values in the app, especially when working with data from different time zones. It will make it easier to perform calculations and comparisons with date and time values, and also will be consistent with the data storage.

Data

In PowerApps, you can store data in a variety of ways, depending on the type of data and the requirements of your app. Here are a few common options:

- **SharePoint lists:** SharePoint lists are a popular option for storing data in PowerApps because they are easy to set up and are well-integrated with PowerApps. You can create a new list in SharePoint, and then connect to it in PowerApps to add, edit, and display data.

- **SQL server:** You can also store data in a SQL Server database, and then connect to it in PowerApps using the SQL connector. This is a good option if you already have a SQL Server database that you want to use, or if you need to work with more complex data structures.

- **Common Data Service** (**CDS**): CDS is a service provided by Microsoft that allows you to store and manage data in a standard format. You can use CDS to create entities (similar to tables in a database) and fields (similar to columns in a table), and then connect to them in PowerApps. CDS is particularly useful if you are building apps that need to integrate with other Power Platform services, such as Power Automate.

- **Excel:** You can also store data in an Excel spreadsheet and then connect to it in PowerApps. This is a simple option for small amounts of data and simple apps.

- **OneDrive, DropBox, Google Drive:** You can also store data in cloud storage services like OneDrive, DropBox, Google Drive and then connect to it in PowerApps. This is a good option for personal use or small team use.

In terms of connectors, PowerApps has a wide range of connectors available, which allow you to connect to various data sources, services, and APIs. Some examples of connectors include:

- **SharePoint:** Allows you to connect to SharePoint lists and libraries.

- **SQL Server:** Allows you to connect to SQL Server databases.

- **Common Data Service:** Allows you to connect to entities and fields in CDS.

- **Excel:** Allows you to connect to Excel spreadsheets.

- **OneDrive:** Allows you to connect to OneDrive files and folders.

- **DropBox:** Allows you to connect to DropBox files and folders.

- **Google Drive:** Allows you to connect to Google Drive files and folders.

- **Outlook:** Allows you to connect to Outlook mail, calendar, and contacts.

- **Dynamics 365:** Allows you to connect to Dynamics 365 data, such as accounts, contacts, and opportunities.

- **Twitter:** Allows you to connect to Twitter and retrieve tweets and user information, and many more.

You can find more information about connectors and how to use them in the official PowerApps documentation.

Limitations

There are a few limitations to keep in mind when working with canvas apps in PowerApps:

- **Record limit:** The maximum number of records that can be retrieved by a single data source in a canvas app is 2,000. If your data source contains more than 2,000 records, you will need to implement paging or filtering to retrieve the data in chunks. REST API usually helps to sort this problem, but requires some advanced development knowledge and prior experience working with APIs.

- **Delegation:** Some functions and operators in PowerApps are not able to be delegated to the data source. This means that when you use these functions or operators, the entire data set needs to be brought back to the device or service where the app is running, which can result in performance issues. Some examples of non-delegable functions are CountRows, Sum, and FirstN.

- **File size limit:** The maximum size of a single file that can be added to a PowerApp is 100 MB.

- **App size limit:** The maximum size of a single PowerApp is 250 MB.

- **Performance:** PowerApps are designed for creating simple, data-driven apps. As the complexity of the app increases, it may start to run slowly, especially if it contains a large number of controls or data sources.

- **Custom connectors:** You can only call custom connectors from a Power App canvas app if the connector is shared with the app.

- **Caching:** PowerApps keeps a cache of data retrieved from data sources to improve the performance of the app. However, this can lead to stale data being displayed in the app if the data source is updated.

- **URL-based navigation:** Canvas app does not support navigation through URL, which means you cannot navigate to a specific screen by specifying a URL.

- **Limited offline support:** PowerApps only supports offline mode for SharePoint and OneDrive data sources.

These limitations are subject to change as the product develops and updates. It is always good to check the official documentation for the latest information.

Solutions

In PowerApps, a solution is a container that holds a set of components, including apps, connections, and custom connectors. Solutions are used to package and distribute apps, as well as to manage and share components across multiple apps.

There are two types of solutions in PowerApps:

- **Managed solutions:** These solutions are created and managed by an administrator or a developer. Managed solutions can be exported from one environment and imported into another environment, making it easy to share and distribute components across multiple environments.

- **Unmanaged solutions:** These solutions are created and managed by individual users. Unmanaged solutions can be exported and imported, but they are only available in the environment where they were created.

When you create a new app in PowerApps, it is automatically added to a default solution, but you can also create new solutions and add apps to them as needed. Solutions can also include custom connectors and connections, which are used to connect to external data sources.

Creating a solution in PowerApps is a way to group together a set of related components, such as apps, connections, and custom connectors. Solutions can be exported and imported, making it easy to share and distribute components across multiple environments. Solutions can be managed or unmanaged, where managed solutions can be created and managed by an administrator and unmanaged solutions can be created and managed by individual users.

Import/export

You can import and export PowerApps using the PowerApps **Command Line Interface (CLI)** or the PowerApps admin center.

To import or export a PowerApp using the PowerApps CLI, you first need to install the CLI on your computer. Once the CLI is installed, you can use the following commands to import or export a PowerApp:

- To export a PowerApp, use the following command:

```
pac paa export -n <appname> -f <filename>.msapp
```

- To import a PowerApp, use the following command:

```
pac paa import -f <filename>.msapp
```

You can also export and import a PowerApp from PowerApps Portal.

To export an app from PowerApps Admin Center, follow the given steps:

1. Go to PowerApps Admin Portal.

2. Select the app you want to export.

3. Click on the "..." button at the top of the screen.

4. Click on "Export".

To import an app from PowerApps Admin Center, follow the given steps:

1. Go to PowerApps Admin Center.

2. Click on "Import" button.

3. Select the file you want to import.

4. Follow the prompts to import the app.

As for customized list forms, you can export and import the SharePoint list which the form is based on. After that, you can open the PowerApps app, open the form and then republish it to the list.

Keep in mind that when you import an app, it will overwrite any existing app with the same name. Moreover, when you import an app, the connections will be imported but they will be disconnected. You will need to reconnect the data sources after importing the app.

Figure 10.5 features PowerApps Canvas app export feature:

Figure 10.5: *PowerApps Canvas app export feature*

Canvas apps and SharePoint Lists and Libraries

As you know, SharePoint lists are a great way to store and organize data, and PowerApps provides a way to create custom forms for SharePoint lists that can be used to add, edit, and view list items.

When you create a custom form in PowerApps, you can use the various layout and control options available to create a user interface that is tailored to your specific requirements. You can use the different layout options, such as Stack, Table, Grid and Flow, to arrange the controls on the form, and you can use controls such as Text Input, Dropdown, and Checkbox to create the fields that will be used to enter and display the data in the form.

When you create a form in PowerApps, the form is linked to a specific SharePoint list, and the fields in the form are automatically mapped to the corresponding fields in the list. You can then use the various data connectors available in PowerApps to work with the data in the SharePoint list, such as the SharePoint connector, which allows you to create, read, update and delete items in a SharePoint list.

In addition to the basic form functionality, PowerApps also provides a number of advanced features that can be used to customize the form further. For example, you can use the Rules and Validation feature to specify validation rules that must be met when a form is submitted, and you can use the Power Automate connector to create workflows that are triggered by events in the form, such as when a new item is added to the list.

To create a custom form for a SharePoint list with PowerApps, you can start by selecting "**Customize forms**" option in the SharePoint list settings, or by creating a new PowerApp from the SharePoint list. Then, you can use the PowerApps Studio to design the form, and use the SharePoint connector to link it to the SharePoint list.

Figure 10.6 features PowerApps SharePoint list form customization:

Figure 10.6: *PowerApps SharePoint list form customization*

PowerApps has become increasingly popular in recent years, because it allows users to quickly and easily create custom business applications without the need for extensive programming knowledge. PowerApps is part of the Microsoft Power Platform, which also includes Flow (for automating workflows) and Power BI (for data visualization and reporting), and together, these tools provide a comprehensive platform for creating custom solutions that can be integrated with other Microsoft products such as SharePoint, Dynamics 365, and Office 365.

With PowerApps, users can create custom forms, workflows, and dashboards to automate and streamline business processes, and they can also connect to a wide range of data sources, such as SharePoint lists, SQL Server databases, and external APIs. Additionally, PowerApps can be easily integrated with other Microsoft products such as Flow, Power BI, and Power Automate, which allows users to create powerful, end-to-end solutions without having to rely on expensive, specialized software.

There are many resources available online to help you learn more about PowerApps, including the Microsoft PowerApps documentation, Microsoft Learn, and YouTube. There are also many community-contributed tutorials and videos on YouTube, which can be a great resource for learning about specific features or getting tips and tricks for working with PowerApps. Some popular YouTube channels that cover PowerApps include:

- TheCRMChamp

- PowerAppsGuy

- Pragmatic Works

- Microsoft PowerApps and Flow Community

- PowerApps and Flow Community

In addition to that, there are many other resources, blogs and websites that dedicated to PowerApps and Power Platform, that you can find helpful.

Power automate overview

Power Automate is a cloud-based service that allows users to automate and streamline business processes across a variety of applications and services. It is part of the Microsoft Power Platform, which also includes PowerApps (for creating custom business applications) and Power BI (for data visualization and reporting), and together these tools provide a comprehensive platform for creating custom solutions that can be integrated with other Microsoft products such as SharePoint, Dynamics 365, and Office 365.

Power Automate allows users to create custom workflows, or "flows," that can be triggered by a wide variety of events, such as the creation or modification of a SharePoint list item, the receipt of an email, or a button press in a PowerApps app. Once a flow is triggered, it can perform a wide variety of actions, such as sending an email, creating a task in Microsoft To Do, or updating a record in Dynamics 365. Flows can also be configured to make decisions based on the data they receive, and they can be connected to other flows to create powerful, end-to-end solutions.

One of the key benefits of Power Automate is its ability to integrate with a wide range of applications and services, both within the Microsoft ecosystem and beyond. Out of the box, Power Automate includes connectors for over 300 different services, including popular apps such as SharePoint, OneDrive, Outlook, Dynamics 365, and Twitter, as well as services such as Azure Functions, SQL Server, and Google Drive.

Additionally, Power Automate allows users to create custom connectors for APIs that are not natively supported, which means that it can be integrated with virtually any system that has an API.

Another key benefit of Power Automate is its ability to automate repetitive tasks, which can help to increase efficiency and reduce the risk of errors. For example, a flow can be configured to automatically create a task in Microsoft To Do, whenever an email is received from a specific sender, or to automatically create a SharePoint list item whenever a new file is added to a OneDrive folder. This can save users a significant amount of time and effort, and it can also help to ensure that important tasks are not forgotten.

Power Automate also allows for collaboration and delegation of tasks, as users can share flows with other users and even embed them in other applications. For example, a manager can create a flow that routes an approval request to the appropriate team members, and then have the approval status automatically updated in a SharePoint list. This way, the manager can keep track of the approval process and delegate tasks to others without having to manually send emails or follow up with team members.

Additionally, Power Automate allows for advanced reporting and monitoring of flows, as users can view run history, performance metrics, and error reports. This can help users to troubleshoot issues and optimize their flows for better performance.

Figure 10.7 features the Power Automate portal interface:

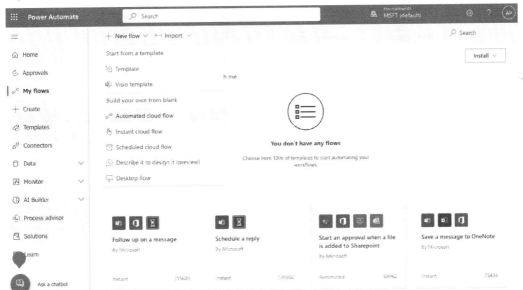

Figure 10.7: *Power Automate portal interface*

In Power Automate (formerly known as Microsoft Flow), there are several types of flows that you can create:

- **Automated flows:** These flows are triggered automatically, based on a specific event or schedule. They can be used to perform tasks such as sending an email when a new item is added to a SharePoint list or creating a new record in Dynamics 365 when a new lead is added in Dynamics 365.

- **Button flows:** These flows can be triggered manually by clicking a button in Power Automate, or via a Power Apps button control. They are useful for quick and simple tasks that do not require a lot of input from the user.

- **Scheduled flows:** These flows run on a specific schedule, such as daily, weekly, or monthly. They can be used to perform tasks such as sending a daily digest email or updating a SharePoint list on a regular basis.

- **Business process flows**: These flows are used to automate business processes and can include multiple stages and steps. They can be used to guide users through a process and ensure that all the necessary steps are completed.

- **UI flows**: These are used to automate repetitive tasks on the UI level. It can help in automating tasks such as filling out a form, login to a website, and more.

- **Event-based flows**: These flows are triggered based on events such as an HTTP request, a message on a queue, or an event from Event Grid.

All these types of flows allow you to connect to a wide range of data sources and services, known as connectors, such as SharePoint, Dynamics 365, Excel, Outlook, OneDrive, and many more. You can also create custom connectors to connect to other services that are not natively supported by Power Automate.

Here are a few examples of how Power Automate (formerly Microsoft Flow) can be used:

- **Automatically sending an email when a new item is added to a SharePoint list:** This flow can be triggered when a new item is added to a SharePoint list, and it can automatically send an email to a specific recipient or group of recipients with the details of the new item.

- **Creating a new record in Dynamics 365 when a new lead is added:** This flow can be triggered when a new lead is added to Dynamics 365, and it can automatically create a new record in Dynamics 365 for the lead.

- **Sending a daily digest email:** This flow can be scheduled to run every day at a specific time, and it can gather information from various sources (for example, SharePoint, Dynamics 365, Outlook) and send a daily digest email to a specific recipient or group of recipients.

- **Creating a new task in a To-Do list when an email is flagged:** This flow can be triggered when an email is flagged in Outlook, and it can automatically create a new task in a To-Do list with the details of the email.

Approval flows

One of the most popular use cases for Power Automate is creating approval workflows. These types of flows can be used to route documents, requests, or other items to the appropriate individuals for review and approval. For example, an approval flow could be used to route a purchase order for approval to the appropriate manager, or to route a vacation request to the employee's manager for approval.

Setting up an approval flow in Power Automate can vary depending on the specific requirements of your use case, but here is a general overview of the steps in this process:

1. Create a new flow in Power Automate and select the "Approval" template.

2. Configure the trigger for your flow. For example, you might choose to trigger the flow when a new item is added to a SharePoint list or when a form is submitted.

3. Define the approval process. You can specify the approvers, the approval type (for example, serial or parallel), and the approval outcome (for example, approved, rejected, or canceled).

4. Add any additional actions to the flow. For example, you might want to send an email notification to the requester when the approval is completed, or update a SharePoint list with the approval status.

5. Test your flow to make sure it is working as expected

6. Finally, Save and publish your flow, so that it is active and can be triggered.

When an approval flow is triggered, it will route the item to the specified approvers for review. The approvers will receive an email notification with a link to the item and the option to approve or reject it. Depending on the approval type, the flow will wait for all approvers to take action, or it will proceed to the next approver as soon as one approves or reject. Once all approvers have taken action, the flow will continue with the next steps according to the approval outcome. For example, if the item was approved, it might update a SharePoint list with the approval status or send a notification to the requester.

You can also customize the approval flow by adding or removing steps, or by making changes to the email templates, conditions and actions to match your specific requirements.

Approval flows in Power Automate can be integrated with Outlook and Teams. This allows users to receive and respond to approval requests directly from within their email or team chat, rather than having to navigate to the Power Automate website.

To set up an approval flow, you will first need to create a flow in Power Automate and choose the "Approval" action. This action will allow you to specify the approvers and the details of the approval request, such as the subject and instructions. You can also customize the response options, such as "Approve" and "Reject."

Once the flow is set up, you can trigger it when a specific event occurs, such as the creation of a new item in a SharePoint list or the receipt of a new email. The approvers will then receive an email or a Microsoft Teams notification with a link to the approval request. Once they click the link, they will be taken to a web page where they can review the details of the request and respond with their approval or rejection.

You can also set up a parallel or serial approval process, with multiple levels of approval, and also set up reminders to be sent to the approvers if they do not respond in a timely manner.

Figure 10.8 features the Power Automate approvals in Teams:

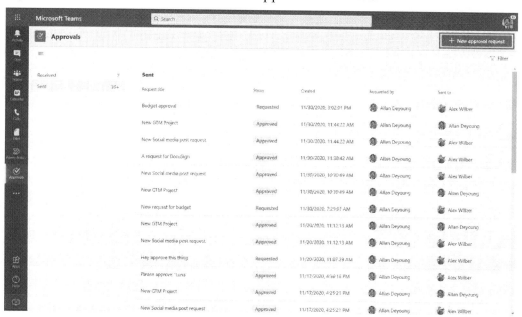

Figure 10.8: *Power Automate approvals in Teams*

Connectors

Power Automate connectors are pre-built integrations that allow you to connect to various data sources and services, such as SharePoint, OneDrive, Dynamics 365, and

Twitter. Connectors can be used to create flows that automate tasks such as creating, reading, updating, and deleting data.

There are two types of connectors in Power Automate:

- Standard
- Premium

Standard connectors are included with the platform and are available to all users. Premium connectors are additional connectors that are available for an additional cost and offer more advanced functionality.

You can also create custom connectors, which allow you to connect to any RESTful API or web service. Custom connectors can be created using the Power Automate Custom Connector feature, which allows you to import an OpenAPI (formerly known as Swagger) specification or create one manually.

To set up a custom connector, you will need to define the connector's metadata, such as its name and icon, and then create the operations that can be performed with the connector, such as creating a new item or retrieving an existing item. You can then use the custom connector in your flows just like you would use any other connector.

Additionally, you can also set up custom connectors with secured endpoints by providing authentication details such as client id and secret. This way, the custom connector can access the secured endpoints and perform the necessary operations.

Please note that creating custom connectors requires knowledge of RESTful APIs and web services, and may require additional development skills.

You can find a list of standard and premium connectors for Power Automate on the Microsoft website. The connectors are organized by category, such as "Business," "Productivity," and "Social & Media." For standard connectors, you can use them without any additional cost and you can use them with your Power Automate flows,

SharePoint Lists/Libraries and workflows

Power Automate can work with SharePoint Online lists in a variety of ways. Some examples of how you can use Power Automate with SharePoint Online lists include:

- Automatically creating new items in a list when an event occurs, such as when an email is received or when a new form is submitted.

- Automatically updating items in a list when certain conditions are met, such as when a specific field value changes or when a certain date is reached.

- Automatically sending notifications or emails when an item is added, modified, or deleted in a list.

- Automatically moving items between lists based on certain conditions, such as when a specific field value changes or when a certain date is reached.

- Automatically creating tasks in a task list based on the items in a document library.

- Automatically creating and updating items in a list based on data from external systems, such as Dynamics 365 or Salesforce.

To set up a flow that works with a SharePoint Online list, you would typically start by creating a new flow in Power Automate and choosing a trigger that corresponds to the action you want to automate. For example, if you want to create a new item in a list when an email is received, you would choose the "When a new email arrives" trigger. Then, you would add actions to the flow that correspond to the actions you want to take, such as creating a new item in a SharePoint list.

You can also use Power Automate to create custom forms that can be used to add, update, and delete items in a SharePoint list. This can be done by creating a custom Power App and connecting it to the SharePoint list using a data connector.

It is worth noting that there is a limit of 100 runs per 24 hour period for a single flow when you working with SharePoint lists. If you exceed this limit, your flow will be paused for 24 hours.

Variables

In Power Automate, variables are used to store and manipulate data within a flow. They can be used to store values, such as strings, numbers, and dates, and can also be used to store collections of data, such as arrays and tables.

To use variables in Power Automate, you first need to create them. This can be done by clicking on the "Variables" button in the flow designer, and then selecting "New variable". Once a variable is created, you can give it a name and set its initial value.

Once a variable is created, you can use it throughout your flow by referencing it by its name. For example, you could use a variable to store the value of an input from a user, and then use that variable to populate a field in a SharePoint list.

You can also manipulate variables using various actions, such as "Assign" action, which allows you to assign a value to a variable, or "Increment variable" action which increments the value of a variable by a specified amount.

There are also several advanced expressions that you can use to work with variables and perform calculations. For example, you can use the "**concat**" function to concatenate two strings together, or use the "**length**" function to determine the number of items in an array.

Additionally, you can use variables in the "**Condition**" action to control the flow based on the value of the variable. You can also use variables in the "Apply to each" action to iterate over a collection of items and perform actions for each item in the collection.

It is also worth noting that, in addition to the built-in variables, you can also create custom variables by creating a variable and giving it a name and a value, or you can use the "Initialize variable" action to initialize a variable with a specific value.

Dynamic expressions

Dynamic expressions in Power Automate (previously known as Microsoft Flow), are a way to use expressions in flow actions that can change at runtime. These expressions use functions and operators to perform calculations and manipulate data in the flow.

For example, you can use the **addDays()** function to calculate a new date by adding a specified number of days to a given date. You can also use the **concat()** function to combine multiple strings of text into one.

You can also use various operators such as **>, <, =, and, or** to perform logical operations on the data.

You can use dynamic expressions in various places throughout a flow, such as in the value of a field when creating an item in a SharePoint list, in the subject of an email, or in the query for a SharePoint search action.

When you use dynamic expressions in a flow, you will typically use the **Expression** tab when configuring an action. Here, you can enter your expression, and the flow will evaluate it at runtime.

For example, you can use a dynamic expression to calculate due date for a task by using **addDays(utcNow(), 7)** in the Due Date field, when creating an item in SharePoint list. This will set the due date 7 days from the current date.

Here is an example of a formula that you could use in the dynamic expression tab to update a "Total" field on a SharePoint list by summing the values of two other fields:

```
add(triggerBody()?['Price'], triggerBody()?['Discount'])
```

Parallel branches and sequential logic

In Power Automate, parallel branches allow you to run multiple actions at the same time, rather than waiting for one action to complete before starting the next. This can be useful in situations where you need to perform multiple tasks simultaneously and do not want the flow to wait for each one to complete before moving on to the next. To create a parallel branch, you can use the "Scope" action, and add multiple actions inside the scope.

Conditions in Power Automate allow you to make decisions based on the data or input you receive. You can use the "Condition" action to check for a specific value or expression, and then take different actions based on the outcome. For example, you can use a condition to check if a value is greater than or less than a certain number, or if a string contains a specific word. You can also use nested conditions to create more complex logic.

You can also use other logic control action like Do until, switch case, apply to each, and so on. These are building block of flow and allows you to control the flow of your data and automate your business process.

Figure 10.9 features the Power Automate view with a parallel branch at the bottom:

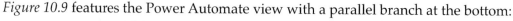
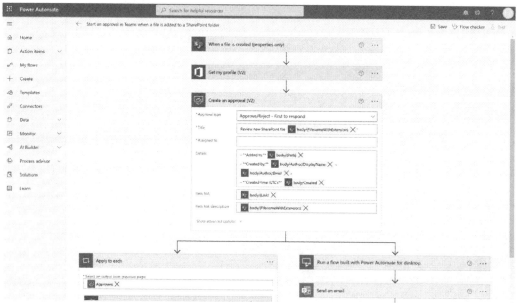

Figure 10.9: *Power Automate view with a parallel branch at the bottom*

Limitations

One of the limitations of Power Automate is the number of runs per month that are allowed on the free plan, which is 750 runs per user per month. If you exceed this limit, you will need to upgrade to a paid plan to continue using the service. Additionally, there is a limit of 30 minutes for how long a flow can run, after which it will be terminated.

There is also a limit of the number of actions that can be included in a single flow, depending on the plan you are using. For example, the free plan allows for only 2,000 actions per month, whereas the premium plan allows for unlimited actions.

Another limitation is that while Power Automate is a very powerful tool, it is not always the best fit for every use case. In some situations, it may be more appropriate to use other tools or programming languages to automate certain processes or perform specific tasks.

Flows may not run for more than 24 hours, and another limitation is that a single flow may not contain more than 50 actions. Additionally, there are limits to the number of runs and number of flows that can be created per month. Moreover, some connectors are labeled as "Premium", which means that they require a paid Power Automate plan to use them or they may have some additional limitations such as number of runs or data volume. Another thing to consider is that some actions in Power Automate require additional permissions to be set up. Additionally, some connectors may not be available for certain regions.

Power Automate does not natively support on-premises data sources. However, you can use the on-premises data gateway to securely connect to on-premises data sources such as SQL Server, SharePoint Server, and more. The gateway acts as a bridge, allowing Power Automate to access the data sources as if they were cloud-based. Keep in mind that the gateway requires an additional installation and configuration, and there are also some limitations to what data sources and actions can be performed when using the gateway.

Power Automate for a Desktop

Power Automate Desktop is a Windows application that allows you to automate repetitive tasks on your computer, such as filling out forms, entering data, and more. It uses the same flow building experience as the web-based version of Power Automate, but it can interact with desktop applications and automate tasks on your local machine. With Power Automate Desktop, you can create flows that automate tasks on your Windows computer, such as opening and manipulating files, automating data entry into a local application, and more. To use Power Automate Desktop, you need to have a Power Automate license and also need to download and install the application on your Windows computer.

Overall, Power Automate is a powerful, flexible tool that can be used to automate a wide variety of business processes across a wide range of applications and services. It can help users to increase efficiency, reduce errors, and improve collaboration, and it can also be integrated with other tools in the Microsoft Power Platform to create comprehensive, end-to-end solutions. You can find many tutorials and examples on

YouTube and other platforms to learn more about PowerApps and Power Automate, but also Microsoft official documentation and Power Automate Community are good resource to start with.

Practical tasks

It has been a lot of content and theory covered in this chapter. Let us strength your newly gained or enhanced knowledge with some practice.

Follow the given steps:

1. Login to Microsoft 365 portal using your account.

2. Once there, click on the squares in the top left corner and select Admin app.

3. From the admin center in the left navigation at the bottom, select Show All and select PowerApps Admin center from the list of available options.

We will not change any configuration as our dev subscription is pretty limited to what we can do here but let us look around. In the left navigation, you can see the option to create and manage your Environments. That is where you can set up DEV, Test and Prod environments and configure rules and policies for them.

Moreover, you have access to analytics from PowerApps admin center and can review different metrics, reports and status of the apps. Setting menu also available from this admin center. There you can set up different configurations.

Resources, Data Integration, and Policies are a few other major features in the admin center. Check them out and look at what configurations are available there.

After you have finished reviewing Admin center, let us go to the **PowerApp portal**. On the home page of Microsoft 365, select **PowerApps** from the list of available applications.

You will be redirected to the PowerApps portal. Then follow the given steps:

1. In the top ribbon, click on '**New app**' and select Canvas.

2. Choose the "**Tablet layout**" for your app.

3. Add a data source, for example, add an Excel spreadsheet to your app by clicking on "**Data sources**" in the left-side menu and choosing "**Add data source**". You can also point to any SharePoint list or library you have already created.

4. Create a gallery to display the data from your data source. To do this, click on "**Insert**" in the top menu and choose "**Gallery**". Choose the "**Vertical**" layout and the type of data source you just added.

5. Add filters to the gallery by selecting the gallery and clicking on "**Filter**" in the right-side menu. Choose the fields you want to filter on and configure the filters as needed.

6. Add a search box to allow users to search for specific data. To do this, click on "**Insert**" in the top menu and choose "**Text input**".

7. Connect the search box to the gallery by selecting the search box and clicking on "**Data**" in the right-side menu. Choose "**OnChange**" from the drop-down list and then choose the gallery you created. In the formula bar, type the following formula to connect the search box to the gallery:

```
"Filter(DataSourceName, SearchBox.Text in ColumnName)"
```

8. Customize the appearance of your app by using the right-side menu to change the background color, font, and other style options.

9. Test your app by clicking on the "**Preview**" button in the top menu.

Now let us see what the process will be to **customize SharePoint list form**. Follow the given steps:

1. Go to SharePoint app and navigate to one of the previously created sites. You can go the first one we created as it is in Modern UI and that is exactly what we need.

2. Once on the site, click on the gear icon in the top right corner and select Site Contents. Look for the List. If there are no lists there – create one.

3. When you are inside the list in the top ribbon, select **Integrate | PowerApp | Customize list forms**. Once clicked, you will be redirected to the PowerApp builder view.

4. In this case, Data connection will be already in place to our SharePoint list. Moreover, you will see that the form is not blank and existing fields are already present on the form layout. You can customize the form as you want by adding some styles or even rules to it. After you finished, you click in the right corner on Save and then Publish buttons.

5. If you go back to the list in SharePoint and click on 'New Item,' you customized form will show up from the right side. You can customize it further at any time if needed.

Follow the given steps:

1. Now let us switch to the **Power Automate** portal. In the list of available apps in Microsoft 365, select Power Automate. From the top ribbon, select '**New Flow**'. Type '**Automated Cloud Flow**'.

2. In a separate tab in SharePoint list, create fields for the status, reason for the change, and any other relevant information.

3. Go back to your Flow and select the trigger '**SharePoint – when item created or modified**'. This will automatically create a trigger in the flow that is activated whenever a new item is added to the SharePoint list or modified.

4. Add an action to the flow that will display a form to the user. The form should have two fields: a drop-down list with two options (Approved, Rejected), and a text field for a comment.

5. After the form, add an action to the flow that will update the status field of the item in the SharePoint list based on the user's input in the form. If the user selected "**Approved**" from the drop-down list, the status field should be set to "**Approved**." If the user selected "**Rejected**," the status field should be set to "**Rejected**."

6. Finally, add an action to the flow that will send an email to the user with a summary of the form data and the updated status.

Power Portals are part of the Power Platform that allow you to create external-facing websites and apps. With Power Portals, you can build and publish custom web portals to engage with customers, partners, and other external stakeholders.

Here are the steps to create a Power Portal:

1. Go to the PowerApps admin center and select the environment where you want to create the portal.

2. Click on the Power Portals option from the navigation menu on the left.

3. On the Power Portals page, click the "**Create**" button to create a new portal.

4. Fill in the required details for the portal such as its name, URL, and the theme you want to use.

5. Define the structure of the portal by adding pages, sections, and widgets. You can choose from a variety of pre-built templates and themes, or create your own custom design.

6. Use the Power Apps Studio to add forms, galleries, and custom components to your pages.

7. Set up data connections to your Dynamics 365 or Excel to retrieve information from your database and display it on your portal pages.

8. Preview your portal to test it, and make any necessary changes.

9. Publish the portal to make it available.

10. Then you can follow the URL you set and check how it looks like.

Power BI is a business intelligence and data visualization tool provided by Microsoft as part of the Power Platform. It allows users to connect to, analyze, and visualize data from a variety of sources in order to gain insights and make data-driven decisions.

To create your first report in Power BI, follow these steps:

1. Install Power BI Desktop on your machine. Simply google it and download.

2. One installed, launch it. Login with your credentials and you can see there is a Workspace called '**My Workspace'** available to you. You can go inside it or create a new one.

3. **Connect to your data:** In Power BI Desktop, you can connect to data from a wide range of sources, such as Excel spreadsheets, SQL Server databases, SharePoint lists, and more.

4. **Import your data:** Once you have connected to your data source, you can import the data into Power BI Desktop by clicking the "**Load**" button in the Home tab.

5. **Build your report:** With your data imported, you can start building your report. You can add visuals such as charts, tables, and maps to represent your data. You can also format your report and apply filters to control what data is displayed.

6. **Publish your report:** Once you have completed your report, you can publish it to the Power BI Service, where you can share it with others and access it from anywhere.

7. From the Microsoft 365 portal you can navigate to the PowerBI app and you will see your published report there.

Conclusion

In this chapter, you learned about Microsoft Power Platform and learned that it includes a set of applications. Among them are PowerApps, Power Automate and PowerBI. Each application has its own purpose and has multiple type of apps available inside it. PowerApps overall are used to build UI and forms, while Power Automate used to build workflow and automate business process. PowerBI is used when data needs visual representation and help with building reports. Each can be connected to a variety of data sources. The Power Platform provides organizations with the ability to build custom solutions quickly and efficiently, with limited technical expertise required. This allows for a more agile approach to software development and can free up IT resources for more complex tasks. Additionally, the Power Platform provides a citizen developer community, where employees can build solutions for their own business needs, leading to increased productivity and innovation.

Points to remember

- The Power Platform is a low-code platform that enables organizations to create custom apps, automate workflows, and create interactive business intelligence reports.

- It consists of three main components: Power Apps, Power Automate, and Power BI.

- Power Apps enables users to create custom apps without the need for extensive coding knowledge.

- Power Automate enables organizations to automate workflows and processes, reducing the amount of manual effort required.

- Power BI provides organizations with interactive data visualization and business intelligence capabilities.

- The Power Platform can be used by organizations of all sizes, across a wide range of industries.

- Citizen development is an important part of the Power Platform, as it allows non-technical employees to create custom solutions to meet their specific business needs.

- To get the most out of the Power Platform, it is important to have a clear understanding of the business requirements and the desired outcomes, as well as the necessary data and resources.

- The Power Platform is highly scalable and can be easily integrated with other Microsoft products and services, making it an attractive option for organizations looking to enhance their productivity and efficiency.

- There are free and Premium connectors available to use inside Power Platform apps.

Join our book's Discord space

Join the book's Discord Workspace for Latest updates, Offers, Tech happenings around the world, New Release and Sessions with the Authors:

https://discord.bpbonline.com

CHAPTER 11
Stream

> "Technology is nothing. What's important is that you have faith in people, that they're basically good and smart, and if you give them tools, they'll do wonderful things with them."
>
> *- Steve Jobs*

Introduction

All of the companies have some sort of media files and videos that should be stored somewhere and be accessible by employees. The whole idea of Stream is to provide an application integrated with Microsoft 365 suite that can store videos, where users can create their channels and publish various media files assigning metadata to them. In this chapter, that is exactly what we will cover, and review how Stream can be integrated with other Microsoft 365 apps such as SharePoint or Teams.

Structure

In this chapter, we will cover the following topics:

- Stream overview
- Search in stream
- Channel set up in Stream

- Hashtags and metadata in Stream
- Integrations from Stream to other apps

Objectives

In this chapter, we will review a video-streaming platform for corporate use from Microsoft, called Stream. It is included in business and enterprise plans and provides users with the ability to store media content and recordings. You will gain knowledge and understanding of how to use the video streaming platform for effective communication and collaboration in an organization. By learning Microsoft Stream, you will be able to streamline the way you share and access videos, making it easier to share important information and updates with your team. Additionally, you can use Microsoft Stream to securely store and share videos, and to provide access to the videos you need, when you need them, with the right people. You can also use the platform to track who is watching your videos, how long they are watching, and where they are located, which can be useful in monitoring the effectiveness of your video content.

Stream overview

Microsoft Stream is a cloud-based video streaming platform designed to help organizations create and manage videos for internal communication, collaboration, and learning. It is a part of Microsoft 365, which allows users to easily access Stream content from within other Microsoft applications such as Teams, SharePoint, and OneDrive.

Stream provides a simple and intuitive user experience, making it easy for users to upload, share, and discover videos. The platform offers a wide range of features to enhance the viewing experience, including automatic speech-to-text transcriptions, closed captions, and customizable video players. Stream also integrates with other Microsoft technologies such as Azure Media Services and AI services, which enables organizations to perform tasks such as video transcoding and object recognition.

One of the key benefits of Stream is its ability to streamline internal communication and collaboration. Stream can be used to share important announcements, conduct virtual meetings, and facilitate video-based learning. For example, organizations can use Stream to create and distribute video training content, making it easier for employees to learn and retain information.

Stream also provides a secure environment for video sharing, ensuring that videos are only accessible to authorized users. The platform allows administrators to control who can access videos and manage permissions, ensuring that sensitive content is not shared with unauthorized users. Additionally, Stream integrates with

Azure Active Directory, which allows administrators to control who can sign in to the platform and view content.

Another important aspect of Stream is its ability to help organizations make better use of their video content. The platform provides powerful search capabilities, which makes it easy for users to find the videos they need. Stream also provides analytics, which helps organizations understand how their videos are being used and how they can be improved. This data can be used to make data-driven decisions about how to improve the video content and the overall video-sharing experience.

Figure 11.1 features the Stream interface as a part of Microsoft 365:

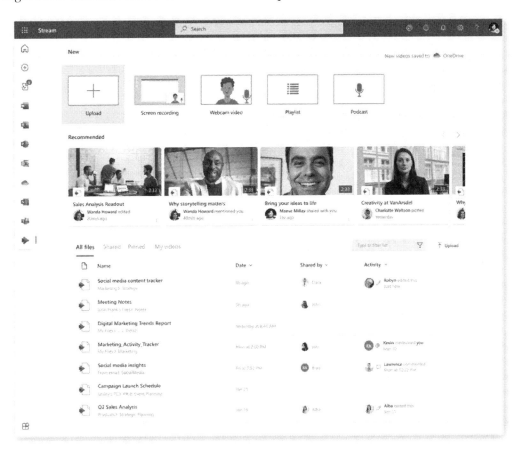

Figure 11.1: *Stream interface as a part of Microsoft 365*

In Stream, you can perform the following tasks:

- **Create a new video**: You can upload a video to Microsoft Stream by clicking the **Create** button on the top right corner of the screen and selecting **Upload video**. You can also record a new video directly in Microsoft Stream.

- **Watch videos**: To watch a video in Microsoft Stream, you can search for it using the search bar or browse through your organization's shared videos. When you find a video you would like to watch, simply click on it to open it.

- **Share videos**: You can share a video in Microsoft Stream by clicking the **Share** button located under the video player. From here, you can choose to share the video with specific people, or you can generate a link to the video that you can share with anyone.

- **Collaborate on videos**: You can collaborate on videos in Microsoft Stream by leaving comments or starting a discussion about the video. You can also tag specific moments in the video with timestamps to make it easier for others to find specific parts of the video.

- **Manage videos**: You can manage videos in Microsoft Stream by organizing them into channels, editing video details, and managing video access permissions.

- **Analyze video engagement:** You can analyze video engagement in Microsoft Stream by looking at metrics such as the number of views, the average watch time, and the number of comments and likes on a video. These metrics can help you understand how your videos are being used and which videos are most engaging to your audience.

Microsoft Stream supports various types of videos, including:

- Screen recordings
- Live events
- Presentations
- Training and educational videos
- Marketing and promotional videos
- Internal and team communication videos
- Customer-facing videos

You can upload, store, and share videos securely within your organization using Stream. The platform provides a range of tools for video management, collaboration, and distribution, such as video editing, captions and subtitles, video search, and access control. Additionally, Microsoft Stream integrates with other Microsoft 365 applications, such as Teams, SharePoint, and OneDrive, making it easier to use and manage videos across an organization.

Microsoft Stream supports a range of video file formats, including MP4, AVI, WMV, and MOV, among others. However, not all video formats may be supported, and there may be restrictions on the type and size of video files that can be uploaded and shared in Stream. Microsoft recommends using the MP4 format for videos uploaded to Stream for optimal compatibility and performance. It is best to check the supported file formats in Microsoft's official documentation to ensure that your videos will work as expected in Stream.

The size and length limitations for videos in Microsoft Stream depend on the plan that you have subscribed to. In general, the maximum file size for uploading a video to Stream is 10 GB, and the maximum length of a video is 2 hours. However, these limits may vary based on the specific plan and the level of service you have.

Microsoft Stream uses Azure Media Services for its back-end. Azure Media Services provides a scalable, highly available, and cost-effective platform for delivering, managing, and protecting audio and video content at scale. The platform provides a wide range of capabilities, including content ingestion, transcoding, and storage, as well as advanced features such as content protection and analytics. These capabilities are integrated into Microsoft Stream to provide a seamless and robust video streaming experience for users.

In Microsoft Stream, transcripts and AI-powered features are generated automatically. The service uses speech-to-text technology to create captions for videos, which can be edited and refined manually if necessary. The captions are synchronized with the video and can be searched and referenced, making it easier to find specific moments in a video. Microsoft Stream also provides an option to translate captions into other languages. This helps to make videos more accessible to a wider audience and can support cross-cultural collaboration and communication. However, it is important to note that the accuracy of the automatic transcriptions and translations will depend on the quality of the audio in the original video, and so, manual refinement may still be necessary in some cases.

Captions can be generated for both uploaded videos and live recordings in Stream. The captions are added as a separate layer on top of the video and can be turned on or off by the user.

In Microsoft Stream, you can control who can view and edit your videos by setting permissions. You can grant permissions to individuals, groups, or everyone in your organization.

The most common types of permissions are:

- **View:** Allows users to watch the video.

- **Edit:** Allows users to make changes to the video's properties, such as title, description, or access permissions.

- **Add comments:** Allows users to add comments to the video.

You can set these permissions at the video level or at the channel level, which applies the permissions to all videos in the channel.

To share a video with others, you can generate a sharing link or embed the video on a website or in another application. You can also share videos with people outside your organization by granting them guest access. It works in the same way as with files in OneDrive or SharePoint.

There are several other special features of Microsoft Stream, which are as follows:

- **Integration with other Microsoft tools:** Microsoft Stream integrates with other Microsoft tools such as Teams, SharePoint, OneDrive, and Yammer.

- **Video Embedding:** Videos can be embedded in other applications, making it easier to share videos and collaborate.

- **Search and Discovery:** Microsoft Stream provides advanced search capabilities, allowing you to find videos based on keywords, captions, tags, and more.

- **Compliance and Retention:** Stream provides several compliance and retention features to help you meet your organization's legal and regulatory requirements.

- **Video Insights:** Microsoft Stream provides analytics and insights into video engagement and usage, making it easier to measure the impact of your videos.

- **Customizable player:** Microsoft Stream provides a customizable video player that you can tailor to meet your needs.

- **Mobile access:** Microsoft Stream provides mobile access for iOS and Android devices, allowing you to watch videos on the go.

Stream is designed to support a variety of video types, including short videos. However, the appearance of the videos in Stream may differ from the appearance of videos on platforms such as Reels or Tik-Toks, if you want to use it to store a short-length videos. Stream has its own user interface and design. Whether or not videos in Stream will look like Reels, will depend on the specific features and design elements that are included in the Stream platform.

Yes, you can add music to videos in Microsoft Stream. The platform does not have a built-in video editor, but you can use other video editing tools to edit your videos and then upload the edited versions to Stream. Once the video is uploaded, you can add background music to the video using the audio feature in Stream. To add audio, you can select an audio file from your device or you can use the audio library in Stream to select from a range of royalty-free audio tracks.

The platform does not have pre-set copyrighted music that can be used in videos. If you want to add music to a video in Stream, you need to ensure that you have the rights to use the music. You can either upload a music file that you have the right to use, or use music from a third-party service that provides royalty-free music.

As for a built-in editor, Microsoft Stream does have basic video editing capabilities, such as trimming the beginning and end of a video, and adding captions, but it is not intended to be a full-featured video editing software.

Search in stream

In Microsoft Stream, the search function enables you to quickly find and locate the video content you need. The search bar is located at the top of the Microsoft Stream web page, and you can use it to search for content within your organization's Microsoft Stream site. The search results will include videos, channels, and people, and will be ranked based on relevance to your search query.

Microsoft Stream uses machine learning algorithms to understand the content of your videos and generate rich metadata, including transcriptions, closed captions, and keywords. This metadata is used to make your videos searchable, so you can easily find what you are looking for.

You can search for specific words, phrases, or topics within the video transcripts, and the search results will highlight the relevant sections of the transcript. This makes it easy to locate the specific information you need, even in long videos.

Additionally, Microsoft Stream also supports advanced search options, such as filtering by video type, date, or channel, and the ability to search for specific people or groups. These options make it easier to find the content you need, and to collaborate with others within your organization.

In Stream, the search functionality is based on the Microsoft search engine and the Azure Cognitive Services. It uses the metadata of the videos, such as the video title, description, and tags, to provide relevant results when a user searches for a specific keyword or phrase. Additionally, the search results can be filtered based on the video owner, channel, and other criteria.

The search functionality in Microsoft Stream can be customized to a certain extent by administrators. For example, you can set up synonyms, so that different terms are mapped to a common keyword, which can improve the search results. You can also set up the content type order, which determines the order in which the content types appear in the search results.

But overall, while there are some customization options available for the search functionality in Microsoft Stream, it is not possible to configure it in the same way as in SharePoint. The focus of the search in Microsoft Stream is on providing relevant results based on the metadata of the videos, rather than on configuring the search settings to a granular level.

As we discussed, Microsoft Stream uses machine learning algorithms for its search functionality. The platform uses speech-to-text technology to transcribe the audio from videos and makes this transcript searchable. This allows users to search for specific words or phrases within videos and quickly find the content they need. Additionally, Microsoft Stream also uses computer vision algorithms to analyze the content of videos, including the text in the video and the visual elements, and make this information searchable as well. By combining speech-to-text and computer vision technology, Microsoft Stream provides a robust and accurate search experience for its users.

Search functionality provides several filters to help you find the content you need. Some of the filters available in Stream include:

- **Keyword:** Allows you to search for videos based on specific keywords or phrases.

- **People:** Lets you search for videos based on the people who have contributed to them.

- **Channel:** Enables you to search for videos within specific channels, which are collections of videos organized around a common theme or subject.

- **Date:** Allows you to search for videos based on the date they were uploaded or last modified.

- **Source:** Lets you search for videos based on the source where they were uploaded, such as from a meeting or from OneDrive.

- **Language:** Enables you to search for videos in specific languages.

These filters can be combined and used in different ways to help you find the specific content you need. Additionally, you can refine your search results by sorting them based on relevance, date, or popularity, and you can also use the search bar to filter the results further by entering additional keywords or phrases.

Channel set up in Stream

In Microsoft Stream, a channel is a container for videos and related information. A channel can be used to organize videos and related information into a logical grouping, such as a department or a project. For example, you might create a channel for each department in your organization, and then add videos related to that department to that channel. You can also customize the channel settings, such as who can view or edit the channel, and what information is displayed about the channel. Additionally, you can use channels to control access to videos and related information and to monitor video usage and engagement.

The channel concept in Microsoft Stream is not the same as on YouTube. A channel in Microsoft Stream is a way to organize and categorize videos within a company or organization. It is essentially a container for videos that have a similar purpose or subject matter. For example, a company might have a channel for product demos, another channel for company-wide announcements, and another channel for training videos. With channels, it becomes easier for users to find and view relevant videos, as well as for administrators to manage the content in a structured manner. The concept of channels in Microsoft Stream is similar to that of playlists in YouTube, but the implementation and features may be different.

Access to Microsoft Stream is typically granted through an organization's Office 365 or Microsoft 365 subscription and is restricted to members of the organization. An individual user cannot create a channel in Stream without being part of an organization that has a subscription. Additionally, the organization can control who has access to create channels, and who can view or contribute content to them.

To set up a channel in Microsoft Stream, you need to follow the given steps:

1. Go to the Microsoft Stream website and sign in with your Microsoft account.
2. Click on the **Channels** tab from the navigation menu on the left.
3. Click on the **Create channel** button.
4. Enter a name for your channel and select the privacy setting for your channel (public, private, or organization).
5. Optionally, you can also add a description and header image for your channel.
6. Click the **Create** button to create your channel.

Once your channel is created, you can start uploading videos, managing your channel's privacy settings, and sharing your channel with others. To upload a video, simply click the **Upload** button, select the video file, and wait for the upload to complete. From the channel page, you can also manage the videos you have uploaded and the members of your channel.

Hashtags and metadata in Stream

Hashtags and metadata are important features in Microsoft Stream that help to organize and categorize videos within the platform.

Hashtags are used to categorize and make videos easily searchable by adding relevant keywords as tags. Hashtags work similarly to those in social media platforms, allowing users to find and discover videos that are relevant to their interests. In Stream, hashtags can be added to the title or description of a video, making it easier for others to find it when searching for specific topics or keywords.

Metadata refers to the information that is associated with a video, such as its title, description, and hashtags. In Stream, metadata can be used to provide additional context and information about a video, making it easier for others to understand its purpose and content. This information can be edited and updated by the video owner or by an administrator with the appropriate permissions.

By effectively utilizing hashtags and metadata, you can ensure that videos are easily discoverable and accessible to the right audience, making it easier to share important information and knowledge within the company.

You can create custom columns to add metadata to videos. This can be useful for organizing your videos and making them easier to search and categorize. To create custom columns, you need to be an administrator of your organization's Stream account. You can then go to the **Settings** section and create a new column under the **Metadata** tab. You can choose the type of data you want to collect for each column, such as text, number, or date. Once you have created the columns, you can add metadata to your videos by editing the video's properties and filling in the relevant columns.

Metadata columns can be customized for the entire tenant or organization, and the same metadata columns will apply to all channels within the tenant. However, it is possible to create different metadata fields for different libraries, which can be used to categorize videos within a channel. These fields can be used for filtering, searching, and organizing videos, and thus, it is possible to have different metadata fields for different channels, to some extent. However, this would require customizing the metadata fields for each library, which may be time-consuming and difficult to manage.

You can use any type of hashtags in Microsoft Stream. However, the hashtags you use should be relevant and descriptive to the video content. This helps users to search for specific content and makes it easier to categorize and organize videos within the platform. You can add hashtags to a video by including them in the video's title, description, or tags.

Integrations from Stream to other apps

Microsoft Stream can be integrated with various other apps and services within the Microsoft ecosystem. This integration allows for seamless collaboration and data sharing between Stream and other apps. Some examples of integrations that are possible with Microsoft Stream include next apps, which are described as follows:

- **Integration with Microsoft Teams:** Microsoft Stream videos can be embedded and played directly within a Teams meeting or chat.

- **Integration with SharePoint:** Microsoft Stream videos can be embedded and played directly within a SharePoint page.

- **Integration with Power Apps:** Microsoft Stream videos can be used as data sources in Power Apps, allowing for creation of custom apps that incorporate video content.

- **Integration with Power Automate:** Automated workflows can be created in Power Automate that trigger based on events in Microsoft Stream, such as a new video being uploaded or a video being deleted.

These integrations can help organizations to streamline their workflows and improve collaboration between teams.

Microsoft Teams is integrated with Microsoft Stream, making it easier for users to share and access videos within their Teams environment. The integration allows users to upload videos directly to Stream from Teams, and to share videos with Teams channels. Additionally, users can view, search, and share Stream videos within Teams, and can also access video content directly from the Teams video library. The integration of Teams and Stream enhances video collaboration and makes it easier for teams to work together on projects and share information. To integrate Teams and Stream, you will need to have both services set up in your organization and be a member of a team in Teams. The integration can be set up in the Teams settings and is typically done by an administrator. Once set up, users will be able to access Stream videos and content directly from Teams.

As for SharePoint, there is a separate web part for it that can be used to integrate Microsoft Stream with SharePoint. This web part allows you to easily embed videos from Microsoft Stream into a SharePoint page. Additionally, the web part provides access to the video metadata and allows users to search for videos directly from the SharePoint page. The integration between Microsoft Stream and SharePoint can help organizations improve collaboration and communication by making it easier to share and access video content.

Microsoft Stream can be integrated with external apps. Microsoft provides APIs and webhooks that allow developers to programmatically interact with Stream and integrate it into other applications. Some examples of integration include automatically posting new videos to Stream from an external system, displaying Stream videos in other websites, or automatically creating transcripts of Stream videos and storing them in another system. The specific steps to integrate Microsoft Stream with external apps will depend on the specific requirements and use case.

In conclusion, Microsoft Stream is a powerful platform that can help organizations enhance their internal communication, collaboration, and learning. The platform offers a simple and intuitive user experience, powerful features to enhance the viewing experience, and robust security features to ensure that videos are only accessible to authorized users. Additionally, Stream provides organizations with the ability to make better use of their video content, allowing them to understand how their videos are being used and make data-driven decisions about how to improve their video content and the overall video-sharing experience.

Figure 11.2 features Stream webpart in SharePoint online:

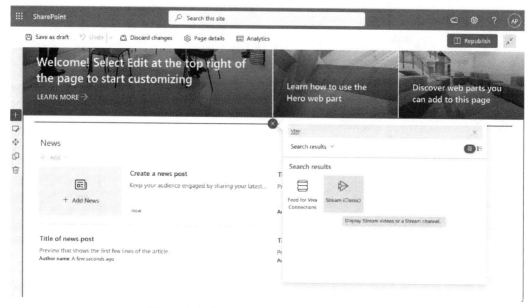

Figure 11.2: *Stream webpart in SharePoint online*

Practical tasks

It is time to strengthen your newly gained or enhanced knowledge, with some practice. Let us now follow the given steps:

1. Log in to Microsoft 365 Using your account.

2. From the list of available applications, select **Stream**.

3. From there, you will see an option to create new recording. If you have any existing video, you can click on **Upload** button to upload them too. Please note that all recordings that you will have from the Microsoft Teams meeting will be stored in SharePoint, and Stream will be used as a player.

Figure 11.3 features new recording and upload buttons in Stream:

Figure 11.3: *New recording and upload buttons in Stream*

4. Feel free to discover both options and create one recording on your own. You can upload any .mp4 or other media files too.

5. Once uploaded or created, you will see settings for recording (make sure to allow pop-up window in your browser as by default, it will be blocked).

Figure 11.4 features video settings and configuration on the right and metadata at the bottom of the video:

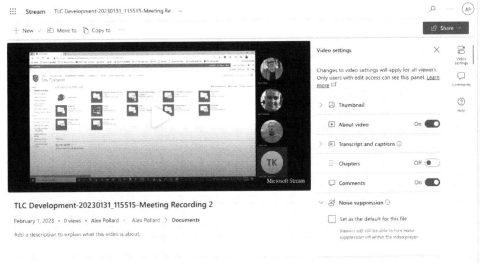

Figure 11.4: *Video settings and configuration on the right and metadata at the bottom of the video*

6. From the top right corner, if you click on the right side of **Share** button, you will see options to set up permissions, share and embed code for this video.

Some of the features are cut in our version of the M365 subscription as we are using the Dev version. So we will not be able to set up a channel or do some other things – these options are available in Stream (Classic). In Dev instance, we have Stream (on SharePoint).

Overall, to set up a channel in Stream, you would need to:

1. Click on the **Channels** option on the left side of the screen.

2. Click on the **Create channel** button in the top right of the screen.

3. Give your channel a name, and optionally, add a description and image.

4. Choose whether you want your channel to be public or private.

5. Choose the members who will have access to the channel. You can add members by email address, or you can add an entire group of people at once.

6. Click the **Create** button to create the channel.

Once you have created a channel, you can upload videos, add metadata and hashtags, and start sharing your videos with others. You can also manage your channel's settings and members, and customize your channel with a logo, background image, and custom color scheme.

Figure 11.5 features the Stream classic view and Create Channel option:

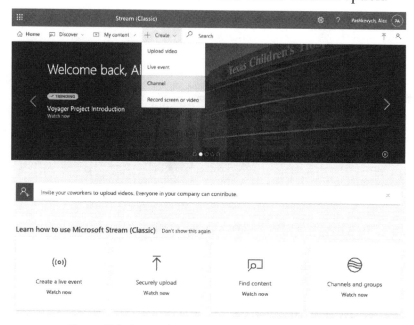

Figure 11.5: *Stream classic view and Create Channel option*

To integrate some of the videos or the entire channel with MS Teams, you would need to go to the Teams. It can be web or desktop client, either will work.

1. Go to any of the teams you have there and in the top right, select plus sign.

2. It will show the pop-up to add application to the channel.

3. In Search, type **Stream**.

Figure 11.6 features adding Stream to a Teams channel:

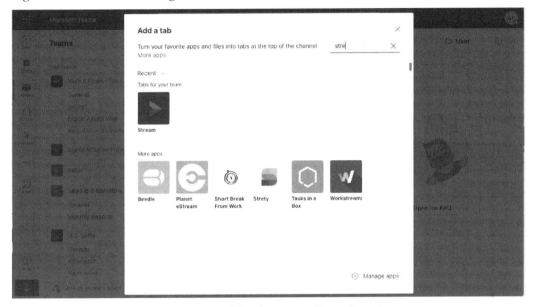

Figure 11.6*: Adding Stream to a Teams channel*

From there, you can provide a name of the channel or set the URL to a specific video.

Once done, this channel or video will be visible on your channel in teams.

Conclusion

In this chapter, you learned about the Microsoft Stream video streaming platform that allows organizations to share, upload, and manage videos in one central location. With features such as automatic transcription, automatic caption generation, and AI-powered video search, Stream makes it easy to find and view relevant video content. Additionally, the platform supports sharing and collaboration through the integration with Microsoft Teams and SharePoint, and allows for customization of metadata and hashtags to help categorize and search for videos. Overall, Microsoft Stream offers a comprehensive and integrated solution for organizations looking to manage and share video content.

Points to remember

- Microsoft Stream is a video streaming platform that allows you to upload, view, and share videos within your organization.

- It supports a variety of video formats and has certain size and length limitations.

- Stream has built-in AI capabilities, such as automatic captions and search, that can help make it easier to manage and access your videos.

- You can organize your videos by creating channels and adding metadata and hashtags to help with discovery and organization.

- Microsoft Stream integrates with other Microsoft products, such as Teams and SharePoint, and can be embedded in external applications as well.

- Permission and sharing can be managed through the platform, giving you control over who can access and view your videos.

Join our book's Discord space

Join the book's Discord Workspace for Latest updates, Offers, Tech happenings around the world, New Release and Sessions with the Authors:

https://discord.bpbonline.com

CHAPTER 12
PowerApps

> "Low-code platforms are transforming the way businesses create and deploy software applications, making it easier for organizations of all sizes to automate processes and meet the demands of a digital-first world."
>
> *- John Wilson*

Introduction

In this chapter, we will dive deeper into the topic of PowerApps. As you already know, there are multiple different versions of PowerApps: Canvas and Model Driven. Information can be stored in SharePoint, Dataverse, SQL or even in Excel. We will review how to build a simple Canvas and Model Driven app. You will learn how to connect your app to the proper data source, how to operate and manipulate the data from there and add various validations to the form.

Structure

In this chapter, we will cover the following topics:

- Canvas PowerApps
- Model Driven PowerApps

- Connections in PowerApps (Datasources)

- Dataverse

- Validations in PowerApps

- View and Formulas

Objectives

To become proficient in creating custom business applications that solve specific business problems, let us review more deep examples of the use of the Power Platform. This includes gaining a solid understanding of the differences and capabilities between Model-Driven and Canvas app development, as well as understanding how to use PowerApps to access, manage, and manipulate data stored in Dataverse. Additionally, you should become familiar with advanced concepts such as customizing the user interface, integrating with external data sources, creating and managing custom data entities, and automating business processes. Automation can be done within the form itself without using Power Automate. By the end of this learning journey, you should be able to design, develop, and deploy custom PowerApps to support business operations and processes, making the most of the Power Platform's capabilities and features.

Canvas PowerApps

To refresh our memory, let us have an overview of the Canvas apps definition.

Canvas PowerApps are a type of low-code application platform that allow users to quickly and easily create custom business applications without writing any code. They are designed to be used by a wide range of users, including business users, developers, citizen developers, and IT professionals.

The main advantage of Canvas PowerApps is their ease of use and quick time-to-market. With a drag-and-drop interface, you can quickly build custom applications that meet their specific needs, without having to rely on expensive developers or IT resources.

Canvas PowerApps are also highly customizable, allowing you to configure the look and feel of the application to match your brand and style. Additionally, apps can be integrated with a wide range of data sources, including cloud services, databases, and SharePoint, allowing you to easily access and manage data within the application.

Another advantage of Canvas PowerApps is the ability to run on a variety of platforms, including mobile devices and web browsers, making them accessible from anywhere and on any device. Additionally, they can be easily shared and collaborated on, allowing teams to work together to create and refine applications.

Canvas Power Apps offer a number of advantages to developers too, and some of them are as follows:

- **Rapid development:** Canvas Power Apps provide a low-code platform that enables developers to create custom apps quickly and easily, without having to write complex code. This can speed up the development process and allow developers to focus on more strategic projects.

- **Easy to use:** The drag-and-drop interface of Canvas Power Apps makes it easy for developers to create and edit apps, even if they do not have a lot of experience with coding. This makes it possible for developers to create custom apps without having to spend a lot of time learning how to code.

- **Flexibility:** Canvas Power Apps are highly flexible, allowing developers to customize the look and feel of their apps to match the needs of their users. This makes it possible for developers to create apps that are tailored to specific business needs and requirements.

- **Integration with other tools:** Canvas Power Apps can be integrated with other Microsoft tools and services, such as SharePoint, Teams, and Dynamics 365, providing developers with a seamless workflow and reducing the time and effort required to switch between different tools.

- **Easy deployment:** Canvas Power Apps can be deployed to the cloud, making it easy for developers to share their apps with others and ensure that they are always up-to-date. This makes it possible for developers to create and deploy custom apps with minimal effort, even if they do not have access to complex IT infrastructure.

Figure 12.1 features the PowerApp builder view in the browser:

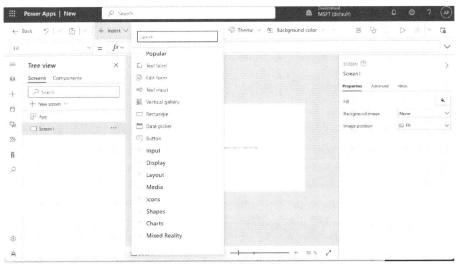

Figure 12.1: *PowerApp builder view in the browser*

Canvas PowerApps and model-driven apps both have different advantages, and the choice between the two will depend on the specific needs of the organization and the nature of the app being developed.

Canvas PowerApps offer more flexibility in design, as they are built on a blank canvas and the developer has full control over the user interface. Canvas apps also allow developers to build custom forms, use custom code and business logic, and create rich interactive experiences. They are ideal for creating simple or ad-hoc apps that do not require a lot of data integration, or for creating custom UI for existing data sources.

Model-driven apps, on the other hand, are designed for more complex app scenarios and have built-in features for data management, security, and business process automation. They are typically faster to develop, as they use pre-built templates and entities, and provide more robust data management capabilities. Model-driven apps are ideal for building apps that have complex business processes, require integration with other systems, or have a large amount of data that needs to be managed.

In summary, canvas PowerApps are best for quick, simple apps with a custom UI, while model-driven apps are best for more complex apps with built-in data management and process automation capabilities that rely on the data structure.

In canvas PowerApps, formulas (expressions) are used to perform calculations and define relationships between data sources, screens, controls, and variables. Formulas are written in a simple language called the "formula language" that is similar to Excel formulas.

The main advantage of using formulas in canvas PowerApps is that they allow developers to perform complex calculations and automate tasks without having to write custom code. For example, formulas can be used to calculate the sum of a column in a data source, or to determine the number of days between two dates.

Another advantage is that formulas in canvas PowerApps are flexible and can be easily changed or updated. This allows developers to quickly respond to changing requirements or business needs, without having to completely rewrite the code. Additionally, formulas can be used to perform complex validations and data transformations, making it easier for developers to ensure that data entered into the app is accurate and consistent.

To learn about expressions and formulas in Canvas PowerApps, a good starting point is the official Microsoft documentation. This provides detailed information on the syntax and usage of formulas in Canvas PowerApps, as well as examples and tutorials to help you get started. Additionally, there are many online resources, tutorials, and forums where you can find help and guidance on using formulas in Canvas PowerApps, including blogs, videos, and community groups. You can also take advantage of online courses or attend in-person training classes to gain hands-on experience with Canvas PowerApps and its features, including formulas and expressions.

There are many third-party solutions available for PowerApps that can be used to extend its capabilities and add new features. For example, some popular third-party solutions for PowerApps include the following:

- **Plumsail actions:** A set of more than 80 connectors for PowerApps that allow you to perform a variety of tasks, such as sending emails, working with SharePoint and OneDrive, and automating workflow processes.

- **CDM+ PowerApps connector**: A connector that enables PowerApps to read and write data directly to CDM+ databases, allowing you to create custom apps that work with your organization's data.

- **PowerApps Custom Connectors**: A set of connectors that enable you to connect to custom APIs and services, allowing you to add new data sources and functionality to your apps.

There are many examples of customized canvas apps, including apps for inventory management, employee training, and customer feedback. You can find many case studies and examples of customized canvas apps on the Microsoft PowerApps website, as well as in the PowerApps community forums.

To find a custom solution for PowerApps, follow the given steps:

1. Visit the **Power Apps Component Framework (PCF)** gallery on the Microsoft Power Apps website. The PCF gallery contains a growing collection of custom controls and components created by both Microsoft and the Power Apps community.

2. Search for the component you need, either by typing a keyword into the search bar or by browsing the categories. You can sort the results by relevance, popularity, or creation date.

3. Preview the component to see a description of its features and capabilities, as well as screenshots or videos that demonstrate how it works.

4. If you like what you see, click the **Get it now** button to download the component to your local machine.

5. Once you have the component file, open Power Apps Studio and go to the **Components** section, of the left-side menu.

6. Click the **Import package** button, select the component file you just downloaded, and click **Import**. The component will now be available for you to add to your app.

7. To use the component in your app, simply drag it from the Components section of the left-side menu onto the canvas. You can then customize its appearance and behavior using the Properties panel on the right-side of the screen.

There is a growing number of third-party solutions available for PowerApps, ranging from custom controls and components, to full-fledged apps that you can import into your own environment. Some examples of customized apps include CRM systems, expense management systems, and inventory management systems. These apps can be a great way to get started with PowerApps and see what is possible with this low-code platform.

Figure 12.2 features solutions view in the PowerApps portal:

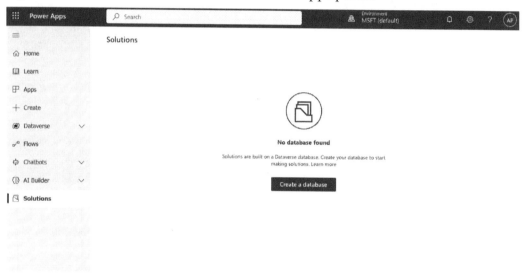

Figure 12.2: *Solutions view in the PowerApps portal*

Model Driven PowerApps

Model-driven apps in PowerApps are a type of application that provides a more traditional, form-based interface for business users. They are built on top of the Common Data Service and Dataverse, which is a secure and scalable data platform that allows you to manage business data and relationships. Model-driven apps are typically used to automate business processes and workflows, such as expense approvals, customer service requests, and project management.

Model-driven apps are designed to be easy to use and customize, with a drag-and-drop interface that makes it simple to create and manage forms, views, and dashboards. They also provide built-in security, with role-based access control that allows you to manage who can access and make changes to the data. Additionally, model-driven apps can be integrated with other Microsoft Power Platform services and technologies, such as Power Automate and Power BI, to provide a comprehensive solution for business automation and data visualization.

Figure 12.3 features an example of a model-driven PowerApp:

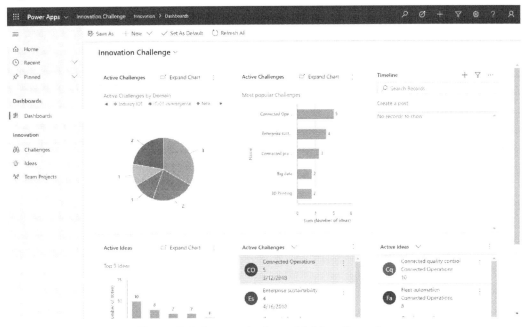

Figure 12.3: *An example of a model-driven PowerApp*

Model-driven apps can be customized, but the extent of customization may be different compared to canvas apps. Model-driven apps provide a more structured way to build and manage your app, and typically have a more limited set of customization options. For example, you can configure the behavior and appearance of forms, views, and dashboards, but you may not have the same level of control over the overall layout and user experience as you would with a canvas app. However, model-driven apps can also provide some advantages over canvas apps, such as more advanced data management capabilities, and improved performance and scalability in some cases. Whether you choose to build a canvas app or a model-driven app, will depend on the specific requirements of your project and your preferred development style.

Model-driven apps have a more structured approach to customizing, compared to canvas apps, which have more flexibility. Customizations to model-driven apps typically involve modifying the metadata of entities, such as adding or modifying fields, creating relationships between entities, customizing forms and views, and so on. Custom logic can be added using JavaScript, but the scope of customizations is more limited compared to canvas apps.

Some examples of customizations that can be done in a model-driven app include the following:

- **Customizing forms:** You can modify the layout and add new fields to forms to meet your business requirements.

- **Customizing views:** You can modify the columns that are displayed in a view, change the order in which they are displayed, and add new views.

- **Customizing business processes:** You can create and modify business processes, such as workflows, to automate business processes.

- **Adding custom logic:** You can add custom JavaScript code to extend the functionality of a model-driven app.

Examples of customizations that cannot be done in a model-driven app without writing custom code include the following:

- **More complex UI designs**: Model-driven apps have a more structured and limited UI design compared to canvas apps.

- **Custom data sources**: Model-driven apps are limited to using the data sources provided by the Common Data Service for Apps. Custom data sources cannot be easily added without writing custom code.

In a model-driven app, the layout is determined by the metadata of the entity. The metadata includes information about the fields, forms, views, and relationships of the entity. It is all usually stored in Dataverse (which we will learn about later in this chapter). The metadata is used to generate a default user interface for the entity, but you can also customize the layout of the user interface by adding custom elements, rearranging fields, and modifying form properties. The metadata also defines the behavior of the entity, such as the validation rules, calculated fields, and workflows.

You can insert a canvas app within a model-driven app on a separate form or provide a link to canvas app screens within the model driven one. However, you cannot insert the Model Driven app inside the Canvas one. Canvas apps and model-driven apps are two distinct types of applications within Power Apps, each with its own unique set of capabilities, strengths, and limitations. The choice between a canvas app and a model-driven app depends on the specific requirements of your solution and the type of user experience you want to provide.

The data model in a model-driven app refers to the structure of the data that is used by the app. It typically includes entities, relationships, and fields that define the data and how it is organized. The data model forms the basis for creating views, forms, and other components of the app, and is used to manage and manipulate the data within the app. It is a key aspect of model-driven apps, as it provides a clear and consistent structure for the data that is used by the app, and enables the app to work with the data in a consistent and intuitive way.

To put it in more simple words, it is all up to the structure of your lists/tables and columns inside them. The layout will be generated automatically based on that structure. Moreover, it can be customized only to a certain extent like setting a color for a header or so on.

Connections in PowerApps (Datasources)

In PowerApps, a connection is a link to a data source, such as a database, web API, or cloud service. A data source is a collection of information that can be used to populate the fields in an app, including the data that the app displays and the data that users can add, modify, or delete.

You can create a connection in PowerApps to access a data source and bring the data into your app. There are several types of data sources that you can connect to, including the following:

- **Dataverse:** A cloud-based data platform that enables users to store, manage, and share data within their organization.

- **SharePoint:** A web-based platform that enables users to store, organize, and share information in a collaborative environment.

- **OneDrive:** A cloud-based file storage and sharing platform.

- **SQL Server:** A relational database management system.

- **Excel:** A spreadsheet application.

By connecting to a data source, you can access and display data in your app, and you can also use the data to perform actions, such as sending an email, creating a record, or updating a database.

There are both free and premium connectors available in PowerApps. Free connectors are basic and are available for common data sources such as Excel, OneDrive, and SharePoint. Premium connectors provide more advanced functionality and access to a wider range of data sources, such as Salesforce, Dynamics 365, and Common Data Service. These premium connectors require a separate subscription or license.

The cost of a premium connector in PowerApps depends on the specific connector and the licensing model of the service that the connector integrates with. There are different pricing models for premium connectors, including *per-user, per-app,* or *per-transaction.*

Generally, a premium connector provides more advanced or premium features compared to a free connector, such as increased limits on data retrieval or manipulation, or additional functionality not available in a free connector. To use a premium connector, you will typically need to purchase a license or subscription to the service that the connector integrates with, and configure your PowerApps environment to use the premium connector.

You also can set up custom connectors to connect to any data source you want in PowerApps. PowerApps supports connecting to a wide range of data sources, including cloud-based sources such as Microsoft 365 and Salesforce, as well as on-premises sources like SQL Server and SharePoint. To set up a custom connector, you will need to use the PowerApps Connectors API. With the API, you can define the connection properties, authentication method, and operations that your connector will support. Once you have defined your connector, you can use it in your PowerApps to access data from your data source.

The cost of using a custom connector in PowerApps depends on the specific connector and its usage. Some custom connectors may be available for free, while others may require a subscription or license fee. The fees for using a custom connector will vary depending on the complexity and capabilities of the connector, as well as the level of support provided. If you are interested in using a specific custom connector, it is recommended to check with the vendor or service provider for more information on their pricing and usage model. There you can also find out about their APIs and webhooks available.

A *data gateway* is a component that enables secure, bi-directional communication between PowerApps and on-premises data sources. The data gateway acts as a bridge, allowing you to access and use your on-premises data sources in PowerApps without having to expose your data to the internet. A data gateway can be installed on a computer within your organization's network and is used to connect to a variety of data sources, including SQL Server, Oracle, and other databases, as well as file shares and other sources. The data gateway is used to securely transfer data from on-premises data sources to PowerApps and vice versa. The cost of a data gateway depends on the plan you choose, with options ranging from free to premium. The data gateway for on-premises connections is available for download from the Microsoft website.

PowerApps provides APIs that allow you to call your PowerApp from another app. The APIs allow you to access and interact with the data and functionality of your PowerApp. With these APIs, you can automate processes, integrate your PowerApp with other systems, and build custom experiences for your users. The PowerApps APIs are REST-based and can be accessed from any programming language or platform that supports HTTP requests.

The API provides a RESTful interface for programmatically creating, retrieving, updating, and deleting data in PowerApps. The available queries and operations for the API are documented in the PowerApps API reference. To use the API, you will need to have a valid authentication token and be familiar with making HTTP requests and parsing JSON responses. You can use tools such as Postman or curl to test and debug your API calls, or you can use a library in your programming language of choice to make the API calls programmatically. The specific steps for using the API will depend on your specific use case and the tools and technologies you are using.

Please note that there are some data sources that are not available in PowerApps. The list of available data sources depends on the version of PowerApps you are using and the plan you have subscribed to. Some of the data sources that are not available in PowerApps include databases hosted on-premises, custom APIs, and some cloud-based data sources that require custom authentication. Before using a particular data source in PowerApps, it is a good idea to check the documentation to see if it is supported.

To set up a connection in PowerApps, you need to add a data source to your app. You can do this by clicking on the **Connections** button in the left-side menu of the PowerApps studio and then selecting **Add a connection**. You can then select from a list of built-in data sources, such as Excel, SharePoint, or OneDrive, or you can add a custom connection by selecting **Custom connector** and entering the connection details manually. Once you have added a connection, you can use it in your app by selecting it as the data source for a control or by using it in a formula. The specific steps you need to follow to set up a connection will depend on the type of data source you are connecting to and the connection details that are required.

Figure 12.4 features some of the data connectors available in PowerApps (Canvas):

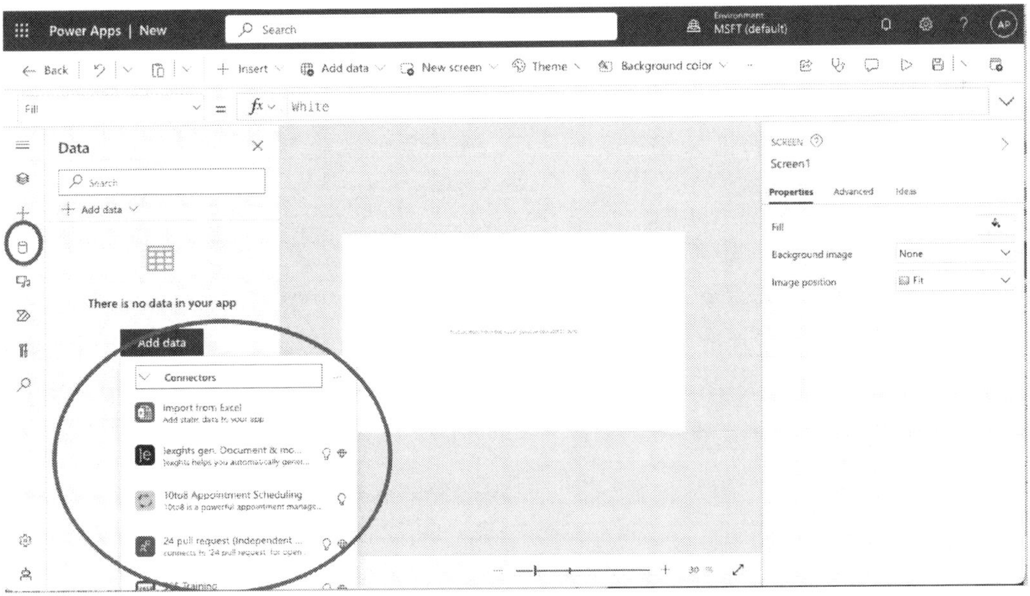

Figure 12.4: *Some of the data connectors available in PowerApps (Canvas)*

In PowerApps, the refresh of data from the data source is typically done automatically. However, you have the option to refresh the data manually if needed. To refresh the data, you can go to the **Home** tab in the PowerApps Studio, and then click the **Refresh** button. The data from the connected data source will be updated in the app, and any changes will be reflected in the app's user interface.

The same connectors are generally available in both canvas and model-driven apps in PowerApps. However, the availability of specific connectors may vary based on the platform and the specific requirements of the app. It is best to check the PowerApps documentation or the Microsoft Power Platform documentation to see which connectors are available and what limitations there may be for a specific connector in either a canvas or model-driven app.

Dataverse

Dataverse (previously known as Common Data Service) is a data platform that provides a centralized repository for managing and sharing data within organizations. It is a part of the Power Platform offered by Microsoft. Dataverse enables users to store, manage, and share data from a variety of sources, including PowerApps, Dynamics 365, and Excel, in a secure and governed manner. Dataverse provides data management capabilities, such as data modeling, data relationships, and data validation, which can be used to build custom business applications with PowerApps. The platform provides a low-code, no-code environment for building and deploying business applications, making it easy for organizations to quickly develop custom applications that meet their specific business requirements.

It is a cloud-based database service provided as part of Power Apps. It allows you to store and manage data for use in Power Apps and other services. Dataverse provides a data model that can be customized to fit the needs of your organization, as well as a set of tools for managing the data stored in the database, including data import/export, data management, and data security.

Figure 12.5 features Dataverse view from the PowerApps portal:

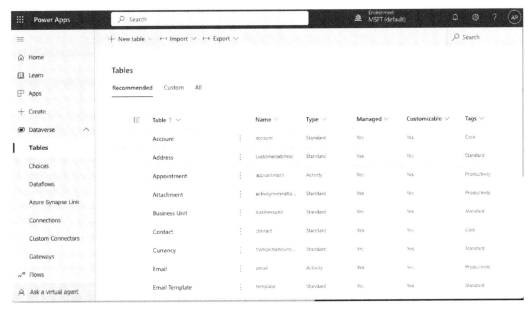

Figure 12.5: Dataverse view from the PowerApps portal

You can define the data structure of your app using entities, fields, and relationships, and then use that data structure to build custom forms, views, and reports. You can also use Power Apps to create custom flows that automate business processes, and to extend the capabilities of your app with custom code, if necessary. To get started with Dataverse, you need to have a Power Apps Plan 1 or 2 subscriptions.

Basically, Dataverse is just a set of tables. You can create new tables or modify those that are available out of the box. You can create and modify columns and build structures based on your needs.

Figure 12.6 features Dataverse table view in the PowerApp portal:

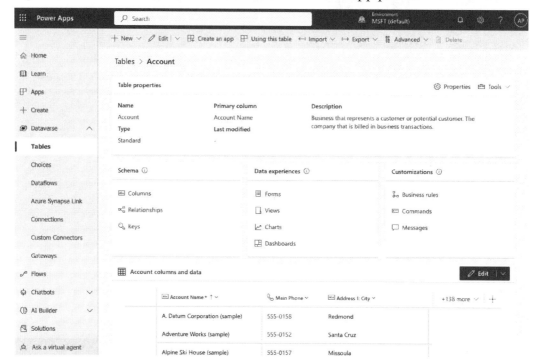

Figure 12.6: *Dataverse table view in the PowerApp portal*

To start working with Dataverse, you should have a basic understanding of how databases work, including concepts such as entities, fields, relationships, and data types. Additionally, you should be familiar with the basic structure of PowerApps and how to create and use data sources within the platform.

Once you have this foundational knowledge, you can start learning about Dataverse by exploring its features, such as its data management capabilities, data modeling tools, and API. This may involve reading the Dataverse documentation, exploring tutorials and examples, or working through hands-on exercises to gain practical experience.

As you continue to learn and work with Dataverse, you may also want to familiarize yourself with additional features and capabilities, such as custom connectors (already briefly discussed previously), data integration and migration tools, and advanced security and access controls.

Dataverse and SharePoint are different technologies that can be used for different purposes. SharePoint is a web-based collaboration and document management platform, while Dataverse is a low-code platform for building and extending applications. Dataverse provides a rich data model, with entities, relationships, and fields, which can be used to build and extend applications, while SharePoint provides a document management system, team collaboration sites, and other features.

When deciding between using Dataverse and SharePoint, to store your data, it is important to consider the specific needs of your project and organization, and the type of application you are trying to build. If you are looking to build an app that can access the data stored in SharePoint already or retrieve information from documents, then SharePoint may be a better option. However, if you are looking to build a custom application with a rich data model, Dataverse may be a better choice.

Dataverse provides several advantages over SharePoint for storing data, and they are as follows:

- **Scalability:** Dataverse is designed to scale and support large amounts of data, making it a good choice for organizations with significant data storage needs.

- **Data Structure:** Dataverse allows for a more flexible and scalable data structure, making it easier to manage and analyze large amounts of data.

- **Data Management:** Dataverse provides a central place to manage and govern data, ensuring that all data is stored, managed, and governed consistently.

- **Performance:** Dataverse is optimized for performance, with fast data retrieval and search capabilities. Applications using SharePoint to store data might luck performance comparing to those using Dataverse.

- **Security:** Dataverse provides robust security features, including role-based access control, data protection, and privacy controls.

It is especially good to use Dataverse when you work with large sets of items and data (more than 5,000 items). SharePoint has a limitation on data retrieval and passing it over to PowerApps. So, if your application needs to have a Dashboard or some large view, it is better to choose Dataverse to store your data.

Validations in PowerApps

Validations in PowerApps are a set of rules and conditions that are used to ensure that the data entered into an app meets certain criteria. Validations can be used to enforce specific business rules, such as ensuring that a date entered into a form is within a certain range, or that a field is required before a form can be submitted. Validations can be implemented in both canvas apps and model-driven apps, and can be set up using a variety of tools and techniques, including formulas, custom code, and conditional formatting. The goal of validations is to improve the accuracy and quality of the data entered into an app, and to ensure that the app is being used in the way that it was intended.

Here are some additional examples of validations that can be implemented in PowerApps:

- **Field-level validation**: You can validate individual fields to ensure that they contain the required information before submitting the form. For example, you can validate that an email address field is a valid email format.

- **Record-level validation**: You can validate the entire record to ensure that it contains all required information before saving it. For example, you can validate that a customer record contains a valid email address and phone number.

- **Business rule validation**: You can enforce business rules using validations. For example, you can validate that a discount percentage does not exceed a certain limit, or that a date is within a specified range.

- **Cross-field validation**: You can validate the relationship between different fields in a record. For example, you can validate that the end date of an event is after the start date.

- **Dependent field validation**: You can validate fields based on the values of other fields in the same record. For example, you can validate that a payment method is selected only if the payment amount is greater than zero.

To implement a validation in PowerApps, you can use formulas or custom JavaScript code (packaged into a solution) to define the conditions that must be met for a user-entered value to be considered valid. For example, you can use a formula to check if a value falls within a certain range or if it matches a specific pattern. You can then display an error message or take other actions if the validation fails. The specific steps to implement a validation will vary depending on the type of validation you want to implement, but typically, you will use the following general steps:

1. Determine the type of validation you want to implement.

2. Define the conditions that must be met for the validation to pass. This can be done using a formula or custom JavaScript code.

3. Apply the validation to the control or set of controls where the user will enter data. You can do this using the Properties panel in the PowerApps Studio or using code.

4. Handle the case where the validation fails. You can display an error message, prevent the user from submitting the form, or take other actions.

The exact steps will depend on the specifics of your validation and the version of PowerApps you are using.

To add validation to a field in a PowerApp, you can use the **Validate** function. Here is an example:

1. Create a new blank app and add a new screen.

2. Add a text input control to the screen and give it a name, such as **EmailAddress**.

3. Add a label control under the text input control, to display a validation message.

4. In the label control, set the **Text** property to (in the function area at the top):

```
If( !IsMatch(EmailAddress.Text, "^[a-zA-Z0-9._%+-]+@
[a-zA-Z0-9.-]+\.[a-zA-Z]{2,}$"), "Invalid email address", "" )
```

This expression checks whether the text entered into the **EmailAddress** text input control is a valid email address, by using a regular expression. If the entered text is not a valid email address, the label control will display the message "Invalid email address". If the entered text is a valid email address, the label control will display an empty string.

Lastly, you can save and preview the app to test the validation.

Views and formulas

Formulas in PowerApps are expressions that you can use to perform a variety of operations and calculations within the app. Formulas can be used to calculate values, perform string operations, manipulate data and records, and more. The syntax used to create formulas in PowerApps is similar to that used in Microsoft Excel. Formulas can be used in a number of different contexts within PowerApps, including the calculation of field values, in the creation of data sources, in custom connectors, and more.

We used formula in the preceding example to implement validation.

There are different types of formulas in PowerApps. Some of the most commonly used types of formulas include the following:

- **Arithmetic formulas:** Used for performing mathematical operations such as addition, subtraction, multiplication, and division.

- **Text formulas:** Used for combining and manipulating text values, such as concatenating strings, extracting sub-strings, and converting text to uppercase or lowercase.

- **Logical formulas:** Used for making decisions based on the values of variables and expressions, such as the IF and SWITCH functions.

- **Date and time formulas:** Used for working with date and time values, such as adding and subtracting time intervals, converting dates to text, and calculating the difference between two dates.

- **Aggregation formulas:** Used for working with collections of data, such as counting the number of items in a collection, finding the minimum or maximum value, and calculating the average of a set of values.

Here are examples of different types of formulas with the code used in PowerApps:

- Arithmetic formulas:

```
= 5 + 10
```

- Text formulas:

```
= "Hello " & "World"
```

- Logical formulas:

```
= IF(5 > 10, "5 is greater than 10", "5 is not greater than 10")
```

- Date and time formulas:

```
= Today()
```

The **Today()** formula returns the current date. You can use this formula in various ways within your app, such as in a control's default value or in a calculation to determine the number of days between two dates.

```
DateAdd(StartDate, 7, Days)
```

The **DateAdd** formula adds a specified number of days, months, or years to a given start date. In this example, it adds 7 days to the StartDate field.

- Lookup formulas:

```
= LookUp(Orders, OrderID = 1, Total)
```

- Aggregate formulas:

```
= Sum(Orders, Total)
```

- Information formulas:

```
= IsBlank(TextInput1.Text)
```

- Table formulas:

```
= Table( { Column1: "A", Column2: "B" }, { Column1: "C", Column2: "D" } )
```

These are just a few examples, but there are many other types of formulas available in PowerApps that you can use to perform different operations and manipulations of data.

You can build different views in PowerApps. For example, you can create a form-style view for data entry, a gallery-style view for data browsing, and a chart-style view for data analysis. In addition, you can also create custom views using canvas apps. These views can be used to present data in a way that is meaningful and actionable to users, and they can be configured to meet specific business needs. You can also create a view that displays data in a grid format, or a view that shows data in a form format. Views can be customized to meet specific requirements, such as displaying a subset of data, or showing data in a specific format. Additionally, different views can be created for different purposes, such as an edit view and a read-only view. The use of views in PowerApps makes it easier to work with large amounts of data, and to present information in a clear and organized manner.

Building a view in PowerApps involves the following steps:

1. **Choose a data source:** Decide which data source you want to use to build the view. PowerApps supports many different data sources including SharePoint, Excel, OneDrive, SQL Server, and more.

2. **Choose a template:** PowerApps provides several templates for building views. Choose a template that best fits the type of view you want to build.

3. **Customize the template:** Customize the template by changing the layout, adding or removing fields, and customizing the formatting of the fields.

4. **Preview the view:** Preview the view to see how it will look on different devices.

5. **Save the view:** Once you are satisfied with the view, save it.

6. **Connect the view to your data source:** This lets you see the data in the view.

7. **Test the view:** Test the view to make sure it works as expected and that all the data is displayed correctly.

8. **Publish the view:** Once you are satisfied with the view, publish it so that others can use it.

You can build navigation between views in PowerApps. Navigation in PowerApps allows you to control the flow of the app and create a more structured and organized experience for the user. You can navigate between screens, which are the individual pages in your app, using controls such as buttons, links, and swipe gestures. To build navigation in PowerApps, you can use the **Navigate** function to specify the target screen and any relevant data to pass to that screen. You can also use the **Back** button to return to the previous screen. The specific steps for building navigation will depend on the specific requirements of your app, but the process typically involves adding controls, defining the navigation behavior, and testing the navigation to ensure it works as expected.

Practical tasks

You have already practiced creating a Canvas PowerApp in one of the previous chapters. But this time, lets dive a bit deeper into it. Follow the given steps:

1. As the first step, login to Microsoft 365 portal using your credentials. From the list of available applications, select **PowerApps**.

2. In the power apps portal, select **Apps** on the left navigation. Click **New App | Canvas**. Provide the name of the app, and the app builder will open. As the first step in building PowerApps, you would need to select a data source. As this is a stand-alone PowerApp, it is not automatically tied to the SharePoint list or any other sources. We would need to connect it manually.

3. In the left navigation, select **Data** option. Then click on the **Add data** button.

4. In a search of available data sources, type **SharePoint** and select the one named **SharePoint**.

Figure 12.7 features SharePoint connection in the list of available connections:

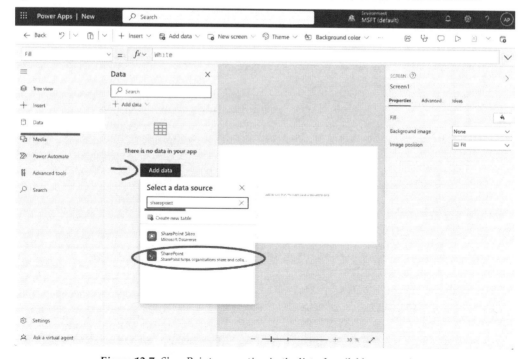

Figure 12.7: *SharePoint connection in the list of available connections*

5. Select SharePoint connection and the choice **Connect Directly** (as we will be using SharePoint online in our task and do not need to connect to the on-prem source of data).

6. The list of available sites will appear. You will mainly see sites that you have created before.

7. Select one of them, preferably the one where you have create a list before.

8. After the site is selected, you will see available options: lists and libraries you can connect to.

9. Select one of them. After selecting, the connection will be established and you will see it on the left side in the data tab.

10. You have a screen added by default when you created an app and now, we can add some controls and data to it. In the left navigation, click on **Insert**. In a search, type **Form**. You will see multiple options available for a form.

11. Select **Edit form** (you can either double-click on it or just drag it into the white screen zone in the middle). Resize the appeared control to take the whole space of your white screen in the middle.

You will see that it shows the message that no data sources were selected. In the right panel, you will see a dropdown where you can connect your previously added data source. Just click on the dropdown and select it from there.

Figure 12.8 features data source selection for the **Edit** form:

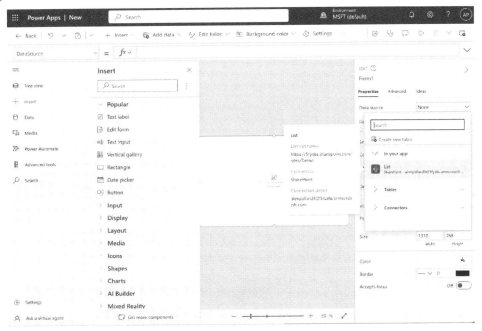

Figure 12.8: *Data source selection for the Edit form*

12. After the data source is selected, you will see fields appearing in your screen. In this case, you will be able to edit them.

13. Below the **Data Source** dropdown, you can click on **Edit fields** and see fields available to you from your data source. There, you can add some fields to your view or edit them.

Now let us configure the form to capture new information and create new records in the list. Follow the given steps:

1. In the same right panel, look for **Default mode** property and set it to **New**.

2. From the left panel, select **Insert** and search for a button control.

3. Add it and position it properly on the screen below your fields.

4. Now select the button on the screen and check in the top left corner of builder. The option should be set to **OnSelect** and next to it a formula bar.

Figure 12.9 features adding Submit button logic on the form:

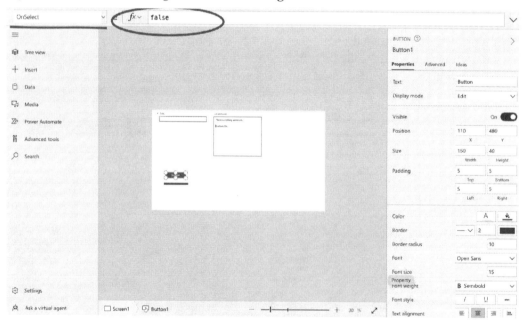

Figure 12.9: *Adding Submit button logic on the form*

5. In the formula bar, add the following formula to submit entered data back into the SharePoint list:

```
SubmitForm(Form1);

NewForm(Form1);
```

6. Rename the button you added to **Submit** or **Save** (whatever you prefer). That can be done from the right panel in the Text property.

Now you can launch the app and test if your data gets submitted to the list you connected to. To test it, click on the play icon in the top right corner. After you are done with your changes, you can publish the app (icon on the right from play icon).

You can also enhance your app by adding gallery view to it to see records that already exist and some search capabilities. You can find rest of the steps and more practical example of how to work with apps at

https://learn.microsoft.com/en-us/power-apps/maker/canvas-apps/add-editable-tables

Play around with styles and functionality within your app and try to add more features to it to become familiar with a platform.

Now after you done with all the changes and you published the app, you can share it with other users. For that, you need to close the app builder (click back in the top left corner) and follow the given steps:

1. Select the app from the list of available apps and click on three dots next to it and **Share**. Or you can click on it from the top ribbon.

Figure 12.10 features sharing Canvas PowerApp from the PowerApp portal:

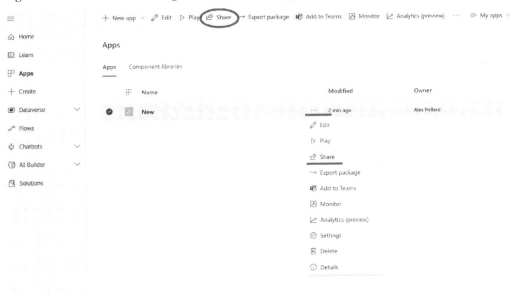

Figure 12.10: *Sharing Canvas PowerApp from the PowerApp portal*

2. A pop-up will be shown from the ride side. There on the left, you can type the user name. Some test users are created when you set up a new Dev env. Then select the person from the list of available names.

3. On the right side, you can set him as a co-owner. In this case, he will be able to make changes to the app. Otherwise he will just be able to interact with it and the functionality you built.

Figure 12.11 features sharing Canvas PowerApp and assigning user with the owner permissions:

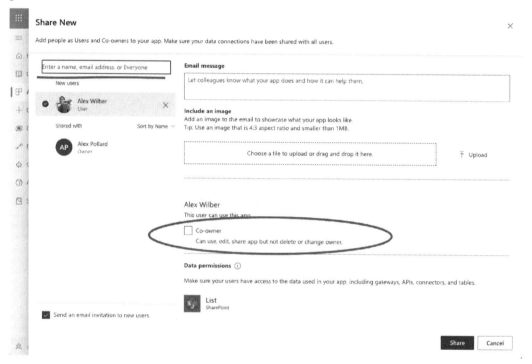

Figure 12.11: Sharing Canvas PowerApp and assigning user with the owner permissions

4. You also can share this app with everyone within the organization or just with a specific group of people. To share with everyone, type **Everyone** in the people search field and select the **Everyone in MSFT** option. Otherwise, you can type the name of the Microsoft group we previously created in another chapter. Please note that you cannot make the whole group of people as co-owners. Each owner should be set individually.

5. Click on the **Share** button after completing.

Now, let us create a model-driven app, by following the given steps:

1. In the left menu in PowerApp portal, click on the **Dataverse** tab. This will create your Dataverse database. Please note that it may take a few minutes to finish up the set up.

2. In the PowerApp portal in the App tab from the top ribbon, select **New app | Model Driven**. Provide the name of your app.

3. It will open in the same way as with canvas builder, but you will see that it is slightly different. To start with, you need to add a new page to the app. Click on **Add page** button in the middle of the screen and select **Dataverse table**. You will see the list of available tables there and you can select a few of them to work with the data there

Figure 12.12 features adding a page and selecting tables for a model-driven app:

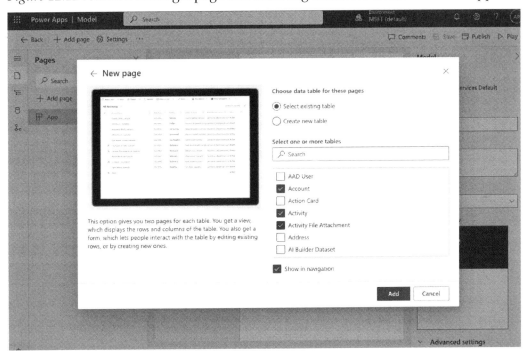

Figure 12.12: *Features adding a page and selecting tables for a model-driven app*

After this is done, you will see how the tables you selected are added to the navigation on the main screen. From there, you can click on different records pre-created in the table and modify fields and forms created for you automatically. Play around with it and see how it works.

You can also refer to the Microsoft PowerApp learning site for a particular use case to work on.

After you are done with making changes in the app, you can click on the **Publish** icon at the top right corner.

Conclusion

In this chapter, we reviewed in more depth various types of PowerApps and how to work with them. There are different ways to build custom business applications in the Power Platform. Canvas apps offer a low-code, drag-and-drop interface for building custom applications, while model-driven apps use a pre-built data model to create more structured and form-based applications. Dataverse is a low-code data platform that serves as the back-end for PowerApps and model-driven apps, providing a scalable and secure way to store and manage data. Ultimately, the choice between canvas, model-driven, and Dataverse will depend on the specific requirements of your project and the level of customization and control that you need over your app and data.

Points to remember

- Canvas and model-driven PowerApps are two types of app development models in PowerApps that have different features and functionalities.

- Canvas apps provide more flexibility and customization, while model-driven apps have a more structured approach and come with pre-built forms, views, and business logic.

- Dataverse is a data platform for PowerApps that provides a centralized and secure place to store and manage data. It can be used with both canvas and model-driven PowerApps.

- Connectors are used to connect PowerApps to external data sources, and there are both free and premium connectors available.

- The data gateway can be used to connect PowerApps to on-premises data sources.

- There is an API that can be used to call PowerApps from another app.

- Validation rules can be added to PowerApps to ensure that data entered into the app meets specific criteria.

- Formulas are used to perform calculations and manipulate data within PowerApps.

- Views in PowerApps can be used to display data in different ways and provide different perspectives on the data.

- Navigation can be set up between views in PowerApps to allow users to easily switch between views.

## CHAPTER 13

Power Automate

> "The future belongs to businesses that embrace automation and harness its power to create a better world."
>
> *- Satya Nadella*

Introduction

In this chapter, we will dive deeper into the topic of Power automate and find out how to build various versions of Flows: running on start, on modify, or scheduled. You will learn a few basic actions commonly used to automate processes in Power Automate. We will also review connections to API and how to make queries directly from the Flow.

Structure

In this chapter, we will cover the following topics:

- Power Automate (Flow)
- Solutions in Power Automate
- Running on start, modify and scheduled flows
- Connections inside Power Automate

- Working with API from Flow
- Sharing flows

Objectives

We will review Power Automate in more depth to gain a thorough understanding of how to automate workflows, processes, and tasks to increase efficiency and productivity. By using Power Automate, you can connect different applications and services, create and run workflows, and integrate with other Microsoft tools and services. This can help you automate repetitive tasks, streamline workflows, and improve communication and collaboration across your organization. By learning Power Automate deeply, you can become an expert in automating business processes and improving your organization's overall efficiency.

Power Automate (Flow)

As you have learned before, Power Automate is a cloud-based service that makes it possible for users to automate tasks and workflows across a variety of applications and services. The service is also sometimes referred to as Microsoft Flow, which was the original name when it was introduced in 2016. Power Automate enables users to build, run, and share automated workflows that can help increase efficiency, save time, and reduce manual effort. With Power Automate, users can automate tasks such as data collection, file transfers, email notifications, and more, by using a simple, visual interface to create automated workflows or "flows."

SharePoint Designer Workflow is a legacy workflow platform that was used to automate business processes within SharePoint. It was designed to be used by business users and developers who were familiar with SharePoint, and allowed them to build workflows using a graphical designer. The workflows created in SharePoint Designer could automate tasks such as document approval, sending notifications, or updating data.

Power Automate is a cloud-based platform that provides a modern and more powerful way to automate workflows. It is a part of the Microsoft Power Platform and can be used to automate a wide range of business processes both within and outside of SharePoint. Power Automate provides a low-code solution that is easy to use and enables users to automate workflows using a visual designer, as well as programmatic solutions that allow developers to build more complex workflows.

Nintex is a company that provides a workflow automation platform that is similar to Power Automate. The Nintex platform allows users to automate business processes using drag-and-drop tools and pre-built connectors to integrate with various systems. It is a popular alternative to Power Automate and SharePoint Designer workflows, and is often used to build complex workflows in SharePoint. Nintex has been there since SharePoint 2013 and has a pretty similar visual interface and builder as Power Automate does. However, both platforms should not be mistaken as they come from different companies. Power Automate is the native platform that comes together with Microsoft 365 subscription.

The two types of flows in Power Automate are Cloud flows and Desktop flows:

- **Cloud flows** are created and run on the cloud, and they can be triggered by events or other systems that are accessible from the cloud. These flows can be triggered by external services such as Microsoft PowerApps or Microsoft Dynamics 365, and they can also interact with other services in the Microsoft Power Platform, such as Common Data Service.

- Desktop flows are created and run on the desktop and they can be triggered by events on the desktop, such as new file creation or changes to a file. Desktop flows can also interact with other services, such as Microsoft OneDrive or Microsoft Teams.

Both types of flows can automate a wide range of tasks, from simple data integration to complex business processes, and they can be customized with a variety of connectors and actions.

The **Shared with Me** section in Power Automate refers to a collection of workflows that have been shared with the user by other Power Automate users. This section provides an easy way for users to find and access workflows that have been shared with them. The workflows can include any type of automation that has been created in Power Automate, such as automated data processing, custom integrations with other apps, or even custom business processes. This feature helps users collaborate with others by sharing workflows and automate tasks.

Please note that if you share a Flow with someone, it will be displayed in Shared with me section and not in the list of all of the Flows in the Cloud flows section.

Power Automate allows you to automate a wide range of processes, including the following:

- **Business process automation:** Automate repetitive manual processes such as approvals, data collection, and form submissions.

- **IT process automation:** Automate IT tasks such as provisioning, data backup and recovery, and incident response.

- **Business-to-business (B2B) integration:** Automate the exchange of data and transactions between different systems, applications, and organizations.

- **Business-to-consumer (B2C) integration:** Automate customer-facing processes such as lead generation, customer service, and order processing.

- **Integration with other Microsoft products:** Automate tasks and processes within other Microsoft products such as Dynamics 365, SharePoint, and OneDrive.

- **Collaboration workflows:** Automate workflows that involve multiple stakeholders, such as task assignments, approvals, and feedback collection.

- **Data integration and migration:** Automate data integration and migration tasks such as data transfer, data validation, and data reconciliation.

In Power Automate, there are two types of flows that you can create:

- **Flow templates** are pre-built flows that automate common tasks, such as sending an email when a new file is added to a SharePoint library or creating a new item in a database when a form is submitted. These templates are designed to make it easy for you to quickly automate processes without having to build a flow from scratch.

- **Blank flows**, on the other hand, allow you to create custom workflows from scratch. You can use blank flows to automate a wide range of tasks and processes, such as sending notifications, updating data, and integrating with other services. With blank flows, you have complete control over the actions and conditions that are included in the flow, allowing you to create highly customized workflows that meet the specific needs of your organization.

In Power Automate, there are several types of blank flows and triggers available. Some of the most commonly used triggers include the following:

- **Manual trigger:** Allows users to manually start a flow when they need it.

- **Scheduled trigger:** Allows users to set up a flow to run on a specific date and time.

- **Button trigger:** Allows users to start a flow from a button within an application.

- **Recurrence trigger:** Allows users to set up a flow to run repeatedly at set intervals.

- **When a new item is created trigger:** Allows users to set up a flow to run whenever a new item is created in a specified data source.

- **When an item is modified trigger:** Allows users to set up a flow to run whenever an item in a specified data source is modified.

- **When a file is created or modified (properties only) trigger:** Allows users to set up a flow to run whenever a file is created or modified in a specified location.

- **When a HTTP request is received trigger:** Allows users to set up a flow to run whenever a HTTP request is received.

In Power Automate, there are several types of cloud flows that can be created and they are as follows:

- **Automated cloud flow:** An automated cloud flow is triggered when a specific event occurs, such as when a new item is created in a data source, or when a form is submitted.

- **Instant cloud flow:** An instant cloud flow is manually triggered by the user. It can be used to perform a specific action, such as sending an email or updating data in a data source.

- **Scheduled cloud flow:** A scheduled cloud flow runs at a specific time, either once or on a recurring basis. It can be used to perform tasks such as sending periodic reminders or updating data in a data source.

- **Power Automate Desktop:** A desktop flow is a type of workflow in Microsoft Power Automate that can be triggered manually or by an event on your desktop, such as the creation of a file or the addition of an item to a database. Unlike cloud flows, which are hosted in the cloud and can run automatically on a schedule, desktop flows run on your local computer or server. Some examples of tasks that can be automated with a desktop flow include copying files, generating reports, and updating databases. Because desktop flows run on your local computer, they can take advantage of the resources and tools available on your machine, such as local files, installed software, and connected devices.

Figure 13.1 features Power Automate Flow types prompt selection when creating a new Flow:

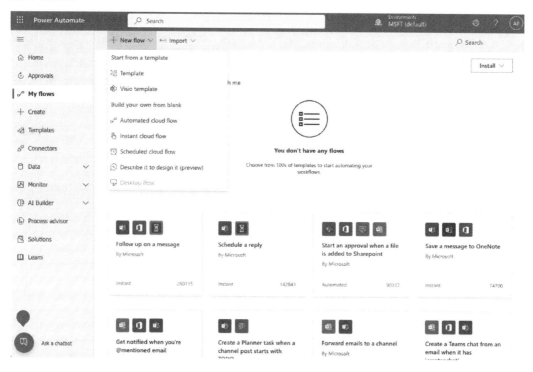

Figure 13.1: *Power Automate Flow types prompt selection when creating a new Flow*

In Power Automate, there are many pre-built **Templates** available that can be used as a starting point to automate specific scenarios or workflows. The templates cover a wide range of scenarios such as sending an email, creating a file, syncing data between services, and much more. These templates can be customized to meet your specific needs and requirements. Basic actions are already pre-defined and pre-built-in templates. By using them, you can save time and effort in setting up your workflows and processes. Additionally, you can also share these templates with others and reuse them across different workflows and processes.

AI Builder is a component of Microsoft Power Automate that enables users to build custom machine learning models without having to write code. It provides a visual interface that allows users to train and test models, and then deploy them within their Power Automate workflows. AI Builder includes pre-built models for common use cases such as text classification, sentiment analysis, and form processing, and also provides the ability to create custom models for specific business needs. This component provides a low-code, user-friendly way for organizations to incorporate artificial intelligence into their workflows and automate tasks that previously required manual effort.

The **Monitor** section in Power Automate is used to monitor and manage the workflows and flows that you have created. This section provides a central location to view the status and details of your workflows and flows, as well as any errors or issues that may have arisen. You can monitor your flows by viewing the history and details of each flow run, as well as by viewing the status of each flow, including the number of runs, the start and end times, and the success or failure of each run. You can also use the monitor section to view performance metrics, such as run time and the number of steps completed, and to view any related errors or issues.

Figure 13.2 features the Power Automate Monitor section to check Flows activity and metrics:

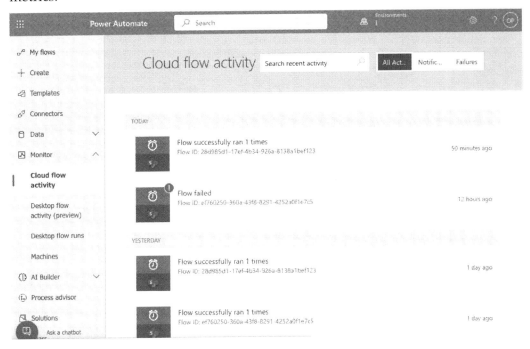

Figure 13.2: *Power Automate Monitor section to check Flows activity and metrics*

The concept of environments in Power Automate is similar to that in PowerApps. Environments allow you to manage your resources, data, and connections in separate spaces, making it easier to test, deploy, and manage your workflows. In Power Automate, you can create and manage environments in the Power Platform Admin Center. In each environment, you can manage connections, flows, and other resources, and you can monitor the usage and performance of your flows in the environment. The process of creating and managing environments in Power Automate is similar to that in PowerApps, and you can use the same environment templates to create new environments.

Solutions in Power Automate

In Power Automate, a Solution is a container for holding one or more flows, as well as other components such as entities, views, dashboards, and processes. Solutions can be used to package a set of related flows, entities, and components so that they can be easily deployed to other environments or shared with other users.

Solutions are useful for organizing and managing flows, as well as for streamlining the deployment and management of flows across environments. With solutions, you can also control which users have access to flows and other components, and you can version your flows to keep track of changes over time.

A solution is a collection of components that can be packaged and managed as a single unit. This allows you to organize your components in a way that makes sense for your organization and makes it easier to share and manage your components. To create a solution, you need to have the necessary permissions, and you can create a solution from the Power Automate portal by clicking on the **New solution** button and following the steps to create your solution. You can then add the necessary components to your solution, including flows, apps, and other components, and manage them as a single unit.

You can add existing components to a solution in Power Automate. To do this, navigate to the solution in which you want to add the existing components, and then click the **Add existing** button. From there, you can select the components you want to add, such as flows, PowerApps, Dataverse tables and more.

Figure 13.3 features the Solutions section inside the Power Automate portal:

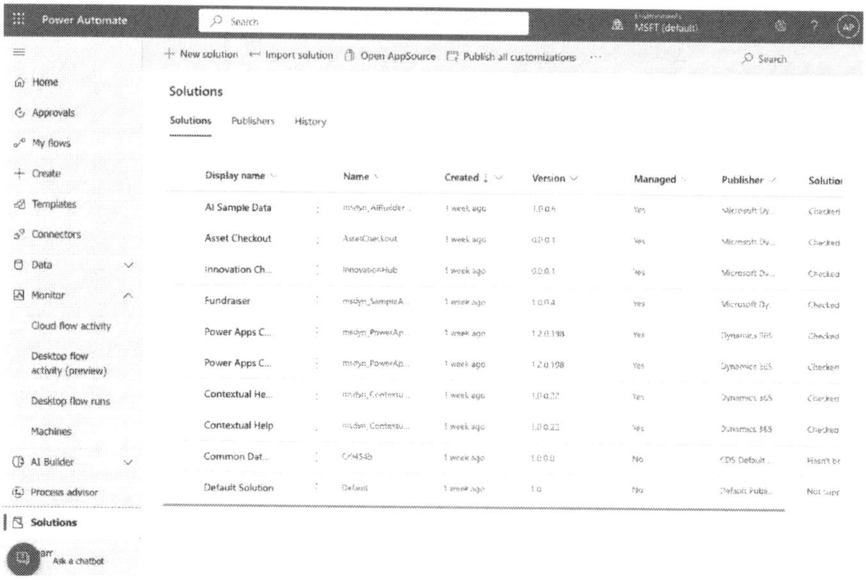

Figure 13.3: *The Solutions section inside the Power Automate portal*

In Power Automate, you can add the following types of components inside Solutions:

- **Flows**: You can add automated, instant, and scheduled cloud flows, as well as desktop flows.

- **Connectors**: You can add connectors, which are used to connect to different data sources and systems.

- **Custom connectors**: You can add custom connectors, which are connectors that you have created to connect to specific systems or APIs.

- **API connections**: You can add API connections, which are used to manage the connection to an API, including the authentication and settings for the API.

- **Power Apps**: You can add canvas and model-driven Power Apps, which can be used to build custom business applications.

- **Power Automate custom connectors**: You can add custom connectors that you have created to connect to specific systems or APIs.

- **Power Virtual Agents**: You can add Power Virtual Agents, which are chatbots that you can use to automate customer interactions and support.

- **Custom APIs**: You can add custom APIs, which are APIs that you have created to expose data and functionality to other systems and services.

- **Power Apps Portals**: You can add Power Apps Portals, which are websites that you can use to expose data and functionality to external users.

Overall, whatever can be integrated with Power Automate can be added inside a solution.

Figure 13.4 features the view inside a Solution and various components added there on the right:

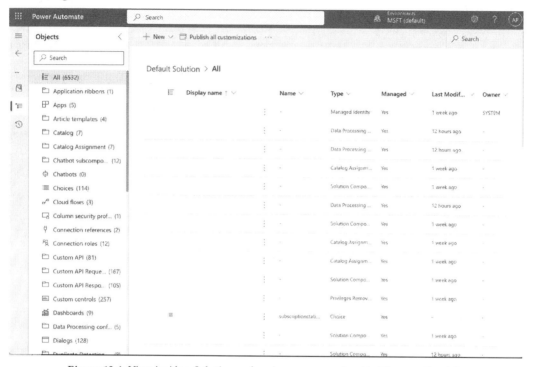

Figure 13.4: *View inside a Solution and various components added there on the right*

The history inside a solution in Power Automate refers to a record of changes made to the components within the solution over time. This can include updates to existing components, as well as the addition or removal of components. The history can be used to track the evolution of a solution and to identify who made specific changes. This information can be useful for auditing purposes and for ensuring that the solution is being developed and maintained in a consistent and controlled manner.

Running on start, modify and scheduled flows

Power Automate provides various options to run flows. The most common trigger types are **on start** and **modify**:

* A flow that is triggered "**on start**" is executed immediately when it is created or when the trigger conditions are met. For example, you can set up a flow that is triggered "on start" when a new item is created in a SharePoint list. When the new item is added, the flow will run automatically, without manual intervention.

- A flow that is triggered "**modify**" is executed whenever the data that the flow is monitoring changes. For example, you can set up a flow that is triggered "modify" when an item in a SharePoint list is updated. When the item is updated, the flow will run automatically, updating or processing the data as required.

- Another option to run flows is through **scheduling**. This allows you to run flows on a recurring basis or at a specific time. For example, you can set up a flow to run every day at a specific time to check for new items in a SharePoint list and then process the data as required.

You can combine multiple triggers together in Power Automate to create a more complex and sophisticated workflow. A trigger is an event that initiates the flow and sets it in motion. By combining multiple triggers, you can create workflows that respond to different events and circumstances in different ways. For example, you can create a flow that is triggered by a form submission, and then also triggered by a change in a specific SharePoint list or by the arrival of a new email in a particular mailbox.

Once the flow is triggered, the steps specified in the flow logic are executed, and the workflow can take a variety of actions, such as sending emails, updating records, and creating new items in a database. You can also add conditions and branching to the flow, allowing it to make decisions and take different actions based on the data it receives.

Combining multiple triggers in a flow allows you to automate a wide range of business processes and workflows, increasing efficiency and reducing the amount of manual effort required. Additionally, by combining triggers with other features in Power Automate, such as conditional statements and looping constructs, you can create complex workflows that can adapt to changing conditions and respond to different scenarios in real-time.

In Power Automate, triggers define when a flow starts running. Advanced settings for triggers allow you to control various aspects of the trigger behavior. Here are some examples of the advanced settings you can configure for a trigger:

- **Run only when specific conditions are met:** You can specify conditions that must be met in order for the flow to run.

- **Run only once per item:** When you enable this setting, the flow will only run once for each item in the trigger event, even if the item is updated multiple times.

- **Concurrent execution:** You can control how many instances of the flow can run at the same time.

- **Time zone:** You can set the time zone that is used when running the flow.

- **Event source time zone:** You can control whether the time zone of the event source is used or whether the flow time zone is used.

These advanced settings allow you to create more complex and sophisticated workflows that run exactly when you need them to, without interfering with each other.

Figure 13.5 features the **Advanced options** section in the Flow trigger:

Figure 13.5: *The Advanced options section in the Flow trigger*

In Power Automate, the settings of a flow trigger determine how the flow runs and when it is triggered. Some of the common settings include:

- **Connection Settings:** This section determines the data source for the flow, such as the SharePoint list or the Dynamics 365 database that the flow will use.

- **Run Settings:** This section determines when and how often the flow should run. You can choose to run the flow on demand, at a specific time, or on a recurring basis.

- **Retry Policy:** This section determines what should happen if the flow fails to run. You can choose to have the flow retry a certain number of times, or you can choose to have it stop running after a certain number of failures.

- **Run After:** This section determines what actions should be taken after the flow has run. For example, you can choose to send an email notification or to update a database record.

- **Parameters:** This section allows you to pass values into the flow, such as the date range for a report or the recipient of an email notification.

Figure 13.6 features the Settings view in the trigger (called by clicking on three dots in trigger):

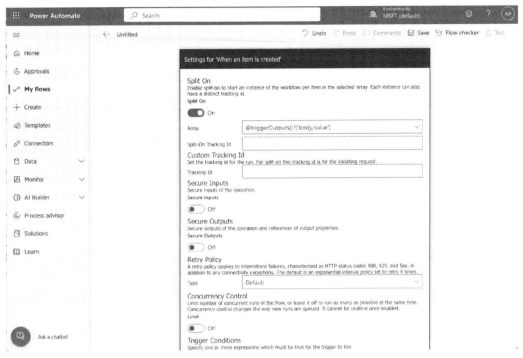

Figure 13.6: *Settings view in the trigger (called by clicking on three dots in trigger)*

These are just a few examples of the settings that are available in flow triggers. To learn more about the specific settings for each type of trigger, you may refer to the Microsoft documentation or other resources.

Connections inside Power Automate

In Power Automate, a connection is a means by which to access data from a particular external service, such as SharePoint, Microsoft Teams, Dynamics 365, or a REST API. Connections define the authentication methods and the access rights for the flows to access the data.

In Power Automate, there are several types of connections that you can use, including:

- Office 365
- OneDrive
- SharePoint
- Microsoft Teams
- Exchange Online

- Dynamics 365
- **Common Data Service (CDS)**
- Power Apps
- Power BI
- Azure

Each connection type has its own set of required credentials and specific parameters to allow Power Automate to access the data in that service.

To establish a connection in Power Automate, you need to add a connection to the service that you want to connect to. You can do this by selecting the **Connections** option from the left navigation menu, then clicking the **+ New connection** button, and selecting the service you want to connect to.

You may be asked to sign in to the service you are connecting to and provide any necessary authentication information such as your username and password or an API key. Once you have provided the required information, you can create the connection and it will be available for use in your flows.

After creating a connection, you can use it in a flow by adding an action from the service you connected to and configuring it with the necessary information. The information you need to provide will depend on the specific action you are using, but it may include things like the list or library you want to interact with, the item you want to update or retrieve, or the message you want to send.

Figure 13.7 features connections to Office 365 user profile and Outlook from Power Automate:

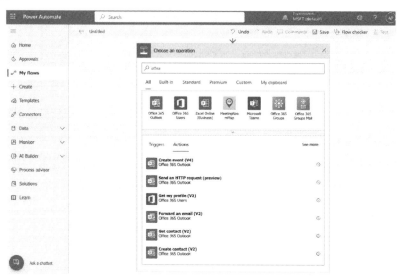

Figure 13.7: *Connections to Office 365 user profile and Outlook from Power Automate*

There are some limitations to keep in mind when working with connections in Power Automate, and they are as follows:

- Not all services offer the same level of integration with Power Automate. Some services may offer a more limited set of actions or triggers, while others may not be supported at all.

- Some services may require an API key or other credentials in order to establish a connection. Make sure you have the necessary information and access rights to the service before you attempt to create a connection.

- Some services may have rate limits or other usage restrictions that you need to be aware of in order to avoid issues with your flows.

- If you are using a custom API or other custom service, you may need to create a custom connector in order to connect to it. This can require additional development work and may not be suitable for everyone.

- Connections can also be disrupted if the service you are connecting to changes its API or updates its integration with Power Automate. You may need to update your connection in order to continue using it effectively.

A custom connector in Power Automate is a type of connection that you can create to connect to an API that is not already available as a standard connection. To create a custom connector, you will need to provide information about the API, including the endpoint URL, authentication methods, and the operations that are available through the API. Once you have created the custom connector, you can use it in your flows just like you would use any other connection. When you create a custom connector, you can define the operations and parameters for the API, as well as the response format. You can also define how authentication should be handled for the API, such as by providing a bearer token or an API key. When you use a custom connector in a flow, you will have access to the operations and parameters that you defined when you created the connector, and you can configure the steps in your flow to work with the data that the API returns. There may be limitations on the use of custom connectors, such as the size of the response or the rate at which requests can be made to the API, but these will depend on the specific API that you are connecting to and the terms of service for that API.

Custom connectors are usually configured by exporting a set of queries from Postman, and originally, they can be found on the system API documentation (the one you are trying to connect to). After that, by setting up a webhook, you can trigger a Flow using an action '**waiting a response from url'**. In this way, pass a data between sharepoint, dataverse or other sources and systems you are connecting to with custom connector.

Working with API from Flow

To work with APIs in Power Automate (previously known as Microsoft Flow), you can use a built-in "HTTP" action to send HTTP requests to the API, and then process the response from the API using additional actions.

Here is a general overview of the steps involved:

1. **Connect to the API:** You can use the "HTTP" action to connect to the API by specifying the API endpoint in the "URL" field. Depending on the API, you may need to provide an API key or token in the "Authorization" header.

2. **Send the API request:** You can customize the HTTP request by specifying the HTTP method (for example, GET, POST, PUT, DELETE), headers, and body.

3. **Process the API response:** After sending the API request, you can use other actions to process the API response. For example, you might parse the JSON response and extract the data you need, or check the response status code to see if the API call was successful.

It is important to note that not all APIs are available for use in Power Automate. Some APIs may be restricted based on the API provider's policies or due to technical limitations. Before using an API in Power Automate, you should review the API documentation to ensure that it is suitable for use in this context.

REST API and Microsoft Graph API are two different types of APIs that can be used with Power Automate to connect to various services and resources within Microsoft 365:

• REST API is a widely used web standard for making API requests to retrieve or manipulate data. REST APIs typically use HTTP requests (such as GET, POST, PUT, and DELETE) to interact with resources, which are identified by URIs.

• Microsoft Graph API, on the other hand, is a RESTful web API that enables developers to access Microsoft 365 data and services. It provides a single endpoint to access data and insights from various Microsoft services, including Exchange, OneDrive, and Teams.

In terms of differences, Microsoft Graph API provides a more unified and consistent way to access data and insights across various Microsoft services, while REST APIs can be used to access a specific service or resource. Additionally, Microsoft Graph API may have some unique capabilities or features that are not available through REST APIs.

To use the Microsoft Graph API in Power Automate, you need to obtain approval from your organization's administrator. The administrator must grant permissions to your Power Automate account to access the Microsoft Graph API. Once the permissions have been granted, you can use the Microsoft Graph API to retrieve and manipulate data from various Microsoft services, such as Exchange, OneDrive, and SharePoint, among others.

To grant permission to use the Microsoft Graph API in Power Automate, you need to follow these steps:

1. Go to the Microsoft 365 admin center.

2. In the left navigation, select **Show all**, and then select **Admin centers**.

3. Select **Azure Active Directory**.

4. In the left navigation, select **App registrations**.

5. Select the app that you want to grant permission to.

6. In the left navigation, select **API permissions**.

7. Select the **Microsoft Graph API**, and then select the desired permissions.

8. Select **Add a permission**.

9. Select Grant admin consent for [tenant name].

This will allow the app to use the Microsoft Graph API on behalf of users in your organization. Please note that you need to have the necessary administrative privileges to perform these steps.

Sharing flows

In Power Automate, you can share your flows with others in your organization. Sharing a flow with others allows them to use it in their own flows, and you can grant different levels of access to different users. There are several ways to share flows, including:

- **Sharing through the flow's run history:** From the flow's run history, you can share the flow with others by clicking on the "**Share**" button. You can then select the users or groups you want to share the flow with and set their access level to "**Can use**."

- **Sharing through the flow's details page:** From the flow's details page, you can share the flow by clicking on the "**Share**" button. You can then select the users or groups you want to share the flow with and set their access level to "**Can use**."

- **Sharing through a solution:** If you have added the flow to a solution, you can share the solution with others. This will give them access to all the components inside the solution, including the flow.

You can also control who can edit the flow, who can see the flow, and who can use the flow by setting appropriate access levels for each user or group.

To set owners and members of a flow in Power Automate, you can follow these steps:

1. Open the flow you want to set owners and members for.

2. In the flow's menu, select the **Sharing** option.

3. On the **Sharing** page, you can see the list of current owners and members of the flow. To add new owners or members, click the **Add owner** or **Add member** button.

4. In the **Add owner** or **Add member** dialog box, enter the email address of the person you want to add as an owner or member. If the person is in your organization, their name should appear as you type.

5. Select the person's name or email address, and then choose the level of access you want to give them. You can choose to give them owner or member access.

6. Click the **Add** button to add the person as an owner or member.

7. Repeat the process to add additional owners or members.

8. When you are done adding owners and members, click the **Save** button to save the changes.

Once you have added owners and members, they will be able to see and modify the flow, depending on the level of access you have given them.

In Power Automate, the **Cloud flows** section displays all the flows that you have created. On the other hand, the **Shared with me** section displays all the flows that have been shared with you by other users.

When you create a flow, you are the owner of that flow and have full control over it. You can choose to share the flow with other users, giving them access to the flow and allowing them to run it or make changes to it. To share a flow, you can add users or groups as members and specify their level of access, such as **can view** or **can edit**.

When a flow is shared with you, it appears in the **Shared with me** section, and you have the level of access specified by the owner. You can run the flow, view its details, and make changes to it, depending on the level of access you have been granted.

It is important to note that, when a flow is shared with you, it still belongs to the original owner and they have the final say on what changes can be made to the flow.

However, if you have been granted **can edit** access, you can make changes to the flow, which can be saved and reflected for all members of the flow.

Practical tasks

Let us jump to practice and play around with Power Automate and Flows. Follow the given steps:

1. Use your account to sign into the Microsoft 365 portal. From there, select **Power Automate** from the list of available applications.

2. As you saw already on the left side, you have multiple features of Power Automate.

3. For this exercise, we will build a flow that triggers upon new item creation or modification from the list, and it will update records inside the list that match a specific category. And after that, it will send an email to the person who submitted or modified an item in the list.

4. Select **My Flows** from the left navigation. We will create a new flow. You will see a popup to provide initial properties.

Figure 13.8 features popup to provide initial properties when creating a Flow:

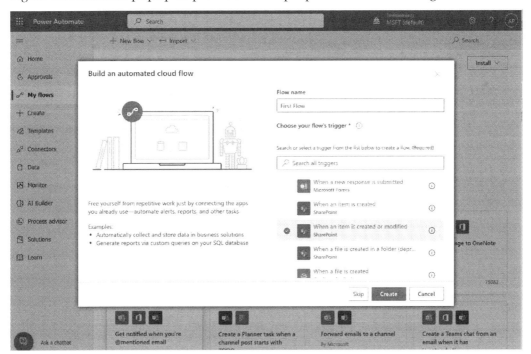

***Figure 13.8:** Popup to provide initial properties when creating a Flow*

5. Name your Flow as you like. We will be working with SharePoint in this exercise, so select the trigger **When an item is created or modified** SharePoint type.

6. Click **Create**. You will be redirected to a Flow builder page.

Once the Flow is created, as the first step, we need to configure trigger to know when to execute our Flow. Follow these steps:

1. In a site address, select the address to one of the available sites you already have in your tenant. From the List name, you will be able to select available lists or libraries form that site.

2. After configured, click on the **New step** button right below your action.

3. Search for **Get Items action** with SharePoint type.

Figure 13.9 features adding new Get Items action into the Flow:

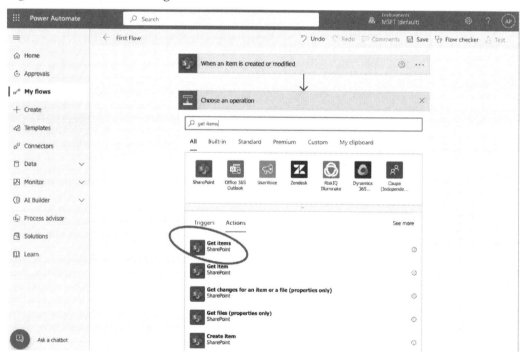

Figure 13.9: *Adding new Get Items action into the Flow*

4. Double-click on the action to add it to the flow.

5. You have an option here to update records in the same list where the original item was created or you can configure it to point to another list on the same or different site. It depends entirely on you. Thus, you would need to provide site name and select list from the configurable properties in that action.

6. Save your Flow by clicking on the icon in the top right corner.

7. Let us navigate to the list in SharePoint where your records will be updated (the one you connected in step 5). In that list, create multiple new columns. *Table 13.1* is the table of columns to be created and data types:

Category	Choice: - HR - IT - Finance
Comments	Multiple Line Text
Record updated	Yes/No (default No)

Table 13.1: Columns to be created along with data types

Thus, your list view will look as shown in *Figure 13.10*, which features the list view in SharePoint with all the columns created:

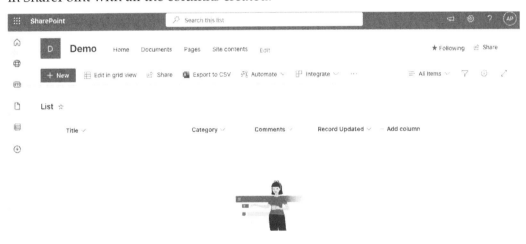

Figure 13.10: List view in SharePoint with all the columns created

8. Now go back to your Flow, and refresh the page there to make sure it pulls up all the new columns created. Add a **New step** and search for **Condition action Control** type.

9. Inside Condition, select **Category column is equal to** and type **IT**.

10. Multiple things will happen here. Your condition will be automatically wrapped in Apply to each block. This happens because in a previous step, you got an array of items from the list. Now, when you update item, it will not be just one item that you need to look into but rather, you will loop

through all of the items in the list. Flow is smart enough to wrap your block into Apply to each to do crawling through the array or received items.

Figure 13.11 features flow Condition action inside Apply to each block:

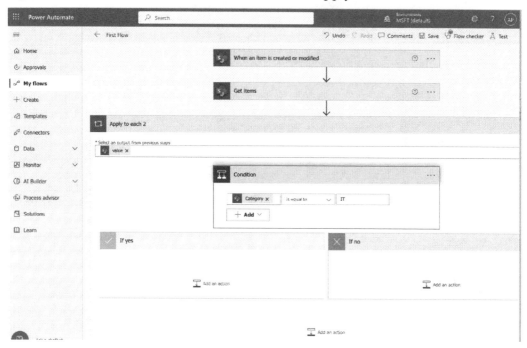

Figure 13.11: *Flow Condition action inside Apply to each block*

Now you have a condition and two branches to build the logic on what should happen if items with **Category=IT** were found.

Inside '**if no**' branch, let us add an action. Search for **send an email (v2) action** and add it, and follow the given steps:

1. Inside '**To**' section, set your email address (you can use your personal one or the one you are using to login to M365). In the **Subject** property, write the subject of your email; for example, 'No items found'. Inside **Body** field, put some text that will be sent over in your email. You can also insert links and images there if you want. For example,

    'Hello, Dear [Created by Display name]

    There were no items found to match the category IT.

    Here is the link to the list [link to your list]

    Thank you'

Figure 13.12 features email Body text in the Flow in '**if no**' block:

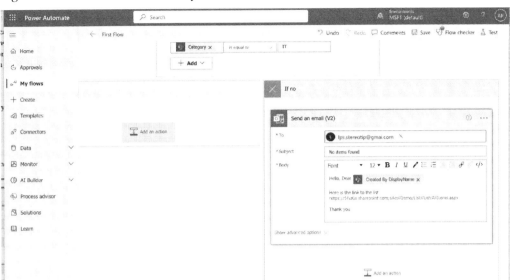

Figure 13.12: *Email Body text in the Flow in 'if no' block*

2. To add a dynamic expression as [Created by Display name], just click multiple times in the body field area and you will see a pop-up where you can select a dynamic value from.

3. Now let us go inside the **If yes** block. Add a new action and select **Update Item** action SharePoint type.

4. Add all configurations as:

   a. **Site Address**: your site url

   b. **List name**: select your list

   c. **ID**: select dynamic value ID

   d. **Title**: null

   e. **Comments**: The item was update

   f. **Record updated**: yes

Figure 13.13 features **Update item** action with properties filled in:

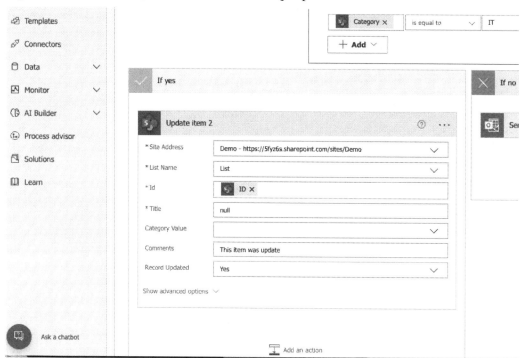

Figure 13.13: Update item action with properties filled in

Now let us save and test it. Follow the given steps:

1. Add multiple items to your list in SharePoint and check Flow behavior.

2. You can track how Flow works from the Flow page where it will show Flow runs. Just click the back arrow in Power Automate, when you are in Flow builder and you will land on that page. You will see the following:

   a. Sharing the Flow.

   b. Sending email notifications from flow when Item created.

   c. Updating fields in the list from the Flow.

   d. Importing and Exporting Flow.

Figure 13.14 features flow run history for the past 28 days:

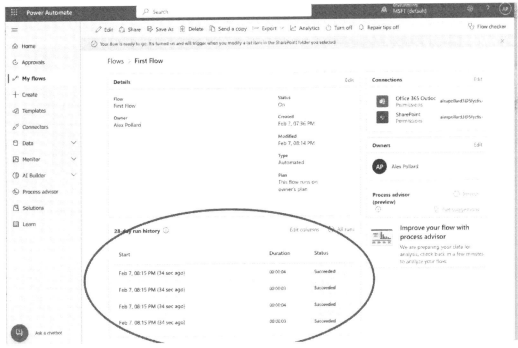

Figure 13.14: *Flow run history for the past 28 days*

Did you notice the warning when you were publishing your flow stating that your applying to each block can be potentially result in an Infinite loop?

Try to solve this warning by adding more conditions into your flow to eliminate infinite loops.

One of the ways would be to track **Record Updated** property and only update those that have value set to '**No**'. Moreover, you may have noticed that you received an email for each record in your list when in reality, you want to receive only 1 email for all records.

By playing around with logic and conditions, you can solve this issue too. Spend some time modifying your flow and adjust it and look through the Microsoft documentation to find a potential solution.

Flows can be shared in the same way as PowerApps. When inside the flow, you can click on Share button and share it with people who should be able to make changes inside the flow. Remember that once you share it the flow will be in the **Shared with me** section.

You can always import and export flows to move them across sites, to transfer owner permissions and to simply create copies and back-ups.

When you are inside the flow, select the **Export** option at the top and select the **Package .zip** option. You will see a page where you can set the name of your exported file and set some properties.

The Import step by default is set to **Update** and this means that during the export, you will update some existing flow. If you want to create a new flow when exporting, then click on the **Update** option and select **Create as new**. All connections can stay as **Select during import**. Click on the **Export** button at the bottom. It will generate and download zip archive to your local machine.

To import Flow, follow the same approach. Go to **My Flows** and from the top, select **Import** option, followed by **Import package (legacy)**. It will prompt you to select the file from your local machine. Select the .zip archive that was exported. It will take a few seconds to analyze the file and it will ask you to provide the name of your new Flow and set up connections. After you finish, the new Flow will be added to your list of the Cloud Flows.

In this way, you can send back-up files to other team members and they can create copies of their own flows where their accounts will be used for connections. In a same way, you can do Flow ownership transfer or just create duplicates to be used on a different lists or sites.

Conclusion

In this chapter, we reviewed Power Automate in more depth. Power Automate (also known as Microsoft Flow) is a powerful platform for automating workflows and business processes. It allows users to automate tasks and streamline processes across a variety of different apps and services, including Microsoft services such as SharePoint and OneDrive, as well as third-party services such as Salesforce and Dropbox. Power Automate provides a wide range of features, including triggers, actions, templates, and custom connectors, making it a versatile and flexible solution for businesses of all sizes. The platform is user-friendly and accessible, allowing users to quickly and easily automate tasks without requiring extensive technical knowledge. With its robust set of features, Power Automate is an excellent solution for businesses looking to streamline their operations and improve productivity.

Points to remember

- Power Automate is a cloud-based service that enables users to automate repetitive tasks and workflows across multiple applications and services.

- Power Automate offers a wide range of pre-built templates and connectors for popular applications and services, as well as the ability to create custom flows from scratch using a drag-and-drop interface.

- Power Automate supports two types of flows: cloud flows and desktop flows. Cloud flows are designed to run in the cloud and can be triggered by a variety of events, while desktop flows run on the user's computer and can be triggered by changes to a file or folder.

- The Power Automate portal provides a central place to manage and monitor flows, and includes tools for collaboration, version control, and access management.

- Power Automate includes AI Builder, a tool that enables users to build custom machine learning models without having to write code.

- Power Automate supports connections to a wide range of applications and services, including popular Microsoft services like SharePoint and OneDrive, as well as many third-party services like Salesforce and Dropbox.

- Power Automate also supports custom connectors, which allow users to connect to APIs and other services not supported by the built-in connectors.

- Sharing and collaboration are an important part of Power Automate, and users can share their flows with others and work together on flows as a team.

Join our book's Discord space

Join the book's Discord Workspace for Latest updates, Offers, Tech happenings around the world, New Release and Sessions with the Authors:

https://discord.bpbonline.com

## CHAPTER 14

Power BI

> **"Good reporting is not just about the numbers; it's about the story behind the numbers."**
>
> *- Bob Garfield*

Introduction

PowerBI is a powerful tool for creating dashboards, analytics reports, and data visualization. In this chapter, you will learn about PowerBI licensing, PowerBI Desktop, how to create reports and publish them, and how to integrate and prepare reports back to SharePoint and make them visible to other users. Moreover, we will overview different data sources and connectors available in the tool and how filters, sorting, and different views can be implemented based on your needs.

Structure

In this chapter, we will cover the following topics:

- PowerBI Overview
- Common controls in PowerBI
- Available data sources in Power BI

- PowerBI Desktop
- Publishing PowerBI report
- Sharing reports with others

Objectives

In this chapter, you will learn about Power BI as a part of Microsoft 365 and SharePoint ecosystem. We will aim to gain proficiency in creating and visualizing data insights and business intelligence reports. With PowerBI, you can connect to various data sources, transform the data into meaningful insights, and create interactive, shareable reports and dashboards. PowerBI provides an end-to-end solution for data analysis, from data extraction and transformation to reporting and visualization, enabling users to make informed decisions based on their data. By learning PowerBI, you can gain a competitive edge by making data-driven decisions, optimizing processes, and identifying new business opportunities.

PowerBI Overview

PowerBI is a cloud-based business intelligence and data visualization tool provided by Microsoft. It allows users to connect, analyze, and visualize data from a wide variety of sources in a single interface. With PowerBI, users can quickly create interactive reports, dashboards, and data visualizations that enable them to make better data-driven decisions. PowerBI is designed to be user-friendly, with a drag-and-drop interface and a wide range of pre-built data connectors.

PowerBI also provides a range of advanced data analytics features, including machine learning algorithms, data modeling, and data exploration. This makes it an ideal solution for businesses and organizations of all sizes that need to analyze and understand large and complex data sets. PowerBI also offers robust collaboration features, allowing teams to work together on reports and dashboards and share data insights with others.

In addition to its web-based interface, PowerBI also provides a range of mobile and desktop apps, allowing users to access their data insights from anywhere. This makes it an ideal solution for organizations with remote workers or field-based employees who need to access data on the go.

The availability of PowerBI is determined by the licensing plan that an organization has with Microsoft. PowerBI offers several licensing options, including PowerBI Free, PowerBI Pro, and PowerBI Premium.

By default, PowerBI is not included for all users. However, some organizations may have a licensing plan that includes PowerBI for all users, or they may have purchased individual licenses for specific users. It is important to check with the organization's IT department to determine what licensing is available and who has access to PowerBI.

PowerBI can be accessed through the PowerBI service, which is a cloud-based service provided by Microsoft. To access PowerBI, you need to use a Microsoft account and sign in to the PowerBI service using your account credentials. Once you have signed in, you can create new reports, access existing reports, and collaborate with others on shared reports. PowerBI is available as a standalone service or as part of the Microsoft Power Platform, which includes other tools such as PowerApps and Power Automate. To access PowerBI, you can go to the PowerBI website and sign in with your Microsoft account. Alternatively, you can access it from Microsoft 365 portal and select PowerBI application once there.

To work with PowerBI, you typically start by connecting to your data sources, which can include databases, spreadsheets, cloud services, and other data sources. You can then use the PowerBI Desktop application to build reports, which can include visualizations such as charts, tables, and maps, as well as other components like calculations and KPIs. Once you have created your reports, you can publish them to the PowerBI service, where you can share them with others, embed them in other applications, or view them on the web or mobile devices.

In the PowerBI service, you can also create and manage dashboards, which provide a consolidated view of your data across multiple reports. You can use the dashboards to monitor key metrics, explore your data, and gain insights into your business.

PowerBI also provides a range of collaboration and data management features, such as data refresh schedules, version history, and low-level security. This allows you to work with your data in a secure and controlled manner, and ensures that your reports and dashboards remain up-to-date and accurate.

Figure 14.1 features the PowerBI home page view:

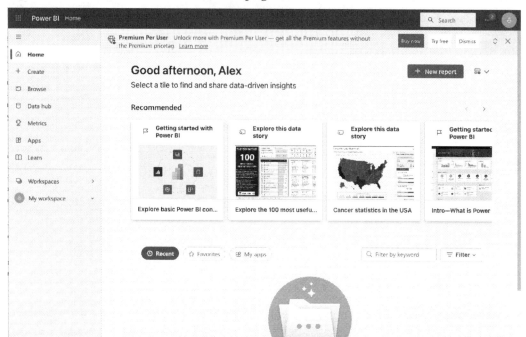

Figure 14.1: *PowerBI home page view*

The **Browse** section in PowerBI is where you can explore and interact with the visualizations, reports, and dashboards in your PowerBI workspace. You can navigate through the different views by clicking on the items in the report navigation pane, and you can interact with the data in the visualizations by selecting different elements, filtering, and drilling down into the data. The browse section provides an intuitive way to interact with the data in your PowerBI workspace, allowing you to explore and analyze the information in a visual and interactive way.

The **Data hub** in PowerBI is a central repository that enables organizations to manage and share their data sources, metadata, and PowerBI content such as reports, dashboards, and datasets. The Data hub enables the IT department to monitor and manage all the data sources in an organization, as well as to establish a data governance framework that includes role-based access control, version control, and approval workflows. The Data hub provides a single source of truth for the data that is used in PowerBI, which helps ensure that all stakeholders are using the most up-to-date and accurate data. Additionally, the Data hub allows users to find and reuse data sources, which can help save time and reduce the effort required to create new reports and dashboards.

The **Metrics** section in PowerBI is a type of visualization that displays data in a way that makes it easy to understand and measure performance. Metrics typically display numerical data, such as sales figures, profit margins, or other **Key Performance Indicators** (**KPIs**), in a way that highlights trends and helps users quickly identify areas that need improvement. Some common types of metrics include bar graphs, pie charts, line graphs, and dashboard gauges. In PowerBI, you can create metrics using a wide range of data sources and use them to monitor performance, track progress, and make informed business decisions.

PowerBI apps are pre-built collections of dashboards, reports, and data sets that provide organizations with insights into specific business domains or scenarios. You can access PowerBI apps from the PowerBI service by clicking on the **Apps** section in the menu. From there, you can search for and select a PowerBI app that fits your needs, or you can create your own custom app by combining existing reports, dashboards, and datasets. PowerBI apps are designed to be shared and re-used within an organization, making it easier to collaborate on data analysis and insights.

Workspaces, reports, and dashboards are all core components of PowerBI:

- A workspace is a container for PowerBI content that enables collaboration and sharing among a group of users. Workspaces can be created to hold reports, dashboards, and other PowerBI content, and they can be used to organize content and control access to it.

- A report is a collection of visualizations, such as charts, tables, and maps, that represent data and insights. Reports are built from one or more data sources and can be viewed, shared, and published to the PowerBI service or embedded in an application or website.

- A dashboard is a single-page, interactive report that provides an at-a-glance view of your most important data. Dashboards are built using a collection of tiles, each of which can display a different type of visualization or data.

You can use workspaces to organize your reports and dashboards and to control access to them. For example, you might create a workspace for each department in your organization, or you might create a workspace for a specific project. You can also control access to the workspaces, reports, and dashboards by setting permissions and sharing with specific individuals or groups.

My workspace refers to a personal area in PowerBI where you can store, organize, and share your reports, dashboards, and data. You can share workspaces with others, and you can also assign someone else as an administrator of the workspace. This allows them to manage the content and members of the workspace, and to perform certain actions, such as publishing reports, granting access to others, and modifying the settings of the workspace. When you share a workspace, you can choose to share it with specific individuals, or with the entire organization, depending on your needs and the level of collaboration you want to achieve.

Please note that you cannot assign someone else as the administrator inside **My Workspace**, but you can do it for all other workspaces.

Here are some main components inside PowerBI:

- **Dashboards:** This section provides an overview of all the dashboards created in your organization. You can create and manage your PowerBI dashboards from this section.

- **Reports:** This section provides a list of all the reports created in your organization. You can create new reports, edit existing reports, and publish reports from this section.

- **Workspaces:** This section provides a list of workspaces in your organization. Workspaces allow you to collaborate with other users on a set of reports and dashboards.

- **Content packs:** This section provides a list of content packs that have been created in your organization. Content packs allow you to share reports and dashboards with other users in your organization.

- **Dataflows:** This section provides a list of dataflows that have been created in your organization. Dataflows allow you to connect to and transform data from various sources.

- **Power BI Premium:** This section provides information about Power BI Premium and allows you to manage the allocation of premium capacity.

- **Settings:** This section provides various settings for PowerBI, such as security and privacy, data source settings, and more.

In PowerBI, there are several settings that allow you to customize your experience. Some of the settings you can adjust include:

- **Workspace settings:** You can set the settings for your workspaces, such as the security settings, content approval, and members.

- **Report settings:** You can set the settings for your reports, such as the privacy settings, visual level security, and data refresh options.

- **Dashboard settings:** You can set the settings for your dashboards, such as the layout, visuals, and background image.

- **Dataset settings:** You can set the settings for your datasets, such as the data source connections, privacy, and security.

- **User settings:** You can set your personal settings, such as the language, theme, and notification preferences.

- **Service settings:** You can set the global service settings, such as the system settings, telemetry, and administrator settings.

Common controls in PowerBI

PowerBI provides a variety of controls that can be used to create interactive and visually appealing dashboards and reports. Some of the common controls in PowerBI include:

- **Tables and matrices:** Used to display data in a tabular format.

- **Charts:** Including bar, column, line, pie, and scatter charts, used to display data in a visual format.

- **Maps:** Used to display geographic data.

- **Slicers:** Used to filter data on a report or dashboard.

- **Drillthrough:** Used to navigate from one report to another.

- **Drilldown:** Used to view more detailed data by expanding the data hierarchy.

- **Bookmarks:** Used to save a specific state of a report and quickly return to it.

- **Buttons:** Used to initiate actions, such as navigating to other pages or triggering a flow.

- **Textboxes:** Used to add annotations, headings, and labels to a report or dashboard.

- **Image:** Used to display images on a report or dashboard.

Figure 14.2 features PowerBI builder view in the browser:

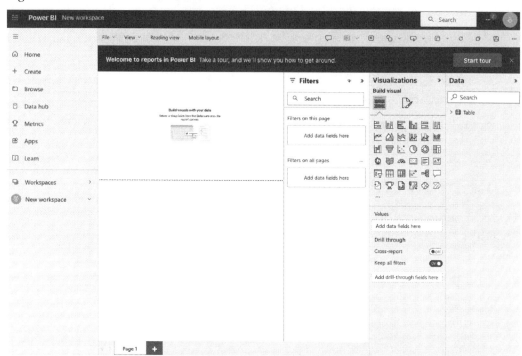

Figure 14.2: *PowerBI builder view in the browser*

The **Visualizations** tab in PowerBI provides a variety of controls to help you visualize your data and communicate insights effectively. Some of the common controls available in the Visualizations tab include:

- **Table:** A table is a simple representation of your data in rows and columns, similar to a spreadsheet. You can use a table to display your data, sort and filter it, and perform basic calculations.

- **Matrix:** A matrix is similar to a table, but with more advanced options for organizing and summarizing your data. With a matrix, you can arrange your data by rows and columns, perform calculations, and visualize data hierarchies.

- **Card:** A card is a compact visual that provides a summary of your data. You can use a card to display KPIs, such as total sales, average order value, or top-selling products.

- **Pie chart:** A pie chart is a circular chart that displays your data as a series of pie slices, where each slice represents a category or a data point. You can use a pie chart to show the relative proportions of different categories in your data.

- **Bar chart:** A bar chart displays your data as a series of bars, where each bar represents a category or a data point. You can use a bar chart to compare values across categories, or to show trends over time.

- **Line chart:** A line chart displays your data as a series of connected points, where each point represents a data point. You can use a line chart to show trends over time, or to compare multiple series of data.

- **Area chart:** An area chart is similar to a line chart, but with the area under the line filled with color. You can use an area chart to visualize data trends over time and to emphasize differences between series.

- **Scatter chart:** A scatter chart displays your data as a set of points on a two-dimensional plane, where each point represents a data point. You can use a scatter chart to show the relationship between two variables, or to visualize trends over time.

These are some of the common controls available in the **Visualizations** tab in PowerBI, but there are many others as well. Each control provides different options for visualizing and summarizing your data, and you can use them in combination to communicate insights effectively.

In PowerBI, the **Filters** and **Data** tabs allow you to control and manipulate the data used in your report:

- The **Filters** tab allows you to apply filters to your data so that you only see the information you want to see in your report. You can apply filters based on specific conditions or values, and you can also use drill-through filters to enable more detailed exploration of your data.

- The **Data** tab provides a view of the data sources used in your report, as well as options for managing your data such as refreshing data, defining relationships between tables, and creating calculated columns. This tab also provides access to **Data Analysis Expressions** (**DAX**), a powerful formula language that you can use to create calculated columns and measures, and to perform complex calculations on your data.

Here is an example of a DAX expression:

$$Total\ Sales = SUM(Sales[Amount])$$

In this example, the DAX expression Total Sales calculates the sum of all values in the Amount column of the Sales table. The result of the expression is displayed as a calculated field in the PowerBI report.

Pages in PowerBI are individual visualizations that you can create, customize, and share in a report. Each page provides a visual representation of your data and helps you to explore and analyze information. Pages can include a variety of elements such as charts, tables, maps, and KPIs. You can use pages to focus on specific aspects of your data or to create a summary of the information in your report. By creating multiple pages, you can provide different views of your data and help others to better understand the information you are presenting. It is similar to a Tabs concept in Excel.

Available data sources in Power BI

In PowerBI, there are several available data sources, including the following:

- **Files:** PowerBI can import data from a wide range of file types, such as Excel, CSV, XML, JSON, and more.

- **Databases:** PowerBI can connect to a variety of databases, including SQL Server, Oracle, PostgreSQL, and more.

- **Cloud Services:** PowerBI can connect to popular cloud services such as Salesforce, Dynamics 365, Google Analytics, and more.

- **Web Content**: PowerBI can scrape data from websites and APIs.

- **Power Platform:** PowerBI can integrate data from other Power Platform services, such as PowerApps and Power Automate.

- **Power BI datasets:** PowerBI datasets can be used as a source of data for other PowerBI reports.

- **DirectQuery/Live Connection**: PowerBI allows to connect to databases and data sources using DirectQuery or Live Connection, allowing the user to create a report based on the data source without copying the data into PowerBI.

These are some of the commonly used data sources in PowerBI. The available data sources may vary depending on the type of PowerBI license you have and the region you are in.

You can use custom data sources or connect your own data sources in PowerBI. PowerBI provides a variety of built-in data connectors for popular services and databases, but you can also use custom connectors to access other data sources. The custom data connectors can be created using the Power Query Editor, which allows you to access, manipulate, and transform data from a wide range of sources, including REST APIs, OData feeds, and databases.

To create a custom connector in PowerBI, you need to use the PowerBI Developer Tools and Microsoft Power Apps. The process of creating a custom connector involves the following steps:

1. **Create a custom API:** You will need to build a custom API that exposes the data you want to connect to. This can be a REST API, an OData feed, or a SOAP web service.

2. **Build the custom connector:** You will use the PowerBI Developer Tools to build the custom connector. This involves defining the metadata for your custom API, such as the endpoint, authentication type, and available operations.

3. **Publish the custom connector:** After you have built the custom connector, you will need to publish it to the PowerBI Service. This will make the custom connector available to all users in your organization.

4. **Connect to the custom data source:** To use the custom connector in PowerBI, you will need to create a new data connection. This involves specifying the custom API endpoint and entering any authentication credentials if required. You will then be able to use the custom data source to build reports, dashboards, and other visualizations in PowerBI.

It is important to note that creating a custom connector requires some technical expertise and a good understanding of APIs, web services, and authentication methods. If you are not familiar with these concepts, you may need to seek assistance from a developer.

In PowerBI, you can refresh your data either manually or automatically. Manual refresh allows you to manually update the data in your report by clicking the **Refresh** button in the **Home** tab of the PowerBI Desktop or in the PowerBI Service. Automatic refresh allows you to schedule data refreshes at specific times or intervals so that the data in your report is always up-to-date. To enable automatic refresh, you need to set up a refresh schedule for your data source in the PowerBI Service. This schedule can be set for daily, weekly, or monthly refresh, and you can specify the time and frequency of the refresh. Additionally, you can set up refresh alerts to be notified when a refresh fails or if the data source cannot be reached.

The number of automatic data refreshes per day that are available in Power BI depends on the type of license you have. For Power BI Free, there is a limit of 8 refreshes per day. For Power BI Pro, there is a limit of 8 refreshes per day. For Power BI Premium, there are no limits on the number of refreshes per day, but the refresh frequency is subject to availability and may vary based on other usage of the service. It is always best to check with Microsoft for the most up-to-date information on automatic data refreshes limitations for Power BI.

PowerBI Desktop

PowerBI Desktop is a Windows application that provides a rich environment for creating, editing, and publishing interactive data visualizations, reports, and dashboards. PowerBI Desktop allows users to connect to a variety of data sources, such as databases, spreadsheets, and cloud services, and transform the data into meaningful insights. PowerBI Desktop provides a user-friendly interface for building data models and creating charts, tables, and other visualizations that can be published to the PowerBI Service and shared with others. PowerBI Desktop also includes DAX functions that allow users to perform complex calculations on their data, including aggregating and filtering data, creating calculated columns and measures, and generating calculated tables. PowerBI Desktop is often used by business intelligence professionals and data analysts to develop rich, interactive data reports that can be used to monitor business performance, detect trends, and make informed decisions.

Figure 14.3 features the PowerBI desktop view:

***Figure 14.3**: PowerBI desktop view*

PowerBI Desktop is a standalone Windows application that provides a more powerful and feature-rich experience for creating, enhancing, and publishing reports to the PowerBI service compared to the web browser version. Some of the key differences between PowerBI Desktop and PowerBI in a web browser include:

- **Advanced authoring features:** PowerBI Desktop provides a wider range of report authoring features, including more advanced data modeling, calculated fields, and custom visuals.

- **Offline report authoring:** With PowerBI Desktop, you can create and modify reports offline, even when you do not have an internet connection. You can then publish the report to the PowerBI service once you are back online.

- **Performance optimizations:** PowerBI Desktop is optimized for performance, with the ability to work with large datasets and provide fast data refresh times.

- **Custom visualizations:** PowerBI Desktop provides the ability to create custom visuals, which are not available in the web browser version.

- **Integration with other Microsoft products:** PowerBI Desktop provides integration with other Microsoft products, such as Excel, allowing you to easily import data from spreadsheets and perform advanced data manipulations.

Overall, if you are a frequent report author and need more advanced features, it is recommended to use PowerBI Desktop.

You can work with both the desktop and web version of PowerBI by saving and publishing reports created in PowerBI Desktop to the PowerBI Service, which is the web version of PowerBI. This allows you to access your reports from any device with internet access and collaborate with others by sharing access to the reports. When you make changes to the report in PowerBI Desktop, you can publish the updated report to the PowerBI Service, which will automatically update the report for all users who have access to it. Conversely, if you make changes to the report in the PowerBI Service, these changes will not be reflected in the PowerBI Desktop version of the report until you refresh the report in PowerBI Desktop.

PowerBI Desktop can be downloaded for free from the Microsoft website. PowerBI Desktop allows you to create, publish, and manage PowerBI reports and dashboards, and provides additional functionality and features not available in the web version, such as advanced data modeling, query authoring, and report design. However, the web version of PowerBI is required for sharing and collaborating with others, and for publishing reports and dashboards to the PowerBI service. There is no cost to download and use PowerBI Desktop, but there may be costs associated with using the PowerBI service, depending on the level of usage and the features required.

Publishing PowerBI report

Publishing in PowerBI refers to the process of sharing your PowerBI report with others. After you create a report in PowerBI Desktop, you can publish it to the PowerBI service, so that others can access it. The report will be stored in a workspace and can be accessed through a web browser or the PowerBI mobile app. The report can be customized and filtered by the end user, but the underlying data is not exposed. To publish a report, you need to save it to a workspace in the PowerBI service and then share the workspace with others. You can control who has access to the report and what they can do with it.

To publish a report in PowerBI, you need to follow these steps:

1. Open the report in PowerBI Desktop.

2. Click on the **Publish** button in the **Home** tab.

3. The report will be uploaded to the PowerBI service and made available to others.

> **Note: You need to have a PowerBI Pro or PowerBI Premium license to publish reports. The reports can be viewed by others who have access to the PowerBI service, either through a shared workspace or through a shared link.**

You can also embed PowerBI reports in SharePoint. To embed a PowerBI report in SharePoint, you need to have a PowerBI Pro or PowerBI Premium license. Once you have a license, you can create a report in PowerBI Desktop, publish it to the PowerBI Service, and then embed the report in SharePoint using the PowerBI Report Web Part.

As for embedding PowerBI reports in 3rd party sites outside of Microsoft 365, this is possible by using the PowerBI Embed API. The PowerBI Embed API allows you to embed PowerBI reports and dashboards into custom web applications, portals, and other web-based solutions. However, the exact steps for doing this will depend on the specific platform you are using and the requirements of the application.

Sharing reports with others

In PowerBI, you can share reports and workspaces with others by granting them access to the content. To share a report or workspace, you need to follow these steps:

1. Open the report or workspace that you want to share.

2. Click on the **Share** button, which is typically located in the upper-right corner of the screen.

3. Enter the email addresses of the people you want to share the report or workspace with.

4. Choose the level of access you want to grant the people you are sharing with. There are typically three options: View, Interact, and Edit. The "View" option allows users to view the report or workspace, but not make any changes. The "Interact" option allows users to view the report or workspace and interact with the visualizations and data, but not make any changes. The "Edit" option allows users to view, interact with, and make changes to the report or workspace.

5. Click the **Share** button to complete the sharing process.

Once you have shared a report or workspace, the people you shared it with will receive an email with a link to the content. They will be able to access the report or workspace by clicking the link and logging in to their PowerBI account.

In addition to sharing reports and workspaces within PowerBI, you can also embed PowerBI reports in SharePoint and other third-party websites outside of Microsoft 365. To embed a PowerBI report, you need to follow these steps:

1. Open the report that you want to embed.

2. Click the **File** menu, then select **Publish to Web**.

3. Choose the level of access you want to grant to people who view the embedded report. There are typically three options: View, Interact, and Edit.

4. Click the **Create embed code** button to generate the embed code.

5. Copy the embed code and paste it into the HTML code of your SharePoint or third-party website.

Once you have embedded the report, people who view your SharePoint or third-party website will be able to see the report and interact with it, based on the level of access you granted.

There are also various levels of permission that you can assign to users, including Member, Contributor, and Admin. Members can only view and interact with the report, Contributors can create and edit reports, and Admins have full control over the workspace and can add or remove members and set permissions.

You can set these permissions and access levels from the **Access and Permissions** section in the Workspace settings.

Practical tasks

As always, it is now time to get back to practice.

Log in to Microsoft 365 portal using your credentials, and from the list of available applications, select PowerBI. You will have a web version of the application open. It gives you functionality to develop reports, dashboards, and other data sets. But to use PowerBI to the maximum, PowerBI Desktop is the way to go.

So, you need to download and install it. You can get a PowerBI desktop from: **https://www.microsoft.com/en-us/download/details.aspx?id=58494** or simply google '**PowerBI Desktop download**' phrase. Download the package and follow the installation prompts.

You already have PowerBI license and everything included with your admin account and sandbox environment. But in real life, you would need to assign the license to each user separately as PowerBI, in most of the cases comes with extra cost, unless you have E5 or G5 license, which is not very common. To assign the license, you would typically go to the Microsoft 365 admin center – Active users section. Select the required user from there and go to Licenses and apps tab and assign PowerBI license there.

Figure 14.4 features PowerBI license assignment from the Admin center:

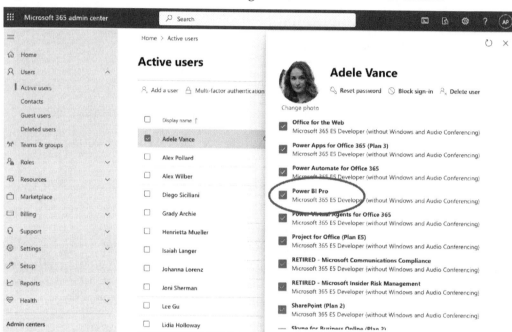

Figure 14.4: *PowerBI license assignment from the Admin center*

To start working with the PowerBI desktop, you would need to create a workspace first. You cannot create a workspace from PowerBI Desktop. Workspaces are a feature in the PowerBI Service, which is the web-based version.

To create a workspace, you need to sign in to PowerBI Service and navigate to the Workspaces section. From there, you can create a new workspace, add members, and specify roles and level of access. In this case, check that you are set as a admin of the workspace.

Figure 14.5 features the creation of the new workspace in the PowerBI web:

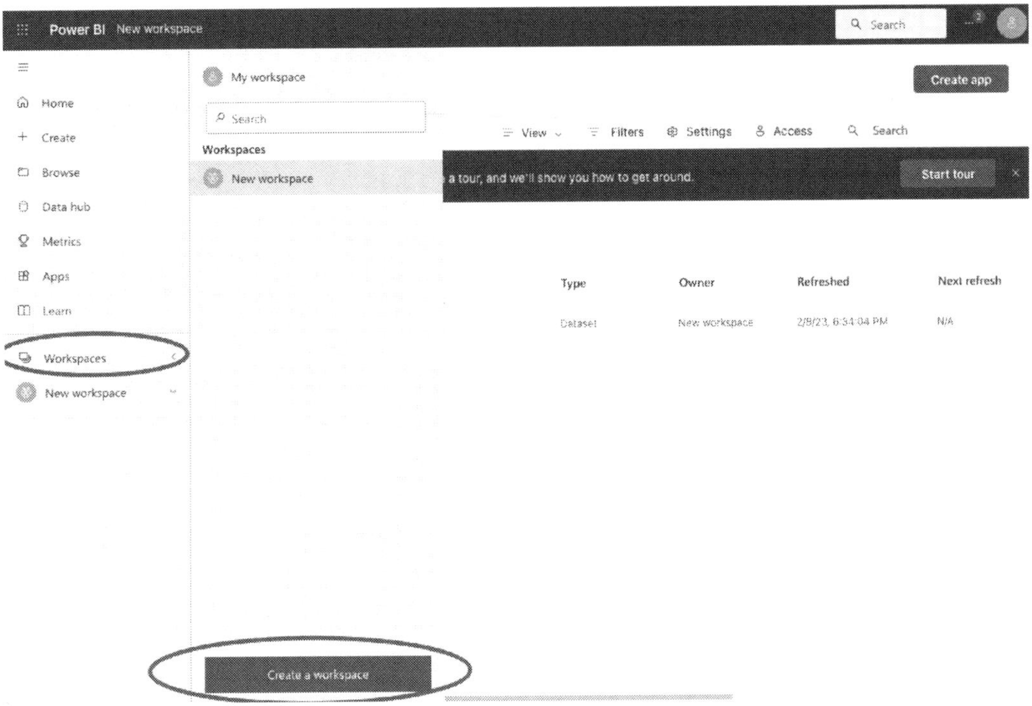

Figure 14.5: *The creation of the new workspace in the PowerBI web*

Once the workspace is created, you can switch back to PowerBI desktop and sign in with your account. Once logged in, you will see a workspace you created in the list of available workspaces.

Let us create a simple report and publish it.

> **Note: There are a lot of exercises, and great examples available at Microsoft learn website. You can google it or just type the link manually: https://learn.microsoft. com/en-us/power-bi/create-reports/sample-datasets**

To build your own report, follow these steps:

1. Open PowerBI Desktop and click on **Get Data** in the Home ribbon.

2. Select **SharePoint Online List** as the data source and click on **Connect**. You can use the same list that we used in previous example with PowerApps and Power Automate. In the majority of situations, PowerApp, Power Automate and PowerBI work together retrieving data from the same data set.

3. Enter the URL of your SharePoint site and select the appropriate authentication method.

4. Select the SharePoint list you want to connect to and click on **Load**.

5. In the PowerBI Desktop report view, you can add fields to the report by dragging them from the Fields panel to the report canvas.

6. To add filters, right-click on the field you want to filter and select **Filter**. You can add multiple filters to limit the data shown in the report.

7. To create a visualization, select the field you want to visualize in the **Fields** panel, then click on the appropriate visualization type in the **Visualizations** panel. You can customize the visualization as needed by using the Format and Analyze ribbons.

8. To add additional pages to the report, click on **Page tools** in the Home ribbon and select **Add Page**.

9. To save the report, click on **Save** in the Home ribbon. To publish the report, select **Publish** in the Home ribbon.

In this exercise, use fields that are already there in the list or you can add new columns and pull it into your report. If you have any Excel files handy – feel free to connect them too, into your report and combine data from both data sets together to see how it works. Apply some filters and build table view.

After getting published, your report will be available for viewing in the PowerBI web and from there, it can be shared with other users or integrated to other apps such as SharePoint.

To integrate the PowerBI report with SharePoint, go to SharePoint online. You can go to any of the previously created sites or create a new one. Click **Edit Page** and look for the PowerBI web part.

Figure 14.6 features PowerBI web-part in SharePoint online:

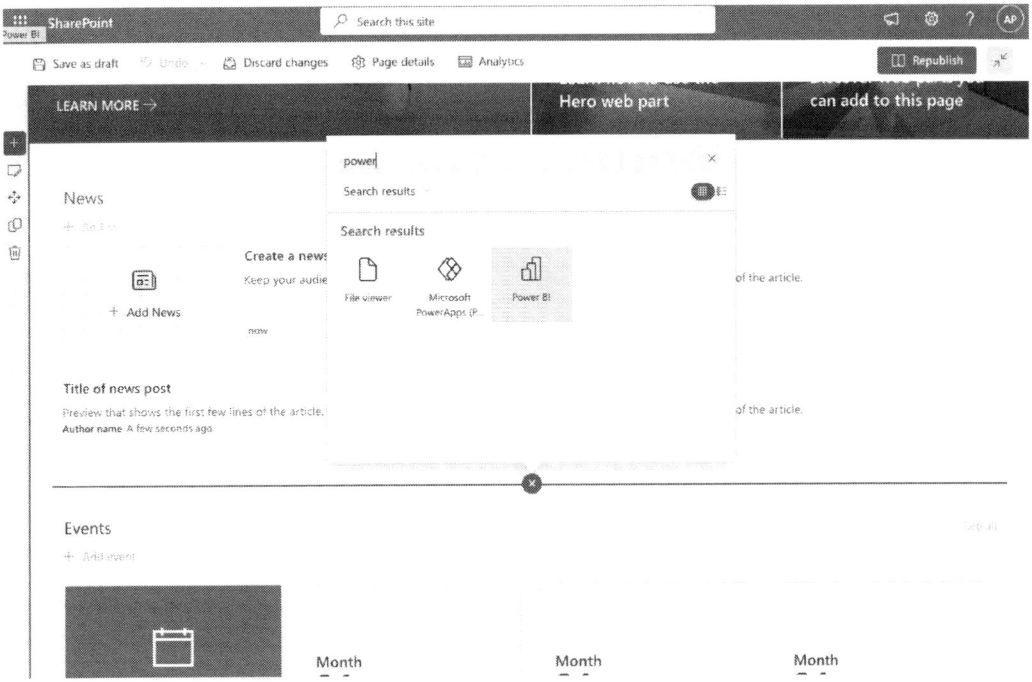

Figure 14.6: *PowerBI web-part in SharePoint online*

After the web part is added, you would need to click on it to edit it and provide your report ID inside the web part property. You can find ID in the PowerBI service itself (web version).

Open a report in the Power BI service.

On the **File** menu, select **Embed report | SharePoint Online**.

Figure 14.7 features PowerBI report copying embed link:

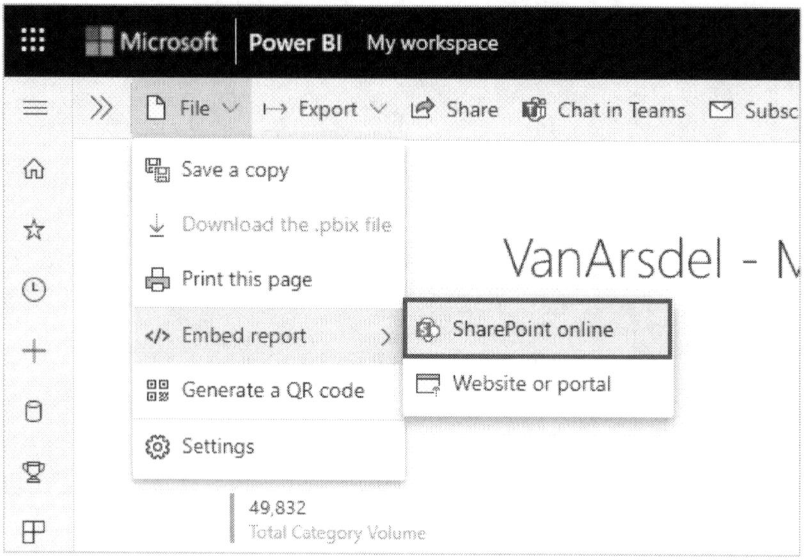

Figure 14.7: *PowerBI report copying embed link*

Copy the report URL from the dialog box. Then, insert it into the web part property on a SharePoint page inside the PowerBI report link field.

You will see how your report is now embedded into the SharePoint page.

You can publish a page now.

Conclusion

In this chapter, you learned about Power BI and its core functionality and features. There is much more to learn about Power BI as a service and you can find out more information from learning sites such as Microsoft learning or some videos and dedicated to this topic courses on the web. In conclusion, we can state that PowerBI is a powerful business intelligence and data visualization tool that allows users to quickly and easily transform data into actionable insights. With a wide range of data sources and an intuitive user interface, PowerBI makes it easy for users to connect, model, and visualize data from a variety of sources, including SharePoint, Excel, and other cloud-based data sources. Whether you are creating a simple report or a complex dashboard, PowerBI has the tools and features you need to effectively communicate data insights to your stakeholders.

Points to remember

- PowerBI is a cloud-based business intelligence and data visualization tool.

- It offers a wide range of data visualization options and integrates with various data sources, including Microsoft Excel and SharePoint.

- PowerBI Desktop is a powerful tool for creating and analyzing data in PowerBI, while PowerBI in a web browser is a good option for consuming and sharing reports.

- Workspaces in PowerBI allow you to share and collaborate on reports with others.

- There are several data visualization controls available in PowerBI, including charts, tables, and maps.

- PowerBI supports automatic and manual data refresh, and you can use DAX to create custom calculations.

- PowerBI reports can be published and embedded in SharePoint and other 3rd party websites, and you can share workspaces with others with different levels of access and permissions.

- PowerBI Desktop is free to download, but you may need a PowerBI Pro or PowerBI Premium license for advanced features and capabilities.

Join our book's Discord space

Join the book's Discord Workspace for Latest updates, Offers, Tech happenings around the world, New Release and Sessions with the Authors:

https://discord.bpbonline.com

## CHAPTER 15

Office 365 Admin Center

> "Good system administration is not just about being able to restore service quickly, but also about making it less likely that problems will occur in the first place"
>
> *- Thomas Limoncelli*

Introduction

As you become familiar with the primary applications of Microsoft 365 from previous chapters, in this one, you will learn how to administrate and manage all of the applications using the Microsoft 365 Admin center. It includes various admin centers and their capabilities to configure policies, set up users and manage billing.

Structure

In this chapter, we will cover the following topics:

- SharePoint Admin Center
- PowerApps Admin Center
- Exchange Admin Center
- Teams Admin Center

- OneDrive Admin Center
- Users and licenses management

Objectives

The objective of learning about the various Office 365 admin centers is to understand the different tools and features available for managing an Office 365 environment. By learning about the different admin centers, you will gain an understanding of how to manage different aspects of an Office 365 deployment, including users, services, security, and more. This can help you to better support your organization's needs, increase efficiency, and streamline administrative tasks. We have already reviewed a lot of functionality of different admin centers. In this chapter, we will recap some of the previously gained knowledge and will get some additional ones as well.

SharePoint Admin Center

The SharePoint Admin Center is a central location for administrators to manage SharePoint Online environments. It provides a variety of tools and settings to help manage SharePoint sites, users, and content. You can use the SharePoint Admin Center to control access to sites and manage site collections, perform site and content management tasks, manage user profiles, and control service applications. The SharePoint Admin Center also provides access to monitoring and reporting tools to help administrators keep track of the health and performance of your SharePoint environment. The SharePoint Admin Center is a crucial tool, as it provides the means to control and manage the SharePoint platform effectively.

Figure 15.1 features the SharePoint Admin center Home page with some report metrics:

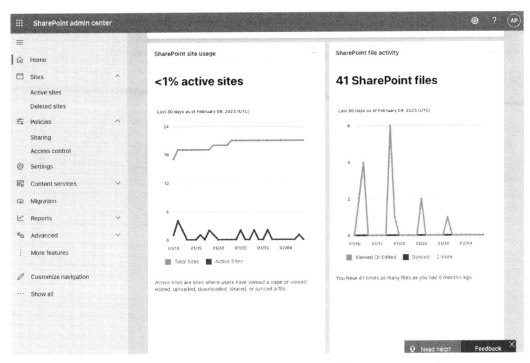

***Figure 15.1:** SharePoint Admin center Home page with some report metrics*

The *home page* of the SharePoint admin center provides an overview of the SharePoint environment, including the current usage and storage status, and any recent service issues. You can also see recent activity, including changes to the SharePoint environment, such as site collections created or deleted, and changes to permissions. Additionally, you can access various SharePoint management tools and settings from the home page, such as the site collections and user profiles management pages.

The *navigation* in the SharePoint admin center is structured in a left-side menu that contains links to various administrative pages. These pages allow you to manage different aspects of your SharePoint environment, such as users and permissions, site collections, policies and settings, and health and performance.

In the **Sites** section of the SharePoint admin center, you can view a list of all the SharePoint sites and site collections that are within your organization. You can use the Sites section to manage various aspects of your SharePoint sites, such as setting up and configuring sites, managing user access, and monitoring site usage and performance. In this section, you can also view detailed information about each site, such as its URL, storage usage, and the number of users who have access to it. Additionally, you can perform actions such as creating new sites, editing existing sites, and deleting sites that are no longer needed.

Figure 15.2 features the SharePoint Admin center Site section site properties panel:

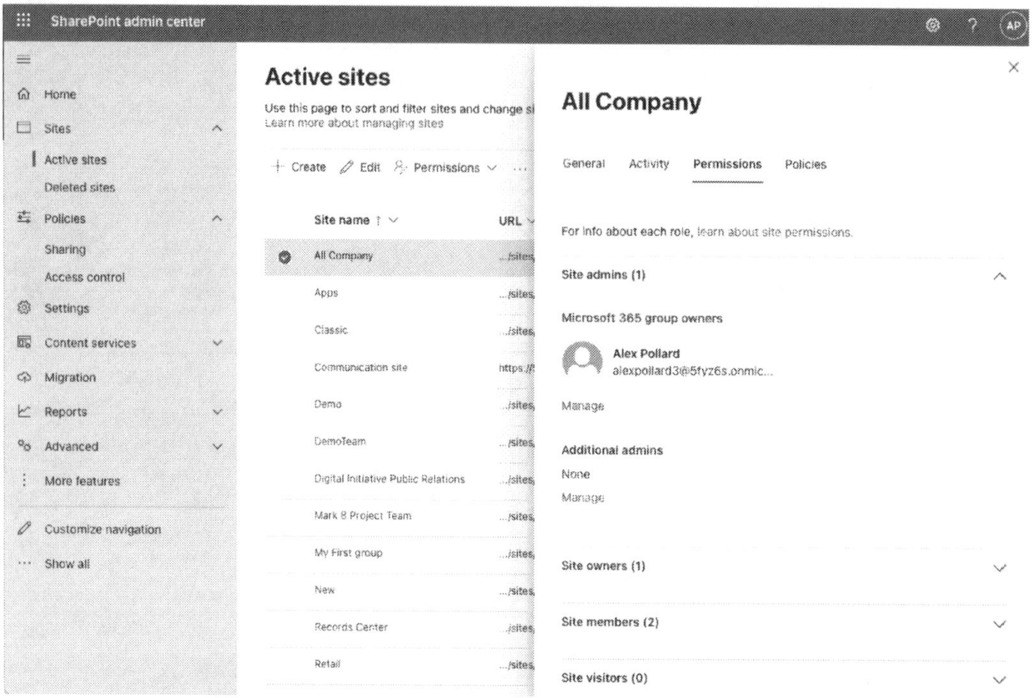

Figure 15.2: SharePoint Admin center Site section site properties panel

The **Policies** section in the SharePoint Admin Center allows you to manage various policies related to your SharePoint environment. Some of the policies that you can manage include:

- **Sharing:** You can manage sharing policies, such as external sharing, to determine who can share content outside of your organization.

- **User Profiles:** You can manage user profile policies, such as who can view or edit user profiles.

- **Compliance:** You can manage compliance policies, such as retention policies, to ensure that your content is retained for the appropriate amount of time.

- **Classification:** You can manage classification policies, such as labeling and protection, to help keep your content secure.

- **Sites:** You can manage site policies, such as site collection policies and site usage policies, to determine who can create and use sites in your environment.

In the **Settings** section of the SharePoint Admin Center, administrators can manage various settings for SharePoint sites and environments. Some of the options available under this section include:

- **Authentication:** Manage the authentication methods used by SharePoint, such as Windows authentication, forms-based authentication, and SAML-based authentication.

- **Security:** Manage various security-related settings, such as password policies, user authentication, and IP address access restrictions.

- **Sharing:** Control how content is shared and who it is shared with, including external sharing and anonymous links.

- **User profiles:** Manage the user profile service, including settings for user profiles, social features, and activity feeds.

- **Resource Quotas:** Monitor and manage the use of resources by SharePoint sites, including the number of sites, storage, and data transfers.

- **Health Analyzer:** Monitor the health and performance of SharePoint sites and identify potential issues that need to be addressed.

The **Content Services** section provides features to help manage and optimize SharePoint content. This includes options for managing the content lifecycle, such as retention policies, records management, and eDiscovery. It also includes options for managing and configuring search and metadata management. The content services section is where administrators can configure settings for SharePoint content, such as content types, site columns, and managed metadata. Additionally, administrators can manage hybrid scenarios and configure connectors to other systems.

The **Migration** section in SharePoint Admin Center provides the ability to move sites and content from other locations to SharePoint in the Microsoft 365 environment.

The **Reports** section provides an overview of usage and activity data, such as site usage and storage metrics, as well as information about sites, content and activity trends.

The **Advanced** section in SharePoint Admin Center provides access to more technical and administrative controls, such as service health, settings for features such as sharing, OneDrive for Business and other cloud-based services, and APIs for custom and advanced solutions.

The **More Features** section in the SharePoint Admin Center can contain various administrative features, such as the Term Store, User Profiles, Search, Apps, and others. These features provide administrators with additional capabilities to manage SharePoint and control various aspects of the platform. For example, the Term Store is used to manage metadata and taxonomy, while User Profiles are used to manage information about users and their activity on the platform. The Search feature can be used to manage search settings and configure the search experience for users. It also has configuration for Infopath, **Business Connectivity Services** (**BCS**) and so on.

PowerApps Admin Center

The Power Platform from the Office 365 admin center provides an administrative interface for managing PowerApps, Power Automate (formerly Microsoft Flow), and Power BI, which are low-code/no-code platforms for creating custom business apps, automating workflows, and analyzing data, respectively.

As an administrator, you can use the Power Platform section of the Office 365 admin center to manage the deployment and usage of these platforms across your organization, including setting policies and permissions, monitoring usage and performance, and controlling the data that is accessed and used.

Additionally, the Power Platform can help you streamline processes, automate repetitive tasks, and gain insights into business data. By providing a centralized location to manage these tools, the Power Platform can help administrators increase efficiency and promote adoption of these tools across the organization.

The *home page* of the Power Platform admin center provides an overview of the environment and displays a dashboard with key performance indicators, such as the number of Power Apps, Power Automate flows, and Power Virtual Agents in use, as well as the usage data of each. The home page also provides quick access to the most common administrative tasks, such as managing licenses, monitoring data usage, and accessing the app settings.

The **Environments** section in the Power Platform admin center provides administrators with a view of the environments that have been created in their organization, as well as the ability to manage those environments. In this section, you can see a list of all the environments in their organization, including the environment type, the name of the environment, the state of the environment, and the date it was last modified. You can also perform tasks such as creating new environments, deleting existing environments, and managing the settings and configuration of the environments. This section provides a centralized location for administrators to manage the environment and infrastructure components required to support Power Platform applications.

The **Analytics** section in the Power Platform Admin Center provides information and insights into the usage of the Power Apps, Power Automate, and Power Virtual Agents in your organization. You can view data such as the number of apps and flows created, the number of runs and executions, and the average response time for flows. This section also provides information on the usage of connectors, premium features, and data sources. With this information, you can monitor the health and usage of the Power Platform and make informed decisions about your organization's needs and usage.

The **Billing** section in the Power Platform Admin Center provides a centralized location for managing the costs associated with using Power Platform. This section allows you to view and manage the licenses and subscriptions for your organization's Power Platform usage, view invoices and payment history, and set up billing notifications to stay informed of your organization's Power Platform spending. You can also set budgets and alerts to help manage costs and allocate funds accordingly.

The **Settings** section of the Power Platform admin center provides access to various configuration options and settings for your Power Platform environments. This section allows you to control the behavior of your environment and manage the users who have access to it. Some of the options you can configure in the settings section include:

- **Environment settings:** This section allows you to configure general settings for your environment, such as the display name, environment URL, and the location of your data.

- **User settings:** This section allows you to manage users and their access to your environment, including granting or revoking access and setting up custom roles.

- **Security and Compliance:** This section provides tools and resources to help you maintain the security and compliance of your environment, including options for data privacy and data retention.

- **Integration:** This section allows you to set up integration between your environment and other systems, such as Microsoft Power Apps and Microsoft Power Automate.

- **Support:** This section provides resources and support options for troubleshooting and resolving issues with your environment.

The **Resources** section in the Power Platform admin center provides access to resources that are related to the Power Platform, such as documentation, videos, and community resources. In this section, administrators can access resources that can help them get started with the platform, troubleshoot any issues that they may encounter, and learn about best practices for using the platform effectively. Additionally, the Resources section may also include links to resources that are specific to a particular component of the Power Platform, such as Power Apps or Power Automate. The resources available in this section will depend on the specific version of the Power Platform that is being used, as well as the region and the type of subscription that is in place.

In the Power Platform admin center, the **Data integration** section is where you can manage data integration and migration. You can see a list of your data integrations and manage their settings, run migration jobs, and access the **Common Data Service** (**CDS**).

The Data section provides a view into the data that is stored in the CDS and other connected sources. You can manage entities, fields, and relationships, create custom entities, and add and manage data sources.

The **Policies** section lets you manage policies for your environment, such as security policies and data privacy policies. You can set up policies for data masking, data encryption, and data retention. This section also provides a view into the policy enforcement and compliance of your environment.

Figure 15.3 features Power Platform admin center **Dataverse Analytics** section:

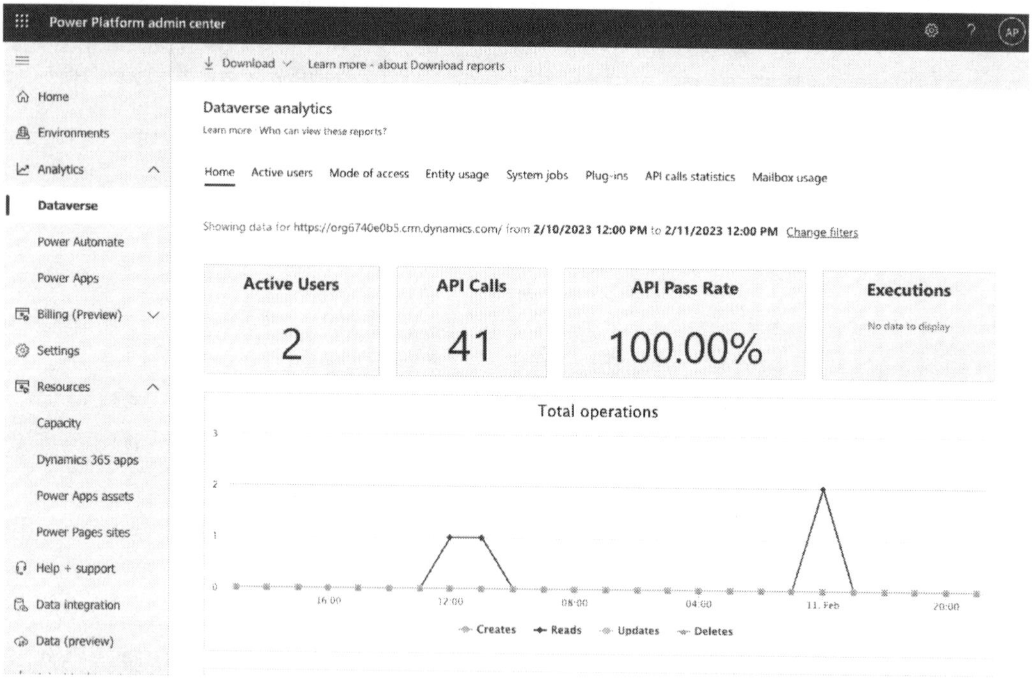

Figure 15.3: Power Platform admin center Analytics section

Exchange Admin Center

The **Exchange Admin Center** (**EAC**) is a web-based management console for Exchange Server that allows administrators to manage various aspects of an Exchange organization, such as mailboxes, recipients, servers, and email addresses, through a web interface. The EAC provides a consolidated view of Exchange-related management tasks and reduces the need to use the Exchange Management Shell. With the EAC, administrators can perform common tasks, such as creating and managing mailboxes, and setting up email addresses and distribution groups, with ease. Additionally, the EAC provides various reporting and diagnostic tools, such as message trace, that help administrators monitor and troubleshoot their Exchange environment.

The *home page* of the Exchange admin center typically provides an overview of the organization's current status and provides quick access to commonly used tasks and reports. Some of the information that may be displayed on the home page of the Exchange admin center includes:

- Information about the number of mailboxes, distribution groups, and other messaging components in the organization.

- Overviews of the overall health of the Exchange organization, including alerts, service status, and performance statistics.

- Quick access to frequently used tasks, such as managing mailboxes, configuring email addresses, and creating distribution groups.

- Access to detailed reports, such as usage statistics, message trace data, and performance reports.

The **Recipients** section is where you can manage various aspects of the email accounts in the organization, such as email addresses, email addresses, distribution groups, shared mailboxes, and user accounts. Within this section, administrators can perform tasks such as creating new email addresses, modifying existing email addresses, setting up distribution groups, and managing shared mailboxes. Additionally, they can perform tasks related to user accounts, such as resetting passwords and enabling or disabling accounts.

The **Mail flow** section in the Exchange Admin Center provides administrative controls for the email messages in your organization's Exchange environment. This section is used to manage the routing of incoming and outgoing email messages, including the rules and configurations for message transport and delivery. Some of the features you can access in the Mail flow section include:

- Mailbox rules

- Transport rules

- Mail flow configuration

- Connectors

- Email address policies

These features allow you to set up and manage the flow of email messages for your organization, helping to ensure the secure and efficient delivery of messages between your users.

The **Roles** section in the Exchange Admin Center is where you can manage and assign various roles to different users in your organization. Roles in Exchange are used to control what users have access to and what they can do within the Exchange system. Some of the roles available in Exchange include:

- **Mailbox administrator:** Responsible for managing mailboxes, such as creating, deleting, and modifying mailbox settings.

- **Compliance administrator:** Responsible for managing compliance features, such as retention policies, eDiscovery searches, and auditing.

- **Help desk administrator:** Responsible for providing support for users, such as resetting passwords, unlocking accounts, and managing distribution groups.

- **Recipient administrator:** Responsible for managing recipients, such as mailboxes, distribution groups, and mail contacts.

By assigning roles to different users in your organization, you can delegate administrative tasks and ensure that the right people have access to the information and tools they need to do their jobs.

The **Migration** section of the Exchange Admin Center allows you to manage email migrations between different email systems. In this section, administrators can create and manage migration batches, view the status of ongoing migrations, and access detailed reports on migration progress.

The **Mobile** section of the Exchange Admin Center provides you with tools to manage and secure mobile access to Exchange email. This section includes options for setting up device policies, monitoring mobile device usage, and configuring device access rules. Administrators can also use this section to manage mobile device security, such as requiring device encryption and setting up password policies.

The **Report** section in Exchange Admin Center provides information about the activity and usage of your Exchange environment, such as the number of messages sent and received, the number of active mailboxes, and the amount of mailbox storage used.

The **Organization** section provides a centralized location where you can manage settings and features that affect your entire organization, such as the Global Address List, Outlook Web App policies, and email address policies.

The **Public Folders** section provides the ability to manage public folders, which are shared folders that can be used to store and exchange information within an organization. In this section, you can create and manage public folder mailboxes, and set permissions for users to access and manage the folders.

In the **Settings** section of Exchange Admin Center, you can manage various settings for your Exchange Online organization. This includes configuration options for mail flow, recipients, compliance, permissions, and more. The **Other Features** section provides access to advanced features such as data loss prevention, role-based access control, and the ability to manage your organization's domain names. The exact features that are available in the Other Features section may vary depending on your specific Exchange Online configuration.

Figure 15.4 features the Exchange admin center Other features section:

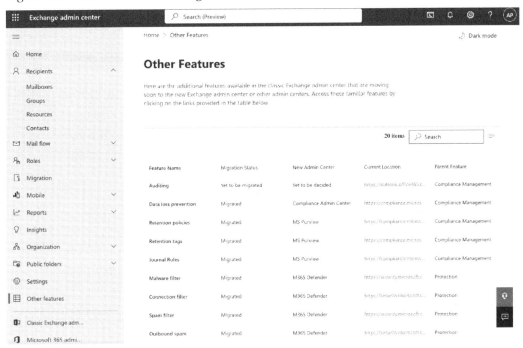

Figure 15.4: *Exchange admin center Other features section*

Teams Admin Center

The Teams Admin Center is a web-based interface for you to manage and configure Microsoft Teams settings for their organization. The Teams Admin Center provides visibility and control over various Teams settings and features, including user management, meeting and calling policies, org-wide settings, and more. The Teams Admin Center is accessible to administrators with the appropriate permissions and can be used to make changes that affect the entire organization. With the Teams Admin Center, administrators can help ensure that Teams is being used effectively and efficiently, and that the right settings are in place to support their organization's needs.

The Teams admin center **dashboard** provides an overview of your organization's Teams usage and allows you to monitor and manage various aspects of your Teams deployment. On the dashboard, you can see information such as the number of active users, the number of teams created, the number of channels, and the amount of storage used. You can also view charts and graphs that provide insights into how Teams is being used in your organization, such as the frequency of chat and call activity, and the distribution of usage across different devices. Additionally, the dashboard may also include alerts and notifications that help you stay informed about important issues or changes in your Teams deployment.

The **Teams** section in the Teams admin center provides the ability to manage various aspects of Teams for your organization. You can use it to:

- Create and manage Teams and channels.

- Manage members and their permissions within Teams.

- Set policies for Teams, such as who can create teams and what type of content can be shared.

- Monitor usage and activity within Teams, such as the number of active users and the number of messages sent.

- Manage apps and services available in Teams, such as bots and connectors.

Additionally, you can use the Teams admin center to monitor and troubleshoot issues with Teams, as well as access and manage settings related to Teams.

The **Users** section contains information and settings related to the users in your organization who are using Microsoft Teams. This section allows you to manage and view the list of users, and perform various tasks such as adding new users, editing existing user information, assigning licenses, and more. You can also see usage and adoption information for Teams and its related services, such as OneDrive and Exchange. The Users section can be used to ensure that your users have the necessary licenses, permissions, and resources to effectively use Teams and other related services.

The **Teams Apps and Meetings** sections in the Teams admin center provide administrators with the ability to manage and configure the apps and meetings experience for users within their organization. In the **Teams Apps** section, administrators can view, manage, and approve apps that have been added to Teams by users, as well as manage policies for app installation and usage. In the **Meetings** section, administrators can manage settings for meetings, such as the ability to join meetings before the host arrives, virtual backgrounds, and recording settings. They can also manage policies related to meetings, such as the use of the meeting lobby, who can present, and audio and video settings.

Some other sections in the Teams Admin center include:

- The **messaging policies** section in Teams Admin Center allows you to manage the policies that control how users can communicate within Teams, such as message and file content restrictions, retention policies, and more.

- The **voice section** allows you to manage telephony settings for Teams, such as call routing, emergency services, and call quality.

- The **locations** section allows you to manage settings for emergency calling, emergency location information, and country/region-specific settings.

- The **enhanced encryption** section provides a way to manage end-to-end encryption settings for Teams.

- The **planning** section provides guidance on how to plan and deploy Teams in your organization.

- The **analytics** section provides insights and usage data on Teams usage in your organization.

- The **notifications** section allows you to manage email notifications and alerts related to Teams.

- The **policy packages** section allows you to create and manage policy packages that can be assigned to groups of users in your organization.

Figure 15.5 features Microsoft Teams admin center dashboard:

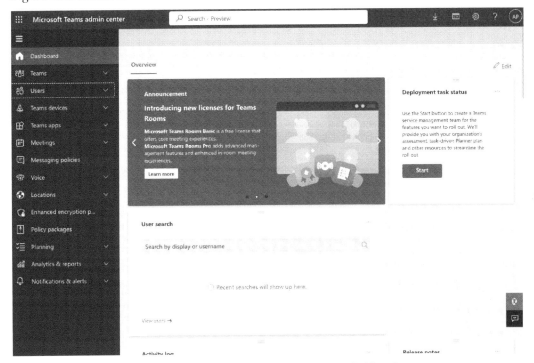

Figure 15.5: *Microsoft Teams admin center dashboard*

The Teams telemetry setup provides administrators with information about the usage and performance of Microsoft Teams in their organization. This information can be used to identify trends, track adoption, and monitor compliance with policies. With telemetry, administrators can see data on things like the number of teams created, the number of users and devices accessing Teams, the frequency of usage, and the performance of audio and video calls. This information can help administrators identify areas where they need to focus their efforts to improve the user experience, troubleshoot issues, and optimize the deployment of Teams. To set up telemetry, administrators can use the Office 365 Management API or the Teams Admin Center. They can also use Power BI to create custom reports and dashboards that display the telemetry data in a format that is easy to understand and analyze.

OneDrive Admin Center

The OneDrive admin center is a web-based interface that provides you with control over your organization's OneDrive for Business deployment. The OneDrive admin center provides administrators with the ability to manage user access and usage, as well as configure settings for OneDrive for Business. In the OneDrive admin center, you can view and manage usage reports, configure policies for data loss prevention, and control access to OneDrive for Business. Administrators can also use the OneDrive admin center to set up auditing and reporting, and configure the OneDrive for Business sync client to meet the needs of their organization.

The OneDrive admin center has been merged into the SharePoint admin center in Microsoft 365. This means that you can manage both OneDrive and SharePoint from the same location in the Microsoft 365 admin center. The functionality of the OneDrive admin center has been integrated into the SharePoint admin center, so that administrators can access the same settings and features for OneDrive as they would for SharePoint.

From the SharePoint admin center, you can manage the following settings for OneDrive:

- **User accounts:** Manage user accounts and access, monitor usage and activity, and set up user permissions.

- **Storage:** Monitor storage usage and set storage quotas for users.

- **Sharing:** Manage sharing settings for files and folders, and set up sharing policies for the organization.

- **Devices:** Manage device access and device policies for OneDrive.

- **Auditing and reporting:** View audit logs and reports for OneDrive activity, and monitor user activity.

- **Data Loss Prevention:** Manage data loss prevention policies for OneDrive, and set up alerts for sensitive content.

- **Compliance:** Manage compliance policies for OneDrive and monitor compliance activities.

Users and licenses management

In Microsoft 365, you can manage user licenses by assigning or reassigning licenses to users, or by changing the number of licenses that you have. This can be done in the Microsoft 365 admin center.

Here are the steps to manage user licenses in Microsoft 365:

1. Sign in to the Microsoft 365 admin center.

2. Click on **Users**, then select **Active users**.

3. Select the user you want to manage.

4. Click on **Licenses and services**.

5. Use the toggle switch to turn on or turn off the services for the selected user.

6. If you want to assign a new license to a user, click **Add license**, and then select the license you want to assign from the list of available licenses.

7. Click **Save changes**.

You can also bulk manage licenses for multiple users by selecting multiple users and following the abovementioned steps.

To purchase additional licenses for Office 365 or Microsoft 365, you can go to the Microsoft 365 admin center and follow these steps:

1. Sign in to the Microsoft 365 admin center using your admin account.

2. Click on the **Billing** option from the main menu.

3. From the **Billing** section, click on the **Purchase services** option.

4. Select the plan you want to purchase and follow the steps to complete the purchase process.

To see your current licenses, you can go to the Microsoft 365 admin center and follow these steps:

1. Sign in to the Microsoft 365 admin center using your admin account.

2. Click on the **Users** option from the main menu.

3. Click on the **Active Users** option.

4. On the **Active Users** page, you will see a list of all the users in your organization and their assigned licenses.

You can use this information to manage and allocate licenses as needed.

In Microsoft 365, only billing administrators and global administrators have the ability to purchase new licenses. Administrators with these roles assigned, have access to the Microsoft 365 admin center, where they can manage licenses for users and services. The billing administrator is responsible for managing the billing and payment information for the organization, while the global administrator is responsible for managing the overall setup and configuration of Microsoft 365 services.

Practical tasks

As always, it is time to get back to practice.

You are aware of a majority of the admin centers from previous chapters and have done some practice there.

You know that in SharePoint, Teams, Exchange, and Power Platform admin centers, you can configure policies that will apply to the content, emails, or chats stored in relative applications.

For instance, to configure some policies for Teams, you have Policies packages available. That is basically a pre-defined set of policies for various organizations such as educational institutes or healthcare providers. Log in to Microsoft 365 with your account and go to **Admin | Teams Admin center**. From the left menu, select **policy packages**.

You can see some policies that are added as an example to the sandbox environment. You can also click on the **Add** button to add new one. When you add a new policy, you can select the type of policy that it will be applied to. It can be a policy for meetings or chats, or calls.

Figure 15.6 features the Microsoft Teams admin center adding new policy package:

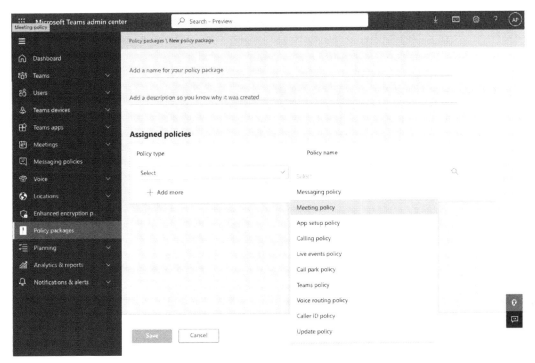

Figure 15.6: Microsoft Teams admin center adding new policy package

You will be prompted to set the name for your new policy.

Once created, you will see a bunch of configurations available in policy related to transcription, music, spam, and so on. Look around to see what configurations are available that you will be aware of them.

Try to create various policy types and see what configurations are available in different types.

From the Microsoft 365 admin center (root one), you can see all of the users and their licenses and permissions. Click in the top left corner on squares and select **Admin app** to navigate to the admin center. Now on the left side, you can select **Active users** and see the list of all users. If you click on any user you will see **Accounts**, **License**, **Devices**, **Mail**, and **OneDrive** tabs. In **Licenses and apps**, you can select what roles will be assigned to a particular user; hence this user's permissions and admin role will be determined based on the assigned ones. There is also a separate accordion menu under that tab called **Apps**. There you will be to select/unselect what apps user should have access too.

Under the **Account** tab, the user's generic information can be changed or updated.

Accordingly, under OneDrive and Mail, some configurations can be done on the user-level.

Sometimes there might be situations when you need help from the Microsoft support team. It can be because some site was permanently deleted, and you need help recovering it. With SharePoint Online, you do not have access to the Database or back-ups. Thus, you cannot restore something permanently deleted on your own. Sometimes some users experience slowness or some features do not work. In this case, contacting Microsoft Support team will be helpful too.

To raise a support request, you need to you Microsoft 365 admin center. From the left menu select the **Support** option and click on **New service request**.

Figure 15.7 features the Microsoft admin center Support section:

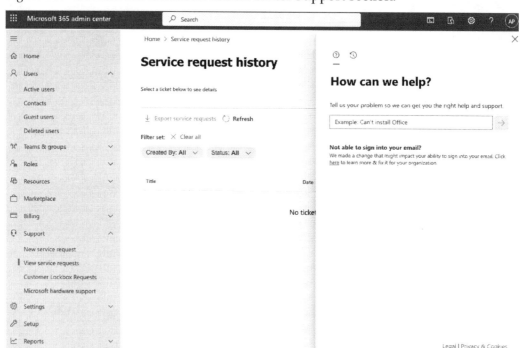

Figure 15.7: *Microsoft admin center Support section*

When creating new service ticket, you will be prompted to type the topic issue is related to. For example, let us assume a scenario where SharePoint is not loading. It will show you all relevant articles that can potentially help solve the issue. If you do not see anything that might be helpful, then at the bottom of the pop-up on the right, you can click **Contact support** button. You will have the option to be contacted back via phone, email or schedule a specific time when you should be contacted. You would need to type details on the issue you have and click on the **Contact me** button. Depending on the license in your organization Support team may reach out to you within of couple hours or a couple of days. The higher the license tier, the sooner you can expect the contact. Then the conversation about your issue can continue from there. In the majority of cases, it takes around 1 week on average to solve majority of more complex issues, considering communication back-and-force with Microsoft Support team.

You as admin also would need to track your tenant Health on a scheduled basis. It is a good practice to go the **Health** section inside Microsoft 365 admin center to track notifications and any potential issues from there. Do it at least once a week. Or better yet, do it on a daily basis.

Figure 15.8 features the Microsoft admin center Health Dashboard section:

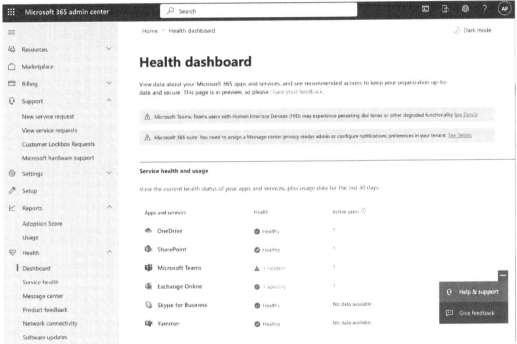

Figure 15.8: *Microsoft admin center Health Dashboard section*

The Health Dashboard in the Microsoft 365 (M365) admin center provides real-time health information and status updates for services in M365, including Exchange, SharePoint, OneDrive, Skype for Business, Microsoft Teams, and Yammer. The dashboard displays the health status of key services, any current incidents, and a history of past incidents. This information can help you quickly identify and resolve issues, ensuring that your users have a seamless experience with the M365 services. Additionally, you can use the Health Dashboard to subscribe to notifications for service incidents and to access support resources for troubleshooting and problem resolution.

If you see any messages in the Health center, you can click on them and details will be shown. From there, you can take actions needed to solve issues or warnings.

Moreover, if there is any delay or issues with the Microsoft 365 services, you will see them there too.

Conclusion

In this chapter, you learned more about various admin centers available in Microsoft 365. Office 365 Admin Center is a central location where you can manage various aspects of your organization's Office 365 environment, including user accounts, Exchange email, SharePoint sites, OneDrive for Business, Teams, and more. Each of these services has its own admin center, which provides a specific set of tools and options for managing that service. The Health dashboard in the Microsoft 365 Admin Center provides real-time health information and alerts for services across Office 365. It is important for administrators to have a good understanding of the various admin centers in order to effectively manage and maintain their organization's Office 365 environment.

Points to remember

- Each service in Microsoft 365 (for example, Exchange, SharePoint, Teams, OneDrive) has its own admin center with its own set of management tools and options.

- The home pages of the various admin centers provide an overview of the current status and health of the service, as well as quick access to common tasks.

- The sections and sub-sections within the admin centers vary depending on the service, but typically include areas for managing users, policies, settings, and resources.

- Some admin centers also provide analytics and reporting features, allowing you to track usage and identify trends.

- To access the various admin centers, you must have the appropriate permissions, such as being a Global Administrator, Billing Administrator, or Exchange Administrator.

- You can manage user licenses from the Microsoft 365 admin center, but only a Billing Administrator or Global Administrator can purchase additional licenses.

- The Health Dashboard in the Microsoft 365 admin center provides information about the overall health and status of your Microsoft 365 services.

## CHAPTER 16

Security and Compliance Policies

> "Cyber security is not just a technical issue; it's also a behavioral issue. Human error is often the weakest link in cyber security."
>
> *- Brian Lord*

Introduction

Security is a big topic in the Microsoft 365 ecosystem and it covers all applications included in the suite. Thus we shall learn all about it in this dedicated chapter. Here, you will learn how to protect your environment from unwanted data leakage or information sharing with external sources, how to set up an environment in a way that would be compliant with policies like HIPAA, and that it would cover all possible applications starting from SharePoint and finishing with Exchange. You also will learn about eDiscovery, Labels and other tools available as a part of the Security and Compliance Center.

Structure

In this chapter, we will cover the following topics:

- Security and compliance center overview
- Security and compliance roles

- Compliance manager
- Data classifications
- Labels
- eDiscovery

Objectives

In every system, you will deal with security. It is especially relevant in cyberspace. To understand how to secure and protect sensitive information, ensure regulatory compliance, and mitigate risks to your organization's data and systems, we will cover Security and Compliance center in M365. The security and compliance center provides a centralized and integrated platform for managing security and compliance for your M365 environment. By using the security and compliance center, you can manage data loss prevention policies, eDiscovery cases, retention policies, threat protection, and more, all from one place. The goal is to help you ensure the security and compliance of your organization's information, reduce the risk of data breaches, and comply with relevant regulations and standards.

Security and compliance center overview

The Microsoft 365 Security & Compliance Center is a central location where you can manage security and compliance for your organization's data. The center provides a range of tools and features to help administrators monitor, protect, and secure your organization's data, as well as meet regulatory and compliance requirements. Some of the key features of the Security & Compliance Center include:

- **Threat protection:** Administrators can use the Security & Compliance Center to monitor and respond to threats, such as viruses, malware, and spam, across Microsoft 365 services such as Exchange, SharePoint, and OneDrive.

- **Data loss prevention (DLP):** Administrators can create and enforce policies to help prevent sensitive information from being leaked, such as by email or through file sharing.

- **eDiscovery:** Administrators can search for and preserve data across Microsoft 365 services in preparation for legal or regulatory proceedings.

- **Compliance management:** Administrators can assess their organization's compliance with various regulations, such as GDPR, HIPAA, and ISO 27001, and implement policies to meet those requirements.

- **Auditing and reporting:** Administrators can view and generate reports on various aspects of their organization's security and compliance posture, such as who is accessing sensitive data and when.

The **Security & Compliance Center in Microsoft 365** (**M365**) has been split into two separate centers to provide administrators with more focused and streamlined experiences. The Security Center provides a comprehensive overview of security-related information and services, while the Compliance Center provides information and tools for meeting compliance requirements and managing data governance. By dividing the information and tools into two separate centers, you can more easily focus on your specific responsibilities and find the information and tools you need more quickly.

Figure 16.1 features SharePoint Security Admin center Home page:

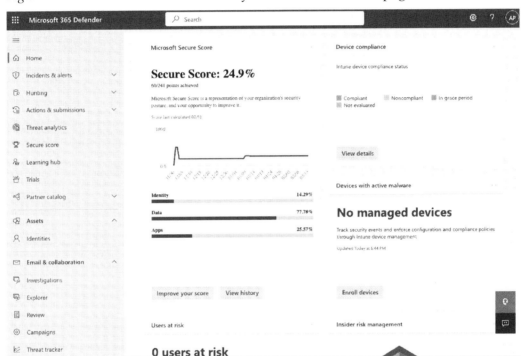

Figure 16.1: *SharePoint Security Admin center Home page*

The Secure Score is a measure of an organization's security posture, based on its adherence to Microsoft's recommended security configurations, practices, and policies. The Secure Score provides a summary of the organization's current security posture, identifies areas where the organization can improve, and provides guidance and recommendations on how to do so. The score ranges from 0 to 100, with a higher score indicating a stronger security posture.

The Security & Compliance Center in Microsoft 365 allows administrators to monitor and respond to security threats to their organization's data. Some of the sections included in the admin center are as follows:

- **Hunting:** The Hunting feature allows administrators to search for, and respond to, potential security threats in their organization's data.

- **Actions and Submissions:** The Actions and Submissions feature allows administrators to take actions on security alerts and incidents, as well as to view submissions from other security tools and services.

- **Threat Analytics:** Threat Analytics is a feature that provides administrators with a view into the current state of security threats affecting their organization. It provides information about security incidents, the types of threats, and how they are affecting the organization.

- **Assets and Identities:** Assets and Identities is a feature that provides administrators with a view into the data assets and identities in their organization. This information can help administrators understand which assets and identities are at risk, and take appropriate actions to protect them.

- **Threat Tracker:** Threat Tracker is a feature that provides administrators with a view into the current state of security threats affecting their organization. It provides information about security incidents, the types of threats, and how they are affecting the organization.

In the Microsoft 365 compliance center, you can manage and monitor your organization's compliance with various regulations and standards such as the **General Data Protection Regulation (GDPR)**, the **Health Insurance Portability and Accountability Act (HIPAA)**, and others. Some of the tasks that can be performed in the compliance center include the following:

- Defining and monitoring compliance policies and standards, such as data retention policies and information protection policies.

- Searching for and identifying sensitive data, such as credit card numbers or social security numbers, and taking appropriate actions to protect this data.

- Classifying and protecting sensitive data using data labeling and **Data Loss Prevention (DLP)** policies.

- Auditing and reporting on activities related to sensitive data, such as access to and usage of the data.

- Creating and managing eDiscovery cases to search for and preserve data relevant to legal and regulatory investigations.

Here are some of the sections you can find in the Compliance Center:

- **Compliance Manager:** The Compliance Manager provides a centralized dashboard for monitoring and managing your organization's compliance posture. You can use it to assess your organization's compliance with various regulations and standards, such as GDPR and HIPAA.

- **Data Classification:** Data classification allows you to categorize and label sensitive data within your organization. This helps to ensure that sensitive data is properly managed, protected, and deleted when necessary.

- **Data Connectors:** Data Connectors allow you to integrate data from various sources into the Compliance Center. This helps you to get a more complete view of your organization's compliance posture.

- **Trials and Solutions:** The Trials and Solutions section provides information on new and existing solutions that can help you address compliance requirements. You can explore available solutions, start trials, and purchase the ones that meet your needs.

Security and compliance roles

In Microsoft 365, there are several security and compliance roles that are designed to give specific permissions to users who need to perform tasks related to security and compliance. These roles include the following:

- **Security Administrator:** This role is responsible for managing the security-related aspects of Microsoft 365. Security Administrators have access to the Security and Compliance Center and can perform tasks such as managing security policies, reviewing security reports, and managing alerts.

- **Compliance Administrator:** This role is responsible for managing the compliance-related aspects of Microsoft 365. Compliance Administrators have access to the Security and Compliance Center and can perform tasks such as managing compliance policies, reviewing compliance reports, and managing eDiscovery cases.

- **Security Reader:** This role has read-only access to the Security and Compliance Center and can view all security-related reports, policies, and settings.

- **Compliance Reader:** This role has read-only access to the Security and Compliance Center and can view all compliance-related reports, policies, and settings.

- **Security Operator:** This role is responsible for managing security incidents and alerts. Security Operators have access to the Security and Compliance Center and can perform tasks such as investigating security incidents and responding to alerts.

- **Compliance Data Administrator:** This role is responsible for managing data governance and classification. Compliance Data Administrators have access to the Microsoft 365 Compliance Center and can perform tasks such as managing data classification labels and policies.

- **Compliance Search Administrator:** This role is responsible for managing eDiscovery cases. Compliance Search Administrators have access to the Microsoft 365 Compliance Center and can perform tasks such as creating and managing eDiscovery cases.

You can assign security and compliance roles in the Microsoft 365 admin center by going to the **Users** page and selecting **Active users**. From there, you can click on a user and select **Roles** to view and assign roles.

You can also create custom roles in the Security and Compliance Center using the **Security roles** or **Compliance roles** pages. Custom roles allow you to define specific permissions for a role that are not covered by the built-in roles.

To create a custom role, you can use the **New-Role Group PowerShell cmdlet** or use the **Role Group Editor** in the Security and Compliance Center. Once you have created a custom role, you can assign it to users or groups in the same way as built-in roles.

Compliance manager

Compliance Manager is a tool within the Microsoft Compliance Center that provides a dashboard for tracking and assessing an organization's compliance posture against industry standards and regulations. The tool provides guidance and recommended actions to help organizations meet regulatory requirements and best practices for data protection and privacy. Compliance Manager can help organizations with compliance in areas such as GDPR, ISO 27001, HIPAA, and more.

Figure 16.2 features the SharePoint Compliance Admin center Compliance Manager:

Figure 16.2: *SharePoint Compliance Admin center Compliance Manager*

In the Compliance Manager, the **Overview** tab provides a summary of the compliance status of your organization, highlighting the progress of assessments, controls, and improvement actions. This tab provides information on the number of assessments you have created, the number of controls within each assessment, the progress of your assessments, the compliance score, the status of improvement actions, and recommendations for the improvement of your organization's compliance posture. You can also access detailed information on your compliance assessments and controls from the Overview tab.

Improvement actions are specific tasks that are recommended for an organization to take, in order to improve its compliance posture. These tasks are based on the results of assessments performed by the Compliance Manager. They are intended to help the organization mitigate identified risks and improve its overall compliance with industry regulations and standards. Improvement actions are assigned to specific roles within the organization, and Compliance Manager tracks the progress of these actions over time to ensure that they are completed.

The **Solutions** tab provides a list of Microsoft and third-party solutions that are available to help with compliance management. The solutions are organized by the regulation, standard, or best practice they address, such as GDPR or ISO 27001. Each solution provides a summary of what the solution does, the associated risks and controls, and links to documentation and other resources. The Solutions tab can help you identify and choose the appropriate solution to help meet your compliance requirements. The Solutions tab can help you identify and choose the appropriate solution to help meet your compliance requirements.

In **Compliance Manager**, assessments are used to evaluate your organization's compliance with various regulations and standards, such as GDPR or HIPAA. Assessment templates are pre-configured sets of controls and requirements specific to each regulation or standard, designed to help organizations evaluate their compliance posture.

The **Assessments** section in Compliance Manager allows you to create and manage assessments for your organization's compliance posture. You can use the built-in assessment templates, customize them to fit your organization's specific needs, or create your own assessments from scratch. Once an assessment is created, you can assign it to specific users in your organization to complete.

The **Assessment templates** section in **Compliance Manager** allows you to view the list of built-in templates that are available for your use in creating and managing assessments. You can also create your own custom assessment templates based on specific regulations, standards, or other requirements relevant to your organization.

In the Compliance Manager, you can configure alerts and alert policies to notify you of compliance-related events and to help you stay on top of your organization's compliance posture, as shown:

- **Alerts** are notifications about specific events, such as the creation or deletion of a sensitive file, that can potentially impact compliance.

- **Alert policies** are sets of conditions that you can configure to trigger specific alerts when they are met. You can use the built-in alert policies, create your own custom alert policies, or modify existing policies.

The Alerts and Alert policies feature can help you monitor your organization's compliance posture and respond quickly to potential compliance issues.

The Compliance Manager in Microsoft 365 provides several templates by default that can help organizations meet various compliance requirements. These templates include:

- **General Data Protection Regulation (GDPR)**
- ISO 27001:2013
- ISO 27018:2019
- **National Institute of Standards and Technology (NIST)**, **Cybersecurity Framework (CSF)**
- NIST SP 800-53
- **System and Organization Controls (SOC)** 1 and 2
- UK OFFICIAL and UK NHS
- **California Consumer Privacy Act (CCPA)**

It is important to note that the templates are designed to provide guidance, and may not be a complete solution for an organization's specific compliance requirements. Organizations may need to supplement the templates with additional controls and processes as necessary.

Data classifications

In Microsoft 365, data classification is the process of categorizing and labeling data based on its level of sensitivity and regulatory requirements. This process can help organizations to manage and protect sensitive information by ensuring that it is identified and handled appropriately throughout its lifecycle.

With data classification in Microsoft 365, you can create and apply sensitivity labels to your content, such as documents and emails. Sensitivity labels are metadata that can help you to identify and protect sensitive information, such as personal or financial data. They can also be used to control access to content, based on the user's need-to-know and the sensitivity of the information. Additionally, you can configure policies that can automatically apply sensitivity labels based on certain conditions, such as the content of the document or the sender of an email.

The **Overview** tab in the Data Classification section of the Microsoft 365 Compliance Center provides an overview of the data sensitivity labels that have been created, applied, and analyzed within your organization. It also includes information about how sensitive data is being shared, and where it is being stored. From the Overview tab, you can create new sensitivity labels, edit existing ones, and configure settings related to data classification. You can also view statistics on the use of sensitivity labels, such as the number of labeled files, email messages, and SharePoint sites.

Trainable classifiers is a feature that allows you to classify and protect data in your organization by creating and training your own machine learning models. These models can then be used to classify sensitive information such as financial data, medical records, or other confidential information, and apply labels or protection policies to that data. The trainable classifiers feature can be used in combination with other data protection and information governance features in Microsoft 365, such as sensitivity labels and **Data Loss Prevention** (**DLP**) policies.

Sensitive info types are pre-defined types of sensitive information that the system can automatically detect, based on content analysis, including data patterns, keywords, and regular expressions. These sensitive info types can be used to create policies to protect sensitive information and help organizations comply with data protection regulations. Examples of sensitive info types include credit card numbers, social security numbers, passport numbers, and driver's license numbers.

Figure 16.3 features the SharePoint Compliance Admin center Data Classification section:

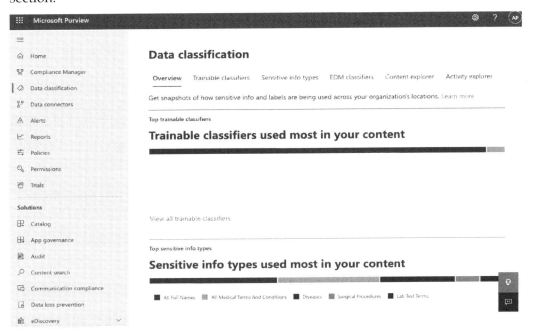

Figure 16.3: SharePoint Compliance Admin center Data Classification section

EDM classifiers, or Exact Data Match classifiers, are a type of data classification that helps identify and manage sensitive information based on a predefined set of rules. These classifiers are used to identify specific types of sensitive data, such as credit card or social security numbers, within a document or file.

Content explorer is a tool within the Compliance Center that allows you to search for content across different locations, such as SharePoint and OneDrive, using specific criteria or queries. You can use this tool to help with eDiscovery or content management tasks.

Activity explorer is another tool within the Compliance Center that provides visibility into the user and admin activities in your organization. You can use this tool to monitor and audit activity in your environment, and to identify potential security or compliance risks.

Labels

In the context of Microsoft 365, labels are used to classify and protect content in your organization. Labels can be applied to various types of content, such as documents, email messages, and other data in your organization. Labels can help you meet regulatory compliance requirements, protect sensitive data, and manage content more effectively.

Labels can be configured to automatically classify content based on a number of criteria, such as content type, location, or user-defined keywords. Once classified, labels can be used to apply policies such as retention, encryption, or rights management. For example, you can use labels to automatically classify all credit card numbers in your organization and apply a retention policy to that data to meet regulatory compliance requirements.

Labels are a key part of data lifecycle management in Microsoft 365.

You can apply labels both manually and automatically in Microsoft 365, as follows:

- You can manually apply labels to documents, email messages, or other content by selecting the appropriate label in the relevant application (for example, Outlook, Teams, OneDrive, and SharePoint).

- You can also configure auto-labeling policies in the Microsoft 365 compliance center to automatically apply labels to content based on certain conditions or criteria. For example, you might configure an auto-labeling policy to automatically apply a "Confidential" label to any document that contains credit card numbers.

By applying labels, you can help ensure that content is appropriately handled, retained, or disposed of, based on the organization's data retention policies and compliance requirements.

Labels can be applied to content in many different Microsoft 365 services, including SharePoint, Teams, Exchange, and OneDrive. In addition, many third-party applications support Microsoft Information Protection and can therefore use the same labels to classify and protect content. The availability of label-based policies and their specific capabilities can vary depending on the service, and so it is important to review the documentation for the particular service you are using to understand how labels are used.

Retention policies in Microsoft 365 are used to apply retention settings to content in different locations such as Exchange email, SharePoint and OneDrive files, and Teams messages. Retention policies can be used to help organizations comply with internal policies and external regulations by retaining content for a specified period of time, and then deleting it when that period has elapsed. Retention policies can also be used to prevent the deletion of content that is still required by an organization.

Labels and label policies are both part of the Data Classification and Data Loss Prevention features in Microsoft 365, but they serve slightly different purposes.

- **Labels** are used to classify and protect individual documents and emails. With labels, you can apply visual markings or metadata to content to help users understand the sensitivity of the information and take appropriate actions to protect it.

- **Label policies**, on the other hand, are used to automatically apply labels to content based on pre-defined conditions. For example, you can create a label policy that applies a "Confidential" label to all documents that contain credit card numbers. This way, you do not have to rely on users to manually apply the label – it happens automatically based on the content of the document.

Label policies can also be used to enforce retention policies, which dictate how long content should be kept or when it should be deleted. For example, you can create a label policy that applies a "Retain for 5 years" label to all financial records, which will ensure that the records are retained for the appropriate amount of time and then automatically deleted when they are no longer needed.

Adaptive Scopes is a way to scope content that is covered by a retention policy, by automatically discovering new locations or data sources that are relevant to the policy as they are created.

Policy Lookup is a feature that allows you to check which retention policies apply to a particular piece of content.

Import is a way to import policies that were created in another tenant.

eDiscovery

eDiscovery is the process of searching and locating electronic information in order to be used as evidence in a legal or regulatory matter. In the context of Microsoft 365, eDiscovery is a set of tools and features available in the Security and Compliance Center that enable organizations to search, identify, and export content from various sources, including Exchange, SharePoint, OneDrive, Teams, and Yammer. The eDiscovery process typically involves identifying relevant content, preserving it, analyzing it, and then producing it as needed. Microsoft 365 provides a range of eDiscovery capabilities, including case management, search, legal hold, and export, to help organizations meet their eDiscovery requirements.

The process of using eDiscovery in Microsoft 365 involves the following steps:

1. **Set up eDiscovery:** Before you can start using eDiscovery, you need to set it up in the Microsoft 365 Compliance Center. This involves creating an eDiscovery case, assigning permissions to the case, and specifying the data sources that will be searched.

2. **Create a search:** Once you have set up the eDiscovery case, you can create a search to find the data you are looking for. You can search for content in a variety of locations, such as Exchange mailboxes, SharePoint sites, OneDrive for Business, and Teams.

3. **Run the search:** After you have created the search, you can run it to find the relevant content. You can preview the results and refine the search criteria as needed.

4. **Export the results:** Once you have found the relevant content, you can export it to a file for further review and analysis.

5. **Close the case:** After you have completed the eDiscovery process, you can close the case to indicate that the matter has been resolved.

It is worth noting that eDiscovery is a powerful tool and should be used carefully to ensure that data is not accidentally deleted or modified. It is also important to follow best practices for eDiscovery to ensure that legal and regulatory requirements are met.

The "**Create a case**" option is a feature of the eDiscovery tool in Microsoft 365's Security & Compliance Center. It allows you to create a new eDiscovery case that you can use to search for and preserve content across your organization. When you create a new case, you can specify the scope of the search, such as the specific mailboxes, sites, or users you want to include, and the type of content you want to search for. You can also specify the specific search terms or keywords you want to use to find the content you are looking for.

The main difference between Standard and Premium (Advanced) eDiscovery in Microsoft 365 is their feature sets. Advanced eDiscovery offers additional functionality, such as more powerful search capabilities, automated data processing, and analytics tools that can help users identify important patterns and insights.

Advanced eDiscovery is available as part of the Microsoft 365 E5 plan, while Standard eDiscovery is available in most other plans, including the E3 plan. Therefore, E5 plan costs more than the E3 plan.

Figure 16.4 features the SharePoint Compliance Admin center eDiscovery section:

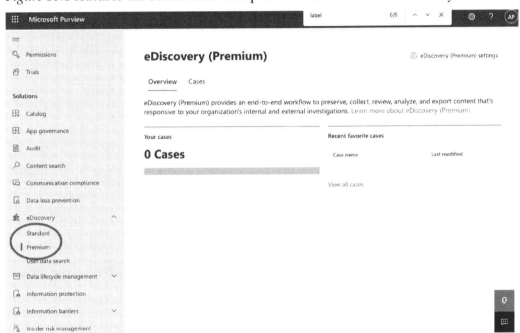

Figure 16.4*: SharePoint Compliance Admin center eDiscovery section*

One important thing to keep in mind when using eDiscovery is that it can be a complex process, and it is important to have a clear understanding of what you are looking for and what tools and techniques are available to help you. In addition, it is important to understand the legal and regulatory requirements that may impact your eDiscovery efforts, such as rules around data privacy, data retention, and the preservation of electronic evidence. Finally, it is important to consider the potential impact that eDiscovery can have on your organization's IT infrastructure and resources, particularly if you are dealing with large volumes of data.

Practical tasks

In your sandbox environment, as a global admin, you already have access to all admin centers and configurations. However, if you would need to assign a Security compliance role, then you would go to the **Microsoft 365 | Admin center | Users**. From there, select the user you need, and in the Licenses and roles section, assign the Compliance admin role.

Please note that Security and compliance roles are totally separate roles and need to be assigned to each user separately, even if they already have SharePoint or Exchange or any other app admin roles already assigned.

As a practice task, let us create some labels and set up rules for them to be automatically assigned to some of the documents. To do so, go to Microsoft 365 and login with your account, and follow the given steps:

1. Go to the Admin center and select **Show All Admin centers** from the left menu and select **Compliance Admin center**.

2. And there from the left menu, select the **Information protection** link.

3. You will be redirected to the page where you can configure labels and related policies.

4. Click on the **Labels** tab.

Figure 16.5 features the Labels configuration in Compliance Admin center:

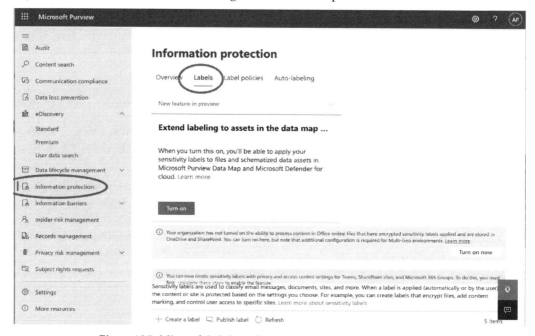

Figure 16.5: *Microsoft Labels configuration in Compliance Admin center*

If you scroll down, you will see that there are already a bunch of labels pre-created on your sandbox environment. Let us create a new label, by following the given steps:

1. Click on the **Create a label** link.

2. Fill up the information in the required columns and select label color that will be assigned to it. Click on the **Next** button.

3. In the **Scope** section, you can leave all checkboxes selected. Read through them to become familiar with those configurations.

4. Next, in the **Items** section, you can select what will happen to documents or items that have this label applied. For instance, you can force to have a unique header or footer, or apply encryption.

5. Let us select the **Apply Content marking** checkbox. Once selected, you will see a next section after you click the **Next** button. It will prompt you to select a watermark or header/footer that you want to apply with this label. Configure footer.

6. Click on the **Next** button.

In the next section, you can configure auto-labeling policy. This can be done from the Label policies tab on the main page, or right from here when you creating a new label.

So, let us turn on that switch for the auto-labeling of files and emails.

Figure 16.6 features the Labels configuration Auto-labeling condition logic set up:

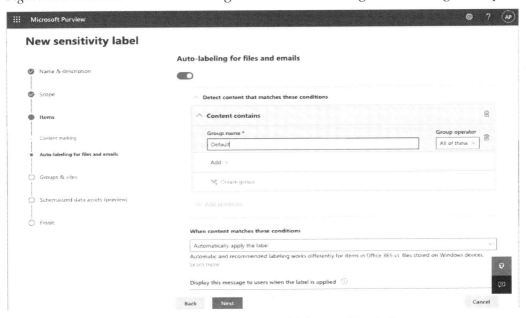

Figure 16.6: *Labels configuration Auto-labeling condition logic set up*

You will be prompted to set a condition logic when the label should be auto-applied.

Click on the **Add** link under Group name column and select **Sensitive info types** from the available options. Search for something familiar such as credit card numbers or SSN (U.S. Social security number). You can select multiple sensitive types if you want. Your condition will be created and you can set a level of confidence on the right from the dropdown. The lower the confidence, the higher the likelihood that the label will be applied. So, if you select 'Low confidence' option then the label will be applied to all of the documents where the system has at least any confidence that the content contains Social security number in a document or in the email or any other type of content.

From the dropdown below, you can select if label should be automatically applied. Otherwise, give the user a notice to apply a label.

You can also set a message that will be displayed to users when the label is applied.

Once configured, click on the **Next** button and go through the screens that are left and follow the prompts.

At the end, you would need to click **Finish** and select if you want your label to be automatically applied to all of the content that is already present in your environment in various apps. That is when you will be prompted to create a label policy.

You also have an option to not Publish your label right away. In this case, it will not be applied, until you select it and click **Publish label** button.

In the same way as with Labels, you can set up Alerts too. Alerts are designed to notify dedicated users or admins when something happens, for instance, when someone tries to share a document with sensitive information to an outside email. To configure Alerts, follow the given steps:

1. Select **Compliance manager** from the left navigation and go to the **Alert Policies** tab there.

2. Click on **Add** button.

3. You would need to provide the name of your alert and then set some conditions when it will be fired. For instance, you can select the **Assignment change** event. Then, you would need to set who will be notified when the event happened. Events (sub-conditions) can be configured and set up separately to expand the list of available sub-conditions out of the box. This will provide you as admin with more agility towards the configuration of alerts.

Next, let us become familiar with eDiscovery. Follow the given steps:

1. Select eDiscovery from the left navigation and create the new case there.

2. After new case is created, click on it.

3. You will go inside the case and will be able to create a new search to look for the documents you need. Or create a new legal-hold if you need to lock some documents and prevent them from being modified or deleted.

4. Go to the **Search** tab and create a new Search from there.

5. Set the name and then select the locations where the search will look for results.

Figure 16.7 features the eDiscovery new Search configuration tab:

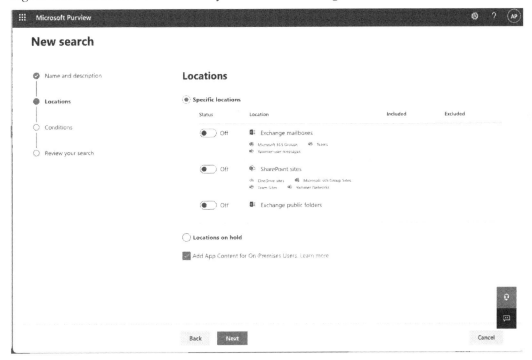

Figure 16.7: eDiscovery new Search configuration tab

You can set specific sites that will be included in the search, or those that should be excluded. By default, once the location is selected, it will be searched across the whole tenant. The same applies for mailboxes in Exchange. After locations are configured, you can set up conditions, for instance, a specific Keyword you are looking for in the subject, body of the document and so on. At the end, you can review your configured search. Once configured, it will take some time to run. So, give it around 10 to 24 hours. Then, you will be able to come back and export search results to see what it returned.

Now you can go back to M365 admin center and select the Security Admin center to see how security policies can be configured from there.

Once there, from the left menu, select **Policies and Policy management** option. You can create a new policy there. There are multiple policy types that can be created. This time, select **Activity policy**. Fill out the required information and set filters and alerts when the policy is applied to become familiar with the configuration.

Figure 16.8 features the activity policy configuration window in Security Admin center:

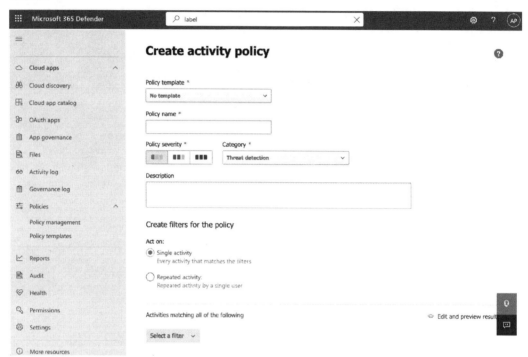

Figure 16.8: *The activity policy configuration window in Security Admin center*

Conclusion

Microsoft 365 includes a range of powerful tools for security and compliance management. The Security and Compliance Center provides a centralized location for managing security and compliance across the Microsoft 365 environment, while also offering a range of advanced features, such as threat intelligence, hunting, and analytics. The Compliance Manager provides a framework for tracking compliance activities, and the Data Lifecycle Management features allow for the creation and enforcement of policies for managing data throughout its lifecycle. eDiscovery provides a powerful tool for searching and discovering data in a legal or compliance context. By leveraging the security and compliance features of Microsoft 365, organizations can better protect their sensitive data and ensure regulatory compliance.

Points to remember

- The Microsoft 365 Admin Center is a central hub for managing your Microsoft 365 subscription.

- The Security and Compliance Center is where you can manage security and compliance for your Microsoft 365 environment.

- The Security Center helps you monitor and improve the security of your environment.

- The Compliance Center helps you manage compliance with legal and regulatory requirements.

- Compliance Manager is a tool for tracking compliance activities and assessing compliance risks.

- Data classification and labeling can help you identify and protect sensitive data.

- Retention policies can help you retain or delete content based on business or regulatory requirements.

- eDiscovery tools can help you search for and export content for legal or compliance purposes.

- To manage security and compliance effectively, it is important to understand the roles and permissions of different user types and to establish clear policies and procedures.

- Regularly reviewing your security and compliance posture and taking action to address identified risks, is critical for protecting your organization's data and reputation.

Join our book's Discord space

Join the book's Discord Workspace for Latest updates, Offers, Tech happenings around the world, New Release and Sessions with the Authors:

https://discord.bpbonline.com

## CHAPTER 17

Term Store and Content Sorts in SharePoint Online

"Content management is not just about reducing storage costs, it's about making sure that the right people have access to the right information at the right time."

- Geoff Bentley

Introduction

To expand metadata capabilities and navigation options, SharePoint has Term Store, where terms, also known as managed metadata, can be created in a proper structure and later be assigned to specific documents or items in SharePoint, or even can be used to build the navigation. In this chapter, you will learn how to access Term store, create Term groups and Terms, and later use them for your content or navigation management needs.

Structure

In this chapter, we will cover the following topics:

- Term Store management

- Global and site level term groups

- Term store main components

- Managed metadata overview
- Content type gallery

Objectives

In this chapter, we will review SharePoint's online term store in more depth and various content types available. The objective is to understand how to organize and manage content in a consistent and effective manner. By using the term store and content types, you can apply consistent metadata to your content, making it easier to search, discover, and manage. This can improve the overall usability and governance of your SharePoint environment. Understanding these concepts can also help you to tailor your SharePoint sites and libraries to the specific needs of your organization, making it a more efficient and effective platform for collaboration and content management.

Term store management

As you have learned before, the Term Store in SharePoint Online is a centralized repository of commonly used terms or metadata, which can be used to apply consistent classification to content across sites and site collections. It allows for the management of taxonomies, keywords, and terms used to tag and classify content in SharePoint Online. The Term Store can be accessed through the SharePoint Online Admin Center, as well as from individual site collections. The Term Store is an important component of SharePoint Online, as it helps ensure that content is classified and tagged consistently, which makes it easier to find and organize.

In SharePoint Online, you can manage the term store using the Term Store Management Tool. Here are the general steps to manage a term store:

1. Navigate to the SharePoint admin center.

2. Under **Admin centers**, select **Term store**.

3. In the Term Store Management Tool, you can create, edit, and delete groups, term sets, and terms. You can also import term sets and export the term store.

4. To create a new term set or term, select the appropriate group and click on **New Term Set** or **New Term**, respectively.

5. To edit or delete a group, term set, or term, select it and click on the appropriate action from the ribbon.

6. You can also set properties for each term or term set, such as descriptions, synonyms, and custom properties.

To manage the term store, you need to have the appropriate permissions. There, you can create term groups, term sets, and individual terms, as well as import term sets and export the term store.

Best practices for term store management include planning and defining your metadata architecture, creating a governance plan, designing your term set structure with clear and consistent labeling, using appropriate terms and avoiding synonyms, creating relationships between terms, and training users on how to use the term store effectively. Additionally, it is recommended to limit the number of people who have permission to manage the term store to ensure consistency and accuracy.

Figure 17.1 features a Term store management tool from the SharePoint Admin center:

Term store

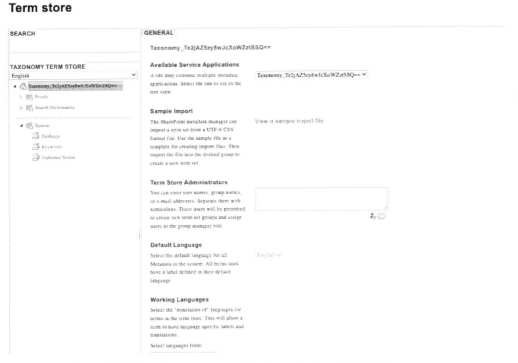

Figure 17.1: Term store management tool from the SharePoint Admin center

In the SharePoint Online term store, the **People** dictionary contains a list of user profiles, while the **Search Dictionaries** folder contains terms that are used to help refine search results. The **Search Dictionaries** folder includes the following subfolders: **Query Rules**, **Result Sources**, **Schema**, and **Synonyms**. These folders allow you to manage search-related terms and rules to help users find the content they need more easily.

The System folder is a special folder that is created automatically and is used to store system-defined terms, such as terms used by SharePoint itself. This folder cannot be deleted or renamed. The System folder in the SharePoint Term Store has several subfolders, including Hashtags, Keywords, and Orphaned Terms. The Hashtags folder contains terms that are automatically generated, based on social tags used in SharePoint sites. The Keywords folder also contains terms that are automatically generated based on search queries entered by users. The Orphaned Terms folder contains terms that are not associated with any groups and can be used to manage terms that are no longer used in the term store.

In SharePoint, a Service Application is a unit of functionality that provides a specific service to other parts of the SharePoint tenant. Available Service Applications are the different types of Service Applications that have been configured in the SharePoint tenant and are available for use. Examples of Service Applications include the Managed Metadata Service, the User Profile Service, and the Search Service. These Service Applications can be managed through the SharePoint Admin Center. Previously on the on-perm version of SharePoint, admins could manage all of these services directly. With SharePoint online, some of them are managed by Microsoft directly though.

In SharePoint Online, **Managed Metadata Service** (**MMS**) is the service application that provides the infrastructure for creating and managing terms and term sets. The MMS enables the creation and maintenance of the Term Store, which is a hierarchical collection of reusable terms and their associated metadata.

So, in SharePoint Online, the Term Store is a component of the Managed Metadata Service. The Managed Metadata Service also includes features such as content type publishing, which allows content types to be shared across site collections, and the ability to use managed metadata as a column in a list or library. The Managed Metadata Service is a crucial component of SharePoint Online, as it enables the use of metadata to classify and manage content consistently across sites and site collections.

The User Profile Service in SharePoint Online is a service application that allows administrators to manage user profiles and properties. It provides a centralized location for storing and managing user profile information such as contact details, job title, department, and other attributes. User profile information is used to enhance social computing features in SharePoint Online, such as My Sites, social tagging, and activity feeds. The User Profile Service can also be used to import user profiles from Active Directory or other external systems.

Global and site level term groups

In SharePoint Online, the term store is a hierarchical collection of centrally managed metadata that you can use as global or site level terms. Global term sets are created and managed at the tenant level, and they can be used across all sites within the tenant. Site-level term sets are specific to a particular site collection, and they can only be used within that site collection. When you create a site-level term set, you can choose to inherit terms from a global term set or create a new set of terms that is specific to that site collection. By using global and site-level term sets, you can ensure consistency and accuracy in the way that metadata is used throughout your organization.

In SharePoint Online, the Term Store Management tool allows you to manage a hierarchy of terms and keywords that can be used across site collections in your organization. Within the Term Store, there are several global term groups, including:

- **People:** This term group is used for organizing and managing user profile information, such as job titles, departments, and skills.

- **Search Dictionaries:** This term group is used for defining synonyms and variations for search queries.

- **System:** This term group is used for system-managed terms, such as hashtags, keywords, and orphaned terms. It includes three subfolders: "Hashtags," "Keywords," and "Orphaned Terms."

These global term groups are available to all site collections in your SharePoint Online environment, and can be managed by administrators with the appropriate permissions.

Site level term groups in SharePoint Online are created within individual SharePoint sites and contain terms specific to that site's content. These site level term groups can be linked to the global term groups to ensure consistency in the use of terms across the entire organization, while still allowing for flexibility at the site level. Site owners and administrators can create, manage, and share their own site level term groups within their respective SharePoint sites.

Figure 17.2 features a Term store Global term groups and Site level term groups:

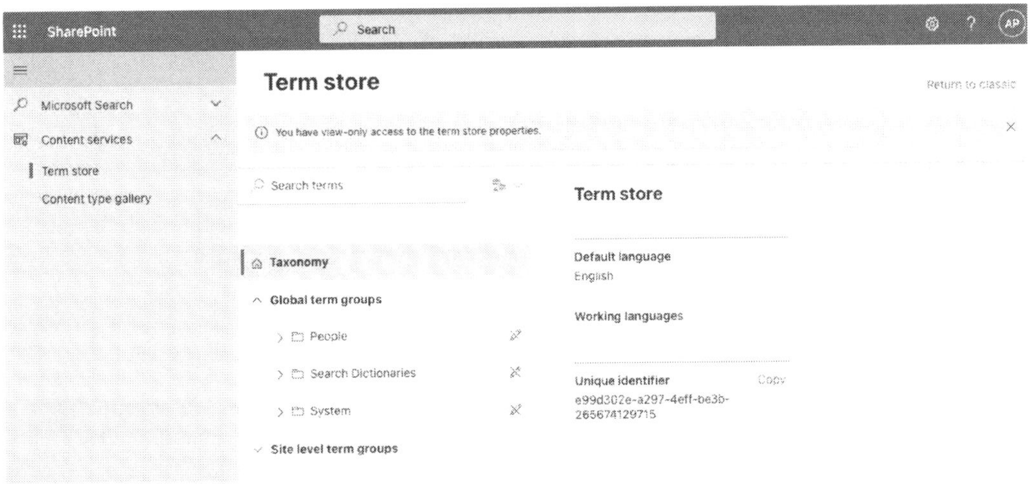

Figure 17.2: *Term store Global term groups and Site level term groups*

It is also worth noting that term sets can be shared across different term groups, both at the global and site level. Additionally, global term groups can be created and managed using the SharePoint Online admin center, while site-level term groups can be created and managed using the Term Store Management tool within the site collection (can be accessed via Site settings).

Term store main components

The main components of the term store in SharePoint Online are as follows:

- **Term groups:** A container for related term sets. Term groups are the highest level of organization in the SharePoint Term Store. They are used to group related sets of terms, and they can be used to manage metadata across multiple site collections or web applications. A term group can contain multiple term sets, and each term set can contain multiple terms. The term group can also have a default language associated with it, which is used when displaying term labels in the SharePoint user interface. In addition, term groups can be managed by one or more term store administrators, who are responsible for creating, editing, and deleting term sets and terms within the group.

- **Term sets:** A collection of related terms organized in a hierarchical structure. In SharePoint, a term set is a collection of related terms that are grouped together. Term sets are a way to organize and manage terms in a hierarchical structure that makes it easy to find and use terms consistently throughout a site or organization. Each term set has a unique name and can contain one or more terms, which can themselves be organized into subgroups within the term set. Term sets can be used to define metadata, which can be used to tag documents and other content in SharePoint. This makes it easier to find and manage content, especially in large and complex sites.

- **Terms:** A label or keyword that is assigned to content to help categorize and describe it. Terms are individual labels or keywords that are used to classify content in a consistent and meaningful way. They are part of a hierarchical taxonomy structure that is created and managed in the Term Store Management Tool. Terms can be organized into term sets, which can in turn be organized into term groups. The use of terms enables users to more easily find and categorize content within SharePoint Online.

- **Term store administrator:** A user with permission to manage the term store and its components.

- **Enterprise keywords:** A special type of term set that allows users to add keywords to items such as documents, pages, or images in SharePoint. Enterprise keywords are a type of managed metadata in SharePoint Online that allows users to add relevant keywords or tags to items such as documents, lists, and libraries. These keywords can then be used for search, filtering, and grouping of items based on common themes. To work with enterprise keywords in SPO, you first need to ensure that the feature is enabled at the site collection level. Once enabled, you can add enterprise keywords to individual items by editing the item properties and entering the keywords in the "Enterprise Keywords" field. You can also bulk-edit items to add or remove enterprise keywords.

Enterprise keywords are stored in a separate term set within the term store, called the "Keywords" term set. This term set can be managed separately from other term sets, and you can configure settings such as whether or not to allow users to add new keywords or require keyword fields for specific types of items. Additionally, you can use the "Keyword term set" page to view and manage all of the enterprise keywords used across your site collection.

To assign Term Store Administrators in SharePoint Online, follow these steps:

1. Go to the SharePoint admin center.

2. Click on **Term store** under the **Content services** section.

3. Click on the three dots next to the term store you want to manage, and select **Manage administrators**.

4. Click **Add users**.

5. Enter the name or email address of the user you want to add as an administrator, and select the role you want to assign (either **Term store administrator** or **Term group manager**).

6. Click **OK** to save the changes.

Only SharePoint Online administrators or users with the **Term store administrator** or **Term group manager** role can assign Term Store Administrators.

Managed metadata overview

So, to recap, managed metadata in SharePoint Online is a way to define and manage metadata in a hierarchical structure called a term store. Managed metadata helps improve the consistency and accuracy of information in SharePoint by providing a way to categorize and tag content with standardized terms, called metadata terms.

In SPO, the term store can be managed at the global level for the entire organization or at the site level for specific sites or site collections. The term store is organized into term groups, which are groups of related terms. Term groups can have one or more term sets, which are collections of related terms. Terms are the individual metadata values that are applied to content in SharePoint.

Managed metadata in SPO can also include enterprise keywords, which are free-form keywords that can be added to content by users. Enterprise keywords are stored separately from the formal term store and can be managed by site administrators.

Managed metadata can be used for a variety of purposes, such as improving search results, making it easier to find and classify information, ensuring consistency across sites and content types, and enabling content-based routing and records management. It can also facilitate navigation and browsing of content, and support the use of content types and workflows. By using managed metadata in SharePoint Online, organizations can better organize and manage their content, which can lead to increased productivity, better decision-making, and improved compliance with regulatory requirements.

You can use managed metadata with lists and libraries in SharePoint Online by creating columns that are based on a term set from the term store. When you create a column, you can specify the term set that it should use, and then users can select terms from that term set when they add or edit items in the list or library. You can also use managed metadata to create views and filters that are based on specific terms, and to group items by term in a list or library view. Additionally, you can use managed metadata to enforce content types and to apply retention policies to items based on their metadata values.

Managed metadata can be used for navigation in SharePoint by creating a managed metadata navigation, which allows users to navigate content using the terms in the term store instead of relying on the site's structure. This can help users to more easily find the content they need, regardless of where it is stored on the site. To use managed metadata for navigation, you will need to create a term set that contains the terms you want to use for navigation, and then configure the site to use the managed metadata navigation. Once the navigation is set up, users can browse the site using the terms in the term set, which will filter the content displayed on the site accordingly.

Figure 17.3 features managed metadata used for Navigation:

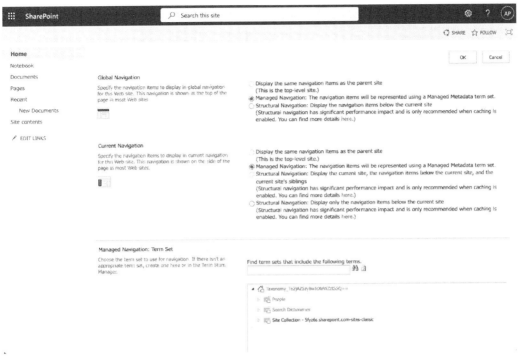

Figure 17.3: Managed metadata used for Navigation

Managed metadata can also be used to improve search results by defining search terms and keywords that users can use to search for content. This can help to standardize search queries and make it easier for users to find the information they need. Managed metadata can also be used to create refinement filters for search results, which can help users to narrow down their search results based on specific criteria. This can help to improve the relevancy of search results and make it easier for users to find what they are looking for. Additionally, managed metadata can be used to define synonyms for search terms, which can help to improve search results by including alternative terms that users may use to search for content.

Content type gallery

Content types are a way of defining and managing the metadata and behaviors of a specific type of content in a SharePoint environment. A content type defines a set of columns or fields that can be associated with a particular type of document, such as a contract, expense report, or proposal. It can also define workflows, templates, and other settings that determine how the content is managed and used within a SharePoint site or site collection. Content types help organizations ensure that consistent metadata is used across all content of a particular type, making it easier to manage, search for, and share information.

SharePoint Online comes with a number of built-in content types, including:

- **Document:** This content type is used for creating and managing documents. It includes several default document templates, such as Word document, Excel workbook, and PowerPoint presentation.

- **Item:** This content type is used for creating list items, such as tasks, issues, and contacts.

- **Folder:** This content type is used for organizing files and documents in a hierarchical structure.

- **Picture:** This content type is used for storing and managing images and photos.

- **Announcement:** This content type is used for creating and publishing news and announcements.

- **Event:** This content type is used for creating and managing calendar events.

- **Link:** This content type is used for storing and managing links to external web pages or documents.

- **Task:** This content type is used for creating and managing tasks and workflows.

- **Issue:** This content type is used for tracking and managing issues and bugs.

- **Survey:** This content type is used for creating and conducting surveys and questionnaires.

In addition to these, you can also create your own custom content types to suit the specific needs of your organization.

Content types can be thought of as templates or blueprints for different types of content in your organization. By using content types, you can define and enforce metadata and behaviors consistently across different types of content, which can make it easier to manage and find content in SharePoint.

For example, you might have a content type for contracts, which includes metadata such as the contract number, vendor, and expiration date. You might also have a content type for project proposals, which includes metadata such as the project manager, budget, and start date. By using these content types, you can ensure that all contracts and project proposals have consistent metadata, and you can easily search for and manage content based on these attributes.

Content types can also include specific settings for workflows, information management policies, and other behaviors, which can help you automate processes and enforce governance policies across different types of content.

To access the Content Type Gallery in SharePoint Online, follow these steps:

1. Go to the **Site Settings** page of your site.

2. Under the **Web Designer Galleries** section, select **Site content types**.

3. You will be taken to the **Content Type Gallery**, which displays all the content types that are available for your site.

In the Content Type Gallery, you can perform the following tasks:

- Create new content types based on existing ones or from scratch.

- Modify existing content types by adding or removing columns, changing the order of columns, or changing the default values of columns.

- Manage the properties of content types, such as the name, description, and group.

- Publish content types to other site collections or to the Content Type Hub.

- Delete content types that are no longer needed.

Overall, the Content Type Gallery is where you can create and manage content types for your SharePoint site, which can help standardize content across your organization and improve searchability and discoverability of content.

Practical tasks

As usual, let us first log in to the Microsoft 365 portal with your account.

From the list of available applications, select SharePoint and go to one of your sites. Select the site that you created in classic mode before, because it will easily allow you to apply managed metadata navigation later.

Launch the site to Site Settings, by clicking on the gear icon in the top right corner and selecting **Site settings** link. Under Site Administration section, click on the **Term store management** link.

Figure 17.4 features a term store management link from the Site Settings menu:

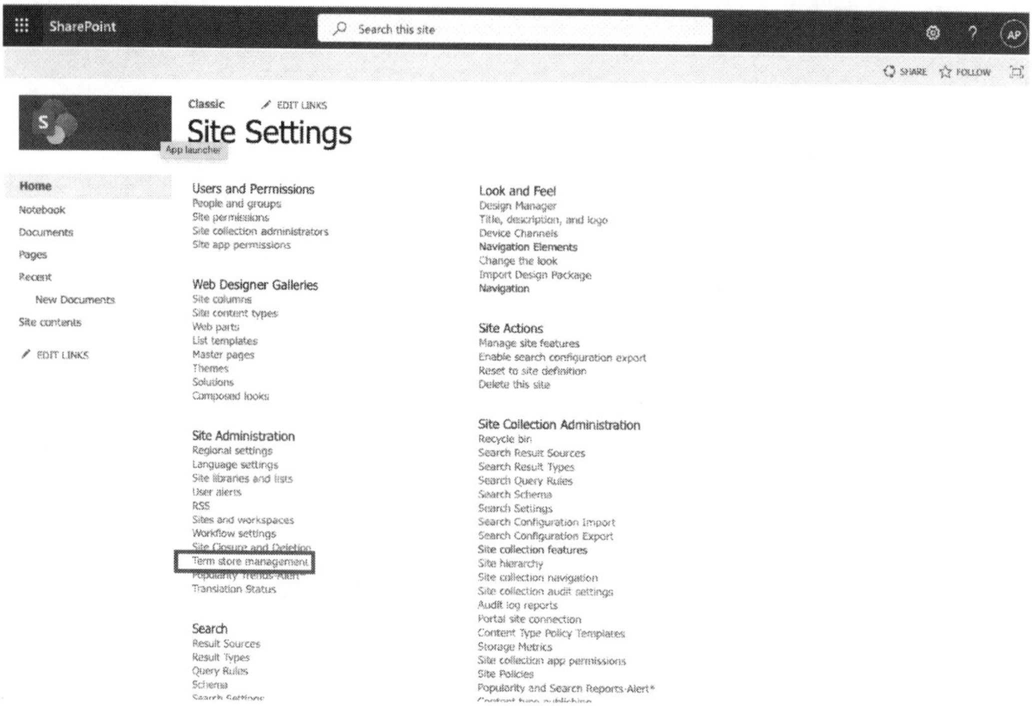

Figure 17.4: *Term store management link from the Site Settings menu*

Inside term store management, as we discussed before, you will see Global and Site level term groups.

Let us create a new term group under a site level. Follow the given steps:

1. Click on the Site level term groups dropdown.

2. Select your site collection under it.

3. Then from the top ribbon, click on **Add term set** button.

4. It will prompt you to set a name for your new term set in the term tree.

5. After created select your new term, and from the top ribbon, select the **Add term** button.

6. Add a few terms there. Please note that terms have a hierarchical structure. So, every time you create a new term, you need to select your term set and not the term you just created. Otherwise term will be created under another term.

Now, as this is done and a few terms are created, we can apply them in the list or library.

Let us go back to your SharePoint site. From there, access any list or library that is already present there. You can create a new one if you would like.

In the list, go to the top right corner and click on the settings gear. Select List/Library settings. Click on **More library settings** when pop-up on the right side shows up.

Scroll a little bit down and select **Create column** link.

Figure 17.5 features a create column option from the list setting page:

Figure 17.5: *Create column option from the list setting page*

You will be prompted to set the name of your column and select a data type.

Set any name you want and select the **Managed metadata type**.

If you scroll down the page, you will see your metadata tree and will be able to select a site level term set you created before.

Click **Ok** at the bottom of the page.

Now if you create a new item/document, you will have a new column available where you can choose values from the terms available in the term set that was created before.

You can implement the same column with this metadata on other lists/libraries and they all will refer to the same terms inside the term set. Search refiners and criterias can be built later based on this metadata.

You can also build navigation based on the managed metadata.

To configure navigation, click on the gear icon in the top right corner of the screen and select **Site settings**.

Then find **Site Collection Administration** section and link **Site Colleciton features**. You will be redirected to page with features that expand default SharePoint functionality. Scroll all the way down and look for **SharePoint Server Publishing Infrastructure** feature. Click **Activate**.

It may take a couple of minutes for a feature to be activated.

After it is activated, you can go back to the Site settings page, and under **Look and Feel** section, you will see the Navigation link available at the bottom. Click on it.

On the Navigation page, you will be able to configure top-level and left-side navigation. You could select multiple properties how navigation should be configured and displayed. Select the **Managed navigation** option for the current navigation (left side navigation). The terms tree will appear and you will be able to select your previously created term set from there.

Figure 17.6 features managed metadata navigation set up on Navigation page:

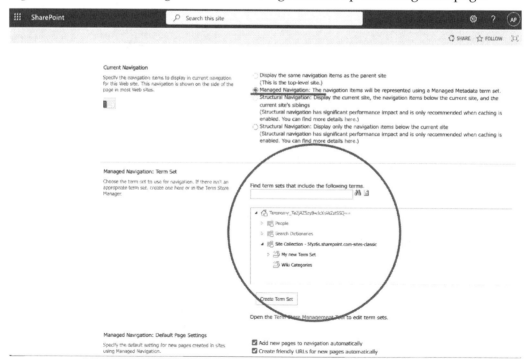

Figure 17.6: *Managed metadata navigation set up on the Navigation page*

You can use the managed metadata terms to define the structure and hierarchy of the navigation menus, and the menus will be automatically updated as you add or modify the terms in the Term Store. Managed Navigation provides a more flexible and customizable way to create navigation menus on your site, and it can be particularly useful for large, complex sites with a lot of content.

As the last exercise, let us review content types and create a new one on your site. Go back to site settings. Under **Web Designer Galleries** section, select **Site Content types** link.

You will be redirected to the page where you can find all content types that already present on your site. You can see that each content type has a parent content type already assigned. Parent content types on their top-level cannot be modified. However, you can create new content types or modify child content types.

For example, you can click on the **Create content type** button in the top ribbon and create a new content type with **Document** content type as a parent. You can attach a new template that can be used as a part of HR documentation and add this content type in any of the document libraries present on the site.

Later search references and criterias can be built based on content types. Retention policies can also be applied based on the content type associated with items/documents.

Conclusion

The Term Store and Content Types are important components of SharePoint Online that enable organizations to manage and organize their information and metadata effectively. The Term Store provides a centralized location for creating and managing taxonomy and metadata, while Content Types enable the standardization and reuse of metadata and other settings across multiple lists and libraries. By using the Term Store and Content Types, organizations can improve search, navigation, and information management, leading to more efficient and effective collaboration and decision-making.

Points to remember

- The term store is a centralized location for storing and managing reusable metadata, such as keywords, terms, and tags.

- Managed metadata and the term store can be used to provide consistent metadata across a SharePoint site, which can help with search, navigation, and content management.

- Content types are used to define and manage the metadata, workflows, and behaviors of a particular type of content, such as a document or item in a list.

- Content types can inherit from other content types, and they can be added to lists and libraries to provide consistency and help enforce governance policies.

- The Content Type Gallery is the central location for managing content types at the site collection level in SharePoint Online.

- Managed navigation can be used to provide a consistent navigation experience across a site collection by using managed metadata to define the navigation structure.

- When using managed navigation, terms from the term store are used as navigation nodes, and changes to the term store will be reflected in the navigation automatically.

- When working with the term store and content types, it is important to plan and design your taxonomy and metadata strategy carefully to ensure that it meets the needs of your organization and supports your governance policies.

Join our book's Discord space

Join the book's Discord Workspace for Latest updates, Offers, Tech happenings around the world, New Release and Sessions with the Authors:

https://discord.bpbonline.com

## CHAPTER 18

Custom Solutions Development SPFX

"Custom solutions development is not just about writing code. It's about solving problems, understanding requirements, and delivering value to customers."

- Joel Spolsky

Introduction

SharePoint offers advanced customization when it comes to updating features based on the company's needs, compared to what SPO can offer out of the box. That is why SPFX solutions might be needed. Using React, Angular or any other JavaScript framework of your choice, you can develop custom web-parts, custom look and feel, dashboards, reports, and much more. In this chapter, we will review the history of customization support for various SharePoint platforms and what approaches are available nowadays.

Structure

In this chapter, we will cover the following topics:

- Custom solutions, sppkg and SPFX
- Key features of the SharePoint framework

- Best practices development for SharePoint
- Application Catalog
- REST and GRAPH API in SharePoint

Objectives

In this chapter, the objective will be to gain the knowledge and skills necessary to create custom SharePoint solutions that meet specific business needs using modern web development tools and frameworks. This includes learning how to use SPFx to build and deploy client-side web parts, extensions, and other customizations in SharePoint Online, as well as integrating external data and services into SharePoint using REST APIs and other methods. By mastering custom solutions development and SPFx in SharePoint Online, you and your organization can enhance the functionality and usability of your SharePoint environment and streamline business processes.

Custom solutions, sppkg, and SPFX

Custom solutions in SharePoint Online are customizations or extensions that are developed and deployed on the SharePoint Online platform to meet specific business needs that are not provided out of the box. These can be developed using various technologies, such as JavaScript, HTML, CSS, or .NET, and can include custom web parts, workflows, forms, and other SharePoint components. Custom solutions can be created for both classic and modern SharePoint environments and can be deployed either on-premises or in the cloud.

Custom solutions development in SharePoint online is generally considered an advanced topic that requires additional skills and knowledge beyond basic SharePoint usage. To develop custom solutions, you would typically need to be proficient in web development technologies such as HTML, CSS, JavaScript, and TypeScript, as well as have a good understanding of SharePoint's development framework and APIs. It may also be helpful to have experience with modern web development frameworks such as React or Angular, as many custom solutions in SharePoint online are built using these technologies.

There are many types of custom solutions that can be developed for SharePoint Online. Some examples include the following:

- Custom web parts and apps.
- Custom workflows and forms.
- Custom themes and branding.

- Custom integration with external systems.

- Custom search solutions.

- Custom reporting and analytics.

- Custom document management solutions.

- Custom security and access controls.

These solutions can be developed using various programming languages and frameworks, such as JavaScript, .NET, and **SharePoint Framework** (**SPFx**).

To develop a custom web part or custom form in SharePoint Online, you would typically use SPFx. Here is a high-level overview of the steps you would follow:

1. **Set up your development environment:** You would need to set up your development environment with the necessary tools and software, such as Node.js, Yeoman, and Visual Studio Code.

2. **Create a new SPFx project:** You can create a new SPFx project using the Yeoman generator for SharePoint.

3. **Develop your web part or form:** Once you have your project set up, you can use your preferred development tools to create your custom web part or form. You can use TypeScript, React, or any other supported framework to build your solution.

4. **Package and deploy your solution:** When you are finished developing your solution, you would package it and deploy it to SharePoint Online. You can use the SharePoint Framework's build and packaging tools to do this.

5. **Test and debug your solution:** Finally, you would test and debug your solution to ensure it works as expected. You can use tools such as the SharePoint Workbench to test your web part or form in a simulated SharePoint environment.

Here is an example of the code for a "Hello World" web part using SPFx.

This code defines a web part that displays the message "Hello World" and includes a text field in the web part properties pane for entering a description. The web part uses React for rendering the content. Please refer to the following code:

```
import * as React from 'react';
import * as ReactDom from 'react-dom';
import { Version } from '@microsoft/sp-core-library';
import {
  IPropertyPaneConfiguration,
  PropertyPaneTextField
```

```typescript
} from '@microsoft/sp-property-pane';
import { BaseClientSideWebPart } from '@microsoft/sp-webpart-base';

import * as strings from 'HelloWorldWebPartStrings';
import HelloWorld from './components/HelloWorld';
import { IhelloWorldProps } from './components/IhelloWorldProps';

export interface IhelloWorldWebPartProps {
  description: string;
}

export default class HelloWorldWebPart extends
BaseClientSideWebPart<IhelloWorldWebPartProps> {

  public render(): void {
    const element: React.ReactElement<IhelloWorldProps> = React.
createElement(
      HelloWorld,
      {
        description: this.properties.description
      }
    );

    ReactDom.render(element, this.domElement);
  }

  protected onDispose(): void {
    ReactDom.unmountComponentAtNode(this.domElement);
  }

  protected get dataVersion(): Version {
    return Version.parse('1.0');
  }

  protected getPropertyPaneConfiguration(): IpropertyPaneConfiguration
{
    return {
      pages: [
        {
          header: {
            description: strings.PropertyPaneDescription
          },
```

```
groups: [
    {
        groupName: strings.BasicGroupName,
        groupFields: [
            PropertyPaneTextField('description', {
                label: strings.DescriptionFieldLabel
            })
        ]
    }
    ]
    };
}
}
```

To package and deploy your custom solution in SharePoint Online, you can follow the given steps:

1. **Create a package for your solution:** You can create a package for your solution by running the **gulp bundle --ship** and **gulp package-solution --ship** commands. These commands will create a .sppkg file that you can upload to the App Catalog.

2. **Upload the package to the App Catalog:** The App Catalog is a central location in SharePoint Online where you can upload and manage your custom solutions. You can upload your .sppkg file to the App Catalog using the web interface or the SharePoint Online Management Shell.

3. **Deploy the solution:** Once your solution is uploaded to the App Catalog, you can deploy it to your site collections. You can do this using the web interface or the SharePoint Online Management Shell.

4. **Add the web part to a page:** After deploying the solution to a site collection, you can add the web part to a page by editing the page and selecting the web part from the web part gallery.

These are general steps, and the specifics may vary depending on your solution and your organization's deployment process. It is important to thoroughly test your solution and ensure it does not negatively impact the performance or stability of your SharePoint Online environment before deploying it to production.

In SharePoint Online, the Application Customizer is the extension that enables you to customize the look and feel of your SharePoint site or application. It allows you to add scripts to the header or footer of a page, inject custom CSS styles, and modify the existing UI elements of a page. The Application Customizer is a popular way to add your own branding, logos, and themes to SharePoint sites, and it provides a lot of flexibility and control over the user experience. It can also be used to add custom business logic to SharePoint pages and to integrate with other external systems.

In order to make your web part available on a SharePoint site, you will need to package and deploy it to the site. Depending on how you have packaged and deployed your solution, you may need to activate a feature or add an app to the site as well. Once your solution is deployed, you can add your web part to a page by editing the page and adding the web part to a web part zone. Once uploaded, the solution can be deployed to the individual site collections in the tenant.

To make a web part available on a site, you would typically deploy it to the app catalog, either by adding it as a site collection app or by deploying it as a feature at the site collection level. Deploying a web part as a feature involves creating an XML file that specifies the web part, and then deploying that file to the site collection using PowerShell.

Adding a web part as a feature or an app to a site collection ensures that it is available for use by all users of the site. Once it is added, users can add the web part to their pages just like any other web part.

When creating a SharePoint Framework solution, you can specify whether the solution should be added as an app or a feature. This can be done in the **config/package-solution.json** file. Once the solution is packaged, it can be uploaded to the app catalog and deployed to site collections using the SharePoint Online Management Shell or the SharePoint admin center.

Customizing the classic UI in SharePoint typically involves using SharePoint Designer or creating custom JavaScript solutions that leverage the SharePoint object model.

To add custom script to classic pages, you can use the Script Editor web part or Content Editor web part, which allow you to add custom HTML, JavaScript, and CSS to a page.

When using the Script Editor web part, it is recommended to host the custom script on a separate location, such as a document library, and reference it in the Script Editor web part. This allows you to more easily manage the custom script and update it as needed.

Overall, the process for developing custom solutions for classic UI involves creating the custom script, hosting it in a location accessible to the SharePoint site, and then adding the Script Editor or Content Editor web part to the page and referencing the custom script. It is important to thoroughly test the custom solution before deploying it to a production environment.

With the Classic UI, there are mainly 2 ways of customizing pages or adding new custom scripts to pages:

- Embed approach via Content editor or Script Editor.

- Direct modification via SP Designer modifying aspx pages.

The embed approach is much safer to execute. You just prepare your html file with structure and all references to .js and .css files. Place them all into SiteAssets document library or any other library you want. Then refer to that .html file from the content editor web-part. It will bootstrap the application and launch it on the page.

The other approach requires you to open page in edit mode in the SP Designer, modify it there and save it. Let us say, sometimes SP Designer likes to insert peaces of code on its own, which potentially makes the code of the whole page messy and there is a high probability that something will be broken.

You can also customize out of the box forms in the Classic UI, without use of PowerApps. To customize the out-of-the-box forms for a list in SharePoint, you can use XSLT to modify the appearance and behavior of the form. XSLT is a markup language used to transform XML documents into other formats, such as HTML. In SharePoint, XSLT is used to transform the data stored in SharePoint lists and libraries into the HTML that is displayed in the user interface.

To customize the out-of-the-box forms, you can use SharePoint Designer, which allows you to modify the XSLT, that is used to generate the forms. Using SharePoint Designer, you can create custom XSLT templates and apply them to the list forms to modify the look and feel of the form.

You can also use third-party tools or frameworks, such as InfoPath, to create custom forms with a richer set of features and functionality. However, keep in mind that InfoPath is no longer supported by Microsoft, and it is recommended to use the SharePoint Framework or other modern development approaches to create custom solutions.

Figure 18.1 features a SP Designer view of the list with 3 forms in there:

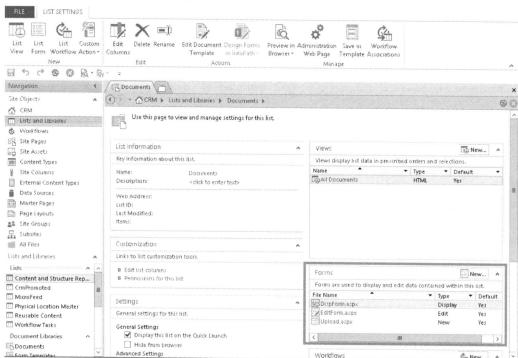

Figure 18.1: *SP Designer view of the list with 3 forms in there*

Key features of the SharePoint framework

Some key features of the SharePoint Framework include the ability to use modern web technologies such as React, Angular, and TypeScript; support for SharePoint Online and SharePoint on-premises; the ability to create web parts, extensions, and application customizers; integration with the SharePoint web parts and content management system; and seamless integration with Office 365 services such as Microsoft Graph and Microsoft Teams. Additionally, the SharePoint Framework is designed to be extensible, meaning that developers can create their own custom controls and components to add to the framework

Its key features include:

- It is a client-side development model based on open-source tools and libraries.

- It enables developers to build responsive and mobile-friendly web parts, extensions, and applications using popular web technologies such as TypeScript, React, and Node.js.

- It allows developers to use modern development tools and frameworks, such as Visual Studio Code, Yeoman, Gulp, and Webpack.

- It provides a flexible and modular development approach, where web parts and extensions can be built and deployed independently and can be reused across sites and tenants.

- It offers a comprehensive set of APIs and controls that allow developers to interact with SharePoint data and services and to customize the look and feel of their applications.

- It supports both SharePoint Online and SharePoint on-premises, and can be used to build solutions for Microsoft Teams, Microsoft Graph, and other Microsoft 365 services.

- It is continuously evolving, with new features and capabilities being added with each release and with a strong and active community of developers contributing to its growth and improvement.

Here is a typical structure for an SPFx project:

- **config**: contains the JSON configuration files for the project.

- **lib**: contains external libraries used in the project.

- **node_modules**: contains the Node.js modules used in the project.

- **src**: contains the TypeScript source files for the project.

- **temp**: contains temporary files used during build and package creation.

- **test**: contains the test files for the project.

- **.gitignore**: specifies the files and directories that Git should ignore.

- **gulpfile.js**: the Gulp.js file that specifies the build tasks for the project.

- **package.json**: the Node.js package file that specifies the project's dependencies and build scripts.

- **README.md**: the project's readme file.

- **tsconfig.json**: the TypeScript configuration file for the project.

- **tslint.json**: the configuration file for the TSLint code linter.

To prepare a new SharePoint Framework project, you can follow these steps

1. Install Node.js on your machine.

2. Install Yeoman and the SharePoint Framework Yeoman generator using the command: `npm install -g yo @microsoft/generator-sharepoint`

3. Create a new directory for your project.

4. Open a command prompt or terminal and navigate to the project directory.

5. Run the following command to generate a new SharePoint Framework project: `yo @microsoft/sharepoint`

6. Follow the prompts to specify the project details, such as the project name and description, and select the desired project options, such as the framework version and web part options.

7. Once the project has been generated, you can open it in your preferred code editor and start developing your custom solutions.

The SharePoint Framework has specific requirements for the version of Node.js that you use. The current version of the SharePoint Framework requires Node.js LTS version 10.x or 12.x. It is always a good idea to check the official documentation for the SharePoint Framework to verify the current requirements before starting a new project.

Yeoman is a tool used to generate scaffolding for modern web applications, including SPFx projects. It is a **command-line interface (CLI)** that helps developers automate the process of creating new projects, adding components, and other tasks. Yeoman is built on top of Node.js and utilizes various generators to create the scaffolding for different types of applications. In the case of SPFx development, Yeoman is used to generate the basic file structure and project configuration for the new project. Once you run the commands to create a new project, the structure that was outlined previously, will be created.

Figure 18.2 features a new project structure in Visual Studio Code:

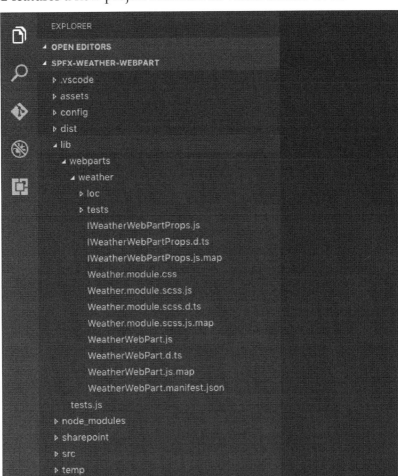

Figure 18.2: New project structure in Visual Studio Code

You need to install Yeoman to generate a new SharePoint Framework project. Yeoman is a command-line tool that helps automate project creation and provides project templates. You can install Yeoman by running the following command in a command prompt or terminal window:

```
npm install -g yo
```

Once Yeoman is installed, you can generate a new SharePoint Framework project by running the SharePoint Framework generator.

You can store your code in a Git repository, which can be hosted on GitHub, Azure DevOps, or other Git hosting services. SharePoint Framework projects are designed to work with version control systems, and Git is the recommended version control system to use with SharePoint Framework projects. This allows you to keep your code under version control, collaborate with others, and manage changes to your code over time.

You can also set up CI/CD pipelines for your solutions deployemnts.

To set up a pipeline for an SPFx project, you can use a **continuous integration/ continuous delivery (CI/CD)** tool such as Azure DevOps or GitHub Actions.

Here are some general steps to follow to set up a pipeline for an SPFx project:

1. **Create a build pipeline:** A build pipeline is responsible for building and packaging the SPFx solution. You can define the steps of the build pipeline using a YAML file in Azure DevOps or GitHub Actions.

2. **Create a release pipeline:** A release pipeline is responsible for deploying the packaged solution to SharePoint Online or on-premises SharePoint. You can define the steps of the release pipeline using a YAML file in Azure DevOps or GitHub Actions.

3. **Configure environment variables:** In both Azure DevOps and GitHub Actions, you can define environment variables that your pipeline will use. For example, you may need to specify the target SharePoint site URL, or the authentication credentials to connect to SharePoint.

4. **Run your pipeline:** Once you have set up your build and release pipelines, you can run them to build and deploy your SPFx solution.

Best practices development for SharePoint

Microsoft provides a set of guidelines and best practices for SharePoint Framework development. Some of these best practices include:

- Following the principle of least privilege for API access.

- Minimizing the use of external dependencies.

- Using the latest version of the SharePoint Framework.

- Adhering to the TypeScript coding standards.

- Ensuring compatibility with modern SharePoint pages and lists.

- Implementing responsive design and cross-browser compatibility.

- Optimizing performance through caching, lazy loading, and other techniques.

- Using Microsoft Graph APIs for accessing data in Microsoft 365.

- Implementing proper error handling and logging.

- Testing the solution on different environments and configurations.

These are just a few examples of the best practices recommended by Microsoft for SharePoint Framework development. Following these guidelines can help ensure the reliability, scalability, and security of your custom solutions.

You should also follow overall best practices for solutions development. They include some of this for SharePoint development:

- **Use the latest tools and frameworks:** SharePoint development is constantly evolving, and so, it is important to use the latest tools and frameworks to take advantage of the latest features and improve your productivity.

- **Use version control**: Use a version control system such as Git to track changes to your code and collaborate with other developers. This ensures that you have a history of your code changes and can easily revert to a previous version if necessary.

- **Follow a modular approach**: Break your code into modular components and use proper naming conventions. This makes it easier to maintain and debug your code.

- **Optimize for performance**: Optimize your code for performance by minimizing the use of server resources, minimizing the amount of data transferred between the server and client, and minimizing the use of third-party libraries and plugins.

- **Write secure code**: Ensure that your code is secure by using authentication and authorization mechanisms, validating user input, and minimizing the risk of SQL injection attacks.

- **Test your code**: Test your code thoroughly using automated tests, unit tests, and integration tests. This helps to catch bugs early and ensures that your code is working as expected.

- **Follow the SharePoint development guidelines**: SharePoint has specific development guidelines and best practices that you should follow. These guidelines cover topics such as code structure, naming conventions, and deployment methods.

- **Use third-party tools and frameworks sparingly:** While third-party tools and frameworks can save you time, they can also introduce security vulnerabilities and make your code harder to maintain. Only use third-party tools and frameworks when necessary and carefully evaluate their security and maintenance impact.

- **Use PowerShell for automation**: PowerShell is a powerful tool for automating SharePoint development tasks, such as deploying code and configuring sites. Learn to use PowerShell effectively to increase your productivity.

- **Document your code:** Document your code thoroughly to make it easier for other developers to understand and maintain your code. Use clear and concise comments and provide documentation on how to use your code.

When developing SPFX solutions, you can use various tools to test and debug your code, including the following:

- **Browser Developer Tools:** You can use the browser developer tools to inspect the HTML, CSS, and JavaScript code in your web parts, as well as to debug your code by setting breakpoints and stepping through it.

- **Debug configuration files:** You can use the debug configuration files to specify the URL of the site where you want to deploy and test your web part. This enables you to test your code in a development environment before deploying it to a production environment.

- **Unit testing:** You can use automated unit testing frameworks such as Jest or Mocha to test your code and ensure that it works as expected.

- **Fiddler:** Fiddler is a web debugging tool that you can use to inspect and debug HTTP traffic between your web part and the SharePoint server.

- **Visual Studio Code Debugger:** You can also use the Visual Studio Code Debugger to debug your SPFX code. The debugger allows you to set breakpoints, inspect variables, and step through your code to help identify and fix issues.

- **Logging:** You can use `console.log()` statements in your code to log messages to the browser console, which can help you debug issues and understand the flow of your code. SharePoint also provides a logging framework that you can use to log messages to the SharePoint logs.

- **Office 365 CLI:** The Office 365 CLI is a command-line interface that you can use to automate tasks related to SPFX development, including building, packaging, and deploying your web parts. It also includes commands to help with testing and debugging your web parts.

Overall, testing and debugging SPFX solutions is similar to testing and debugging any other web application, and requires a combination of tools, techniques, and best practices to ensure that your code is reliable and performs as expected.

When you create a new SPFx project, you can run it locally using the `gulp serve` command. This command will start a local development server and launch your project in a web browser. You can make changes to your code and see the results immediately in the web browser without having to deploy your code to SharePoint. This is a great way to test and debug your code during development.

Once you are ready to deploy your code to SharePoint, you can package your code and deploy it to SharePoint. You can then see the results on your SharePoint site. Note that you will need to have the appropriate permissions to deploy custom solutions to SharePoint, and you should always test your solutions thoroughly in a non-production environment before deploying them to a production environment.

Application catalog

The application catalog in SharePoint Online is a central location where you can upload, manage, and share custom SharePoint applications. The application catalog can be used to deploy SPFx solutions, add-ins, and other customizations. It is a place where you can control access to the apps and add-ins that your organization has deployed in SharePoint Online, and manage the licenses for those solutions. The application catalog is typically created at the tenant level, and administrators can use it to ensure that custom solutions are properly tested and approved before being made available to users.

In SharePoint Online, there are two types of app catalogs:

- **tenant-level:** The tenant-level app catalog is created at the tenant level and can be used by any site collection within the tenant.

- **site-level:** The site-level app catalog is created at the site collection level and can only be used by that site collection.

You should use a tenant-level app catalog when you want to deploy apps that can be used across multiple sites within your SharePoint Online tenant. This makes it easier to manage and deploy apps centrally.

On the other hand, you should use a site-level app catalog when you want to deploy apps to a specific site or set of sites within your SharePoint Online environment. This can be useful if you have customizations that are specific to a particular site or group of sites.

In general, it is recommended to use a tenant-level app catalog if you have apps that can be used across multiple sites, and use a site-level app catalog if you have customizations that are specific to a particular site or group of sites.

The app catalog is not created by default in SharePoint Online. You need to create it manually. Here are the steps to create a new app catalog:

1. Open the SharePoint Online Admin Center.

2. Click on **More features** in the left navigation menu and then select **Apps** under the **Apps** section.

3. Click on **App Catalog** in the top navigation menu.

4. If you already have a tenant-level app catalog, you will see a link to it on this page. If you do not have one, click on **Create a new app catalog site**.

5. Choose whether you want to create the app catalog at the tenant level or at the site collection level.

6. Fill in the required information, such as the name and URL for the new app catalog site.

7. Click **OK** to create the new app catalog.

After creating the app catalog, you can upload custom apps and add-ins to it and then deploy them to your SharePoint sites.

To create a site-level app catalog in SharePoint Online, follow these steps. Please note that this can be done only using PowerShell.

To set up a site level app catalog using PowerShell, you can use the following steps:

- Open the SharePoint Online Management Shell or connect to SharePoint Online using PowerShell.

- Type the following command to create a new app catalog site:

```
New-SPOSite -Url <AppCatalogSiteURL> -Owner <UserPrincipalName>
-StorageQuota <StorageQuota> -Title <Title> -Template STS#0
```

Replace the placeholders with the following values:

- `<AppCatalogSiteURL>`: The URL of the site collection where you want to create the app catalog. For example, **https://contoso.sharepoint.com/sites/appcatalog**.

- `<UserPrincipalName>`: The user principal name of the site collection owner. For example, **john@contoso.onmicrosoft.com**.

- **<StorageQuota>**: The storage quota for the site collection in megabytes. For example, 100.

- **<Title>**: The title of the site collection. For example, App Catalog.

Refer to the following code:

```
Connect-PnPOnline -Url https://<your-tenant>.sharepoint.com/sites/<site-url> -UseWebLogin


# create site collection app catalog

Add-PnPSiteCollectionAppCatalog


# or alternatively, create subsite app catalog

Add-PnPAzureStorageApplicationPrincipal -TenantId <your-tenant-id> -ApplicationId <your-app-client-id> -ClientSecret <your-app-client-secret>

New-PnPSite -Type TeamSite -Title "<Site Title>" -Url "<Site URL>" -SiteDesign <site-design-name> -Description "<Site Description>" -Owner "<User Principal Name>"

Add-PnPAppCatalog -Site "<Site URL>"
```

Replace **<your-tenant>**, **<site-url>**, **<your-tenant-id>**, **<your-app-client-id>**, **<your-app-client-secret>**, **<Site Title>**, **<Site URL>**, and **<site-design-name>** with appropriate values.

> **Note: The user running the PowerShell command needs to have the SharePoint Online Administrator role and must be a SharePoint Online global administrator or a SharePoint Online administrator in the tenant.**

To publish a solution in the app catalog and track versions, you can follow these general steps:

1. **Build your solution:** Before publishing, you need to build your solution code in either debug or release mode.

2. **Package the solution:** Create a package of your solution using either the SharePoint Framework's built-in packaging tool (gulp bundle --ship) or a packaging tool of your choice.

3. **Upload the package to the app catalog:** Once you have packaged the solution, upload it to the app catalog by dragging and dropping it into the app catalog or using the **Add an app** option in the site contents page.

4. **Add version information:** When you upload the package to the app catalog, you will be prompted to provide version information for your solution. This is important to track the version of your solution and ensure that the latest version is being used.

5. **Deploy the solution:** Once the package is uploaded, you need to deploy it to the site or sites where you want it to be available. You can do this by going to the **Apps for SharePoint** page in the site contents and selecting the solution to deploy.

6. **Test and validate the solution:** After deploying the solution, you should test it thoroughly to ensure it is functioning as expected.

7. **Update the version as needed**: When you make changes to your solution, you should update the version number and repeat the deployment process to ensure that the latest version is being used.

Overall, it is important to maintain good version control and track changes to your solutions to avoid conflicts and ensure that the latest and most stable version is being used.

The version information for a SPFx solution is typically set in the `package.json` file, under the version property. This is the standard way of specifying the version number for any npm package, which SPFx solutions are also considered to be. When you package and deploy your SPFx solution, the version number specified in the package.json file is included in the package file and can be seen in the app catalog or wherever the solution is deployed.

REST and GRAPH API in SharePoint

There are many APIs available in **SharePoint Online** (**SPO**) for developers to use in their custom solutions, including:

- **SharePoint REST API:** This API allows developers to interact with SharePoint resources using the RESTful interface. It can be used to create, read, update, and delete SharePoint resources such as sites, lists, and documents.

- **Microsoft Graph API:** This API allows developers to interact with Microsoft 365 services, including SharePoint, using a single REST API endpoint. It provides a unified programming model to access data and services across Microsoft 365.

- **Client-Side Object Model (CSOM):** This API provides a client-side object model for SharePoint. It allows developers to interact with SharePoint resources using managed code. It can be used in .NET Framework and .NET Core applications.

- **JavaScript Object Model (JSOM):** This API provides a client-side object model for SharePoint using JavaScript. It can be used to interact with SharePoint resources from a web page.

- **SharePoint Add-in model:** This API allows developers to create add-ins for SharePoint. Add-ins are deployed separately from SharePoint and can be hosted on different platforms, such as Azure or a local server.

- **Power Automate (formerly Microsoft Flow):** This API allows developers to create workflows and automation solutions that interact with SharePoint.

The main difference between the SharePoint REST API and the Microsoft Graph API is the scope of resources that each API can access.

The SharePoint REST API provides access to SharePoint-specific resources, such as lists, libraries, and sites. It can be used to perform **Create, Read, Update, Delete (CRUD)** operations on these resources and to execute queries using the Data protocol. It is useful for SharePoint-specific scenarios, such as customizing list views or building custom web parts.

The Microsoft Graph API, on the other hand, provides access to a wide range of resources across different Microsoft services, including SharePoint, Teams, OneDrive, and more. It uses a consistent schema and authentication model across all the services it supports, making it easier to use and more flexible than the SharePoint REST API. It is useful for scenarios that involve integrating multiple Microsoft services or building custom applications that use data from different sources.

To use the SharePoint REST API, you can send HTTP requests to the SharePoint site that you want to work with. You can use REST API to perform CRUD operations on SharePoint data.

To use the SharePoint REST API, you can use various HTTP methods such as GET, POST, PUT, and DELETE. The API endpoint URL will depend on the type of operation you want to perform and the data you want to access.

Here is an example of a REST API request to get all items from a SharePoint:

```
https://{site_url}/_api/web/lists/getbytitle('{list_title}')/items
```

In the preceding URL:

- `{site_url}` is the URL of the SharePoint site you want to work with.

- `{list_title}` is the title of the SharePoint list you want to get items from.

You can also use various query parameters to filter, sort, and select the data you want to work with. Here is an example of a REST API request to get only the Title and ID fields of all items from a SharePoint list where the Status field is 'Completed':

bashCopy code

```
https://{site_url}/_api/web/lists/getbytitle('{list_title}')/
items?$select=Title,ID&$filter=Status eq 'Completed'
```

In the preceding URL:

- **$select=Title,ID** selects only the Title and ID fields.

- **$filter=Status eq 'Completed'** filters the results to only show items where the Status field is 'Completed'.

You can use various other query parameters like **$orderby** to sort the results, **$top** to limit the number of results, and **$skip** to skip a certain number of results.

To make a REST API request from your SPFx solution, you can use the **@pnp/sp** library or the **fetch()** API. Here is an example of a REST API request using the **@pnp/sp** library:

```
import { sp } from "@pnp/sp";


// Get all items from a SharePoint list

sp.web.lists.getByTitle("My List").items.get().then((items) => {

  console.log(items);

});
```

In the preceding code, the **sp** object is provided by the **@pnp/sp** library and allows you to interact with SharePoint data using REST API requests. The **getByTitle()** method is used to get a reference to the SharePoint list you want to work with, and the **items.get()** method is used to get all items from the list.

When using the REST API to retrieve items from a list, the default maximum number of items returned per request is 100. However, this can be increased up to a maximum of 5,000 using the **$top** parameter. If you need to retrieve more than 5,000 items, you can use paging to retrieve the results in batches.

> Note: There are also other limits and quotas in place for SharePoint Online, such as the maximum file size, maximum number of items in a list or library, and maximum number of indexed columns per list. These limits can vary depending on the specific plan or subscription that you have, so it is important to check the documentation and guidelines for your particular environment.

The *Microsoft Graph API* also has parameters that can be used to filter, sort, and paginate data. The Graph API provides access to a wide range of Microsoft services and allows you to work with data in a more unified way.

Here is an example of using the Graph API to get the profile information for the current user:

```
GET https://graph.microsoft.com/v1.0/me
```

In this example, **me** is a special keyword that represents the current user. You can also use other parameters to retrieve additional information or filter the results, such as:

- **$select:** to retrieve specific properties of an object, such as `?$select=id,displayName`.

- **$filter**: to retrieve only objects that meet certain criteria, such as `?$filter=startswith(displayName,'A')`.

- **$orderby**: to sort the results, such as `?$orderby=displayName`.

- **$top** and **$skip**: to paginate the results, such as `?$top=10&$skip=20`.

Note that the specific parameters and their usage may differ depending on the endpoint you are accessing and the type of data you are working with. You can find more information about the Graph API and its parameters in the Microsoft Graph API documentation.

When using the Microsoft Graph API in SharePoint Online, permissions need to be granted by the SharePoint administrator in order for the API to access SharePoint data. The administrator needs to approve the permissions requested by the application or solution using the Graph API through the Microsoft 365 admin center. Once approved, the application can use the Graph API to access SharePoint data within the permissions granted.

As an admin, you can grant permissions to your app through the **Azure Active Directory** (**Azure AD**) portal. You will need to have an Azure AD tenant associated with your SharePoint Online environment.

Here are the general steps to grant permissions to your app:

1. Register your app in Azure AD and obtain an application ID and secret.

2. In the SharePoint admin center, go to the API access page and grant the necessary permissions to your app.

3. In the Azure AD portal, go to the app registration for your app and add the necessary API permissions.

4. As a developer, request access to your app from an admin in your organization.

Once your app has been granted the necessary permissions, you can authenticate and make requests to the Graph API using an access token. You can find more information about authentication and using the Graph API in the Microsoft Graph documentation.

There are some limitations when using the Microsoft Graph API. Here are a few examples:

- **Throttling:** Microsoft limits the number of requests that can be made per minute, per user or application, and per tenant, to prevent overloading the service.

- **Permissions:** Access to certain resources or operations in Microsoft Graph requires specific permissions to be granted. These permissions need to be requested by the developer and approved by a tenant administrator.

- **Data volume:** The amount of data that can be returned in a single request is limited. If more data is needed, developers will need to use pagination or batching techniques to retrieve additional data.

- **Rate limits:** The Graph API has rate limits that are designed to prevent excessive usage and to maintain the performance and availability of the service.

These are just a few examples of the limitations of the Graph API, and it is important to review the Microsoft documentation to understand the specific limitations and best practices for using the API.

Practical tasks

In this chapter, you learned more about custom solutions development and coding for SharePoint online. The first step before starting development is to set up your local development environment. To do so for SharePoint online development, follow these steps:

1. **Install Node.js:** You can download and install Node.js from the official website: **https://nodejs.org/en/**

2. **Install Yeoman:** Open a command prompt or terminal and run the following command to install Yeoman globally:

   ```
   npm install -g yo
   ```

3. **Install the SharePoint Framework Yeoman generator:** Run the following command to install the SharePoint Framework Yeoman generator:

   ```
   npm install -g @microsoft/generator-sharepoint
   ```

4. **Install a code editor:** You can use any code editor of your choice, but Visual Studio Code is a popular choice among SharePoint developers. You can download and install Visual Studio Code from the official website: **https://code.visualstudio.com/**

5. Set up your SharePoint Online tenant, if you do not already have.

6. Create a new SharePoint Framework project: Open a command prompt or terminal and run the following commands to create a new SharePoint Framework `project`:

```
mkdir MyProject
```

```
cd MyProject
```

```
yo @microsoft/sharepoint
```

Follow the prompts to select the project options you want, such as the framework version, project type, and project name.

7. **Build and test your project:** You can run the following commands to build and test your SharePoint Framework project:

```
npm install
```

```
gulp build
```

```
gulp serve
```

The **gulp serve** command will start a local development server and open your SharePoint Framework project in a web browser.

That's it! You now have a local development environment set up for SharePoint Online and SPFx development. You can start building custom solutions for SharePoint using the SharePoint Framework and test them locally before deploying them to your SharePoint Online tenant.

Now let us create a new hello world web-part that we could deploy to the SharePoint online environment. Follow these steps:

1. Open a command prompt or terminal window on your computer. Or you can use Visual studio code and open a terminal there.

2. Create a new folder for your project by running the following command:

```
mkdir HelloWorldWebPart
```

3. Navigate to the new folder by running the following command:

```
cd HelloWorldWebPart
```

4. Run the following command to create a new SPFx project:

```
yo @microsoft/sharepoint
```

5. When prompted, enter a name for your project (for example, "**HelloWorldWebPart**") and select **WebPart** as the client-side component type.

6. Choose the appropriate options for your project, such as the SharePoint Framework version and your target environment.

7. Once the project is created, open Visual Studio.

8. In Visual Studio Code, open the "**HelloWorldWebPart.ts**" file located in the **src/webparts/helloWorld** folder.

9. Replace the existing code in the file with the following code:

```
import { Version } from '@microsoft/sp-core-library';
import { BaseClientSideWebPart } from '@microsoft/sp-webpart-base';
import { escape } from '@microsoft/sp-lodash-subset';


import styles from './HelloWorldWebPart.module.scss';
import * as strings from 'HelloWorldWebPartStrings';


export interface IHelloWorldWebPartProps {
  description: string;
}

export default class HelloWorldWebPart extends
BaseClientSideWebPart<IHelloWorldWebPartProps> {

  public render(): void {
    this.domElement.innerHTML = `
      <div class="${ styles.helloWorld }">
        <div class="${ styles.container }">
          <div class="ms-Grid-row ms-bgColor-themeDark ms-fontColor-white ${ styles.row }">
            <div class="ms-Grid-col ms-lg10 ms-xl8 ms-xlPush2 ms-lgPush1">
              <span class="ms-font-xl ms-fontColor-white">${escape(this.properties.description)}</span>
            </div>
          </div>
        </div>
      </div>`;
```

```
    }

    protected get dataVersion(): Version {
      return Version.parse('1.0');
    }

    protected getPropertyPaneConfiguration(): any {
      return {
        pages: [
          {
            header: {
              description: strings.PropertyPaneDescription
            },
            groups: [
              {
                groupName: strings.BasicGroupName,
                groupFields: [
                  PropertyPaneTextField('description', {
                    label: strings.DescriptionFieldLabel
                  })
                ]
              }
            ]
          }
        ]
      };
    }
  }
```

10. Save the changes to the file. Run the following command to build and bundle the project:

```
gulp build
```

11. Once the build is complete, run the following command to preview the web part:

```
gulp serve
```

12. Open your web browser and navigate to the local SharePoint Workbench by entering the following URL: **https://localhost:4321/_layouts/workbench. aspx**

13. Add the web part to the workbench by clicking the "+" icon and selecting the "**HelloWorldWebPart**" web part, just as the usual process for adding web parts on the page.

Congratulations! You have now created a "Hello World" SPFx web part using Yeoman.

To package your SPFx solution, you can use the following steps:

1. Run the following command to package the solution:

```
gulp bundle --ship

gulp package-solution --ship
```

The first command (**gulp bundle --ship**) bundles your code into a distributable format, and the second command (**gulp package-solution --ship**) creates the SharePoint package (**.sppkg**) file.

2. Once the package is created, you can find it in the "**sharepoint**" folder, which is located in the "**temp**" folder of your project.

3. You can then upload the .sppkg file to your app catalog and deploy it to your SharePoint site.

4. To upload the file, we would need to create it.

To Create an app catalog, you can follow the steps outlined in Microsoft's official documentation to create an app catalog for your SharePoint Online tenant: **https://docs.microsoft.com/en-us/sharepoint/use-app-catalog**

Otherwise, follow the steps we covered previously, on how to create tenant level app catalog.

After app catalog is configured, you can go to the app catalog site collection.

Go to site content there and select **Apps for SharePoint**. Upload your sppkg there and click on **Deploy** when prompted.

Once done, you can open SharePoint online site and there go to any page, edit it, and add your Hello World web part there.

Let us see also how you can create a custom solution that will interact with the GRAPH API. To connect to Microsoft Graph API from your custom solution, you can use the Microsoft Graph JavaScript client library. Here are the steps:

1. Install the Microsoft Graph client library using the following command:

```
npm install @microsoft/microsoft-graph-client
```

2. Create an instance of the Client class and authenticate the user using the appropriate authentication provider. Here is an example of authenticating with the implicit grant flow:

```
import { Client } from "@microsoft/microsoft-graph-client";


const client = Client.init({
  authProvider: (done) => {
    done(null, {
      accessToken: "<INSERT_ACCESS_TOKEN_HERE>",
      tokenType: "Bearer",
    });
  },
});
```

Note: You can use other authentication providers depending on your authentication flow. Refer to the Microsoft Graph JavaScript client library documentation for more details.

3. Use the client object to call Microsoft Graph API endpoints. Here is an example of getting the user's profile:

```
const user = await client.api('/me').get();
console.log(user);
```

That's it! You can now use the Microsoft Graph API from your custom solution.

Conclusion

Custom development with SharePoint Framework (SPFx) in SharePoint Online provides a powerful way to extend SharePoint capabilities and build custom solutions that can integrate with other systems and services. SPFx supports modern web development practices and tooling, including React, Angular, and TypeScript, and provides a range of features and APIs for interacting with SharePoint data and functionality.

Developers can use SPFx to build custom web parts, extensions, and solutions that run in the browser and can be deployed to SharePoint Online tenant and site-level app catalogs. The SharePoint REST API and Microsoft Graph API provide powerful ways to interact with SharePoint data and external services, and can be used in conjunction with SPFx to build powerful custom solutions.

However, custom development should be approached with care, as it can introduce risks such as security vulnerabilities, performance issues, and compatibility problems. Best practices for custom development in SharePoint Online include the guidance and recommendations provided by Microsoft, such as, using secure coding practices, testing thoroughly, and deploying solutions through proper channels, such as the SharePoint app catalog.

Points to remember

- Always follow best practices and guidelines provided by Microsoft for SPFx development.

- Use the latest version of Node.js and npm for SPFx development.

- Use the latest version of Yeoman generator for creating new SPFx projects.

- Always test your custom solutions thoroughly before deploying to production.

- Use SharePoint app models such as add-ins and SPFx solutions for custom development.

- Use the SharePoint REST API or Microsoft Graph API to access SharePoint data from your custom solutions.

- Use PowerShell to manage SharePoint environments and to perform administrative tasks.

- Follow the principle of least privilege and grant permissions to users and applications only as needed.

- Use version control systems such as Git to manage your custom solutions and to track changes.

- Keep up-to-date with the latest developments and updates from Microsoft regarding SharePoint Online and SPFx development.

Join our book's Discord space

Join the book's Discord Workspace for Latest updates, Offers, Tech happenings around the world, New Release and Sessions with the Authors:

https://discord.bpbonline.com

## CHAPTER 19

PnP, PowerShell and Scripting

> "Scripting is the glue that ties together our modern computing environments."
>
> *- Mike Glover*

Introduction

In addition to customization, scripting is available for the entire Microsoft 365 platform. In this chapter, we will review the main scripting languages supported by Microsoft 365, such as PowerShell, PnP, CSOM, and even CAML. Using scripts, Admins can generate reports faster, retrieve and operate with data in the platform, set up policies and much more, all from cmd interface.

Structure

In this chapter, we will cover the following topics:

- PowerShell
- PnP
- CSOM
- CAML
- Executing scripts for Microsoft 365

Objectives

In this chapter, we will discover scripting languages and capabilities within SharePoint online and Microsoft 365 platform. The primary objective of learning **Patterns and Practices (PnP)** and PowerShell for SharePoint is to automate and simplify repetitive and complex tasks in SharePoint administration and development. PnP is an open-source initiative that provides a library of reusable code and best practices for SharePoint development, while PowerShell is a command-line shell and scripting language that can be used to automate a wide range of SharePoint tasks. By learning these technologies, you can streamline your SharePoint development and administration workflows, save time, and improve productivity. Additionally, PowerShell can help you perform tasks that may not be possible through the SharePoint user interface alone, such as bulk updates, complex queries, and custom reporting.

PowerShell

PowerShell is a command-line shell and scripting language developed by Microsoft for Windows, Linux, and macOS operating systems. It is built on top of the .NET Framework and provides an environment for administrative tasks such as managing Windows machines and servers, automating system tasks, and configuring various services and applications.

PowerShell has a syntax similar to that of other command-line shells, but it also allows for the use of advanced scripting techniques such as object-oriented programming, piping of commands, and use of variables, loops, and conditional statements. It includes a large number of built-in cmdlets (commands) that can be used to perform a wide range of administrative tasks.

PowerShell can be used for both interactive command-line tasks and for scripting tasks to automate system administration tasks. It also has support for remote administration, allowing administrators to manage remote systems from a central location.

Figure 19.1 features a PowerShell CMD in Windows:

Figure 19.1: *PowerShell CMD in Windows*

In SharePoint Online, PowerShell is often used by administrators and developers to automate common tasks, manage site collections and sites, configure permissions and security, and interact with SharePoint content using the SharePoint **Client Side Object Model (CSOM)**. PowerShell can also be used to manage and deploy SharePoint solutions and apps, create and manage lists and libraries, and perform bulk operations on SharePoint content, among other things. Additionally, PowerShell can be used to interact with other Office 365 services, such as Exchange Online, Azure Active Directory, and Microsoft Teams.

Here are a few examples of tasks you can perform with PowerShell in SharePoint Online

- Connect to SharePoint Online site:

```
Connect-SPOService -Url "https://your-domain-admin.sharepoint.
com/"
```

- Create a new SharePoint Online site:

```
New-SPOSite -Title "Site Title" -Url "https://your-domain.share-
point.com/sites/site-name" -Owner "user@your-domain.com" -Tem-
plate "STS#0"
```

- Get a list of all sites in your SharePoint Online tenant:

```
Get-SPOSite
```

- Get a list of all lists in a SharePoint Online site:

```
Get-SPOList -Web "https://your-domain.sharepoint.com/sites/site-
name"
```

- Add a user to a SharePoint Online group:

```
Add-SPOUser -Site "https://your-domain.sharepoint.com/sites/site-
name" -LoginName "user@your-domain.com" -Group "GroupName"
```

These are just a few examples of tasks you can perform with PowerShell in SharePoint Online. The possibilities are endless, and you can automate many tasks and processes with PowerShell to save time and increase efficiency.

There are several advantages to using PowerShell for scripting and automating tasks in SharePoint Online, such as the following:

- **Speed and Efficiency:** PowerShell allows you to execute complex and repetitive tasks quickly and efficiently, saving time and effort.

- **Scalability:** PowerShell scripts can be easily adapted to run on multiple servers, sites, or environments.

- **Consistency:** PowerShell scripts ensure that tasks are executed consistently, reducing the risk of errors caused by manual intervention.

- **Automation:** PowerShell scripts can be scheduled to run automatically, freeing up time for other tasks.

- **Flexibility:** PowerShell scripts can be customized to perform specific tasks, making it a versatile tool for various SharePoint Online administrative tasks.

- **Remote Management:** PowerShell allows you to manage SharePoint Online from a remote machine, eliminating the need to log in to the SharePoint Online portal.

PowerShell is a powerful tool for performing bulk operations in SharePoint Online. Here are some examples of bulk operations that can be done with PowerShell:

- Adding or removing users to/from SharePoint groups in bulk.

- Updating SharePoint list items in bulk.

- Uploading or downloading files in bulk.

- Creating or deleting SharePoint sites or subsites in bulk.

- Enabling or disabling features in bulk.

- Managing SharePoint user profile properties in bulk.

Here is an example of uploading files to a SharePoint document library in bulk using PowerShell:

```
#Connect to SharePoint Online Site

Connect-PnPOnline -Url "https://yourdomain.sharepoint.com/sites/
sitename" -UseWebLogin


#Path of the Folder where files are saved

$FolderPath = "C:\FolderName"


#Get All Files from Folder

$Files = Get-ChildItem $FolderPath


#Loop through each file and upload to SharePoint Online
```

```
ForEach ($File in $Files)

{

    Try

    {

        #Get the Contents of the file

        $FileStream = New-Object IO.FileStream($File.FullName,[Sys-
tem.IO.FileMode]::Open)


        #Upload the file

        Add-PnPFile -Path $File.FullName -Folder "Shared Documents"
-Stream $FileStream -Values @{Modified=$File.LastWriteTime} -ErrorAc-
tion Stop

        Write-Host "File '$($File.Name)' uploaded successfully to
SharePoint." -ForegroundColor Green

    }

    Catch

    {

        Write-Host "Error uploading file '$($File.Name)': $_.Excep-
tion.Message" -ForegroundColor Red

    }

}
```

This script connects to a SharePoint Online site, specifies the folder where the files are stored, gets all the files from that folder, and then loops through each file and uploads it to a SharePoint document library. This is just one example of the many bulk operations that can be done with PowerShell.

PowerShell is a powerful tool for automation and can be used to create scheduled jobs. You can use the Windows Task Scheduler to schedule PowerShell scripts to run at specified intervals or times. This allows you to automate repetitive tasks, such as backups, data exports, or user management.

To create a scheduled task that runs a PowerShell script, you can use the **New-ScheduledTaskTrigger**, **New-ScheduledTaskAction**, and **Register-ScheduledTask** cmdlets in PowerShell. Here is an example:

```
$Trigger = New-ScheduledTaskTrigger -Daily -At 2am

$Action = New-ScheduledTaskAction -Execute 'PowerShell.exe' -Argu-
ment '-File "C:\Scripts\MyScript.ps1"'

Register-ScheduledTask -TaskName "My Scheduled Task" -Trigger $Trig-
ger -Action $Action
```

This creates a scheduled task named "**My Scheduled Task**" that runs daily at 2:00 AM and executes the PowerShell script located at "**C:\Scripts\MyScript.ps1**". You can modify the task's trigger and action settings to suit your needs.

PowerShell also supports background jobs, which allows you to run multiple tasks simultaneously. This can be useful when performing bulk operations or when running long-running scripts that need to continue running in the background.

While PowerShell is a powerful tool for automating tasks and managing systems, there are some limitations and potential disadvantages to keep in mind, and they are as follows:

- **Steep learning curve:** PowerShell is a complex and powerful tool, which can make it challenging for beginners to learn and use effectively.

- **Potential for errors:** Since PowerShell commands can have a significant impact on your system, there is a risk of causing unintended harm if you make a mistake in your script.

- **Security risks:** Running PowerShell scripts can pose a security risk if they are not properly secured, as they can potentially execute malicious code or change system settings.

- **Limited cross-platform compatibility:** While PowerShell is available on multiple platforms, some commands and modules may not be available or function properly on non-Windows systems.

- **Performance issues:** Some complex PowerShell scripts or cmdlets may cause performance issues or even crash your system, especially if they are poorly optimized or executed on large datasets.

It is important to be aware of these potential limitations and take appropriate precautions when using PowerShell for your tasks.

You can use variables in PowerShell. Variables in PowerShell are used to store and manipulate data during the execution of a script. A variable is a name assigned to a value or an object, and the value or object can be accessed by referring to the variable name.

To create a variable, you can use the $ symbol followed by the variable name, as shown:

```
$myVariable = "Hello, World!"
```

This creates a variable called **$myVariable** and assigns it the value "Hello, World!".

You can then reference the variable by typing its name anywhere in the script where you want to use the value, as shown:

```
Write-Host $myVariable
```

This would output the value of the variable to the console. You can also perform operations on variables, such as concatenation, addition, subtraction, and more, depending on the data type of the variable.

In PowerShell, brackets are used to group commands or expressions together, or to indicate parameter values for a command.

When a command is executed in PowerShell, the interpreter evaluates the command line and any expressions in it, and then executes the resulting command. The order of evaluation follows the standard rules of operator precedence, and parentheses can be used to change the order of evaluation.

Here are some examples of using brackets in PowerShell:

- **Grouping commands:** `(Get-ChildItem -Path C:\Temp)`, `(Get-ChildItem -Path C:\Windows)`

- **Grouping expressions:** `($a + 2) * $b`

- **Specifying parameter values:** `New-Item -ItemType Directory -Path C:\Temp\NewFolder`

- **Calling a method on an object:** `$list.Count()`, where **$list** is an object that has a Count method.

In PowerShell, brackets are used to group statements together or to create arrays or hash tables. There are several types of brackets in PowerShell, including round brackets (), square brackets [], and curly braces {}:

- Round brackets are commonly used to group statements together, which can then be passed as a parameter or piped into a cmdlet or function. For example, you might use round brackets to group together a series of commands that retrieve data from SharePoint and then pass that data to another command.

- Square brackets are used to access elements in an array or to index into a hash table. For example, you might use square brackets to retrieve the third element in an array or to access a value in a hash table using its key.

- Curly braces are used to define script blocks, which are groups of statements that can be passed as parameters or assigned to variables. Script blocks are often used in advanced PowerShell programming, such as creating custom functions or modules.

When you run PowerShell code, it is executed in a top-down manner, meaning that each line of code is executed in order from top to bottom. If you use brackets in your code, the statements inside the brackets are executed before the statements outside the brackets.

You can also create a while loop in PowerShell. Here is an example:

```
$i = 1
while ($i -le 10) {
    Write-Host "The value of i is: $i"
    $i++
}
```

This code will output the value of i from 1 to 10. The **while** loop will continue to execute the code within the braces as long as the condition inside the parentheses is true. In this case, the loop will continue as long as **$i** is less than or equal to 10.

PnP

PNP stands for Patterns and Practices. In the context of SharePoint and Office 365 development, PNP refers to a set of open-source initiatives led by Microsoft and the SharePoint community to provide guidance, libraries, and tools for developing solutions on the SharePoint and Office 365 platforms. The PNP initiative provides guidance and examples of best practices for SharePoint and Office 365 development, including PowerShell cmdlets, .NET libraries, and JavaScript libraries for working with SharePoint data and customization.

PnP provides a set of libraries, tools, and documentation that make it easier for developers to work with SharePoint and Office 365 APIs and to create customizations and solutions.

One of the main advantages of using PnP is that it provides a set of pre-built functions and cmdlets that can help automate common tasks and accelerate development. PnP cmdlets can be used to perform tasks such as creating or modifying sites, lists, and fields, managing permissions, uploading files, and more, without having to write custom code from scratch.

PnP also provides guidance on best practices for developing SharePoint and Office 365 solutions and helps ensure that developers are using the latest recommended approaches and techniques.

Overall, PnP can help make development for SharePoint and Office 365 faster, more efficient, and more standardized, while also providing a helpful community of developers and resources for support.

Let us cover another good example of a bulk operation. It might be to restore a large number of files from a Recycle bin that were deleted by a user on accident. Doing it manually would take quite some time for you by restoring 100 documents at a time. What if you need to restore 50,000 of them?

That is when you need scripting, and PowerShell can and should be used. Let us discover how we can use PnP in this case.

```powershell
# Connect to SharePoint Online site

Connect-PnPOnline -Url https://yourtenant.sharepoint.com/sites/your-site -UseWebLogin


# Get recycle bin items deleted before a specified date

$deletedBeforeDate = "2022-12-31"

$recycleBinItems = Get-PnPRecycleBinItem | Where-Object { $_.DeletedDate -lt $deletedBeforeDate -and $_.ItemType -eq "File" }


# Restore each item

foreach ($item in $recycleBinItems) {

    Write-Host "Restoring $($item.LeafName)..."

    Restore-PnPRecycleBinItem -Identity $item.Id

}


Write-Host "Restore operation complete."
```

This script first connects to a SharePoint Online site using the **Connect-PnPOnline** cmdlet. It then uses the **Get-PnPRecycleBinItem** cmdlet to retrieve all recycle bin items that were deleted before a specified date and that are of type "File". It then iterates over each item using a **foreach** loop and calls the **Restore-PnPRecycleBinItem** cmdlet to restore the item. Finally, the script outputs a message indicating that the operation is complete.

Note that this script uses the PnP PowerShell cmdlets, which provide a convenient way to work with SharePoint Online from PowerShell.

Some of the main advantages of using the **Patterns and Practices (PnP)** framework include:

- **Simplifies development:** PnP provides a set of libraries and tools that simplify development tasks, such as site provisioning, branding, and deployment.

- **Supports multiple SharePoint versions:** PnP supports SharePoint 2013, 2016, and SharePoint Online, allowing developers to use the same tools and techniques across different SharePoint environments.

- **Open source:** PnP is an open-source project that is actively maintained by Microsoft and the SharePoint community, which means that developers can contribute to the project and customize it to meet their needs.

- **Integration with PowerShell:** PnP integrates with PowerShell, which makes it easy to automate tasks and perform bulk operations.

Some of the competitors of PnP include **SharePoint Framework (SPFx)** and the SharePoint Object Model. SPFx is a newer framework that provides developers with a client-side development model for building SharePoint customizations. The SharePoint Object Model is a set of classes and methods that developers can use to interact with SharePoint data and functionality. However, unlike PnP, these frameworks do not provide a set of pre-built libraries and tools that simplify development tasks.

CSOM

CSOM stands for **Client-Side Object Model**. It is a set of APIs for SharePoint that enables developers to access SharePoint resources from client applications outside the SharePoint farm. CSOM is available for several programming languages including .NET, JavaScript, and Java.

Using CSOM, developers can perform a variety of tasks such as creating or updating lists and libraries, managing user permissions, and working with SharePoint features like workflows and event receivers.

CSOM is particularly useful for building custom SharePoint solutions that integrate with other applications, as it allows developers to interact with SharePoint using programming languages and tools with which they are already familiar.

CSOM and PowerShell are not the same. CSOM provides a way to interact with SharePoint using code that runs on a client machine, rather than on the SharePoint server.

PowerShell, on the other hand, is a command-line shell and scripting language that enables users to automate administrative tasks and perform various operations on Windows-based systems, including SharePoint. PowerShell can interact with SharePoint using CSOM, but it can also interact with other systems and services using different APIs and protocols.

To use the **Client Side Object Model (CSOM)** in SharePoint, you first need to add the required DLL files to your project or script. These DLL files can be obtained by installing the SharePoint Server or SharePoint Online Client Components SDK on your development machine.

Once you have the DLL files, you can use them in your code to interact with SharePoint. The basic steps to use CSOM in your code are as follows:

1. Create a client context object to represent the SharePoint site you want to interact with.

2. Use the client context object to create an instance of the appropriate CSOM object, such as a List or ListItem.

3. Set the properties of the CSOM object as needed.

4. Use the client context object to execute the CSOM operation, such as adding or updating a list item.

5. Handle any errors that occur during the operation.

Here is an example of using CSOM to add a new list item to a SharePoint list:

```
# Load the SharePoint CSOM Assemblies

Add-Type -Path "C:\Program Files\Common Files\microsoft shared\Web
Server Extensions\16\ISAPI\Microsoft.SharePoint.Client.dll"

Add-Type -Path "C:\Program Files\Common Files\microsoft shared\Web
Server Extensions\16\ISAPI\Microsoft.SharePoint.Client.Runtime.dll"


# Set the URL of the SharePoint site

$siteUrl = "https://contoso.sharepoint.com/sites/marketing"


# Set the credentials to use for authentication
```

```
$creds = Get-Credential


# Create a client context object for the SharePoint site

$ctx = New-Object Microsoft.SharePoint.Client.ClientContext($si-
teUrl)

$ctx.Credentials = New-Object Microsoft.SharePoint.Client.SharePoin-
tOnlineCredentials($creds.UserName, $creds.Password)


# Get the list to add the item to

$list = $ctx.Web.Lists.GetByTitle("Documents")


# Create a new list item

$newItem = $list.AddItem()

$newItem["Title"] = "New Document"

$newItem["Category"] = "Marketing"

$newItem.Update()


# Execute the operation

$ctx.ExecuteQuery()


# Display a message indicating success

Write-Host "New item added to list"
```

This example uses PowerShell to create a client context object for a SharePoint site, get a list by title, create a new list item, and add it to the list. It then executes the operation using the ExecuteQuery method, and displays a message indicating success.

Both CSOM and PnP offer similar functionality for interacting with SharePoint Online. CSOM is a lower-level API that requires more code to accomplish tasks, while PnP is a higher-level API that simplifies many common operations.

You may want to use CSOM if you require fine-grained control over the operations you are performing, or if you are already comfortable with the API. On the other hand, PnP is often easier to use and can be faster to develop with, making it a good choice for many scenarios.

Ultimately, the choice between CSOM and PnP depends on your specific needs and preferences. It is often possible to mix and match the two depending on what makes the most sense for your use case.

Some advantages of using CSOM include:

- Can be used with multiple programming languages, including C#, VB.NET, JavaScript, and others.

- Allows you to perform operations on SharePoint remotely.

- Can be used to work with SharePoint Online and SharePoint On-Premises.

- Provides a way to perform complex queries using **Collaborative Application Markup Language** (**CAML**) query language.

- Supports batching of multiple operations, which can help to reduce the number of round trips between the client and server.

Some disadvantages of using CSOM include:

- Can require more code and setup than other options, such as REST API or PnP.

- May not be the best option for simple operations, as the code can be more complex than other approaches.

- Can require a higher level of technical expertise to use effectively.

- May not be suitable for all scenarios, such as when working with large amounts of data.

Overall, the choice between using CSOM and other approaches (such as REST API or PnP) will depend on the specific requirements of your project and your development team's expertise.

CAML

Collaborative Application Markup Language (**CAML**) is an XML-based query language used in SharePoint to define queries against lists and libraries. CAML is used to retrieve data from SharePoint lists and libraries, and to define the structure of list definitions, content types, and field definitions. It can be used to filter and sort data, and to define complex queries that involve multiple fields and conditions. CAML is an important part of SharePoint development, as it is used extensively in the development of custom solutions, workflows, and web parts. CAML can be used in various ways in SharePoint, including in server-side code, client-side code, and XML-based configuration files.

It is used primarily for querying data from SharePoint lists and libraries, and for defining views and forms in SharePoint. CAML queries can be executed using the **SharePoint Client Object Model (CSOM)** and the SharePoint REST API. However, the trend in recent years has been to use the REST API more often than CSOM or CAML, as the REST API is more flexible and can be used with a wider variety of technologies.

Here is an example of CAML used to retrieve all items from a SharePoint list:

```xml
<View>
   <Query>
      <Where>
         <Eq>
            <FieldRef Name='Status'/>
            <Value Type='Text'>In Progress</Value>
         </Eq>
      </Where>
   </Query>
   <ViewFields>
      <FieldRef Name='Title'/>
      <FieldRef Name='AssignedTo'/>
      <FieldRef Name='DueDate'/>
   </ViewFields>
</View>
```

In this example, the CAML query is used to retrieve all items from a list where the "**Status**" field is set to "**In Progress**". The results will include the "**Title**", "**AssignedTo**", and "**DueDate**" fields for each item.

You can use CAML to sort and filter items in SharePoint. Here is an example of sorting items based on a specific column:

```xml
<View>
   <Query>
      <OrderBy>
```

```
        <FieldRef Name="ColumnName" Ascending="TRUE"/>
    </OrderBy>
  </Query>
</View>
```

Here is an example of filtering items based on a specific condition:

```
<View>
  <Query>
    <Where>
      <Eq>
        <FieldRef Name="ColumnName"/>
        <Value Type="Text">FilterValue</Value>
      </Eq>
    </Where>
  </Query>
</View>
```

In these examples, "**ColumnName**" is the name of the column you want to sort or filter by, and "**FilterValue**" is the value you want to filter by. You can modify the CAML query to suit your specific needs.

Here is an example of using CAML to query items from a SharePoint list using CSOM in C#:

```
using (var ctx = new ClientContext("https://contoso.sharepoint.com/
sites/MySite"))
{
    var list = ctx.Web.Lists.GetByTitle("My List");

    var camlQuery = new CamlQuery();

    camlQuery.ViewXml = "<View><Query><Where><Geq><FieldRef
Name='Created' /><Value IncludeTimeValue='TRUE' Type='Date-
Time'>2022-01-01T00:00:00Z</Value></Geq></Where></Query></View>";

    var items = list.GetItems(camlQuery);
```

```
    ctx.Load(items);
    ctx.ExecuteQuery();


    foreach (var item in items)
    {
        Console.WriteLine(item["Title"]);
    }
}
```

This code queries a list named "**My List**" and retrieves all items created after January 1st, 2022 using a CAML query. The query is defined using the **<View>** and **<Query>** elements, and the **<Where>** element is used to specify the condition for filtering the items. In this case, we are using the **<Geq>** (greater than or equal to) operator to filter by the "**Created**" field, and retrieving only items created after January 1st, 2022.

Some potential limitations and disadvantages of CAML include:

- **Steep learning curve:** CAML can be difficult to learn and use effectively, especially for developers who are new to SharePoint. However, once you understand it and its structure, it is pretty easy to use.

- **Limited functionality:** CAML can be limited in terms of the types of the queries it can perform and the data it can retrieve.

- **Maintenance overhead:** CAML requires developers to write and maintain XML code, which can be time-consuming and error-prone.

- **Performance issues:** Poorly designed CAML queries can cause performance issues, especially when working with large data sets.

- **Not supported in all contexts:** CAML is primarily used in SharePoint server-side code and may not be supported in all contexts, such as **SharePoint Framework (SPFx)** client-side web parts.

Despite these limitations, CAML can still be a powerful tool for querying and manipulating data in SharePoint, especially for complex scenarios where other methods may not be sufficient.

Executing scripts for Microsoft 365

To execute scripts for Microsoft 365, you can use PowerShell or Microsoft Graph API. PowerShell is a command-line shell that provides a way to automate administrative tasks on Microsoft 365. Microsoft Graph API is a RESTful web API that provides a way to interact with various services in Microsoft 365 programmatically.

To execute PowerShell scripts for Microsoft 365, you will need to install the Microsoft Online Services Sign-In Assistant and Azure Active Directory Module for Windows PowerShell on your computer. Once installed, you can connect to your Microsoft 365 tenant by running the following PowerShell command:

```
Connect-MsolService
```

This will prompt you to enter your Microsoft 365 administrator credentials. Once authenticated, you can run PowerShell commands or scripts against your Microsoft 365 environment.

To execute scripts using Microsoft Graph API, you will need to obtain an access token by registering an application in the Azure portal and granting it the necessary permissions. Once you have an access token, you can make API calls to various services in Microsoft 365.

Here is an example of how to obtain an access token using the OAuth 2.0 client credentials flow and make an API call to the Microsoft Graph API using PowerShell:

```
$tenantId = "yourtenant.onmicrosoft.com"
$appId = "yourappid"
$appSecret = "yourappsecret"
$resource = "https://graph.microsoft.com"

# Obtain an access token
$tokenEndpoint = "https://login.microsoftonline.com/$tenantId/
oauth2/token"
$body = @{
    grant_type = "client_credentials"
    client_id = $appId
    client_secret = $appSecret
    resource = $resource
}
$accessTokenResponse = Invoke-RestMethod -Method Post -Uri $to-
kenEndpoint -Body $body
$accessToken = $accessTokenResponse.access_token
```

```
# Make an API call using the access token
$headers = @{
    "Authorization" = "Bearer $accessToken"
}
$apiEndpoint = "https://graph.microsoft.com/v1.0/me"
$user = Invoke-RestMethod -Method Get -Uri $apiEndpoint -Headers
$headers
Write-Output "Hello $($user.displayName)"
```

This example obtains an access token using the client credentials flow, and then makes an API call to retrieve information about the currently authenticated user using the Microsoft Graph API.

Scripting can be used for various tasks in Microsoft 365, such as automating administrative tasks, managing user accounts and permissions, managing Exchange Online, SharePoint Online, OneDrive for Business, and more. Scripting can also be used to customize and extend the functionality of M365 services to meet specific business requirements. Some examples of tasks that can be performed using scripting in M365 include:

- Creating and managing users and groups.

- Modifying user properties and permissions.

- Configuring Exchange Online settings.

- Creating and managing SharePoint sites and content.

- Automating OneDrive for Business tasks.

- Managing Microsoft Teams and related settings.

Scripting can help streamline and automate these tasks, thus saving time and reducing errors. It can also provide more flexibility and customization options than the graphical user interface.

Practical tasks

In this chapter, we discovered PowerShell and various scripting capabilities, extensions, and libraries. Let us do some practice with them now.

Firstly, you would need to update your local dev environment and install additional software for script execution.

To prepare your local dev environment to execute scripts in PowerShell and PnP, you can follow these specific steps:

1. **Install PowerShell:** PowerShell is included in Windows operating system by default, but make sure to install the latest version from the Microsoft website.

2. **Install SharePoint Online Management Shell:** PnP PowerShell requires the SharePoint Online Management Shell to interact with SharePoint Online. You can download the latest version from the Microsoft website.

3. **Install PnP PowerShell:** PnP PowerShell is a set of cmdlets that enable you to perform various SharePoint Online operations. You can install it by running the following command in PowerShell:

```
Install-Module -Name SharePointPnPPowerShellOnline
```

4. **Connect to SharePoint Online:** Once you have installed the SharePoint Online Management Shell and PnP PowerShell, you can connect to SharePoint Online by running the following command in PowerShell:

```
Connect-PnPOnline -Url https://yourtenant.sharepoint.com -UseWebLogin
```

Replace "**yourtenant**" with your SharePoint Online tenant name.

Now we need to install some libraries and packages for SharePoint online.

To install SharePoint Online Management Shell, you can follow these steps:

1. Go to the official Microsoft download page for SharePoint Online Management Shell: **https://www.microsoft.com/en-us/download/details.aspx?id=35588**

2. Select the language of your choice from the dropdown menu and click on the "**Download**" button.

3. On the next page, select the version of SharePoint Online Management Shell that corresponds to your operating system architecture (32-bit or 64-bit).

4. Once the download is complete, run the SharePoint Online Management Shell setup file and follow the prompts to install the software.

5. After the installation is complete, you can launch SharePoint Online Management Shell from the Start menu or by searching for "**SharePoint Online Management Shell**" in the Windows search bar.

6. To connect to SharePoint Online using SharePoint Online Management Shell, run the following command:

```
Connect-SPOService -Url https://yourtenant-admin.sharepoint.com
-Credential admin@yourtenant.onmicrosoft.com
```

Replace "**yourtenant**" with your SharePoint Online tenant name and "**admin@ yourtenant.onmicrosoft.com**" with the username of a user who has administrative privileges in SharePoint Online. In this case, that is your account for a sandbox environment.

You should now be able to use SharePoint Online Management Shell to manage your SharePoint Online environment.

Let us review an example of how to prepare a simple script using PnP PowerShell to retrieve the titles of all SharePoint Online lists in a site collection:

1. Open a code editor such as Visual Studio Code.

2. Create a new file with a **.ps1** extension. You can save it anywhere locally.

3. In the file, add the following code:

```
# Load PnP PowerShell module
Import-Module SharePointPnPPowerShellOnline

# Connect to SharePoint Online
Connect-PnPOnline -Url https://yourtenant.sharepoint.com -UseWebLogin

# Get all lists in the site collection
$lists = Get-PnPList

# Loop through each list and display the title
foreach ($list in $lists) {
    Write-Host $list.Title
}
```

4. Replace "**yourtenant**" with your SharePoint Online tenant name in the Connect-PnPOnline command.

5. Save the file.

6. Open PowerShell and navigate to the directory where the script file is saved.

7. Run the script by entering the filename with the .ps1 extension. For example, if your file is named "**Get-ListTitles.ps1**", you would run the script by entering:

```
.\Get-ListTitles.ps1
```

The script will connect to SharePoint Online, retrieve the titles of all lists in the site collection, and display them in the PowerShell console. You can modify the script to perform other tasks such as creating or modifying SharePoint Online resources using PnP PowerShell. You can connect to any of the existing site collections or create a new one for this purpose.

Now, let us review a more practical example, than the one we already covered before in this chapter. We will review how to restore files from recycle bin in bulk, step by step:

1. Create a new file with a .ps1 extension.

2. In the file, add the following code:

```
# Load PnP PowerShell module
Import-Module SharePointPnPPowerShellOnline


# Connect to SharePoint Online
Connect-PnPOnline -Url https://yourtenant.sharepoint.com -UseWe-
bLogin


# Define variables
$daysToRestore = 30 # Number of days to restore items from
$recycleBinItems = Get-PnPRecycleBinItem | Where-Object { $_.De-
letedDate -gt (Get-Date).AddDays(-$daysToRestore) }


# Loop through each item in the recycle bin and restore it
foreach ($item in $recycleBinItems) {
    Write-Host "Restoring item $($item.LeafName) from $($item.
DirName)..."

    Restore-PnPRecycleBinItem -Identity $item.Id

}


# Display completion message
```

```
Write-Host "All items deleted within the last $daysToRestore days
have been restored."
```

3. Replace "**yourtenant**" with your SharePoint Online tenant name in the Connect-PnPOnline command.

4. Modify the **$daysToRestore** variable if you want to restore items that were deleted more or less than 30 days ago.

5. Save the file.

6. Open PowerShell and navigate to the directory where the script file is saved.

7. Run the script by entering the filename with the .ps1 extension. For example, if your file is named "**Restore-RecycleBinItems.ps1**", you would run the script by entering:

```
.\Restore-RecycleBinItems.ps1
```

The script will connect to SharePoint Online, retrieve all items in the recycle bin that were deleted within the last 30 days, and restore them one by one. The progress will be displayed in the PowerShell console. Once all items have been restored, a completion message will be displayed. You can modify the script to restore items that were deleted more or less than 30 days ago, or to perform other bulk operations using PnP PowerShell.

Conclusion

In conclusion, PnP, PowerShell, and scripting can all be powerful tools for managing and automating tasks in SharePoint Online and Microsoft 365.

PnP provides a set of tools and libraries that simplify the development and management of SharePoint Online and Microsoft 365 solutions, making it easier for developers to create customizations and automate tasks. PowerShell provides a powerful scripting environment for automating tasks and managing systems in Microsoft 365, and is particularly useful for managing large numbers of items or performing complex operations.

Scripting allows you to automate repetitive tasks, enforce policies, and streamline processes, improving the efficiency and accuracy of your workflows. It is important to keep in mind that scripting can have limitations and drawbacks, such as increased complexity, the need for technical expertise, and potential security risks. It is important to use scripting tools wisely and follow best practices to ensure the safety and reliability of your environment.

Points to remember

- PnP is an open-source initiative led by Microsoft that provides guidance, code samples, and tools to help developers build custom solutions on top of SharePoint and Microsoft 365.

- PowerShell is a command-line shell and scripting language that is widely used by IT professionals and developers to automate administrative tasks and manage systems.

- Scripting is a powerful tool for SharePoint Online developers that can help automate repetitive tasks, speed up development, and improve the quality of their code.

- PowerShell can be used to interact with SharePoint Online via the **SharePoint Client-Side Object Model (CSOM)** or the REST API, and can be used to perform a wide range of tasks, such as creating or deleting sites, lists, and libraries, managing user permissions, and working with SharePoint features and web parts.

- PnP provides a set of PowerShell cmdlets and scripts that make it easier to work with SharePoint Online, including cmdlets for provisioning sites, lists, and libraries, managing site templates, and working with page layouts.

- **Collaborative Application Markup Language (CAML)** is an XML-based language that can be used to define views and queries for SharePoint lists and libraries. Although CAML is still supported in SharePoint Online, it is not widely used and has been largely replaced by other technologies like the REST API and the Microsoft Graph API.

- When choosing between PnP, PowerShell, and scripting, developers should consider factors like their familiarity with each technology, the complexity of the task at hand, and the performance and scalability requirements of their solution. Each technology has its own strengths and weaknesses, and the choice ultimately depends on the specific needs of the project.

Join our book's Discord space

Join the book's Discord Workspace for Latest updates, Offers, Tech happenings around the world, New Release and Sessions with the Authors:

https://discord.bpbonline.com

Index